SUPPLY CHAIN

Project

Management

A

Structured Collaborative

and

Measurable Approach

James B. Ayers

SUPPLY CHAIN
Project
Management

A
Structured Collaborative
and
Measurable Approach

$$S_L^t$$

ST. LUCIE PRESS

A CRC Press Company

Boca Raton   London   New York   Washington, D.C.

Library of Congress Cataloging-in-Publication Data

Ayers, James B.
  Supply chain project management: a structured collaborative and measurable approach /
    p.   cm.
  Includes bibliographical references and index.
  ISBN 1-57444-350-X (alk. paper)
  1. Business logistics. I. Title.
HD38.5.A94 2003
658.7—dc21   2003046683

This book contains information obtained from authentic and highly regarded sources. Reprinted material is quoted with permission, and sources are indicated. A wide variety of references are listed. Reasonable efforts have been made to publish reliable data and information, but the author and the publisher cannot assume responsibility for the validity of all materials or for the consequences of their use.

Visit the CRC Press Web site at www.crcpress.com

© 2004 by CRC Press LLC
St. Lucie Press is an imprint of CRC Press LLC

No claim to original U.S. Government works
International Standard Book Number 1-57444-350-X
Library of Congress Card Number 2003046683
Printed in the United States of America 2 3 4 5 6 7 8 9 0
Printed on acid-free paper

Dedication

To Paula, household supply chain expert, who undertook the toughest project of them all — raising three kids and taking care of me.

Preface

The *Handbook of Supply Chain Management*, published in 2001, asserted that supply chain management, or SCM, requires new ways of doing old tasks. In many ways, SCM has made the job of running a business harder. Going alone in today's world, without collaborating with supply chain partners, is a dead-end strategy. It will be hard for many to make the transition needed to work with partners.

In other ways, however, successful collaboration may make life easier. Managers have the opportunity to widen their circles, involving partners with mutual interests in making their businesses a success.

This "paradigm shift" requires new ways of working. "Structured, collaborative and measurable" — terms in the title of this book — are undoubtedly virtues worth pursuing. But, in a supply chain world, how? Hopefully, for many, this book answers that question. Fundamentally, managers have the choices represented below. On one side is "business as usual." On the other is a structured, collaborative and measurable approach that exploits project management knowledge and practice.

Business as Usual	Project Management Approach
Functional initiatives	Companywide and multicompany initiatives
"Program" mentality, ambiguous goals	"Project" mentality, "make it happen"
Narrow solutions	Broad solutions
Led by technical staff	Led by senior management
Systems first, processes later	Processes first, systems as enablers
Measured by ROI	Measured by competitive improvement
Get it done in your spare time	Dedicated resources
Launch and forget	Monitor and track

As the name implies, business as usual is the rule, not the exception. The first hurdle is enlisting different parts of the organization in the supply chain effort. If that can be accomplished, moving to a multicompany effort is the next hurdle.

Supply Chain Project Management has three sections and an appendix, described briefly here.

Section I. SCM in the 21st Century

Chapter 1, the first of four chapters in this section, describes the book's foundations. These include knowledge and practice in both SCM and project management. Chapter 1 orients the reader to the book's layout. Remaining chapters in Section I describe SCM knowledge areas. Chapter 4 summarizes models and tools covered in the *Handbook of Supply Chain Management*.

Section II. Project Management and SCM

Section II turns to structured approaches for project management and supply chain analysis and documentation. The section opens in Chapter 5 with a "maturity model" for project management. The maturity model is a tool that measures progress in implementing what we preach in the book. We have two — one for project management knowledge and practice application (Chapter 5 in Section II) and one for SCM knowledge and practice application (Chapter 10 in Section III).

Other Section II chapters are devoted to standards promulgated by national organizations for project management and SCM. The Project Management Institute (PMI) maintains its Project Management Body of Knowledge (PMBOK), which is covered in Chapters 6 and 7. The Supply-Chain Council maintains the Supply-Chain Operations Reference Model (SCOR), described in Chapter 8. Chapter 9 uses experience from projects that missed their goals to develop root causes for project failures.

Section III. SCM Project Processes

This section contains templates for an expansive supply chain project blueprint. It borrows PMBOK process standards for the project structure. Its purpose is to help practitioners shape their own efforts, particularly those who want cross-functional and multicompany participation. Practitioners should pick and choose project components from this section.

Appendices

Appendix A contains case studies from supply chain practitioners. These are well worth reading independently. However, each supports one or more topics covered in the chapters. These links are identified at the beginning of applicable chapters in Section III.

Appendix B lists deliverables from Section III project management process templates and summarizes responsibility recommendations for executing those processes.

Here are a few suggestions on how to use the book. Start with Chapter 1 for a quick overview. Pick topics of interest and explore those chapters. Chapters are designed as standalone descriptions of their topics. Readers will likely be one of two types. The first is a supply chain practitioner seeking background on project management. The other is a project management practitioner wanting knowledge of SCM. Section II might fill in gaps for the former; Section I for the latter. For those charged with managing a supply chain improvement project, Section III should be very helpful.

Good luck in your pursuit of excellence in supply chain project management.

James B. Ayers
Los Angeles, California

Acknowledgments

My consulting career has required working in or running projects. Unfortunately that experience hasn't included all that much formal training in project management. Learning on the job, guided by some fine examples and intuition, has seemed adequate. My acquiring editor at CRC Press, who shepherded this project through the approval process, suggested PMI as a source for the project management side of our SCM/project management "cocktail." That was an inspired suggestion; supply chain management is too important to be left to casual approaches.

Four reviewers checked my work in progress. Katie Kasper, who led the Supply-Chain Council's collaboration effort, reviewed Chapter 8, which describes the Council's SCOR model. Chris Christensen and Lars Rosqvist, both experts in project management, reviewed the entire Section II covering project management and made many important suggestions. Dave Malmberg reviewed Chapter 9 defining project management shortcoming's root causes. Dave has experienced many supply chain technology project successes — and failures.

The book has been an opportunity to report on the work of the Supply-Chain Council's Collaboration Task Force. I was a relative newcomer to the group but was happy to participate in developing proposed revisions to SCOR. Early contributors who laid the foundation for collaboration include Katie Kasper, Kevin McCormack, Herbert Heinzel, Jim McGwin and Dave Hough. Scott Palmer of the Supply-Chain Council kept the effort together. The endeavor to translate collaboration into SCOR included committee members Pat Murrin, Frank Quiett, Togar White, Adrian Despres, Dave Malmberg, Craig Gustin and me. Jim McGwin originated the collaboration hierarchy concept described in Chapter 8.

I would also like to thank case study writers who are listed under "Contributors" along with their affiliations. Comments on my earlier book, *Handbook of Supply Chain Management*, reflect appreciation of the down-to-earth perspective cases provide.

Rob Smith and his supply chain team at Bombardier Transportation have had an opportunity to put many of the tools and techniques described here into practice. The experience, including their feedback, has also been invaluable to this work.

Author

James B. Ayers is a principal with CGR Management Consultants in Los Angeles. (E-mail: jimayers@cgrmc.com) He consults in strategy and operations improvement with clients of all sizes within the United States and internationally. Services include strategy development, profit improvement and new product process improvement. He has served clients delivering services in transportation, healthcare, engineering, utility and financial industries.

Mr. Ayers has authored or edited two other books on supply chain management, plus numerous articles. His books are *The Handbook of Supply Chain Management*, published by CRC Press and APICS, and *Making Supply Chain Management Work: Design, Implementation, Partnerships, Technology and Profits* by Auerbach Publishers.

Mr. Ayers holds a B.S. with distinction from the U.S. Naval Academy and M.B.A. and M.S. in industrial engineering degrees from Stanford University. As a naval officer, he served on nuclear submarines. He is also a member of the Project Management Institute, the Society of Manufacturing Engineers and the Council of Logistics Management. He is a Certified Management Consultant (CMC) by the Institute of Management Consultants. Mr. Ayers is active with Supply-Chain Council efforts to continuously improve its Supply-Chain Operations Reference Model, or SCOR.

Contributors

The following provided case studies to illustrate the profits and pitfalls experienced in implementing supply chain improvement projects.

Peter A. Crosby, Principal
CGR Management Consultants
Los Angeles, CA

Donald J. Derewecki
Gross and Associates
Woodbridge, NJ

Douglas T. Hicks
Olive LLP
Farmington Hills, MI

Emile Lemay, Senior Vice President Operations
Lantis Eyewear Corporation
Secaucus, NJ

Dave Malmberg, Principal
CGR Management Consultants
Los Angeles, CA

Frederick H. Neu, Principal
Frederick H. Neu and Associates
Camarillo, CA

Contents

SECTION II Project Management and Supply Chain Management

SECTION III Supply Chain Management Project Processes

Section I

Supply Chain Management in the 21st Century

1 Purpose and Overview

This chapter describes this book's purpose and how it plans to achieve the contract with its readers implicit in its title.

This work is a sequel to the *Handbook of Supply Chain Management,* published in 2001.[1] In that book, we examined the emerging supply chain management discipline, or SCM for short. Our opinion is that SCM doesn't change management goals, but does call for new knowledge, practices and skills. The *Handbook* described the knowledge and practice needed by managers to effectively apply SCM. This book focuses on the implementation process.

For the user of this book, reading the *Handbook* is helpful, but not necessary. This section, Chapter 4 in particular, recaps its major concepts and tools.

Commentators like academics, analysts and senior managers debate the relative value of strategy and tactics. Great strategies that go unimplemented have little value. On the other hand, well managed projects unguided by strategy may also be of little value. Whatever value they have is purely accidental.

SCM is a discipline that's underappreciated in many boardrooms, according to Shakeel Mazaffar, Group Vice President Global Supply Chain for UK-based Imperial Chemical Industries PLC (ICI). This is surprising, according to Mazaffar, since "SCM has rendered inflation dead in its tracks."[2] No inflation is a benefit, at least for consumers, of global competition from capable SCM organizations. As this is written, there is still a large "space" in many organizations between the people who make the strategy and those who do everyday work. Drivers of supply chain change, described in more detail in Chapter 3, add to the urgency of getting these two groups together. Blending SCM and project management is a logical step in this direction.

1.1 BOOK PURPOSE

A *Handbook* principle is that SCM application requires strategy making as well as operations excellence. SCM is not just a "left-brain" discipline. That is, it is not limited to managing the thousands of transactions needed to get a product from producer to user. SCM also requires "right-brain" thinking to develop strategies that better attend to underserved markets.

We state the purpose of this book in the following way:

To enable managers to use both SCM and project management knowledge and practice to develop and execute supply chain strategies.

TABLE 1.1
Goals for This Book

Title Component	Role of This Book
Supply chain	SCM disciplines continue to be defined. This book contributes to that definition.
Project management	Project management has much to offer any improvement endeavor. We describe the project management practices that support implementation of supply chain strategies.
Structured	A tenet of project management is a disciplined structure. The structured approaches inherent in project management will aid SCM as well.
Collaborative	Collaboration along the supply chain is increasingly seen as indispensable to success. Bringing partners from outside the company into planning and executing supply chain operations makes project management all the more crucial.
Measurable	SCM projects should move you from where you are to where you want to go. We propose a framework for self-assessment and ongoing tracking of progress toward both supply chain and project management excellence.

The extended title of this book runs together themes necessary to fulfill this mission. Table 1.1 breaks down the title and describes how the book addresses each element. We hope the reader finds the promise implicit in the title achieved.

To reach our goal, we describe knowledge and practice in both project management and SCM disciplines. Figure 1.1 illustrates, showing four components that compose *supply chain project management*. "Knowledge" embraces skills developed by experience and education that require judgment in their application. "Practice" encompasses models, procedures, vocabulary, standards and tools that ease the job of applying that knowledge.

Project Management Knowledge	Project Management Practice
SCM Knowledge	SCM Practice

FIGURE 1.1 Component disciplines for supply chain project management.

The scope of knowledge and practice in both project management and SCM disciplines is very, very broad. It would be difficult to capture "everything" in either discipline in a single book. But this work should be a good start — drawing from a number of authoritative sources. A reader should use the book as a foundation document; an ample bibliography points toward additional resources, as needed.

Many company initiatives are pursued without a synthesis of disciplines. After all, busy managers can't be expert in every discipline they need. Our target audience consists of those who must manage supply chain improvement efforts. It will help those who want to proceed in a disciplined way to avoid missteps or even disasters. As many have found, missteps and disasters are a definite possibility. These can be costly in terms of lost business and wasted money and effort. Reading this book, therefore, should be an excellent investment.

1.2 PROJECT MANAGEMENT AND SCM KNOWLEDGE AREAS

Section II reviews project management knowledge and practice as described by the Project Management Institute (PMI). PMI describes these in its Project Management Body of Knowledge (PMBOK). PMBOK frameworks in the form of project structures, descriptions of project management knowledge areas and knowledge area processes will improve execution of SCM projects. Table 1.2 lists the PMBOK and SCM knowledge areas.

TABLE 1.2
Knowledge Areas For Project Management and SCM

Knowledge Areas	
Project Management	**Supply Chain Management**
1. Integration management	1. Designing supply chains for strategic advantage
2. Scope management	2. Implementing collaborative relationships
3. Time management	3. Forging supply chain partnerships
4. Cost management	4. Managing supply chain information
5. Quality management	5. Removing cost from the supply chain
6. Human resource management	
7. Communications management	
8. Risk management	
9. Procurement management	

PMI would describe SCM as an "application area" for project management knowledge and practice. An application area is a field that, by the nature of the work done there, relies on projects to bring needed change. Projects, as the PMBOK defines them, are temporary, unique efforts leading to a "product, service or result." Examples of other project management application areas, including construction, software development and product development, are plentiful. Projects are taking an increasing share of our work, displacing ongoing, repetitive operations. PMI refers to this phenomenon as "management by projects." The consulting industry that includes the practitioners who produced this book is an example of an industry that is managed by projects.

PMI offers organizations the opportunity to develop application area extensions. These extensions become PMI standards if they undergo the rigors of the PMI Project Management Standard-Setting Process. Although we view SCM as an excellent candidate for such certification, we haven't pursued this approval. We do apply PMBOK conventions as much as possible; there is no use reinventing the wheel when proven methods are available.

SCM knowledge and practice, in our view, is broad and includes strategy development, measuring performance and costs and how we organize. It has roots in, but is not limited to, logistics, which includes procurement, transportation and warehousing. Other SCM disciplines include operations research, industrial engineering, information systems, accounting, finance, mechanical engineering and process reengineering.

SCM brings these knowledge areas together. The *Handbook of Supply Chain Management* synthesizes this knowledge and practice into five management tasks that change with the emergence of SCM. This book employs these as knowledge areas for SCM, as shown in Table 1.2. As PMBOK relies on knowledge areas to structure its project management processes, we use the five SCM knowledge areas to structure our recommended SCM improvement project processes (Chapters 12–15).

1.3 BOOK ROADMAP

Figure 1.2 is a roadmap to book chapters. It serves as a reference to sections and chapters. Section I is titled "Supply Chain Management for the 21st Century." It describes why environmental change challenges management and the SCM skills needed to deal with that change.

Section II focuses on knowledge and practice in project management. This overview introduces models and techniques used in these disciplines. It also includes a chapter on the Supply-Chain Operations Reference model called SCOR. Section III integrates Sections I and II concepts and tools into project roadmaps for implementing change.

In the remainder of Section I, we'll describe recent SCM change drivers (Chapter 3) and recap the five management tasks that will change with the emergence of SCM (Chapter 4). The five tasks, listed in Table 1.2, constitute our SCM knowledge areas.

Section II begins with a model by a thought leader on project management, Harold Kerzner (Chapter 5). Kerzner's "maturity model" for project management describes stages in achieving project management excellence. Section II, in Chapter 6, continues with a summary of terminology used by project management professionals. Project management terminology, as well as SCM terminology, varies from organization to organization. The Glossary at the end of the book aids in standardizing our vocabulary.

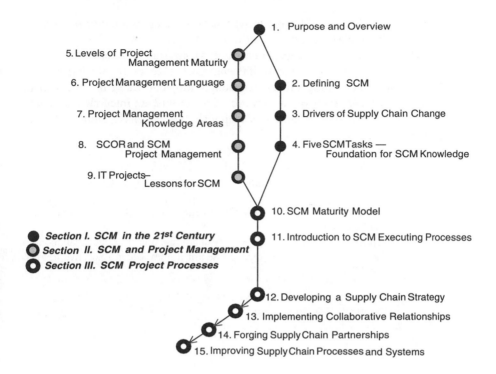

FIGURE 1.2 Book roadmap.

Chapter 7 describes the nine project management knowledge areas and related processes for managing projects. Later, in Section III, we'll follow PMBOK's lead and use SCM knowledge areas as a basis for SCM project processes.

The SCOR model, Chapter 8, contributes to the book's goal of structure for improvement efforts. It is an example of supply chain practice. SCOR is the product of multicompany efforts sponsored by the nonprofit Supply-Chain Council.

Information technology is an important enabler of supply chain processes. Many IT projects fail to meet their goals. We dedicate Chapter 9 to project management lessons learned from IT projects gone awry. These lessons point to root causes that our SCM project designs must address.

Section III integrates the project management and SCM knowledge and practice areas. We begin Section III in Chapter 10 with a five-level maturity model for SCM. It uses the five management tasks and a progression in company maturity ranging from "dysfunctional" (Stage I) to "strategic contribution" (Stage V). The descriptions enable readers to locate their current state and plan for moving to the proverbial next level. This injects the element of "measurability" into our supply chain efforts.

Chapter 11 lifts features of effective project management described in Section II for inclusion in a template for SCM projects. The remainder of Section III, Chapters 12 to 15, describes processes within the SCM knowledge areas for executing supply chain improvement projects.

Throughout the book, we'll point to Appendix A cases to amplify the lessons of the chapter. These pointers will be part of the chapter's introduction.

Figure 1.3 organizes book topics according to the four categories that define world-class supply chain project management. Each chapter from Chapter 2 to Chapter 11 focuses on one of the four categories — project management knowledge and practice and SCM knowledge and practice. Chapters 12–15 integrate knowledge and practice from all four categories. The pointer to the circle around all four categories illustrates this relationship.

ENDNOTES

1. Ayers, James B., *Handbook of Supply Chain Management,* Boca Raton, St. Lucie Press and APICS, 2001.
2. Mazaffar, Shakeel, "Transforming the supply chain function from the stock room to the boardroom in a $7.5 billion company," Senior Supply-Chain Executive Retreat, February 25–27, 2003.

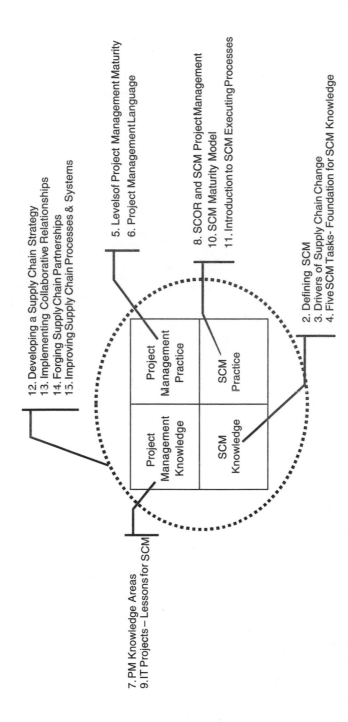

FIGURE 1.3 Book chapters/topics organized by category.

2 Defining SCM

Its people, its industry, its history and its products frame an organization's view of SCM. This chapter recognizes that there are different SCM interpretations for different companies. There is no right, absolute view of SCM. However, each organization should have a working definition that fits its needs. This should include SCM scope, goals, participation and plan for implementation. This chapter will increase awareness of the choices faced in developing that definition.

A review of the current state of efforts to define SCM is warranted. The term *SCM* is relatively new in the business lexicon; and its definition varies from user to user. Before going far in this book, we need to get our arms around the "space" we call SCM and this chapter updates related thinking on that topic. In fact, Chapter 9 describes examples of failed projects that trace their root causes to the lack of adequate scope definition.

Unless there's agreement in the organization about what SCM is, it's going to be tough to get on with improvement projects. Users of methodologies described in this book can help their companies reach agreement on just what constitutes SCM as it applies to them. The definition should include, but not necessarily be limited to, the scope, goals, participation and management plan for SCM efforts.

2.1 CLM PERSPECTIVE

Our update starts with the Council of Logistics Management (CLM). CLM members constitute an industry at the heart of the supply chain space — transportation, software companies, warehousing, system integrators, third-party logistics providers and providers of related services. CLM provides an annual perspective on the logistics industry.[1] Recently, it has had to cope with the rise of supply chain terminology and its impact on the logistics industry. This impact includes the potential confusion between the terms *supply chain* and *logistics*. CLM defines "logistics" as follows:

> Logistics is that part of the supply chain process that plans, implements and controls the efficient, effective flow and storage of goods, services and related information between the point of origin and the point of consumption in order to meet customers' requirements.

CLM observes that discussions defining SCM can be "thoroughly bewildering." To clarify, they quote the Supply Chain Research Group at the University of Tennessee. That group states that the SCM term in reality describes two separate concepts that are easy to confuse. The first is what the university researchers call supply chain *orientation* (SCO). Supply chain orientation is a philosophy of management. A company embracing the SCO philosophy seeks to coordinate the supply chain as an overall system. That system consists of tactical activities crossing multiple companies. This willingness, or "orientation," is a precursor to actually implementing such activities.

SCM, the Tennessee group advocates, has a different meaning. SCM is the "actual implementation of this orientation across various companies." If it's going to implement real supply chain improvements, a firm with an SCO must do business with other firms having the same viewpoint. Without such SCO-inoculated partners, its efforts will be incremental local projects. SCM happens when supply chain partners, all with the SCO viewpoint, collaborate on supply chain design. The resulting collaboration coordinates intra- and inter-company business functions and tactics to improve life for all parties.

This perspective offers important insights. It recognizes that moving forward toward supply chain excellence is at least a two-step process. One must first "get religion" (SCO) and then attempt to live by the precepts of the religion (SCM). Following those principles is very difficult if heretics surround you. This is particularly true if you have little control over those with whom you associate. Also, some of the heretics may be inside the family — not just outside.

There are several supply chain project management lessons here. If you want to play the supply chain game, you and your organization must both "have religion." You must also be dealing with partners who do. With regard to our five SCM tasks listed in Table 1.2, you must work hard at Task 2: *Implementing collaborative relationships* and Task 3: *Forging supply chain partnerships*. The former addresses internal needs, the latter external.

The need for SCO to get the benefits of SCM can also be satisfied through well-planned supply chain improvement projects. Demonstrating business benefits makes a strong argument.

2.2 THE FUTURE OF SCM — EIGHT PROPOSITIONS

In his keynote address to the 2002 Supply-Chain World — North America conference, John Langley of the Georgia Institute of Technology described a view of SCM's future.[2] Dr. Langley is no newcomer to SCM. He was previously at Pennsylvania State University and the University of Tennessee.

His view is that the supply chain is a "network of resources that supports fulfillment and satisfaction of customers." Logistics is about 30% of the supply chain equation, with manufacturing and material acquisition being other major components. His use of the term "network" to describe a supply chain is increasingly common.

Dr. Langley describes several "propositions," a term synonymous with suggestions or proposals, for the future of SCM. These offer valuable perspectives about the dimensions of SCM. His propositions, along with comments and interpretation, are shown in Table 2.1. The following paragraphs amplify these ideas and point to the need for effective project management.

TABLE 2.1
Propositions for the Future of SCM

	Proposition	Description
1	Managers must understand the customers' customer.	If you are far back in the supply chain — one or two levels away from end users, you must understand how end-user needs will affect your customers and you.
2	"Not everything that can be counted counts, not everything that counts can be counted."	Defining useful measures is deceptively difficult. Many traditional financial measures are too simplistic for effective SCM.
3	Failure to use information technology well precludes achievement of objectives.	Examples of technology support include supply chain pipeline visibility, exception-based notification and collaborative information sharing.
4	Logistics/SCM is the sweet spot for collaboration.	This proposition is attributed to Michael Hammer, author of *Reengineering the Corporation*.[7] The theme is that any organization needs the support of others to succeed.
5	Outsourcing will grow in importance.	Services like those provided by 3PL providers and contract manufacturers will continue to grow at rates exceeding 20% annually.
6	"Multinational" and "global" are worlds apart.	Just because a company operates in many countries, it isn't operating a global supply chain. This is true even if the products are the same from country to country. The advice "Think globally, act locally" may lead to isolated local supply chain designs.
7	An organization needs to know its competencies.	Three criteria are helpful in defining these: 1. Do we have the needed skills? 2. Is the activity consistent with the organization's mission? 3. Do we have the ability to invest in this capability? A "No" to any of the above questions makes that activity suspect as a competence. If it is not a competency, it should be the role of a supply chain partner.
8	Winners will identify and implement the best strategies.	The most important feature of this proposition is that winners must have a strategy. Obviously it helps to have a good one. The strategy should be customer-driven and produce the right mix of innovation, differentiation, effectiveness and efficiency.

The absence of Proposition 1, an understanding of your customers' customers, is a consequence of the need to complete day-to-day urgent, but relatively unimportant, tasks. Also, many of our executives never rub shoulders with customers or suppliers, so it's difficult to gain an appreciation for their problems. Even CEOs have difficulty thinking in the shoes of upstream and downstream partners. Effective supply chain projects will capture whatever insights one needs from immediate partners as well as important nonadjacent players in the chain.

Proposition 2 addresses measures. Many measures used to control the supply chain are in conflict. For example, having a lot of inventory raises costs but may be needed to maintain customer service. Higher levels of SCM performance require many trade-offs to decide what measures are needed and what amounts are "too much" or "too little." In the project management context, appropriate measures must accompany supply chain process designs. "You get what you measure," applies in SCM, as it does everywhere else.

Proposition 3 argues that information technology continues to be "front and center" in supply chain design. This is no surprise to those bombarded by an ever-growing range of software options. Langley rightly points to the three listed in Table 2.1 as having particular importance. But, as many anecdotes confirm, implementing complex systems is fraught with risk. Chapter 9 lists principal root causes. Where possible, a supply chain project should stretch the bounds of low-technology com-mon-sense solutions before leaping into complex technology solutions.

Companies traditionally collaborate in areas that clearly require it, like new-product development. Partners bring their own distinct technologies to the product-development effort. As indicated in Proposition 4, the collaboration "sweet spot" will shift toward supply chain development. Certainly project management increases in importance as participation in joint efforts expands.

Few are unaware of the growth of outsourcing, the subject of Proposition 5, in all manner of activities deemed nonessential to a company's competitive posi-tion. Examples are information technology, logistics and manufacturing functions. For many product companies, that leaves technology and product development, marketing and perhaps fulfillment as internal functions. A theme of this book is that, while outsourcing is a tool, supply chain design is a source of competitiveness. That doesn't necessarily mean one has to perform all supply chain functions internally.

In Proposition 6, Dr. Langley draws the distinction between *multinational* and *global*. Our interpretation of his view is that a multinational company thinks of each country as a separate business. A global country will ignore, at least to a practical extent, national boundaries.

This was the dilemma of CEO Robert Lutz at Excide.[3] Lutz has won renown for his leadership at Chrysler and, more recently, at General Motors, where he was tapped to revive product design. Between his stints at the two automakers, Lutz was CEO at Excide, a money-losing maker of batteries. The Excide Lutz joined was a country-focused organization. Each country carried a full product line, but many countries competed across national boundaries, with low or no profits being the result. As a response, the company pursued a product-based organization, but found many problems with that set-up. Ultimately, a hybrid resulted that will likely be changed again.

The dilemma is not uncommon. The Excide article cites Proctor and Gamble, Ford and NCR as having to wrestle with similar trade-offs. By the time the article was written, Excide had experimented with several variants. Referring to these efforts, a company executive stated, "We were searching for the Holy Grail. But there isn't one."

Our view is that global structures along product or end-user lines enjoy the advantages of an international scale. Regional market structures presumably bring the market closer to the company. However, we believe more and more multinationals will favor international, rather than national, supply chains.

Proposition 7, also related to competencies, lists three tests to determine whether an activity performed by the company is a competency. Dr. Langley's talk described the situation of a trucking company performing its own maintenance. This is a closely related activity, but does it really fit the company mission? Can the company invest in the people and technology to be the best at maintenance? A "no" means the company should find someone to take over its maintenance.

Many companies do not consider their strategy for competing to be within the scope of SCM. However, Dr. Langley's Proposition 8 and our own SCM Task 1 (described in Chapter 4) encourage thinking of SCM as a strategic enabler. Thinking of SCM as part of strategy faces a host of barriers, including perceptions by management that SCM equates to cost reduction, lack of operational expertise in executive suites and the view of many that strategic planning itself is a waste of time.

These eight propositions help us frame what we mean by SCM. They reinforce the idea that SCM is indeed a broad, not narrow, effort. SCM, if these propositions are valid, touches strategy, organization, company focus, technology and business partners. The next section describes issues related to thinking of SCM as a competitive weapon.

2.3 COMPETING SUPPLY CHAIN TO SUPPLY CHAIN

SCM and SCO, as described above, reflect a belief that competition will shift from a company-to-company to a supply chain-to-supply chain, or "SC vs. SC," basis. To date, this has been somewhat of a "gut" feeling of many practitioners that seems to make sense.

However the shape of SC vs. SC competition is a nuanced subject. A survey, reported in *Supply Chain Management Review*, examines the perceptions and realities around SC vs. SC competition.[4] The survey was sponsored by the Integrated Supply Chain Management (ISCM) Program at the Massachusetts Institute of Technology (MIT) and canvassed 30 supply chain experts from industry, academia and consulting.

The authors' report has important implications for framing SCM and projects for implementing supply chain change. The survey addresses the following questions:

- "Do we actually compete as supply chains or as individual companies?"
- "What effect does industry structure have on our supply chain decisions?"
- "Is there a continuum for competing on a supply chain basis?"
- "Is there a single supply chain model for competing in an industry?"

More than 70% of respondents said that SC vs. SC competition was real. However, there was far less agreement on the meaning of SC vs. SC competition. By interpreting responses, the surveyors reported three different scenarios for SC vs. SC competition. The respondent percentages represent the 70% who agreed with the SC vs. SC competition view and adds up to 101% due to rounding error. The 30% who disagreed were not included in the results.

1. **Literally competing SC vs. SC**. This entails groups of companies competing with each other. The entity in this scenario is the group composing

the supply chain. Groups are formal or informal. There is little or no overlap of companies among competing supply chains. This was the view of 41%, with 36% being formal arrangements and 5% informal.

2. **Supply chain network capabilities**. In this scenario, individual companies are the principal competitive entity, not the multicompany chains in Scenario 1. These individual companies compete on the basis of their supply networks. The networks support one of two "subscenarios." In the first (2A), the supply chain provides a total capability to compete on cost or service beyond the reach of a single company. The second (2B) is a unique network designed by the lead company. This response was favored by 37% of respondents, with 23% being type 2A and 14% being 2B.

3. **Supply chain networks headed by a channel master**. A single powerful company dictates "terms of trade" in the channel. This was selected by 23%. Examples include Wal-Mart in retail and Dell in computers.

According to the authors, Scenario 1 has many difficulties in reaching true SC vs. SC competition. First, there are often common suppliers in rival supply chains. This is a barrier to any supply chain's being truly unique, at least over those parts of the chain that are common. Second, investments by a customer in one of its suppliers may end up benefiting rivals if that investment is used to meet their needs. Third, proprietary information is difficult to hold close if a supplier can "signal" innovations to rivals with whom he is working. Finally, information-sharing sufficient to establish a proprietary chain is hindered by the threat of disclosure.

The authors also point out that some suppliers compete with their customers. This happens when the component supplier or its sister divisions have competing end products. It is also the case in aftermarket support where the component supplier has control of the design and components in critical subsystems.

The authors report success with SC vs. SC in industries like fashion, food production, products based on proprietary technology or raw materials, or geographically focused supply chains. A vertically integrated company also competes SC vs. SC because it is "completely disconnected" from other supply chain competitors. Its rivals, however, don't have to be integrated also.

SC vs. SC doesn't work, in the authors' view, in industries with "channel masters" like autos, commercial aircraft and personal computers. Dominant customers, like Boeing and Airbus, use a multitude of suppliers, many of which serve both.

Our view is that this doesn't mean those who serve a channel master shouldn't use SCM to improve their competitive positions. They would do so by using Scenario 2 above where an individual company instigates the supply chain design. The 2A scenario is the traditional way a supply chain develops. A company has a product it wants to sell. It picks suppliers based on the competencies it needs. If it needs widgets, it goes to the "best" widget maker. "Best" here may mean the fastest, the cheapest, the most flexible, or having the most advanced technology. If that maker is already providing widgets to competitors, as Intel provides its chips to multiple competitors, the company may look elsewhere. Or it may accept that there is no choice or that it doesn't make much difference.

Scenario 2B is a more proactive approach to improving competitive position. This is akin to "activity systems" recommended in Chapter 4. Our view is that the MIT survey doesn't emphasize the differences between Scenarios 2A and 2B enough. A 2B company has the opportunity to design a differentiated supply chain or activity system focused on the needs of its customers, whether the customer is Boeing-like or a small business.

In Scenario 3, the channel master makes the rules. However, most channel masters have plenty of choices. So a company needs to strive to be the best supplier available in its chosen category. SCM is an important tool in doing so, both in the way it picks suppliers and the way it supports the channel master.

Which scenario best describes your situation? The article provides a useful framework for incorporation into programs for supply chain improvements. This perspective on SC vs. SC competition should be particularly helpful to companies assessing their current environment.

The answer will lead a company along different paths to supply chain improvement. A vertically integrated company, for example, will likely reexamine prospects for farming out supply chain activities. A manufacturer whose suppliers and distributors "sleep with the enemy" may be more selective and reduce the number of business partners. If this isn't possible, then improvement efforts will focus on building internal capabilities.

2.4 THE VALUE CHAIN AND OTHER PERSPECTIVES

This section describes other perspectives that either help define SCM or contribute to confusion around its definition. They are presented here to guide readers toward the definition they choose for their own organizations.

2.4.1 SUPPLY CHAIN DEFINITIONS

The *Handbook of Supply Chain Management*[5] proposed definitions of the terms *supply chain* and *supply chain management*. Table 2.2 repeats the *Handbook* definitions, which have held up well since publication. Note that the definition includes "knowledge," which intends to capture product technology, process technology, embedded software and ongoing after-sale requirements.

Other authors and practitioners use other terminology. For example, as noted earlier in this chapter, supply chains are frequently referred to as *networks*. The

---

TABLE 2.2
Definitions from the Handbook of Supply Chain Management

Supply chain	Life cycle processes supporting physical, information, financial and knowledge flows for moving products and services from suppliers to end users.
Supply chain management	Design, maintenance and operation of supply chain processes for satisfaction of end user needs.

perception of a chain implies linear movement of product, information and money. The reality is closer to simultaneous, concurrent processes so "network" is a good descriptive term.

Also, many take a "company centric" view and split the "chain" between "supply" and "demand" at the company level. This is the case if the company is in the middle of the chain, several steps away from end users. The company-centric company sees the "supply" chain as providing incoming materials to the company — the upstream side. The "demand" chain constitutes the downstream side from the company to the end user. Supporting this terminology is a category of software dealing with "demand chains."

We still favor the view where the "supply chain" term represents all the resources needed to satisfy end-user needs. In other words, to the end user, it's all a supply chain.

2.4.2 The "Value Chain"

Supply chain, the term, gets tangled up with another, *value chain,* at times. It is an assumption on our part that the term supply chain was an adaptation of Michael Porter's value chain terminology, introduced in Porter's books, which were important contributions to strategic planning.[6]

Within a company, the value chain includes product or customer touching activities including *inbound logistics, operations, outbound logistics, marketing* and *sales and service.* Supporting these are value chain components like *procurement, technology development, human resource management* and *infrastructure.* Each linked company has its own value chain with similar generic components.

Porter also adds profit margin to his value chain. This represents the difference between the prices paid by customers and the cost of the value chain activities mentioned above. Higher profits mean that the enterprise deploys its capabilities in a way that delivers more value to customers as measured by their willingness to pay for it. Enterprise strategy leverages value chain components to increase these profits.

One could argue that supply chain activities are a subset of the value chain. Notably, *inbound logistics, operations* and *outbound logistics* are certainly supply chain activities. Excluded from the supply chain would be activities like *human resources, marketing* and *sales and technology development.* But it is harder and harder to discern any difference between supply chain activities and value chain activities. Our view is that the two are nearly synonymous. Certainly, a review of the enabling processes in supply chain models like the Supply-Chain Council's SCOR supports this view. There is more on this in Chapter 8. We include *Task 1. Designing supply chains for strategic advantage* as an SCM knowledge area. Managers everywhere should exploit the supply chain to increase the value they contribute and improve their own profits.

2.4.3 Viewpoints Encountered in Industry

In the *Handbook of Supply Chain Management*, we described viewpoints, shown in Table 2.3, that a company might have toward SCM. Most companies will fit one of the six models in Table 2.3. The views are arranged from the narrowest supply chain point

TABLE 2.3
Viewpoints Toward SCM

	Viewpoint	Focus	Supply Chain Executive
1	Functional	None: Standalone department	None
2	Procurement	Incoming "supplies"	From procurement
3	Logistics	Distribution to channels	From distribution
4	Information	Integration through technology	From IT or operations
5	Process reengineering	Cost reduction	From operations
6	Strategic	Profit-adding capabilities	Multiskilled manager

of view to the broadest. For each, there's a description and a best guess what kind of manager would lead the supply chain in a company with that particular viewpoint.

In Viewpoint 1 there is no supply chain function. Traditional departments are relatively independent, tied together only by a reporting relationship to a CEO or COO. Some companies, typical of those where Viewpoint 1 is embedded, have attempted to apply tools like SCOR at the functional level with limited success.

A company heavily dependent on suppliers will pick a procurement executive as the supply chain executive, Viewpoint 2. The focus in this company will be cost reduction for purchased materials. Large engineered product companies like those in aerospace or automotive fit this model.

A company dependent on its downstream activities might hold Viewpoint 3. The distribution executive advances to the lead supply chain role. Industries with high distribution costs, relative to raw material and manufacturing costs, would follow this direction. Examples include apparel, food and consumer goods.

An information-intensive company might place supply chain responsibility on a technical person. Internet companies might make this choice. Also, companies serving a channel master might feel that responsiveness to their customers lies in technology links and would choose a tech-savvy manager.

Process reengineering companies, representing Viewpoint 5, pursue programs like Six Sigma or "lean" that focus on process improvement. They are often in mature industries where continuous cost reduction is mandatory.

The strategic viewpoint is the broadest and can incorporate the others. It recognizes that SCM is a strategic enabler. Section III project processes will lay out a pathway to implement this viewpoint. Our view is that SCM holds value for improving strategies and a company that fails to take a strategic view forfeits an opportunity to improve its lot in life.

2.5 IMPLICATIONS FOR SCM PROJECT MANAGEMENT

A company's definition of SCM will set the limits for projects pursued under the supply chain banner. An important element of supply chain project management knowledge is "scope management." Chapters 7 and 12 describe the knowledge area and its implication for project definition.

The company viewpoint will expand or limit the scope it is willing to pursue. In too many companies, there is no true supply chain-responsible manager. There are only functional managers in procurement or distribution areas given new titles. Without the recognition that managing supply chains requires a new perspective, a company is likely to be disappointed in its efforts ato improve its supply chains.

ENDNOTES

1. Council of Logistics Management, What It's All About, 2000, pp. 3–4.
2. Langley, John Jr., The future of supply chain management, address to Supply-Chain World North America, annual conference, April 23, 2002.
3. Lublin, JoAnn S., Place vs. product: It's tough to choose a management model, *Wall Street J.,* p. A1, June 27, 2001.
4. Rice, James B. Jr. and Hoppe, Richard M., Supply chain vs. supply chain: The hype and the reality, *Supply Chain Mgmt. Rev.,* (5/5) September–October, 2001.
5. Ayers, James B., *Handbook of Supply Chain Management,* Boca Raton: St. Lucie Press and APICS, 2001, Ch. 1, 2.
6. Porter, Michael E., *Competitive Advantage: Creating and Sustaining Superior Performance*, New York: The Free Press, Macmillan, New York, 1985.
7. Hammer, Michael and Champy, James, *Reengineering the Corporation*, New York, HarperCollins Publishers, 1993.

3 Drivers of Supply Chain Change

"It's not the strongest of the species that survive, not the most intelligent, but the ones most responsive to change."

— **Charles Darwin**

This chapter addresses six change drivers fueling SCM projects. The drivers mirror environmental trends — economic, technological, political and social. Awareness of root causes for change supports formulation of supply chain change projects.

3.1 DRIVERS ARE IMPORTANT

The drivers of supply chain change described here are visible and widely reported in the press. However, supply chain operators don't always connect drivers to what they do daily. Also, most drivers are far beyond a manager's power to control, so their implications may be ignored. Here we make a connection and explain how these drivers for change are at the bottom of many supply chain projects that are either under way or should be under way. In initiating a project as described in Chapter 12, managers formulating projects should understand and acknowledge the project's "roots." This points them to the issues that the project must address.

This chapter acts as a checklist. Readers should examine each supply chain change driver and its impact on their operations. This should lead to questions of whether the organization's project portfolio is sufficient in terms of dealing with the drivers.

Table 3.1 presents a working definition of each driver. Figure 3.1 models the connections among them. *Innovation*, in Figure 3.1, pushes the whole process forward, so we place it first in our sequence. The three drivers, *Extended Products, Globalization* and *Flexibility Imperative,* act in different ways, described later. They shape the direction, scope and form of products and services as well as the supply chains needed to deliver them.

Two-headed arrows connect these three drivers to signify simultaneous collaboration development. In effect, the output of innovation is "digested" and transformed into requirements for processes and collaboration. The next driver is what we call *Process-Centered Management,* encompassing the requirements for supply chain processes. These, in turn, define needs for *Collaboration*, the last driver. Collaborations set in motion more innovations in the form of continuous improvements and more far-reaching changes.

TABLE 4.1
SCM Driver Definition

SCM Drivers	Definition
1 Innovation	Advances in both product and process. Includes material technology, production equipment, software and artistic input.
2 Extended products	The necessity for features and related services beyond the physical product. Also, the commoditization of basic products.
3 Globalization	Having to source and sell worldwide. Includes cross-border trade for raw material, manufacturing support and distribution.
4 Flexibility	The premium on fast responses to environmental changes and short product life cycles. Includes product mix, volume and features.
5 Process-centered management	Improvement of processes, not functions. Shifting focus to business processes as a basis for improvement efforts.
6 Collaboration	The need to break down boundaries. Using intra-company and inter-company cooperative efforts to meet mutual goals.

The following sections discuss the drivers and how each contributes to supply chain change.

3.2 INNOVATION

Our model in Figure 3.1 shows innovation, the first driver, as the "engine" of change in supply chains and their management. Innovation encompasses both products and processes. An innovation in product technology might act indirectly on the supply chain. For example, a totally new product will require new suppliers and new ways to distribute the product. A process innovation may alter the way the product is produced, making it better or lowering its cost. Either type of innovation can broaden the market and bring on the need for supply chain change. Other innovations may lie in the way the product is delivered or in the supply chain itself.

Forbes, in its 85th anniversary issue, listed what it considers the 85 most important innovations since its founding in 1917.[1] Example product, process and supply chain innovations described in the article, along with the date of the innovation, are listed below. The reader should appreciae that the innovations listed here undoubtedly affected their industries and their supply chains at the time of introduction. The effect on supply chains might have been indirect, in the case of new materials, fundamental technology advances and process innovations, or direct, as in the supply chain examples listed.

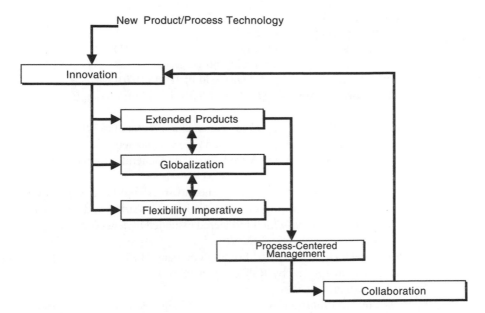

FIGURE 4.1 Drivers of SCM change.

The first group entails technology used in products. The underlined portions are the *Forbes* innovation as it appeared in the article. These are followed by short descriptions of the innovation.

- Breakthroughs in fundamental technologies
  - **Bell Telephone Laboratories**, which developed transistors, data networking and many other innovations (1925)
  - **Synthetic rubber**, which today forms the basis of many products like cable insulation and wet suits (1929)
  - **Transistors** (1947)
  - **Recombinant DNA** using gene splicing (1976)
- New materials
  - **Wallboard**, which reduced building costs (1933)
  - **Nylon** (1934)
- Technology without new material embedded in product designs
  - **Frozen food** by Clarence Birdseye (1924)
  - **Integrated circuits**, which shrank discrete components onto chips (1959)
- Artistic content like motion pictures, books and music
  - **The LP**, or long-playing record (1948)
  - **E-entertainment** beginning with Nolan Bushnell's Pong game (1972)

The following are examples on the process side:

- Advances in process and production technology
  - **Electronic digital computer** (1942)
  - **Microprocessor**, which miniaturized computers (1971)
- Software for managing and executing processes
  - **Relational database** from Edgar Codd of IBM (1970)
  - **UNIX/C programming**, which enabled cross-platform applications (1972)
  - **Spreadsheet**, the "killer app" for personal computers (1979)
- Innovation in management techniques and roles in society
  - **Business management** by Alfred Sloan of General Motors, which formalized corporate structures (1923)
  - **Value investing**, which brought science to stock and bond valuation and many of the motivating measures of industry performance (1934)
  - **United Auto Workers**, which pioneered extended benefits for employees (1935)
  - **Conglomerates**, a diversified holding company (1952)
  - **Consumerism** spurred by Ralph Nader (1965)
- Methods of communication
  - **Pulse code modulation**, which transferred signals into electronic one and zero pulses (1937)
  - **Fiber optics** for high capacity communication (1956)
  - **Modem** for data transfer over phone lines (1962)
  - **Telstar I**, the first commercial communication satellite (1962)
  - **The Internet** (1969)
  - **Ethernet**, used to hook computers into networks (1972)
  - **World Wide Web**, which widened access to the Internet (1991)

The following examples might be considered "pure" or "nearly pure" examples of supply chain innovation. The innovations include many examples of "extended products" and product/service designs focused on market segments.

- Mass marketing of products
  - **Keds** sneakers (1917)
  - **Tupperware**, using new plastics marketed door to door (1947)
- **Mutual funds** as a new way to sell securities to the public (1924)
- **Holiday Inn** utilizing standardized franchises (1952)
- **Fast food** with franchised food outlets (1955)
- **Containerized shipping** speeding up transport of goods (1956)
- **Point of sales data** by Sam Walton leading to information sharing (1962)
- **Discount brokerage** offering basic services at low cost (1973)
- **Index fund** with formula investment policies offering low cost (1976)
- **Customized mass retail** from Dell that bypassed distributors (1984)
- **Internet business** as embodied in Amazon (1995)

We look backward 75 years for the innovations. What about the future? One area that surprises and often confounds us is information technology. There is also no shortage of prognostications on its direction or its impact. In early 2003, InfoWorld published its list of disruptive technologies for IT and the business world.[2] The articles were divided into four groups: platforms, networks, applications and services.

Platform technology, according to Tom Yager, is shifting from proprietary to open technologies. For example, Microsoft Office 11® will support XML to promote file sharing. P.J. Connolly and Wayne Rash point to wireless networking and what they call "virtualization." Virtualization, paraphrasing the authors, is any time, any where, any way connection to the network. Devices like the laptop computer and the cell phone support this trend.

Application development, reported by Jon Udell, will be revolutionized by the combination of XML, a "strategic data format" and Web services that are "fundamentally about moving and transacting XML-based data."[3]

In the services category, Mario Apicella cites "self-service CRM" as a disruptive technology. The technology will continue efforts to remove human intervention from company–customer transactions. Apicella forecasts that self-service will move from buying and selling goods and services, where it is today, to assisting customers with problems. This will call on innovations in portal design, search engines and voice- and text-recognition technology.

It's not easy to know when an innovation will impact your products or their supply chain. However, as the past and future examples demonstrate, the potential for a disruptive technology is always there. It is also not always something that comes out of the lab; it can arise from new ways of organizing or packaging an existing product or service.

Figure 3.2 depicts the interaction of product, process and supply chain innovation. The interactions can overlap or be sequential in their timing. Overlapping innovation is more common. New products, changes in process technology, or new markets often arise in different departments in the organization. They may come together in an annual planning process or when things no longer work well and management is forced to react. At that time, the organization makes a coordinated effort to change. Sequential innovation starts when product or process innovations create a clear need to change an existing supply chain.

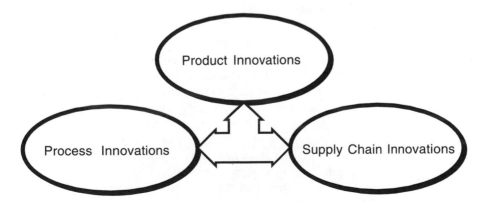

FIGURE 4.2 Interaction of product and process innovations.

Without innovation, the push for supply chain change would be much more limited than it is. Product innovation increases the value of products to customers. This, in turn, generates profits needed to attract new investment, enriches producers and fuels more innovation. The supply chain is called upon to produce the products that generate the profit. The Porter value chain model described in Section 2.4.2 describes this profit contribution. For innovative products, this is not a minimal profit based on cost but the kind of profit exemplified by innovators like some pharmaceutical companies and Microsoft.

Another driver arises from process innovation. Even without new products or markets, few can stand still in the face of competition. As process innovations improve cost and service, products become more affordable increasing potential markets.

The consulting firm McKinsey encapsulated the effects of process innovation by examining U.S. retail sales leader Wal-Mart.[4] The author, Bradford Johnson, notes that, in 1987, Wal-Mart had only a 9% market share, but was 40% more productive than competitors as measured by sales per employee. By 1995, through "big box" stores, electronic communication with suppliers, low prices and central distribution centers, Wal-Mart had a 27% share and a productivity advantage of 48%.

From 1995 to 1999, competitors played catch-up, but Wal-Mart maintained its edge. McKinsey's study of Wal-Mart reported how it achieved the gains.

- **Managerial innovations**. These had nothing to do with IT (information technology). An example cited is cross-training employees to increase flexibility in their assignment.
- **Focused IT investments**. These are investments that enhanced the company's low price objective and did not include more recent investments in real-time sales data collection and dissemination.
- **Higher-value goods**. This reflected the market's desire for more upscale products. For example, the $30 shirt costs as much to sell as the $20 shirt.

Note that the Wal-Mart improvements relied on both process and product innovations. Wal-Mart filled its shelves with products it knew, from its systems, that the consumer would buy.

Wal-Mart is an illustration of the innovation driver for supply chain projects. The company uses its supply chain capability to identify products that yield the highest profit. For a retailer bringing thousands of products to market, pegging profitability at the product level is a vital, if somewhat daunting, task. Relying on data, not the intuition of buyers and merchandisers, is key.

What about the company with only a few products where there's no confusion as to where profitability lies? This is often the case when the product is based on intellectual property (IP), which provides a monopoly of sorts. A *Wall Street Journal* article described the implications of this product category.[5] The products based on IP are fundamentally different. Almost all the cost is in development and almost 100% of every sales dollar is pure profit.

Is SCM important in these cases? The answer is "yes." There are at least three ways SCM supports IP monopoly products along their life cycle.

1. The introduction of these "killer" products
2. Reduction of unseen lost sales "profit leaks"
3. Extensions of product life

First, effective supply chain processes speed moneymaking products to market. Glitches that cause delays in product introduction are tantamount to leaving money on the table. Also, such products require, according to Bill Gates of Microsoft, as quoted in the *Wall Street Journal* article, "monopoly power." This results only if you become an industry standard. Without the domination, your up-front investments will be total losses, not total profits. The supply chain may make the difference in establishing this position ahead of the second-place competitor.

Reducing lost sales, item two above, requires adequate supplies to meet demand. Moneymaking products produce no profit if the sale is lost due to a stock-out. Finally, the innovative product is not innovative forever. It may die a sudden death as it matures if costs aren't brought into line with the competitive market. However, in mature markets where there is no monopoly, supply chain excellence becomes all the more important, as Wal-Mart, a seller of low-tech products, illustrates. Chapter 4 further addresses SCM from a product life cycle point of view, exploring how supply chain needs change with phases in the product life cycle.

3.3 EXTENDED PRODUCTS

Figure 3.1 illustrates how product or process innovations feed the next SCM driver, *Extended Products*. The definition in Chapter 2 describes the supply chain as "physical, information, financial and knowledge flows for moving products and services from suppliers to end users." This includes a lot of intangible services, as well as tangible products. In fact, as a *Wall Street Journal* article stated, "Manufacturers find themselves increasingly in the service sector."[6] The article attributes the trend to manufacturers having to provide services because that is "where the money is."

The *Handbook of Supply Chain Management* provided our definition of *extended product* and *base product*. The **base** product is the physical form of the product — its shape, features and functionality. The **extended** product, illustrated in Figure 3.3, includes other features that influence a purchasing decision. For the automobile shown in Figure 3.3, examples include the dealer network, financing, ease of doing business with the company and its representatives, the warranty and brand image.

Few products and services are commodities in the strictest sense. Features of the extended product may outweigh the importance of the base product, which customers may view as indistinguishable from competing brands. General Electric's former CEO, Jack Welch, points to service development associated with hardware production as fundamental to his success at GE.[7]

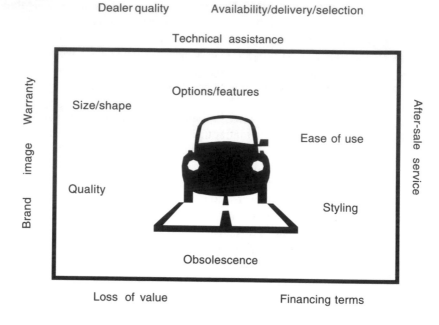

Dealer quality   Availability/delivery/selection

Technical assistance

Options/features

Size/shape

Ease of use

Quality

Styling

Obsolescence

Brand   image   Warranty

After-sale   service

Loss of value   Financing terms

Accessibility --   ease of doing business

FIGURE 4.3 The extended product.

Along with this trend comes, also as reported in a *Wall Street Journal* article, shorter life cycles for product-producing businesses and a shift in their assets.[8] The article charts the trend in the value of total assets away from tangibles like inventory and factories to intangibles like intellectual property, reputation and technology. Since 1955, tangibles have declined from 78% to 53% of total assets in 2001.

The article also reports that investments in intangibles such as RandD, software and advertising have more than doubled as a percentage of GNP in the U.S. since 1978. A downside is that reliance on intangibles may leave companies exposed to rapid changes. This has been the story with recent "meltdowns" in financial markets. Examples include Enron, Polaroid and Global Crossing.

How is the extended product a driver for supply chain change? In Figure 3.3, several extended product features for the automobile, shown outside the base product box, rely on supply chain design. These include the following:

- **Availability, delivery and selection**. These features are certainly determined by supply chain processes like inventory management, the ways orders are placed, a reliable supplier base and physical distribution.
- **After-sales support and dealer quality**. Customers know they are not just making a car purchase but entering into a long-term relationship with the car company and its dealer. Many auto dealers make no money on the sale of a vehicle but rake it in after the sale. So they are relying on

"deferred gratification" in the form of the service relationship to make money.

- **Accessibility and ease of doing business**. Interactions with a company can involve a host of customer contacts over the product's life cycle. These can draw in several supply chain partners like key suppliers, not just the "brand" company. So good choices are important to success.

In an ideal world, supply chain managers methodically monitor the product and process innovations coming their way. They then design a supply chain to incorporate the innovation. Or, in a slightly less ideal situation, the managers slot each innovation into the "best fit" supply chain already in place in the company.

However, many fall short of achieving this ideal. In fact, base product and extended product management are likely to be in separate functions. Base products may be the realm of engineering and manufacturing departments, while marketing and sales rule extended products.

Most managers may also assume every innovation fits into the existing supply chain. Inertia makes it hard to change supply chains. Everyone understands how things work now, even if expensive investments in systems, staff and facilities may be needed to make changes.

3.4 GLOBALIZATION

For supply chain managers, globalization influences range from upstream suppliers to downstream customers. For smaller manufacturers who export to other countries, their executives must not only make sure that the production lines are running but also that currency markets are moving their way.[9] The shift to "off shore" sourcing, usually to cut material cost, provides opportunities for jobs and investment in developing countries. When this occurs, globalization also puts money in people's pockets, widening markets for company products. For example, the market in China for Rolls Royce is limited because few can afford an expensive car, or any car at all. But, as Chinese companies grow through exports, car buyers — even for the Rolls — are created.

Carly Fiorina, CEO of Hewlett-Packard, captured the possibilities for expanding markets around the world in a speech in Los Angeles.[10] Her talk cited a Bill Moyers'[11] speech that profiled a village of 100 people that mirrors the global community.

- Fifty-seven people are from Asia, 21 from Europe, 14 from the Western Hemisphere and 8 from Africa.
- Thirty are Christian.
- Eighty live in substandard housing. Fifty suffer from malnutrition. Twenty have never had a drink of clean water.
- Seventy can't read. Sixty-five have never made a phone call.
- Thirty-five have never made more than $2 a day.
- One is college educated and one owns a computer.

The profile demonstrates that there is much to do to raise living standards and create markets. Many more should enjoy the benefits of the kind of prosperity advanced economies provide.

The numbers cited by Ms. Fiorina also demonstrate the "distance" between rich and poor in terms of living standards. In the global economy, this distance between rich and poor is as important as physical distance. Pankaj Ghemawat tackled the concept of distance in an article in the Harvard Business Review.[12] His approach puts globalization in perspective by enlarging our concept of "distance" by taking in more factors than just physical distance. He proposes a framework called "CAGE" because it addresses cultural, administrative, geographic and economic distance.

Applying CAGE to a country like China puts the large population in that country into perspective. Despite the potential implicit in a big population (over 1 billion people), China is farther away than simple distance implies. Ghemawat cites income level, multiple dialects, reliance on personal connections, high taxes, duties, government involvement in business and corruption as additions to physical distance. With CAGE as a tool, he encourages managers to take an alternative view of distance in assessing potential markets.

Another globalization trend is the need for factories and their supply chains currently focused on national markets to serve a broader audience. An example is Bombardier Transportation, a German-based company that makes rail equipment for use around the globe. In 2001, the company had 21 manufacturing sites in Europe with 25,000 employees. Traditional customers have been governments that favor local suppliers for their rail systems, so plants are positioned in the countries where the company does business.

At the time of this writing, the company is "rationalizing" its supply chain. This involves closing of duplicate or redundant manufacturing capacity. An important criterion for whether a plant has a future is that remaining plants must be competitive in export markets. Propelling this trend is the privatization of national rail systems. Unlike some government buyers, hard-nosed private operating companies go looking for the best deal they can get, regardless of location.

This process will also be propelled by recent decisions by the EU Court of Justice. In June 2002 it rejected "golden shares" that had enabled countries to block acquisitions of local companies by outsiders. The purpose cited by the court is to remove "restrictions on the movement of capital between member states and third countries."

China, a source for many components, is turning its attention to U.S. markets.[13] According to Forbes, Chinese companies, formerly subcontractors, will seek to set their own brands in U.S. markets. Examples include Haier, a maker of appliances with over $7 billion in sales, that has targeted a threefold increase in sales to the U.S. Huawei Technologies serves the same markets as Cisco for network equipment. The company also wants to triple its export sales. To make these goals a reality, the companies are fast obtaining marketing and sales expertise.

Many U.S. companies are watching their business disappear, taken over by competitors in emerging companies. This is not a new process; it has occurred throughout U.S. history, beginning when one low-cost region like the South has captured production from a mature region like New England. Protests are futile; the process in unstoppable. The U.S. producer must change sources or capitalize on its geographic advantage. An example is focusing on customers who value fast response over low cost.

Germany, burdened by a legacy of providing social services, has slowly priced itself out of world markets.[14] The cost of social services causes production to flee Germany for lower-cost alternatives. Globalization is cited by the *Wall Street Journal* as a root cause. Specific causes include the mobility of people and businesses, a common currency and the fall of the Berlin Wall. The owner of a printing business founded in 1825 said his company had failed "to be better, faster and cheaper than our competitors."

In summary, we see three globalization-related drivers for supply chain projects — new sources, new markets and rationalization. New sources expand options upstream in the supply chain. New markets do the same downstream. Rationalization calls for restructuring — shifting one's own operations to different locales — to meet the challenges while eroding the relative importance of national markets.

3.5 FLEXIBILITY IMPERATIVE — THE ULTIMATE CAPABILITY

The last driver arising from innovations is what we call the supply chain "flexibility imperative." Absence of flexibility implies a static supply chain that fails to "flex" as needs change. It also characterizes supply chains that serve different customers who have different needs with a "one-size-fits-all" approach.

Flexibility is a term with different meanings to different people. The need for flexibility raises to an art form management decisions about what "flexible" is actually and what is needed in the way of supply chain flexibility. Here we propose ways to define the need for supply chain flexibility.

Flexibility is a performance metric in the Supply-Chain Operations Reference (SCOR) model by the Supply-Chain Council.[15] Of the five top level SCOR metrics described in Chapter 8 and shown in Table 8.2, flexibility is the most important. The five Level 1 SCOR metrics are of two types. *Customer-facing* metrics are reliability and responsiveness in addition to flexibility. *Internal-facing* metrics are cost and asset utilization. The latter includes both working and fixed capital.

Without flexibility, the other four SCOR metrics are unlikely to be achieved. In fact, flexibility can be both internal and external facing. If a car dealer can deliver a blue, black, or red car to a customer's order, that dealer is considered "flexible" because he offers a range of choices. For this, his supply chain would receive high marks from the SCOR model for satisfying customers.

However, the dealer may gain his flexibility by carrying excess inventory; so all three colors are readily available on demand. This will hurt other metrics like cost and asset utilization. However, if the dealer didn't carry inventory but created the car to order, he would be not only externally flexible but also internally cost and asset efficient. In the make-to-order example, the supply chain uses a different way to provide customers with what they want.

Earlier we stated that "flexibility" could have many meanings. SCOR defines it as being able to move across a range of performance without penalty. The APICS Dictionary provides two sets of meanings: one for manufacturing systems and one for supply chains. For manufacturing systems, The APICS dictionary lists six categories of flexibility.[16] These are:

1. Mix flexibility
2. Design changeover flexibility
3. Modification flexibility
4. Volume flexibility
5. Rerouting flexibility
6. Material flexibility

These are the types of flexibility we might expect of a factory but are no less applicable to an entire supply chain.

At the supply chain level, the dictionary includes the ability to mitigate the following uncertainties:

- Demand forecast uncertainty
- Supply continuity variability
- Cycle time plus lead-time variability
- Transit time plus customs-clearance time uncertainty in the face of changing volume

Most, if not all, supply chain and production planning is based on expectations for these parameters. This supply chain view holds that flexibility is our ability to adapt when expectations prove false. We hold a broader view of flexibility and believe that flexibility exists at three levels. These are:

1. **Management mind set**: Recognition of the need for flexibility and an ability to define what kind of flexibility is needed
2. **Long term**: Matching supply chain design with customer requirements
3. **Short term**: Response time and production flexibility

The levels are interdependent. That is, a company must have #1 to get #2; and it must have #2 to get #3. The SCOR model focuses largely on #3 and is quiet on #1 and #2. The APICS definitions are strong on production planning and scheduling for long- and short-term needs, but lacking in terms of considering external-facing requirements for flexibility.

The next sections define our three levels and their implication for SCM.

3.5.1 MANAGEMENT MINDSET

If one accepts that change is a constant in the marketplace, then one must also accept that flexibility is a necessity. As we said above, flexibility becomes the foundation for achieving any of the other high-level metrics in SCOR. Being flexible creates the ability to move to where the supply chain needs to be with regard to reliability, responsiveness, cost and asset utilization. Without flexibility to cope with change, there can be no reliable delivery, no responsiveness to customers, no efficiency and no appropriate use of assets.

"A clock that's stopped is accurate twice a day." This observation continues with the notion that a clock that's stopped, that's stuck and doesn't move, is of little value. Inflexible supply chains are like this. Possibly, they were correct at one time. But as markets and products changed, unchanging supply chains can jeopardize the company's future.

For flexibility to be a reality, it has to be a real priority in the minds of managers. Often, it is simpler to define when the correct mindset is absent, rather than when it's present. Symptoms of mindset absence often appear in what executives measure and how they organize. Things to look for include the following:

- Company strategies are silent on the topic of flexibility.
- Supply chain departments are frozen and unlinked. Separate budgets exist for the functions — purchasing, manufacturing and distribution.
- The primary performance measure for supply chain managers is cost. A common example is "supply chain cost per dollar of sales."
- The company has an "inventory reduction" program. Inventory is an effect, not a cause.
- Buyers are measured on unit costs of purchased material.
- Lost sales aren't estimated and tracked. No one is accountable for them.
- Inventory and other assets are "free." Their costs are not weighed in performance measures.

The presence of any of these should raise alarms. However, absence of any of the symptoms is not sufficient for achieving a management mind set. In addition, management must articulate the types of flexibility needed for the business. For that task, they need strategies for competing through SCM. Section III, in Chapters 12 and 15, includes flexibility in project processes. There we recommend an approach, described here, for defining supply chain flexibility requirements.

3.5.2 Defining Needed Flexibility

David Upton has focused on the flexibility topic and has recommended a methodology for incorporating flexibility into the planning of manufacturing systems.[17] His definition of flexibility, similar to that in the SCOR model, is the following:

> Flexibility is the ability to change or react with little penalty in time, effort, cost or performance.

Upton proposes three dimensions as a framework for defining flexibility. The framework can easily be translated from the manufacturing system level, where he proposed it, to the supply chain. Table 3.2 summarizes the framework and provides examples.

TABLE 4.2
Characterization of Flexibility

	Component	Description	Examples
1.	Dimensions	What is it that requires flexibility?	Different input materials Mixes of product Different volumes
2.	Time horizon	What is the period over which flexibility is required? • Operational — seconds to days • Tactical — days to months • Strategic — months to years	Operational — schedule changes, daily shipments Tactical — quarterly changes in mix, use of materials Strategic — long range changes often requiring capital
3.	Elements	In what way should we be flexible? • Range — by how much the dimension (#1 above) must be able to change • Mobility — low transition costs for moving in a range • Uniformity — the ability to be consistent over a range	Range — volumes of output, sizes of product, range of products Mobility — having low setup costs to change product mix Uniformity — building the ability to maintain service, yield and cost

Upton recognizes the problems that go with defining flexibility. Just saying, "We need to be flexible," is inadequate due to the many possible interpretations. To define the form of needed flexibility, he poses three questions, paraphrased in Table 3.2.

- Question 1 asks what parameter requires flexibility — in what "dimension" is flexibility needed? The six manufacturing system components identified by APICS and listed above are good examples of what is meant by dimension.
- The answer to Question 2 identifies the "time horizon." Upton uses operational, tactical and strategic for short (seconds, minutes, hours), medium (hours, days, weeks) and long time horizons (weeks, months, years).
- Question 3 addresses "elements" of flexibility. Upton describes three under which most flexibility requirements fall. They are range, mobility and uniformity.

A **range** element will specify the limits of performance. For example, if volume flexibility (dimension) over a short period is sought (time horizon), the range will specify the high and low operating volumes (element). **Mobility** refers to the penalty of moving from one state in the range to another. For example, if there is little cost in moving from 100 units per hour to 150, then mobility is high. On the other hand, if it is very difficult to make this change, mobility is low. **Uniformity** refers to the performance over a range. For example, if the move from 100 to 150 units causes little change in the quality of the product, then flexibility is high.

Figure 3.4 illustrates a supply chain flexibility specification. The example defines supply chain flexibility requirements for product mix, volume and customer response time.

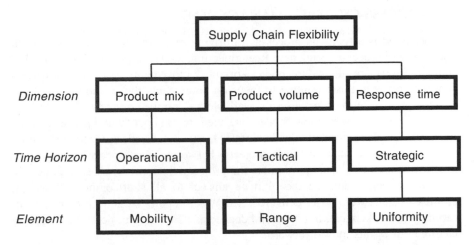

FIGURE 4.4 Taxonomy for defining flexibility — an example.

- **Product mix** changes are required over an operational time frame that, in this case, is daily. The element of flexibility is mobility. So any product mix can be made each day with the supply chain moving quickly from one product to another. A sandwich shop exemplifies this type of flexibility in a short timeframe, with any menu sandwich being produced to order in minutes.
- **Product volume** in our example is to the ability to change overall volume up or down in a tactical, or intermediate, timeframe. Monthly is an example. So the sandwich shop might adjust its schedule up or down based on expected business level by month. If the shop were across the street from a college, then staff would be up during the school year and down during summer vacation. The range component would specify the product volumes used to set staffing levels.
- **Response time** provides a standard that is competitive. It is a "uniformity" element, meaning that customer response time must be uniform over the range of volumes in which the supply chain must operate. So the sandwich shop must provide service within minutes at both high- and low-volume levels. This doesn't mean every customer or customer category must have the same response time. But that the response time for any customer type has to be the same under all volume conditions.

Specifications for flexibility are imperative because they drive design of supply chain processes and shape collaboration with supply chain partners. Static specifications are not acceptable; the Upton method makes possible definition of ranges of operations and expectations for customer service. Also, many CEOs seek some kind of visual cockpit for their operations. One based on defined flexibility parameters like those in the example is an excellent start.

3.6 PROCESS-CENTERED MANAGEMENT

Another trend is a focus on processes in driving improvements. Awareness of the importance of processes is not new. Reengineering, total quality management (TQM) and Six-Sigma are all mature process-oriented movements. Yet there is often a "tension" between those wanting to focus on process and those who want to bring technology — often just because it's available — into the company.

Jack Welch, in the previously cited interview, talks about "world peace" projects requiring complex information technology.[18] In his first decade as General Electric's CEO, he approved many of these projects. His term "world peace" refers to the over-hyped promises made to promote the projects. Such promises assured that the massive projects would be the ultimate answer to all shortcomings. When the promised results were never delivered, Mr. Welch reports he got a lot smarter and certainly more skeptical. In his second decade as CEO, only projects that produced tangible fast results moved forward.

Rich Karlgaard who is publisher of *Forbes*, the financial periodical, observes a similar phenomenon.[19] He notes how decision making for technology investments has shifted back and forth from "bottom-up" to "top-down." The bottom-up phenomenon occurred with the personal computer. The front-line troops got the message first and technology bubbled up to the executive suites. In the reengineering movement of the early 1990s, top-down took over. The rise of enterprise systems linked departments and had to be coordinated from the top. Later, as the Web came to the fore, bottom-up took hold once again. Often, bundles of money were wasted to get companies into the "new economy."

Karlgaard reports from the field that we are back to top-down. Now, CEOs and CFOs, like Mr. Welch, need "hard returns only." No more soft returns, only quantifiable hard returns will sell a project.

What is the implication for SCM? Is top-down or bottom-up the right model for SCM projects? Table 3.3 describes three scenarios framing how projects for supply chain improvement are formulated, justified and managed.

Scenario #1 in Table 3.3 is bottom-up, originating in the department. A project might be purchase of a machine tool in the manufacturing department. "We cut our labor by 60%," is a claim that might describe results from such a project. It is likely a local savings, involving just that portion of the process where the tool is used. It is not necessarily true that overall process cost was reduced.

Scenario #2 is top-down at the business unit level, with projects that cross department boundaries. A customer relationship management (CRM) system is an example. "We increased our sales 5%," might be a claim of success for the system. However, an auditor might have difficulty tracing any "hard" return revenue increases to the system.

Scenario #3 is "beyond" top-down because it extends beyond company boundaries. Projects in this category seek to reduce total cost in the supply chain. There are many obstacles to projects of this type. On the premise that supply chain partners

TABLE 4.3
Three Scenarios For Developing Supply Chain Projects

	Level	Sponsorship	Example Approaches	Goal	Justification
1.	Function	Department head	Machine tools, new production equipment	Department improvement	Return on investment, savings
2.	Business unit	CEO	Enterprise systems, expansions/ contractions	Business unit improvement	Revenue increase or cost reduction
3.	Supply chain	CEO, customer, supplier, alliance	Information sharing, investment sharing	Supply chain competitiveness	Revenue increase

will be more involved in any one company's improvement efforts, those companies must rely on process-centered management approaches. With this approach, company and supply chain processes determine how competitive we are.

To be effective at the supply chain level, #3 in Table 3.3, a process focus, i.e., top-down, is a necessity. Reasons include avoiding local optimums at the expense of the overall system, the basic interdependence of departments and businesses in the supply chain and the advantages of shared knowledge to solve problems.

But there are also many obstacles that include physical separation, suspicion, poor cost accounting, counterproductive performance measures and lack of skills or numbers. So collaboration to improve processes is not easy. But the beginning is a process-centered management focus with processes including those that extend beyond the boundaries of the business unit. Our Section III project management processes will help readers implement process-centered approaches at the supply chain level.

3.7 COLLABORATION

Few today dispute the need for collaboration in improving supply chains. It is apparent in software developers' products for exchanging information. Another example is the Supply Chain Council's initiative to upgrade its SCOR model to incorporate collaboration, described in Chapter 8. In Chapter 4 we'll describe two types of collaboration in more detail: that which is internal between departments and that which is external between business units. Here we describe the role of collaboration in driving supply chain change.

3.7.1 DEFINITIONS OF COLLABORATION

A big push for collaboration is technology based. To many practitioners, the term *collaboration* is a codeword for *information sharing* that is, in turn, code for *new systems*. So a category of software products, supply chain information applications, has emerged to support collaboration. These products enable sharing of production and inventory data, online auctions, marketplaces for buying and selling and production planning along the supply chain.

TABLE 4.4
Definitions of the Term "Collaboration"

	Company Represented and Analyst		
	Yankee Group Jon Derome	AMR Research Larry Lapide	Forester Research Navi Radjou
Level 1	Exchange of structured data	Execution (routine documents like purchase orders)	Monitor. Watch the process together.
Level 2	Free-form interactive sharing (Web tools, chats, on-line)	Information sharing, mostly one-way	Manage. Coordinate activities.
Level 3	Process collaboration (structured, mix of human and automated exchange)	Collaborative relationship (joint planning and scheduling, coordinated execution)	Optimize. Joint decision-making. Win-win partnerships across network.

It should be no surprise, then, that definitions of collaboration have an information technology tone. Table 3.4 shows the definitions of collaboration by industry analysts from three prominent research organizations.[20] These analysts represent concerns that report technology trends, including those taking place in the supply chain.

All three analysts describe collaboration as a three-stage process, as shown in Table 3.4. The levels begin with simpler forms of information sharing that are relatively easy to automate. They proceed to higher levels that involve joint decision-making. These may be aided by technology, but are essentially powered by management decision-making processes that are difficult to automate.

Of the three versions, we favor the Forester Research version because it captures the widest range of decision-making activity going beyond transactions to supply chain structuring. It also most clearly covers collaboration processes like strategy setting and sharing of needed investment to compete on a supply chain basis. Chapter 4 describes an expanded framework for collaboration.

3.7.2 CPFR®

An example is useful to demonstrate how one industry, retail, has coped with the need for collaboration.[21] There's a lot at stake for this industry. Matching supply and robust demand means increased sales. Mismatches from over-production result in write-downs and fire sales.

The industry standard, CPFR, stands for Collaborative Planning, Forecasting and Replenishment and is a trademark of the Voluntary Interindustry Commerce Standards (VICS) Association. The standard addresses a clear problem in retail, where a large number of retail stores and suppliers make collaboration a paying proposition. There are often long supply chains, large inventories and high exposure to write-offs of unsold goods that go out of fashion or miss the sales window, such as mittens in May.

CPFR has nine tasks in its generic business model that trace the collaboration process between manufacturers, retailers and distributors. Listed below, the nine steps provide a flavor for the overall CPFR approach. The first two steps are **planning**; the second six are **forecasting**; the last is **replenishment**.

Planning	1. Develop front-end agreements.
	2. Create joint business plan.
Forecasting	3. Create sales forecast.
	4. Identify exception for sales forecast.
	5. Resolve/collaborate on exception items.
	6. Create order forecast.
	7. Identify exceptions for order forecast.
	8. Resolve/collaborate on exception items.
Replenishment	9. Generate orders.

Each of the high-level steps is decomposed to lower levels of detail. In addition to the generic version, there are models for different levels of participation by manufacturers, distributors and retailers. CPFR is a rather complete model for setting up transactions in situations it covers. Flow charts provide a blueprint for users to follow through all steps of the process so they can benefit by lessons learned elsewhere. The structure is a valuable model for structuring similar arrangements in any industry.

3.7.3 STAGE 3 (MULTICOMPANY) SCM

CPFR is a good example of an industry's response to the need for supply chain change. CPFR is a model to help those who decide to share the information needed to make collaboration work. But what form might collaboration take at a strategic level, particularly when the supply chain is taking shape? An earlier article outlined a vision for "Stage 3" supply chain collaboration efforts.[22] The term "Stage 3" comes from the third, or supply chain, level as described in Table 3.3. Chapter 14 is a project blueprint for establishing this type of collaboration. Multicompany SCM features include the following:

1. Shared goals that include both strategic and tactical improvements. An example of the former is increased market share; examples of the latter are lower cost and reduced inventory.
2. A team effort that includes representatives from participating companies.
3. As needed, an honest broker to facilitate the effort. This can be a trusted team member or third party like a consultant.
4. A multicompany CEO or senior management steering committee. This group would be responsible for the results of the collaboration.
5. Contracting that distributes costs and rewards based on contributions. Negotiations over costs and profits shouldn't fall back on a standard buyer-seller arm's length negotiation model.
6. Process integration using appropriate technology and continuous improvement.

An example of a technology standard in item 6 is a retailer and distributor who decide to employ CPFR data exchange standards for their supply chain improvement effort.

Item 6 also closes the loop, as shown in Figure 3.1, taking collaboration back to further supply chain innovation. A Stage 3 effort shouldn't be a one-shot affair; after the initial effort, improvements should continue. Once established, the supply chain partnership becomes a source of innovations.

3.8 KNOW YOUR DRIVERS

This chapter has addressed the factors that make supply chain change a way of life. Some companies will be slow in becoming aware of which drivers affect them the most. However, the drivers will be there, exerting a force for change that's not recognized in the organization. But the need for coming to grips with change is inevitable. As we move on, we explore in greater depth ways to be successful at proactively managing the drivers rather than having them manage you. A prerequisite for proactive management is knowing which drivers are acting on you.

ENDNOTES

1. Armstrong, David, Burke, Monte, Lambert, Emily, Vardi, Nathan and Wherry, Rob. 85 innovations, *Forbes*, December 2002, pp. 124–210.
2. *InfoWorld,* January 6, 2003.
3. This quote in the article was made by Neil Charney, director of Microsoft's platform strategy group.
4. Johnson, Bradford C., Retail: the Wal-Mart effect, *The McKinsey Quarterly*, 2002, No. 1.
5. Murray, Alan, Intellectual Property: Old Rules Don't Apply, *Wall Street Journal,* August 23, 2001, p. A1.
6. Ansberry, Clare, Manufacturers Find Themselves Increasingly in the Service Sector, *Wall Street Journal*, February 10, 2003, p. A2.
7. Welch, Jack, A conversation with Jack Welch, *MSI Executive Series* (Internet broadcast), April 16, 2002.
8. Ip, Greg, Why many highfliers built on big ideas are such fast fallers, *Wall Street Journal*, April 4, 2002, p. A1.
9. Phillips, Michael M., Ship Those Boxes; Check the Euro! *Wall Street Journal*, February 7, 2003, p. C1.
10. Fiorina, Carleton S., Widening the communities of knowledge, *Town Hall Speaker-Digest*, p. 104, December 18, 2001.
11. Bill Moyers is an American journalist with PBS.
12. Ghemawat, Pankaj, Distance still matters: The hard reality of global expansion, *Harvard Business Review*, September 2001, pp. 137–147.
13. Dolan, Kerry A. and Hardy, Quentin, The challenge from China, *Forbes*, May 13, 2002, pp. 73–76.
14. Rhoads, Christopher, Burden of history: Behind the crisis in Germany, a past that is crippling, *Wall Street Journal*, December 6, 2002, p. A1.

15. Supply-Chain Operations Reference-model: Overview of SCOR Version 5.0, Supply-Chain Council, 2001, p. 1.
16. *APICS Dictionary*, 10th ed., 2002, p. 45.
17. Upton, David M., The management of manufacturing flexibility, *California Business Review*, Winter 1994, pp. 72–89.
18. Welch, Jack, op.cit.
19. Karlgaard, Rich, Digital rules, *Forbes,* May 27, 2002, p. 39.
20. Lapide, Larry, Derome, Jon and Radjou, Navi, Analysts panel discussion, Supply-Chain World North America: Extending Collaboration to End-to-End Synchronization, April 2002.
21. The CPFR model is explained in detail at www.cpfr.org.
22. Ayers, James B., Gustin, Craig and Stephens, Scott, Reengineering the supply chain, *Information Strategy: the Executive's Journal*, Fall, 1997 (14/1), pp. 13–18.

4 Five SCM Tasks — The Foundation for SCM Knowledge

This chapter recaps the five management tasks we define as SCM knowledge areas. They are the foundation for SCM project processes described in Section III.

In Chapter 1 (Table 1.2), we introduced five tasks that SCM requires to be done differently. Our five tasks, also the subject of the *Handbook of Supply Chain Management*, have always been part of the manager's workload. However, the drivers of supply chain change, described in Chapter 3, require new ways of performing these traditional tasks. Table 4.1 lists the five tasks, along with the project management themes associated with each. Together, they constitute our version of the SCM body of knowledge. Incorporating them into executing processes in our projects is the subject of chapters in Section III, as indicated in the final column of Table 4.1.

4.1 INTRODUCTION TO THE FIVE SCM TASKS

Task 1 is supply chain strategy design. It is consistent with the view, described in Chapter 2, that company strategy should include the supply chain. SCM is more than procurement or distribution — which conventional management practice views as costs to be controlled. With regard to change drivers from Chapter 3, Innovation, Extended Products, Flexibility and Globalization are all issues tackled in supply chain strategic planning.

Task 2 refers to internal collaboration. This collaboration is between departments or functions in the organization that need to work together. Gaining such collaboration is not trivial. Companies tinker continuously with organization structures and performance measures. But reorganizing alone is insufficient for gaining lasting improvement.

Effectively partnering with external partners is the goal of Task 3. Different types of partnership are required for different situations. The task describes the alternative forms of partnership and where each form fits best. Also, roles in the supply chain are changing, with companies offloading some functions to partners while acquiring others as core competencies. Effective performance of Tasks 2 and 3 produces collaboration leading to innovation, our primary driver of supply chain change.

Tasks 4 and 5 reflect the drive for process-centered management, another of our drivers identified in Chapter 2. Providers of information technology solutions flood the marketplace with products and accompanying claims for their efficacy. A growing

TABLE 4.1
Five Tasks for Better SCM

Chapter		Description	Section III Chapter
1	Designing supply chains for strategic advantage	Success in the marketplace requires supply chain innovation. A supply chain strategy that supports an overall strategy for competing should guide the effort.	12
2	Implementing collaborative relationships	Organization form, responsibilities and measures enable supply chain innovation. The place to begin is at home. The task covers relationships inside the organization.	13
3	Forging supply chain partnerships	Outside partners are needed to be successful. Old paradigms must be discarded. Effective project management requires an organized multicompany approach.	14
4	Managing supply chain information	Opportunities to succeed wildly or fail miserably abound. Supply chain systems must support supply chain processes.	15
5	Removing cost from the supply chain	Effective change requires understanding and managing root causes of cost in supply chain operating processes. The task embodies goals for both service and cost.	15

consensus is that, to effectively manage supply chain information (our Task 4), the process to be improved must be the focus. Cost cutting (Task 5) never goes out of style and is always an important SCM component. However, it too must be process focused, as supply chain costs are consequences of process design. Not to be ignored while cutting costs is the need to maintain competitive levels of service.

Barriers to effective SCM are outdated paradigms that dominate relationships in supply chains. The buyer–seller arm's-length relationship is one of these. Unintended consequences can be the result of measures geared at cutting material costs. Also, many costs are little understood. Too few organizations work effectively to reduce costs simply because they don't understand root causes for costs.

This is a "how to" book, with project processes for executing these tasks in Section III. Chapters 12–15 describe project management processes needed to execute each SCM task. The remainder of this chapter highlights knowledge, terminology and tools of value in performing these tasks. Many of these will be referred to in Section III.

4.2 TASK 1: DESIGNING SUPPLY CHAINS FOR STRATEGIC ADVANTAGE

Supply chain managers can no longer limit themselves to a functional discipline like procurement, manufacturing, or distribution. They also need an understanding of

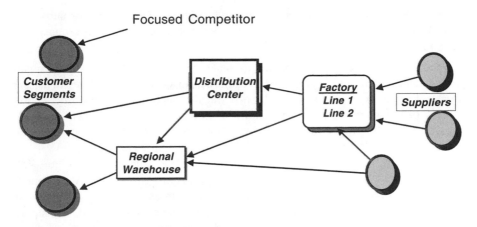

FIGURE 4.1 Penalty for poor SCM strategies.

company markets, needs filled by company products and the competitive landscape. A trait of many low-performing companies is ignorance of these dynamics. This leads to static supply chain designs that leave the company vulnerable to competitors.

4.2.1 THE NATURE OF MARKETS AND PRODUCTS

Fundamental to effective SCM is awareness of market segments. Segments are customer or user groups with common characteristics. In the automobile market, BMW caters to a different segment (sometimes called the high end) from Saturn, which caters to the low end. It is also likely that the BMW buyer will have expectations that differ from the Saturn buyer's. To be a successful dealer for either of these products, a seller must understand those expectations.

Figure 4.1 illustrates the danger. The figure shows a typical supply chain from a company's suppliers to its customers. But, instead of there being one "monolithic" customer on the left, there are customer segments. For example, cost may be a basis for segmentation. Some segments may be cost sensitive; others may not. Quality might be another basis for segmentation. Some segments may be especially demanding in terms of requiring high quality while others may not. Examination of extended product features, described in Chapter 3, also can lead to segmentation alternatives.

Market master Dell attributes its leadership position to segmentation.[1] Dell's COO, Kevin B. Rollins, encouraged Dell to target market segments with strategies focused on the needs of each segment. This enabled its high growth during the mid 1990s. Other successful companies use segmentation and supply chain excellence to differentiate their offerings.

- Enterprise Rent-A-Car established off-airport rentals focusing on nontravelers' rental car needs.
- Furniture maker IKEA sells low-cost unassembled furniture in a self-service environment.
- Contract manufacturers serve original equipment manufacturers with manufacturing and logistics capabilities tailored to each customer's needs.

- U.S. manufacturers in globalizing industries, who face low-cost substitutes, recast their supply chains for greater flexibility and fast response.

Segmentation requires companies to make choices about their supply chain
design. Those who use a single supply chain design to serve several segments are
at risk. Eventually, a competitor will sniff out the opportunity to do a better job
serving one or more segments and run off with that business, as shown in Figure
4.1. It will do this by focusing on that segment's needs with better prices, service
or quality than that provided by a "one-size-fits-all" supply chain.

A second product-market dynamic is the product life cycle, shown in Figure 4.2.
A new product starts life with low sales, shown as the *inception* phase. At inception,
the product is both produced and marketed through an existing supply chain or, if
the product's markets are new to the company, the company must build its supply
chain from scratch. In this stage, most companies will control supply chain processes
because product design is likely to be fluid and production volumes low.

If it's successful, the product moves into the *growth* phase. Growth brings
prosperity and profits are plentiful. Often, the supply chain for the product can't
keep up; products are hard to get with demand that exceeds supply. At this point,
competitors flood the market, sharing the riches. If designs have to be changed, a
company may want to continue to control the supply chain. If designs are stable,
partners may provide the needed capacity to meet demand.

As sales level off, the market for the product enters the *mature* phase. Competitors are still there, attracted by fat profits enjoyed during the growth phase. Design
changes fail to produce incremental sales because the product is "good enough."
Margins tighten and a battle for market share ensues. Now a company will likely
want to outsource supply chain tasks to specialists. This expands company capabilities through the use of specialists who lower costs and provide paths to various
market segments.

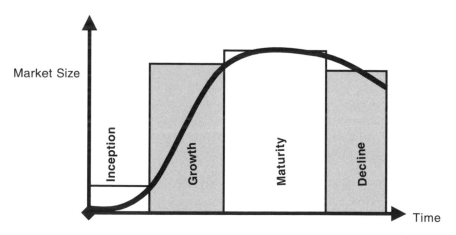

FIGURE 4.2 The product life cycle.

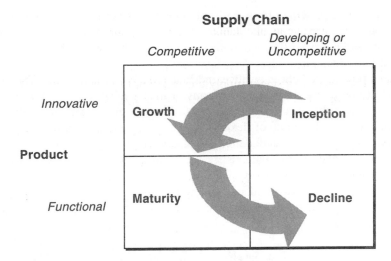

FIGURE 4.3 Market positions of products.

In the last stage, *decline*, sales drop. As they do, those who aren't competitive exit the market.

Marshall Fisher promotes the idea that different types of products require different types of supply chain.[2] He says there are two types of products: innovative and functional. With regard to the product life cycle, innovative products are those in the inception and growth phases. Functional products, like those we buy every day, are in mature or decline stages.

Fisher argues that innovative products require responsive supply chains and that functional products require cost-effective supply chains. This is because the higher profit margins that go with innovative products justify more inventory and other expenses to assure supply.

Figure 4.3 combines Fisher's insight with the product life cycle. In inception and growth phases, competition is based on the product. The supply chain must assure supply. As the product matures, the basis for competitiveness shifts from the product to the supply chain. Product features are increasingly commodity-like, with only minor differences among competing products. The supply chain, part of the extended product described in Chapter 3, must be cost effective for the product to survive.

A mismatch occurs when the responsive model is used for functional products or the cost effective model is used for the innovative product. For innovative products, the cost-effective model leads to lost sales or surplus goods. Thus a supply chain manager measured on costs for logistics and inventory may hurt the company by being too tight fisted when there is robust demand. For functional products, customer service can be too good, leading to excessive inventory and other costs.

Few measure financial losses from either lost sales or excessive supply chain cost. In the best of worlds, such a measure would be an estimate. So accountants are reluctant to ascribe "phantom" numbers requiring guesses as to lost sales.

However, lost sales, write-offs and too high operating expenses are costs incurred from failing to match supply and demand, the primary supply chain mission. When such costs will make a difference to decision-makers, they should be estimated and targeted for reduction.

Can a product be both innovative and functional at the same time? The answer is "yes" if you define the product in terms of its extended features. For example, the cloth maker that can deliver a "hot" fashion material inside a week has an innovative product by virtue of flexibility. The same material ordered 9 months in advance from a Chinese manufacturer is a functional product, probably provided by the low-bid supplier. For manufacturers caught in the globalization vice, extended product features, based on supply chain flexibility, may be their only recourse.

Dr. Hau Lee also uses the idea of functional and innovative product framework to classify supply-demand relationships.[3] His classification uses uncertainty in demand and supply as its basis.

Demand Uncertainty	Supply Uncertainty	Examples
High, innovative product	High	New products, semiconductors
	Low	Fashion apparel, toys, music
Low, functional products	High	Weather-dependent produce, precious metals
	Low	Basic apparel, grocery products

Low demand and supply uncertainty supply chains should stress efficiency. These are particularly enhanced by demand information that is highly predictable. Matching that demand with reliable supply enables a lean supply chain characterized by high inventory turnovers and excellent use of pipeline resources, like shelf space.

Low-demand, high-supply uncertainty supply chains should build risk-hedging methods into their supply chain processes. These include multiple suppliers for critical components, inventory and information sharing along the supply chain.

High-demand, low-supply uncertainty supply chains must emphasize responsiveness. No factories in China for these supply chains. Response times must be minimized; flexibility is key. An example strategy is contingency stocks of raw materials ready to be configured into end products, a postponement approach.

Supply chains where both demand and supply are uncertain require what Dr. Lee calls "agility." This may require a "network" of flexible manufacturers making up the "virtual" enterprise. Designing products with as many common parts as possible can facilitate such a situation.

4.2.2 MODEL FOR COMPETING THROUGH SCM

"Actions speak louder than words" is an old saying. Many are aware that organizations don't always practice what they preach. A way to capture the strategy being pursued by an organization is to examine company change projects. These are funded projects with resources and current action — not wishes or hopes that have only been discussed but never acted upon.

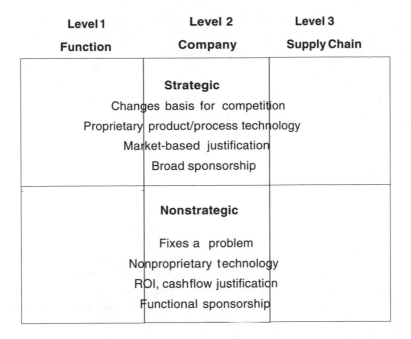

	Level 1 Function	Level 2 Company	Level 3 Supply Chain
	Strategic Changes basis for competition Proprietary product/process technology Market-based justification Broad sponsorship	
	Nonstrategic Fixes a problem Nonproprietary technology ROI, cashflow justification Functional sponsorship	

FIGURE 4.4 Types of SCM improvement projects.

Figure 4.4 is a model for competing through SCM first presented in the *Handbook of Supply Chain Management*.[4] The model displays the levels of project (function, company, supply chain) going from left to right and the type of project (strategic or nonstrategic) from top to bottom. The figure also lists some identifiers for strategic and nonstrategic projects.

The way most companies operate leads to projects in the lower left hand corner. A climate, described in Chapter 3, that encourages fast payback projects supports nonstrategic functional projects. So does the lack of internal collaboration, leading to promotion of projects confined to a single function. If companies improve internal collaboration, Task 2 in our framework, more projects will occur at the business unit level. Effective collaboration along the supply chain will add projects at Level 3.

The model in Figure 4.4 should aid those implementing supply chain strategies. Its use assures that strategy making is indeed generating strategic projects to implement those strategies. From a project management point of view, it is also a useful classification for a funded project portfolio.

4.2.3 SCM Strategy Tools

What constitutes a supply chain strategy? Should it be separate from the rest of the company's strategy? How does a company incorporate the drivers described in Chapter 3 into their SCM strategy? Our view is summarized by the following propositions:

- Processes, including those associated with the supply chain, are a source of competitiveness on a level of importance equivalent to decisions on other key strategic elements, like the product mix.
- The supply chain is not just a "cost," but an opportunity for improving competitive position.
- SCM should be intertwined with what the company calls its "strategy." It may be at the center of the strategy (like Dell and others) or supportive of that strategy.
- SCM as a strategy is necessary, but not sufficient. Customer selection, product design, economics, the social–political environment and other factors need to be considered.
- Supply chain measures should support strategic goals.

There are many ways to develop strategies that incorporate these propositions. Two that can be adapted to company needs are described here. Chapter 12 project processes also incorporate them. The first approach, using the Supply Chain Council's Supply Chain Operations Reference model (SCOR), produces a narrower, operations-oriented strategy for improvement. Users must take additional steps to link strategies produced by the SCOR process with other strategic components.

The second approach, Activity Systems, produces a broader strategy that does incorporate other strategic components. There is no reason the two can't be used in concert to produce operating improvements along with new strategic directions.

4.2.3.1 SCOR Approach

The SCOR model from the Supply-Chain Council, described in Chapter 8, recommends metrics as a basis for a supply chain strategy. The metrics are used to compare one's own company to competitors. A supply chain strategy, based on moving to the head of the competitive pack, can arise from this comparison.

SCOR contains many metrics spread throughout its three levels. Most users of SCOR measures follow an approach similar to that shown in Table 4.2, which shows the top, or Level 1, SCOR metrics. The table helps decide "where to go" in terms of supply chain improvement using the following steps:

1. Pick the metrics of most importance to your business.
2. Set priorities for the metrics. In which areas does the company have to excel?
3. Compare, or benchmark, your company's current performance against competitors. Identify the best opportunities for improvement. Use current measures to establish an "as-is" baseline for the current supply chain.
4. Develop strategies to close gaps in performance.

Table 4.2 shows the SCOR top-level metrics in the two categories — customer-facing and internal-facing. Customer-facing metrics are those that measure performance attributes that are visible to customers. Examples are delivery performance

TABLE 4.2
Using SCOR to Define a Supply Chain Strategy

Priority	Performance Attribute	Customer-Facing			Internal-Facing		Competitive Assessment		
		Reliability	Responsiveness	Flexibility	Cost	Assets	Under-Performs Competitors	Exceeds Competitors	Opportunity
A	Delivery performance	•					•		
B	Fill rate	•					•		
C	Perfect order fulfillment	•					•		
A	Order fulfillment lead-time		•				•		
NA	Supply chain response time		•				NA		
A	Production flexibility			•			•		•
C	SCM cost				•			•	
C	Cost of goods sold				•			•	
A	Value-added productivity				•			•	
NA	Warranty or returns processing cost				•			NA	
C	Cash-to-cash cycle time					•		•	
NA	Inventory days of supply					•		NA	
C	Asset turns					•		•	

and lead-time. Internal-facing components, mostly financial, are those that customers don't see.

In this case, a company using the process above has decided that three Level 1 metrics don't apply (Step 1 above). Perhaps all raw materials are commodity-like and readily available from a variety of suppliers. So, supply chain response and inventory days of supply aren't relevant. The company's product may be relatively low value or inappropriate for returning, so warranty and returns processing costs are also irrelevant.

For Step 2, the company ranks the priority for the metric. This company ranks the most important as As. Metrics of low importance are Cs.

The last three columns, called Competitive Assessment, evaluate the company's position relative to competitors. The data shows the company is under-performing in customer-facing areas (column labeled "Under-Performing Competitors") and "over performing" in internal-facing ones (column labeled "Exceeds Competitors"). From Table 4.2, one should conclude that the company stresses financial performance over customer service.

At Step 4, the analysis identifies production flexibility as an opportunity for improvement. Perhaps improvement here will improve customer service while retaining expected financial performance.

The illustration provides the essence of the SCOR approach. There are many alternatives for gathering and presenting the gathered information. SCOR model process element templates, covered in Chapter 8, will assist definition of improvement projects.

Note that the SCOR approach focuses on logistics measures. In Chapter 3, we identified the "extended product" as a basis for competition. In setting priorities for performance attributes and identifying opportunities for improvement, a company should consider other strategy elements like extended product features. However, this has to be concerted effort involving functions beyond those often associated with the supply chain.

4.2.3.2   Activity Systems

Michael Porter, a strategic planning expert, has formulated the activity system approach.[5] Porter has also embellished his approach with observations on the impact of the Internet on strategy, extending the framework to e-commerce.[6] Porter's premise is that competitiveness arises from a network (system) of company "activities" performed differently from rivals'. These are linked in a way that competitors find difficult to replicate. The company with unique activity systems can better withstand competitive attacks.

A procedure for strategy development using this framework includes the following steps:

1. Pick attractive market segments for your products.
2. Make choices how to compete for the attractive segments.
3. Develop themes to support each choice.
4. Design activities to support the themes.
5. Link the activities into an activity system.

Making choices, required in Steps 1 and 2, is hard for many managers. One might have to forsake customer segments in the process, choosing to serve one customer and not serve another. This is counter-intuitive, especially when one believes any revenue, regardless of profitability, is better than no revenue at all. Also, using a technique described later called spheres, the company is likely to end up with multiple supply chains, each tailored to the needs of different segments. This may seem like added complexity or outright duplication to many.

By creating uniqueness through the activity system, the company can escape "commoditization" where rivals compete solely on price. For instance, our example in Table 4.2 is likely competing on price. But the company's customer service is deemed below industry standards. The only way it can continue to compete is to grind out cost reductions. So far, it seems to have succeeded. But the future could be in doubt if competitors attack profitable segments with focused strategies based on unique activity systems. Perhaps the only way out is to break with the past and use better customer service to differentiate itself.

The *Handbook of Supply Chain Management* used Miller SQA to illustrate the application of the activity system approach.[7] We return to Miller here with an expanded analysis. We'll put to use additional details that the project manager at the time, William Bundy, has provided about the project and motivations for it.[8,9] Since the *Handbook* was published, a down market has caused Herman Miller, the parent company, to discontinue the SQA brand of moderately priced furniture. But the SQA supply chain model lives on and has been extended to the entire Herman Miller operation.

Miller provides office furniture in the form of chairs, panel systems, desks and file cabinets. These are built to order with different designs and mixes of components. Customers order through dealers or the Miller sales force. The back-and-forth nature of major purchases can take many weeks. Also, delays in delivery may lead to buyer's remorse and cancellation of orders. Before Herman Miller implemented its new "model," competitive lead-times were 4 to 6 weeks for delivery and another couple of weeks for installation. Often, furniture was shipped by the manufacturer, stored at the local dealer and then installed on the customer's site.

Herman Miller has worked to transform its entire "value chain," not just a piece of it. Miller defines this chain as having the following components, also shown in Table 4.3, as "phases" in the fulfillment process.

1. Customer contact to order entry
2. Order entry to shipment
3. Shipment to installation

It was important to Herman Miller to take this holistic approach. Manufacturing represented only 20% of total cycle time. If other components couldn't be reduced, customers would see little difference. The company is now capable of reliably filling orders in 10 days.

An important consideration in achieving short lead times was the susceptibility to order changes and outright cancellation. Miller also sought to increase the financial return on its business. This meant reducing the cash-to-cash cycle and lowering inventory and manufacturing assets.

Herman Miller used a combination of management savvy, lean manufacturing techniques and technology to achieve its ends. We can derive an activity system with the features Miller required to accomplish its goals. These are depicted in Table 4.3 and Figure 4.5.

Herman Miller's intent was to rely on its established reputation for product quality and shift the basis of competition to fast, efficient service. The "SQA" in its name provided the themes for this approach, our Step 3 above. SQA stands for "simple, quick and affordable." Our version of the Miller activity system adds ROI, return on investment, as a theme because it was a motivator for the effort. ROI improvement would come from reductions in lost revenue, lower inventory, faster collection of revenue and increases in plant utilization.

TABLE 4.3
Herman Miller Activity System

Phase	Activity/Process	Description
Customer Contact to Order Entry	Easy interface	An activity driven by the philosophy of quickly providing information to customers about the product in order to facilitate decisions.
	Order entry tool — "1.1"	On-line catalog showing products. Acts as order entry mechanism. Transmits the order to the factory.
	Visualization tool — "Z-Axis"	Keeps running price. Generates bill of material. Enables the customer to view the layout in three dimensions, hence the name "Z-axis."
Order entry to Shipment	Build-to-order	A production system capable of starting production after the order is received.
	"Production Metering Center"	A raw material staging area that processes incoming materials, preparing them for production. Interfaces with suppliers, low raw material inventory.
	ERP	Enterprise planning system. Stores bill of materials and financial data.
	Expert Scheduling	A proprietary application and accompanying manual interventions for scheduling production. It is continuous, avoiding MRP problems associated with periodic updates.
	MES	Manufacturing execution system. System for assignment of work to production.
	Visibility	Information sharing so that all partners know what others are doing.
	New contracting	Altered terms for suppliers. Shifted inventory responsibility and set tight schedules for delivery.
	"SupplyNet"	Supplier information sharing. Internet tool for sharing material status throughout the supply chain. Includes stock at Miller and its suppliers.
Shipment to Installation	Direct Delivery	Delivery to the end user's site, bypassing dealers' warehouse facilities.
	Multi-order shipping	Shift from a reliance on less than truckload to full truckloads. Enables efficient routing of multiple orders on a single truck.
All	Empowered customer service	Ability of customers to contact a person who can answer any of many questions and makes decisions on the customers' behalf. Contact points are staffed to provide high access.

Figure 4.5 shows the linkages between activities. If Figure 4.5 resembles a spider web, it's no accident. Lines connect themes (shown in circles) and activities (in boxes). The activities that directly support the themes are also darkened. Other activities, in turn, support these.

A competitive activity system will have interlocking activities that are hard to duplicate. The more there are, the harder it is to duplicate. Directly supporting the four themes are three activities: build-to-order manufacturing, easy customer interface and direct delivery. Supporting these activities are other activities. For example,

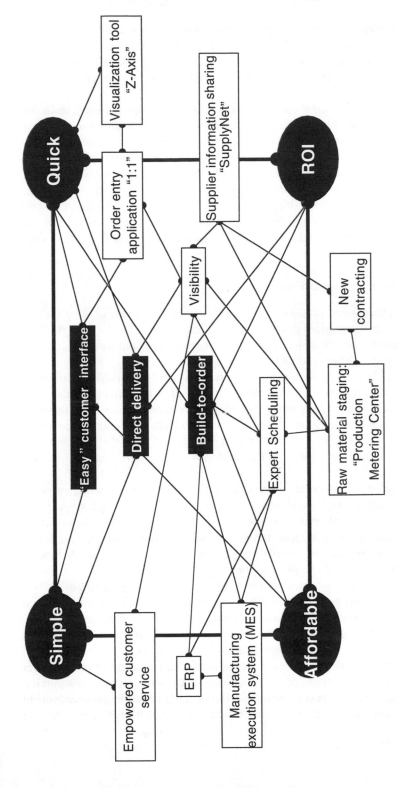

FIGURE 4.5 Herman Miller activity system.

the z-axis application is part of an order entry program. New contracting altered the relationship with suppliers, including the shift of inventory holding to them. This enabled a third-party production metering center that held only a few days' inventory. Since its inception, Miller has made the metering center an internal function.

The activity system is a powerful tool for building company strategies, including missions for the supply chain. The tool enables internal collaboration by drawing on all functions for coordinating disparate functional efforts. It also supports responses to the SCM drivers described in Chapter 3. By identifying how the company will compete, the process defines flexibility requirements. Activity systems, because they are operationally focused, also support process-centered management. Strategy making with the activity system approach develops supply chain process needs and shows where those processes fit into the strategic picture. Finally, where gaps in internal operations need to be filled, collaboration with outside partners can fill the holes.

4.2.4 NEW PRODUCTS AND PROCESSES

Chapter 3 put product and process innovation as the central driver of supply chain change. Figure 4.6 summarizes different types of innovations. The lower right-hand quadrant represents the status quo. From there, each type of innovation can move the organization in a different direction.

The upper right-hand quadrant (new product, old process) describes companies with a constant flow of new products. The record company that produces many new releases has a well-used supply chain. So does the restaurant chain that innovates by developing new menu items. In these cases, products continuously take new shapes, but process changes are incremental. A large part of what the company does is concentrate on operating the product development "machine" that brings new products to market.

The lower left-hand quadrant (old product, new process) happens when a process innovation radically alters the economics of an industry or even enables new products. Process improvements that pack more functions on smaller and smaller silicon chips are an example. Supply chain innovation, like Herman Miller's, also lies in this quadrant. The Internet is another example of process innovation. A flexible machine tool that can quickly shift from product to product is another.

The upper left quadrant (new product, new process) brings changes in two dimensions. These can be breakthrough core products or the fruits of advanced RandD. Technology products like personal computers and copiers were such products when they first reached their markets. Their success required new supply chains to support sales of the new technology.

Process-centered management calls for concurrent development of both product and process. This has the benefit of faster development, a boon in an era of shrinking life cycles. Project management processes should be ready to accelerate supply chain process improvements in response to new product or competitive processes.

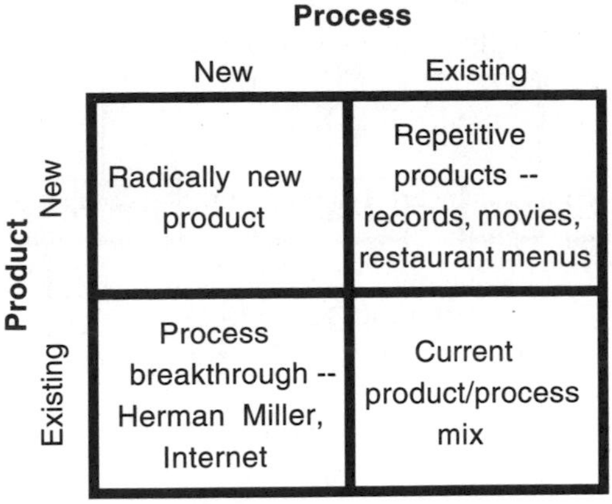

Process

	New	Existing
Product New	Radically new product	Repetitive products -- records, movies, restaurant menus
Existing	Process breakthrough -- Herman Miller, Internet	Current product/process mix

FIGURE 4.6 Types of product and process innovation.

4.3 TASK 2: IMPLEMENTING COLLABORATION RELATIONSHIPS

Task 2 turns inward to issues of collaboration within company walls. One can hardly argue that the company's ability to manage itself and its supply chain initiatives is not a requisite for improvement. For example, if one wants to develop an activity system like Herman Miller's, boundaries must be extended to many departments. These include not only manufacturing but also sales, procurement, systems development and finance.

Also, functional departments, often focused on their own issues, must work with other departments toward common goals. To keep things going, top management must be involved with moral encouragement and financial support. The organization structure and performance measures also must be "in sync" with the direction sought.

These topics are addressed in Chapters 12 and 13 project process descriptions. In this chapter, we want to discuss the "boundary" issues regarding the scope of the improvement effort. This involves market segmentation, which we discussed above, company organizations and dividing the overall supply chain into logical "chunks" for activity systems.

Decisions regarding organization structure fall under this task. The best organization for the future is often not the one that's currently in place, so here we describe options for changing it in some detail. In the next section, we describe "spheres" and how simultaneously addressing internal structure and spheres is a necessary step in any supply chain improvement effort.

Despite the many possible alternative organizations, there are three basic options:

1. Functional (depicted in Figure 4.7)
2. Product-centric (depicted in Figure 4.8)
3. Customer-centric (depicted in Figure 4.9)

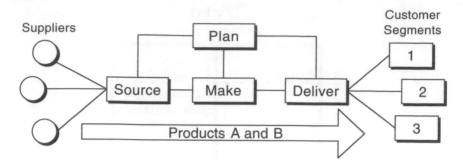

FIGURE 4.7 Functional organization.

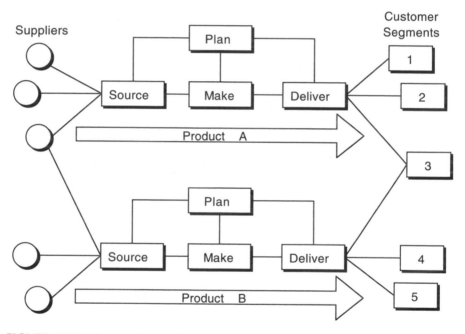

FIGURE 4.8 Product-centric organization.

   The next sections discuss the choices available and the environments that support each alternative.

4.3.1 FUNCTIONAL ORGANIZATIONS

The first organization type is functional, or process-centric. This type defines most mature organizations. Typical functional departments in a manufacturing company include manufacturing operations, distribution, procurement, customer service and finance. Figure 4.7 uses the SCOR core management processes — PLAN, SOURCE, MAKE and DELIVER — to model the functional structure. The figure shows three suppliers and three market segments (1, 2 and 3). Both company products (A and

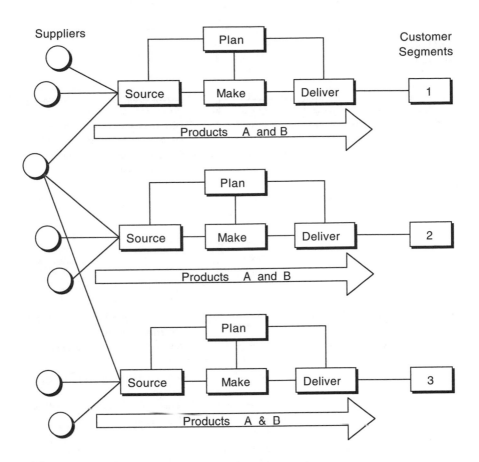

FIGURE 4.9 Customer-centric organization.

B) flow through the same functions. In this structure, shop floor operations (MAKE) may also be functionally organized with equipment distributed into work centers organized by type of equipment.

The functional organization with its focus on specialization is often the product of relentless cost reduction. As such, the functional structure usually does a good job of producing "local optimums" in terms of cost. Examples are the cheapest possible raw materials (low-cost SOURCE), production processes with low labor cost (low-cost MAKE) and cost-optimized distribution channels (low-cost DELIVER).

The functional organization also is likely to rely on Level 1 improvement project types. These are local supply chain improvement projects shown on the left in Figure 4.4. Most of these are nonstrategic, aimed at local cost reductions within a single department.

The functional, process-centric organization fits the small organization. In small companies, informal lines of communication facilitate collaboration across functions since there is little physical separation. A narrow product line also fits well into the

TABLE 4.4
Alternative Organization Forms

Type of Organization	Preferred When:	Not Preferred in Cases Where:
Functional	Narrow product line or small organization All products have similar processes and common needs for cost, service and flexibility. Mature business (Stage 3 and 4 products) with low growth or design change Capital intensive production technology Dominate production competence required, requires technical excellence in a focused area	Diverse product/customer base Products in several life cycle stages Flexibility important in adjusting to changing conditions
Product-centric	Multiple products with differing process technologies New product undergoing changes in growth markets (Stage 1 and 2) Cost driven business, functional products Homogeneous customer base — one or only a few segments	Serving varied customer base with differing requirements Relatively low cost production technology Cost secondary to service in production decision Little in the way of process technology innovation
Customer-centric	Strategy that targets attractive segments Alliances needed in distribution channels Outsource capabilities readily available Style driven business requiring fast response, innovative products Market segments demanding different extended product features Heterogeneous customer base/many segments	Too many segments to serve Lack of scale could cause loss of focus Price sensitive market

functional organization. The firm is a specialist and needn't worry about problems that go with a complex product portfolio.

Another scenario supporting the choice of a functional organization is a dominant production technology. This technology is the center of the business. It is hard to duplicate, requires deep technical skills and is often capital intensive. A semiconductor foundry where the cost of manufacturing facilities runs to billions is an example. Another is an engineering-intensive, high-technology aerospace business such as satellite making.

4.3.2 PRODUCT-CENTRIC ORGANIZATIONS

In the product-centric organization, business units are aligned with product types or brands. In Figure 4.8, there is a minicompany for Product A and another for Product B. Segment 3, which buys both product A and B, is served by both minicompanies.

For example, auto companies organize around "platforms," where a single platform is the basis for several branded products. For a company like the Chrysler division of DaimlerChrysler, platforms include minivan, truck, Jeep, small car and large car. Each platform group is responsible for design, production and marketing plus the assets to fulfill these functions. This choice streamlined an organization of bureaucratic single-function departments that had separate agendas.[10]

A clear case for the product-centric organization is also made when each product demands different process technology. While this is not true for a Chrysler, it would be true for a company marketing two products like beer and wine that require different processes.

Also, a new product may justify a product-centric organization through Stages 1 and 2 in its product life cycle. This would be the case if current supply chains are unsuitable, and process innovation is needed throughout the supply chain from the shop floor to distribution channels. This allows these functions to innovate according to the needs of the business. Later, as the product matures and processes stabilize, pieces may be spun off to specialists, leading to a more functional organization.

Another situation that's perhaps suitable for the product-centered organization occurs when products are distributed across the product life cycle. Two separate supply chains might deliver mature and innovative products, applying the Fisher model described earlier in Section 4.2.1. Those that are mature functional products require a cost-effective supply chain, while those that are innovative require a responsive one.

4.3.3 CUSTOMER-CENTRIC ORGANIZATIONS

Customer-centric organizations are built around targeted segments. Figure 4.9 shows a separate organization for each of three segments. This arrangement is attractive to the company with well-defined segments having distinctively different requirements. Customer-centric also fits when the supply chain is filled with innovative products that change frequently.

Also, tailored extended product features may be important to success. A "grab-and-go" coffee shop business would need a supply chain separate from the coffee house serving customers who linger over their espresso. The customer-centric organization is likely to respond to changes in customer preferences faster than other models. With respect to processes, low investment requirements and flexibility in selecting suppliers and distribution channels encourage the customer-centric choice.

An organization doesn't have to pursue any single organization type from end to end. There are ways to combine types for different steps in the chain. However, one type will likely dominate in any company. Without laying out a structure using the ideas presented here, any attempt at supply chain change may fall short. In the following section, we describe a companion concept, "spheres" for help in making decisions regarding organization.

4.4 TASK 3: FORGING SUPPLY CHAIN PARTNERSHIPS

This section describes tools put to work in Section III project templates, including "spheres" and a classification methodology for partnerships with outside companies.

4.4.1 SPHERES

In the preceding section of this chapter, we encouraged companies to select the best model for their internal organization — process-centric, product-centric, or customer-centric. A sound practice is to make this decision within the context of the company's external environment. A concept we call *spheres* is fundamental to decisions on organization. Recent experience indicates that definition of spheres is vital to the success of supply chain improvement efforts. We describe how to formulate them in Chapter 12.

TABLE 4.5
Components of a Sphere

Dimension	Basis for Sphere
Markets	Defined by segments where end users have common characteristics and buying behavior.
Products	Should include both the physical and the extended product, the services related to the physical product.
Operations	Includes both internal and supply chain partner operations. The latter can include distribution channels, other company divisions and key suppliers.

A sphere is a market–product–operation combination that provides a way to "divide and conquer" in developing and implementing activity systems. The sphere term derives from the fact that a sphere has three dimensions — markets, products and operations — described in Table 4.5. All but the simplest of organizations will operate in multiple spheres. Identifying those spheres to help decide what organization model to follow and what operations are needed makes good sense.

The dimensions, in the left-hand column in Table 4.5, are markets, products and operations. *Markets* are the segments as defined by the company. *Products* are those sold to that segment. *Operations* are the supply chain components (suppliers, manufacturing and distribution facilities) used to make the products.

A functionally organized company, like that shown in Figure 4.7, might draw spheres around each of its functions. Figure 4.10 is one possible result. Using the spheres in the figure, the company will consider one set of initiatives directed at SOURCE to improve processes for obtaining material (Sphere (A) characterized as *all markets-all products-suppliers and inbound material facilities*). Another sphere

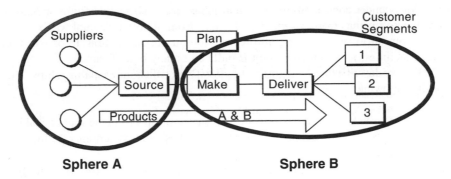

FIGURE 4.10 Spheres for the functionally organized company. A = all markets, all products, suppliers and inbound material facilities; B = all markets, all products, manufacturing and distribution facilities.

(B) will integrate MAKE and DELIVER functions for all products. It is characterized as *"all markets-all products-manufacturing and distribution facilities."*

Suppose our functional company is geographically organized with multiple operations serving market segments (1, 2 and 3) that are in different regions. Then those regions might define the spheres. For example, the choice might be *Asia, Europe* and the *U.S.* or *Eastern, Midwest* and *West*. Such a division would have six spheres, A (for materials) and B (for manufacturing and distribution), for each of the regions.

Spheres for product-centric and customer-centric organizations will also influence organization choice. In fact, starting with sphere designs and then selecting and implementing the organization structure is the recommended sequence for man aging supply chain improvement programs.

Product configuration will also drive sphere definition. A commercial airplane where millions of parts make up one delivered product may shape its spheres around different types of components. On the other hand, a product where a few raw materials make up one base product, like a pill, can produce multiple spheres shaped around downstream distribution channels.

Because they apply to all spheres, a good practice is to create a sphere for ENABLE processes from SCOR. These include shared resources, common business rules and regulatory functions that are justifiably centralized. In Chapter 12 and the Glossary, we differentiate between *product-producing spheres* and *enable spheres*. The first has external customers. The latter has internal customers and serves more than one product-producing sphere.

4.4.2 CLASSIFYING PARTNERSHIPS

Many companies pursue collaborative partnerships. Chapter 3 introduced collaboration as a driver of innovation in supply chain change. Chapter 8 describes Supply Chain Council approaches to collaboration.

Like "flexibility," addressed in Chapter 3, partnership discussions need a way to better describe the nature of a particular partnership arrangement that already exists or is under consideration. A "partnership" can take several forms, bound by agreements ranging from informal to formal, from simple to complex. Examples range from information-sharing all the way to outright acquisition. In between are shared facilities, joint ventures, joint RandD and many other forms.

Here we describe three categories for classifying collaborative partnerships. They are the following:

1. **Purpose.** Whether the partnership creates new "space" in the supply chain. A "yes" or "no" defines the purpose. A "yes" almost certainly defines a strategically important partnership.
2. **Direction.** Whether the partnership goes up, down or across the supply chain. A "vertical," "horizontal" or "both" defines direction.
3. **Choice.** Relative power in the partnership. A "many-to-many," a "one-to-many," a "many-to-one" or a "one-to-one" relationship.

The following paragraphs explain the three categories.

4.4.2.1 Purpose

The term "space" describes the role a company plays in its market. This is the niche carved out by the company and incorporates its operations, its branding and its activity system. A partnership can seek to define new space, perhaps to implement a unique strategy within the supply chain. An example is the Internet retailer that partners with a brick-and-mortar retailer. The combined enterprise provides a fuller range of marketing channels for product sales and returns.

Dell's direct model for selling personal computers is another example. The Dell direct model created a new channel. Herman Miller created new space with its supply chain design, providing a service level that couldn't be matched by any rival. That model was heavily dependent on both supplier agreements and, at least initially, on a third-party logistics provider.

The partnership operates in a new space to the degree it is unique among providers in its marketplace. A "yes" in the purpose category signifies the intent to create new space. By definition this must be a strategic supply chain level endeavor, as defined in Figure 4.4. A "no" in the purpose category will indicate a partnership for other reasons, such as achieving economies of scale, replacement of a current supplier or geographic coverage.

4.4.2.2 Direction

With regard to partnership creation, the direction can be either vertical or horizontal. In some cases, both directions may be involved. Figure 4.11 illustrates the direction property. In the figure, our supply chain is shown with white circles, with our own company represented by a diamond. The chain of another company is shown with darkened circles and a diamond for our direct competitor.

We decide to partner with our competitor in a horizontal partnership, as shown in the figure. If we produce similar products, this partnership is unlikely to create

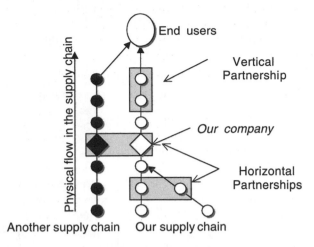

FIGURE 4.11 Direction category in partnerships.

new space. The Hewlett Packard merger with Compaq was this type of combination. However, it could be seen as creating space if our product lines serve common markets but are complementary with little overlap.

Another horizontal partnership takes place in Figure 4.11 between two of our suppliers.They provide different products to one of our immediate suppliers, so this partnership creates new space. A vertical partnership, which is also likely to create new space, is shown downstream of our own operation.

4.4.2.3   Choice

Our final category, choice, reflects the power held by one partner over another. In some cases, a market is a monopsony, where a single buyer controls demand. These powerful partners may not seem like partners at all when they dictate the terms of the relationship. The U.S. Department of Defense, Boeing, the Big 3 U.S. automakers and Wal-Mart definitely have rules suppliers must follow to do business with them. These rules are really not optional. However, your agreement to provide any of these powerful partners with goods and service implies your willingness, if not your eagerness, to enter into a partnership with them.

Figure 4.12 illustrates the "choice" categories. It does this from the perspective of "our company" along the vertical axis on the left-hand side. The company with whom we partner is shown on the horizontal axis. The result is four characterizations of choice in the partnership.

If you are one of many suppliers of your product, you are the weaker partner. This means users of your service or buyers of your goods have *many* options. A partnership of a weak with a strong partner is a "many-to-one" partnership (lower left-hand box in Figure 4.12) meaning that you (a single company in a large field of many) are doing business with the powerful customer (the "one"). Department of Defense, Big 3 and Wal-Mart suppliers have many-to-one partnerships with these large customers. Assuming you do a lot of business with a behemoth, it is quite strategic to you.

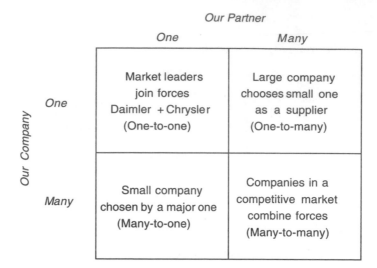

FIGURE 4.12 Partnership choice. Society of ManufacturingEngineers. With permission.

If our company wanted to team with another "weak" company serving a market and we are both small fish in a large pool, we might create a "many-to-many" partnership to chase the business (lower right-hand box in Figure 4.12). If we are two large fish, we might create a "one-to-one" partnership to share risk in a large capital project (upper left-hand box in Figure 4.12).

Sometimes size isn't important. The small company holding a patent for unique technology may be in the driver's seat — the "one." Large companies seeking to license or distribute the technology could, in fact, be the "many."

4.5 TASK 4: MANAGING SUPPLY CHAIN INFORMATION

Chapter 3 pointed to the emergence of process-centered management as a driver of supply chain change. For many companies, this will change their approach to justifying and implementing information technology (IT). Bensaou and Earl drew the contrasts between two "mindsets" that differentiate Western and Japanese companies.[11] Motivating their research were the many complaints about system efforts gone awry in Western companies as compared with the relatively few "disasters" in Japan. (This is a theme developed further in Chapter 9.)

Table 4.6 summarizes the authors' findings. A theme is that Western managers tend to adopt technology for its own sake rather than for what it does for the processes it supports. Too much effort is absorbed in the technical aspects of implementation rather than planning the evolution of the process.

This is hardly surprising, considering the recent rush to deal with Y2K-driven replacements. Initiatives were often reactive to the need to quickly modernize systems just to stay in business, not necessarily to improve processes. At the time of

TABLE 4.6
Mindsets for Framing IT Investments

Issue	Western Mindset	Japanese Mindset
Matching IT with business needs	Align IT with business strategy	Basic way we compete drives IT investments
Return on investment	Capital budgeting process, ROI	Operation performance improvement
Technology and process improvement	Tend to adopt technology — seen as best way to improve	Use the right technology to meet a performance goal
Connections between IT users and specialists	Tech savvy staff and CIOs	Rotation through technical and management roles
Improvement of organization performance	Design elegant system; adapt to it.	Design system to use employee knowledge

Source: Society of Manufacturing Engineers. With permission.

this writing, there is a backlash among technology buyers. Many view their systems as "good enough" and are extending the time between upgrades.

No less important is the flood of aggressively marketed software products in the supply chain management category. Figure 9.2 lists some of the applications covered by the products. Recent categories related to SCM include the following:

- MRP/ERP (materials/enterprise resource planning) — back office systems for fulfilling common functions across the entire company. Replacing these was often the push for Y2K efforts.
- APS (advance planning and scheduling) — planning and scheduling systems that enable faster and more frequent planning of supply chain operations.
- MES (manufacturing execution system) — short-term control applications, including that used in the Herman Miller case, aimed at scheduling operations, particularly in applications requiring fast responses.
- CRM (customer relationship management) — applications that help manage interactions with customers and prospects.
- SRM (supplier relationship management) — an application like CRM for suppliers.
- WMS (warehouse management system) — application designed for the particular needs of larger warehouses and distribution centers.

Many of these applications are designed to facilitate communication over the Internet. This provides a capability among trading partners to share information on the status goods in the supply chain as well as forecasts. CPFR, described in Section 3.7.2, is an example.

We saw, in the Herman Miller case (Section 4.2.32), the importance of information technology in enabling the company's supply chain strategy. Because many companies struggle with new systems, Chapter 9 is dedicated to the project management issues surrounding information technology. In Chapter 15 we integrate Task 4 and Task 5 into project for process improvement enabled by technology.

Information systems requirements for the supply chain will likely occur at the "edges" of the organization. This is the observation of two authors, John Hagel, III and John Seely Brown, who describe the future for "Web services."[12] Getting a major system into place is a formidable, expensive task. Using traditional approaches to system development grows even more complicated when "hooking up" with partners. The advantage to be gained from linking with supply chain partners will spur the growth of Internet protocol software to ease this task.

Another reaction to proliferation of supply chain software applications is finding ways to sort through choices presented by employees and software sellers. Three managers of major e-commerce Web sites described their ways of coping with software sales pitches.[13] In a discussion, conducted appropriately by e-mail, a reporter queried executives from Lands' End, Eddie Bauer and Sears. These executives managed their companies' consumer Web sites. The participants reported that they personally or members of their groups receive more than 50 sales calls a week. To screen these, they make a list of desired features against which to screen the pitches. If the candidate software functionality isn't on that list, you're unlikely to get in the door. This is an example of putting the process needs before the technology.

The move to Web services and specification of needs in advance are logical approaches for dealing with information technology for supply chains. Hagel and Brown, cited above, describe the challenges and roles for the corporate IT department. These include the following:

- IT departments will have to migrate applications to outsourced suppliers of Web services while maintaining existing systems.
- The CIO must be more of a strategist, looking for areas of strategic advantage while building a new IT-based business.
- Nurturing relationships with other companies will become a key IT role as companies become more dependent on their partners for success. This also requires better negotiating skills for CIOs.

Chapter 15 will work these concepts into the supply chain project management plan.

4.6   TASK 5: REMOVING COST FROM THE SUPPLY CHAIN

In this book, we talk of cost reduction that maintains competitive levels of customer service. No other reason comes close to cost reduction as a motivator for supply chain improvement projects in most companies today. There is good reason for this. If the project requires an investment, cash flow from savings will pay for it. A languishing stock price may also be boosted if the project produces an earnings boost or makes a good story for stock analysts and investors.

Having said that, too many cost reduction efforts lash out at the costs themselves and not their root causes. So, when it comes to identifying projects for better cost performance, a first step is understanding the root causes for the costs. The *Handbook of Supply Chain Management* identified six root causes, which were the following:

- **Lack of clarity**. You cannot hit the target if you can't see it. Traditional accounting does a poor job of highlighting cost drivers.
- **Variability in processes and management behavior**. Much cost comes from variation in company processes, a premise that underlies well-publicized Six Sigma efforts to reduce this variation.
- **Expensive product design**. Much of the cost for manufactured projects is "baked in" during design.
- **Information-sharing shortfalls**. Observers are right; the cost of being unintegrated is high.
- **Weak links**. Links are the glue holding the chain together. They are both intra- and intercompany. Designing the links is important to achieve needed levels of flexibility in a cost-effective way.
- **Unintended consequences**. Poorly designed methods of reward and punishment can be a root cause.

Product design as a root cause should be emphasized. It is a rare company that includes product design as part of its SCM improvement program. For companies with short product cycles, this is a big mistake. "Eighty percent of the product cost is determined in the first 20 percent of the product life cycle." This quotation from Steve Church of Avnet applies to electronics.[14] But it is also true for many other lower technology products. "Early" refers to the engineering phases, design and prototyping. Once a product moves into production, the supply chain manager's influence on final cost drops significantly.

Chapter 15 describes projects for cost reduction through either nontechnology or information technology. Templates will include the methods for addressing root causes. Exact solutions will call on many technical disciplines. We'll refer to these in our discussion; references to specific techniques are in the Bibliography.

ENDNOTES

1. McWilliams, Gary, Dell Computer's Kevin Rollins becomes a driving force, *The Wall Street Journal,* April 4, 2002, p B6.
2. Fisher, Marshall L., What is the right supply chain for your product?" *Harvard Business Review,* (75/2), March–April, 1997. 105–116.
3. Lee, Hau L., The right supply chain strategy for value creation, Supply-Chain Council Executive Retreat, February 26, 2003.
4. Adapted from the *Handbook of Supply Chain Management,* Chapter 5.
5. Porter, Michael E., What is strategy? *Harvard Business Review,* (74/6) November–December, 1996. 61–78.
6. Porter, Michael E., Strategy and the Internet, *Harvard Business Review,* (79/3) March 2001. pp. 62–78.

7. *Handbook of Supply Chain Management,* chapter 48.

8. www.menlolog.com/html/NewsViews/ArticlesAbout Menlo/MillerSQAArticle/htm.

9. Bundy, Bill, Brown, Art and Dean, Steve, Changing the rules of the game, Presentation, Council of Logistics Management Annual Meeting, October 1999.

10. Lutz, Robert A., *Guts*, New York: John Wiley & Sons, Inc., 1998, Chapter 2.

11. Bensaou, M. and Earl, Michael, The right mind-set for managing information technology, *Harvard Business Review,* September–October, 1998, pp. 119–128.

12. Hagel III, John and Brown, John Seely, Your next IT strategy, *Harvard Business Review (79/9),* October, 2001, pp. 105–113.

13. *The Wall Street Journal*, Making the sale, January 27, 2003, p. R9.

14. Church, Steve, The impact of globalizing supply networks, Supply-Chain Council Executive Retreat, February 26, 2003.

Section II

Project Management and
Supply Chain Management

5 Levels of Project Management Maturity

Harold Kerzner's five-level Project Management Maturity Model (PMMM) is the subject of this chapter. The model is a tool for measuring an organization's ability to exploit project management knowledge and practice. Tools in Section III should enable a company to reach at least Level 3 in the PMMM for supply chain projects.

This chapter sets the stage for an expanded description of project management vocabulary and structure. One can effectively argue that improving one's supply chain is impossible without competence in project management. Just ask people at one of the many companies that, through lack of focus, patience, skills, or money, generally cannot implement initiatives. When we reach Section III, we'll also see that juggling too many projects may also limit the pace of change.

What comes first — supply chain competence or project management competence? This is a "chicken-and-egg" question. Both are required. The necessity to move ahead with supply chain change may be just the incentive needed for building a project management capability, if it doesn't already exist. Organizations already expert in project management can capitalize on their competence in pursuit of better supply chains.

As the need for rapid change calls for project management skills, many will be challenged. Dr. Harold Kerzner offers a vision of what excellence in project management looks like, captured in his PMMM. The PMMM gages an organization's position on the maturity continuum, providing a *measurable*, as our book's title promises, way to track progress. The description here summarizes Kerzner's PMMM supplemented with comments on its applicability to SCM. For more PMMM information, the reader can turn to either of two references, one short[1] and the other long.[2]

Figure 5.1 displays the five levels of the PMMM beginning with "common language" and progressing to "continuous improvement." The positioning of the levels in Figure 5.1 reflects overlapping in the progression from one level to another. For example, the move from Level 1: Common Language to Level 2: Common Processes is not necessarily sequential. Migration to common processes can begin even while a common language capability is developing. When Level 3: Singular Methodology is implemented, Level 2: Common Processes, is likely to be jettisoned in favor of the single "best" way. So there is little overlap.

Table 5.1 uses elements from Kerzner's descriptions of different levels for a quick reference to assess maturity levels. Table 5.1 is slanted toward supply chain needs but should fit most other project types. To place your company, simply find the description that best fits you. Note, we have added a Level 0 for the organizations

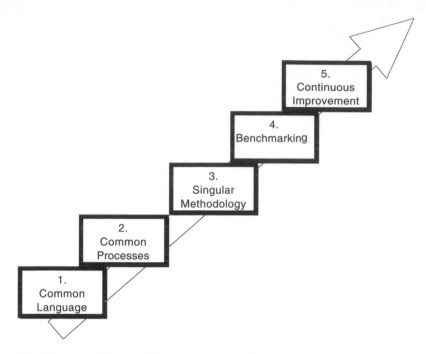

FIGURE 5.1 Kerzner Project Management Maturity Model (PMMM) levels. Kerzner, Harold, *Strategic Planning for Project Management: Using a Project Management Maturity Model*, New York: John Wiley & Sons, 2001. With permission.

without any project management perspective. Unfortunately the Level 0 company, where the need for formalized project management is not on the radar screen, is not rare. Lars Rosqvist of Bombardier Transportation, who reviewed Section II, notes the reluctance of many line managers to get involved in project work at all.

Please note that the PMMM calls for common language and processes in Levels 1–3. Later in this section, we draw on resources from the Project Management Institute and the Supply-Chain Council to suggest the vocabulary and processes for SCM. Section III describes specific SCM project management processes for implementation. These provide a "singular methodology," a requisite for Level 3 of the PMMM.

5.1 LEVEL 1: COMMON LANGUAGE

Use of project management is sporadic at Level 1. At Level 1, an organization has "pockets" of appreciation for project management. Members of the organization are aware of the need, but not competent in its execution. Indeed, the level is based more on awareness of what should be done, not what is actually being done. Top management support is lacking or not persistent. Any implementation that does occur is "bottom up" and variable from project to project.

The organization is also likely to be strongly functional. Managers are protective of their turf and unwilling to join in cross-functional projects. Supply chain projects,

TABLE 5.1
Assessment Tool for PMMM

	0 No Discernible Project Management	1 Common Language	2 Common Processes	3 Singular Methodology	4 Benchmarking	5 Continuous Improvement
Organization awareness	Unaware of the need for project management. Functional orientation.	Awareness exists of need for project management knowledge and language.	Use of project management life cycles (phasing). Scope control. Use of software.	Cultural barriers are eliminated. Individuals can easily shift to "project mode."	Individuals are aware of the need for improving project management processes.	Shared knowledge by project teams. Cultivation of project management talent.
Management support	None. Not on the management agenda.	No investment in project management capability. Little senior management support.	Education provided in project management. Willingness exits to address internal issues.	Support for project management exists throughout the organization. Projects are linked to strategy.	Establishment of a Project Office or Center of Excellence to pursue improvements.	Recognition of continuous improvement as necessary.
Process discipline	None. No project management processes exist.	Occasional use of project management methodology initiated at lower levels.	Concerted effort to use project management. Cost and schedule controls are used.	Single, informal approach used on all types of projects.	Company looks outside for upgrading project management processes.	Changes are made to company's own project management processes.
Motivation	Ignorance. No apparent motivators. Project management not considered important.	Insufficient motivation to take authority away from functional managers.	Company must undertake major important projects in order to survive.	Project management efficiency perceived to be closely linked to company success.	The company strategy is heavily dependent on projects. Examples include new products, internal improvement, major systems, supply chain design and capital investments.	

using the terminology shown in Figure 4.4, are "functional" in scope and "nonstrategic" in their impact. There is little in the way of project management training and development. To graduate to Level 2, the organization must increase its awareness of project management and its benefits. Moving from Level 1 to 2 can take weeks or years.

5.2 LEVEL 2: COMMON PROCESSES

At Level 2, support for project management broadens. It takes the form of support from top to bottom in the organization, training of specialists and other involved staff and a recognition of the need for processes and methodology. Also at Level 2, projects are tracked financially, possibly requiring changes to the cost accounting system.

Motivations for moving to Level 2 often come when an organization faces high-risk projects. Examples include major capital expenditures, big systems implementations, new product development, or supply chain improvements. The last, in fact, can involve all the prior items. Often the realization that project management will help comes from lower in the organization.

Kerzner identifies five "life cycles" at Level 2. These are stepping stones to fully fulfill Level 2 requirements. Getting through the five phases is not trivial and, like Level 1, can involve an extended period of time. The *embryonic* phase, the first in the life cycle, is the acceptance of the need for project management. It is often spurred by the need to take on "survival" projects like those listed above to provide the motivation. If you fail a survival project, your business fails.

The second life cycle phase, *management acceptance,* is entered when senior management endorses project management, often at the behest of those under them, who are performing the project. This phase is over when senior management becomes willing to change the way it does business.

Line management acceptance is gained for project management in the third life cycle phase. This manifests itself in the willingness to free talents for project management training and for the projects themselves. Level 4, the *growth phase*, starts to create the project management process. The following achievements mark the end of this phase:

- Development of project life cycles
- Formulation of a project management methodology accompanied by training
- A commitment to planning by executive management
- Resistance to scope changes, usually in the form of scope creep
- Implementation of project management software that covers cost and schedule

Level 5 is the *initial maturity phase*. A curriculum is available to improve the skills of those working in projects. It includes development and integration of cost or schedule control systems. A major obstacle is the resistance to accountability that comes with "horizontal" accounting for project costs.

5.3 LEVEL 3: SINGULAR METHODOLOGY

At this level, the organization selects a "singular" project management methodology. The term *singular* has several meanings. One is "unique, individual, or separate." This implies that the organization takes the best of the methodologies it has found or developed and adopts them as their own. The resulting project management methodology is likely to be unique, hence "singular," to the organization. Another use of the term is as a synonym for "single." That is, having a common process for use through the organization in lieu of multiple versions developed as ad hoc approaches to individual projects.

Kerzner doesn't directly define the term "singular," but his use of the term implies both meanings. He characterizes a singular methodology as having the following components:

1. **Integrated processes** — there are no separate TQM, product development, or change management projects. The singular project management process covers all. Programs like TQM, because of the discipline required, can be precursors to a singular process.
2. **Cultural support** — the entire organization supports the process. This is a goal of our SCM *Task 2 Implementing collaborative relationships,* where internal friction to effective supply chains is at a minimum.
3. **Management support at all levels** — support for the projects and project managers comes from both line and senior management. Line managers, in particular, support the project manager with joint accountability, staff, alternative plans if necessary and implementation. The project manager is empowered by senior management to make decisions. The project team produces recommendations and alternatives, not just restated problems. Status reporting is formalized with regard to timing, distribution and content.
3. **Informal project management** — the methodology is adapted to the needs of individual projects. Control tools include general guidelines and checklists. An effort to minimize paperwork is made. An example is using red, yellow and green "traffic lights" to report status on work packages and deliverables. Informality provides the flexibility to adapt the project management methodology to a broad range of project types.
4. **Return on investment from project management training and education expense** — project management skills development is ongoing. There is a realization that the return in benefits exceeds the cost of the training and education. A company at Level 3 will have few conflicts rising to senior management since problems are headed off at lower levels.
5. **Behavior excellence** — there is recognition within the organization that project management is different from day-to-day operational management. The needed skills are defined and cultivated.

Kerzner emphasizes that excellence in project management doesn't guarantee the success of the project. However, it does improve the project's chances for success.

In fact, if every project is successful, Kerzner observes, the organization isn't working on enough projects.

5.4 LEVEL 4: BENCHMARKING

Benchmarking is a popular technique for identifying ways to improve the project management culture. Benchmarking might discover new software approaches or adaptable practices from one's own industry or other industries. The latter might encourage broader use of project management internally. The idea of benchmarking is to take the Level 3 singular methodology to the next level by bringing outside ideas into the organization through the benchmarking process.

A supporting structure recommended by Kerzner "cements" project management into the company structure. The recommendations begin with a project office (PO) or a center of excellence (COE) for project management. These differ in that the PO is a permanent line function, while the COE can be a formal or informal committee.

Our own experience with SCM indicates that a broad program of supply chain change should have central control of a project office nature. Each project within the program should have similar formats for tracking progress, including the use of verifiable project milestones. A consolidated form of reporting using an easily accessed project management tool is also indispensable in providing visibility over the progress or lack thereof.

5.5 LEVEL 5: CONTINUOUS IMPROVEMENT

At Level 5, the organization puts benchmarking and other information to work for process improvement. These improvements can occur anywhere in the project management domain. Level 5 lasts "forever." Kerzner cites several examples of continuous improvement. Among them are the following:

1. Procedural documentation, avoiding re-creation of paperwork from project to project.
2. Project management methodologies that are tailored to the organization, not "canned."
3. Capacity planning that assures the best projects will have the resources they need.
4. Competency models in which skills, not deliverables or expectations, define the need for project staff.
5. Multiple projects managed by individual project managers made possible by training and qualification, risk management techniques, project scheduling and joint accountability with line management.
6. End-of-phase reviews that encourage project cancellation if the project is not working, along with rigorous business-oriented scrutiny.
7. Strategic selection of projects that assures that projects align with strategy.
8. Portfolio management wherein proposed projects are evaluated based on risk and the benefits from implementation.

9. Horizontal accounting where costs of implementation are estimated and closely tracked.

Any of these categories could represent a major effort. Kerzner's point is to keep one's project management methodology evolving in advance of progress made by competitors. Project management skills, in his view, are a strategic asset.

The remainder of this section and Section III project templates are a resource for improvement of project management processes. The goal is to provide the reader at any level of project management maturity with workable ideas for improvement. Elements include both necessary vocabulary and processes directed at the needs of supply chain improvement. Cases provided in Appendix A also represent a form of benchmarking, providing ideas for reader adaptation to their own organizations.

ENDNOTES

1. Kerzner, Harold, Strategic Planning for Project Management: Using a Project Management Maturity Model, New York: John Wiley & Sons, 2001.
2. Kerzner, Harold, Project Management: A Systems Approach to Planning, Scheduling and Controlling, 7th ed., New York: John Wiley & Sons, 2001.

6 Project Management Language

The Project Management Institute maintains terminology for project management. Common language will help in reaching higher levels of project management maturity as described in Chapter 5. Our supply chain project approaches in Section III will use the terminology in this chapter.

Project management language for this chapter comes from *A Guide to the Project Management Body of Knowledge* (PMBOK) from the Project Management Institute (PMI).[1] This chapter focuses on the needs within SCM for project management vocabulary and should help achieve Level 1: Common Language of the PMMM covered in this chapter. This summary should alert the reader to significant terms.

- There's a difference between a *program* and a *project*. A program consists of a number of projects. Projects are temporary and unique. In other words, they have a beginning and an end. A program can go on forever containing a number of projects plus some ongoing operation elements.
- *Project life cycle phases* mark important milestones in the project. A phase usually ends with a major deliverable.
- *Processes* are the foundation of project management knowledge. There are nine project management knowledge areas, each containing several processes as shown in Figure 7.1. Knowledge and practice in executing these processes will make one a more skilled project leader or team member.
- Processes are divided into *process groups*. There are five groups: *initiating, planning, executing, controlling* and *closing*.
- A *work breakdown structure*, or WBS, is a "deliverable-oriented" view of a project. This is useful in communicating expectations in terms of scope and products for the project.

There are many opportunities for becoming entangled in project management and supply-chain jargon. Chris Christensen, a project management expert, has pointed to areas of potential confusion. A company may have a safety *program*. However, this is not a project term since it is ongoing. Closer to the project world, an engineer can be assigned, perhaps more or less permanently, to his company's "widget program" that is, a multiproject effort to bring a new product to market.

Also, we should avoid confusing the "product life cycle" described in Section 4.2.1 from the "project life cycle," which is project phasing. Also, the term "product"

TABLE 6.1
Interdisciplinary Examples

	Event	Project Management Challenges	SCM Challenges
A	Partnership with a major supplier	Needed transitions, joint team operation	Inbound logistics, systems requirements, financial terms, target markets, capital commitments
B	New product introduction	Integration of schedules with RandD, facilities planning	Distribution channels, sourcing, manufacturing capability, early supplier involvement
C	Horizontal acquisition of a rival company	Integration of products and operations	Design of combined entity supply and distribution networks and processes
D	Implementation of a strategy based on an activity system	Coordinated implementation of new processes	Operational components of the activity system
E	Plant relocation	Construction management, move coordination	Property acquisition, location analysis, plant design, layout
F	Bill of material cost reduction	Coordination of multiple efforts using different approaches	Supplier interface, value engineering, qualification and testing

in the project management sense refers to project deliverables. "Product" in the broader sense refers to the goods and services our company sells.

6.1 OVERLAPPING DISCIPLINES

The PMBOK points out that project management is not a standalone discipline. In fact, the need for project management disciplines arises because multiple disciplines must work together to make change happen. Figure 1.1 shows that the four cornerstones of world-class project supply chain management include project management knowledge and practice plus SCM knowledge and practice within SCM.

Table 6.1 shows examples of the overlap of project management and SCM disciplines. On the left are possible "events" in the life of an organization. Each event generates work requiring both project management and SCM expertise. To achieve success, each also requires multiple disciplines or even multiple companies. For this reason, project management capabilities will be challenged to bind the effort. Many organizations delegate the work needed in these examples to functional managers. A company at Level 1 or below in the PMMM would not even have a project management function.

Examining the table's examples makes it easy to see the potential for problems with uncoordinated efforts. For example, one can see the pitfalls in Event E, relocation of a manufacturing plant. This project might be traditionally viewed as limited to a single function, manufacturing. However, in addition to manufacturing, there are several tasks associated with Event E for general management that would benefit from project management. For example, the marketing function must decide what to make and in what quantities. Finance should justify the effort and determine how to pay for the plant.

In Chapter 5, we described a Level 3 company as measured by the PMMM as having a singular methodology for project management. This methodology should be capable of coping with the complexity represented by a broad range of different projects like those shown in Table 6.1.

6.2 PROJECT MANAGEMENT STRUCTURE AND VOCABULARY

The PMBOK is an impressive, and a bit intimidating, collection of techniques, procedures and structures for project management. As a "body of knowledge," one would expect no less. Our view is that the PMBOK should be viewed not as holy writ to be followed literally but as a collection of tools to be shaped to the organization's business needs. For those without mature project management, experimentation at Level 2 of the PMMM is meant to lead to the best solution for any particular organization. The following sections provide a starting point for developing a company vocabulary and methodology.

6.2.1 BASIC DEFINITIONS

Understanding PMBOK terminology begins with the components of a project environment. Figure 6.1 is a picture of this environment. At the top are *programs*, which are groups of related projects that have common links of some sort. In addition to projects, a program may have an element of continuous, nonproject repetitive activity. A program, for example, can include development of a product (a project) and subsequent manufacturing of the product (a continuous, routine activity).

Whether a company calls its supply chain effort a program or project could depend on its intent. If the SCM effort were to be an ongoing activity that, from time to time, would have no projects, "program" would be a logical label for the effort. If the SCM effort is to be a one-shot affair, then "project" might fit better. Chris Christensen cautions against the use of "program" over "project." He observes that many companies have "programs" where very little is accomplished. There is no real commitment to the effort; it exists more for window-dressing than for achieving real results. However, the word "project" is more often associated with real effort from real people with definite goals.

Examples in Table 6.1 illustrate possible supply chain programs or projects. Event A, partnership with a major supplier, could involve multiple *projects*, defined as *temporary* efforts that create something *unique* in the form of a product, service or result. In Program A, these separate projects might produce new communications links (a product), coordinated transportation (a result), assembly of components at the supplier (a service), development of inventory policies (a service) and so forth. "A" is also properly a program, not a project, if it involves operations after the partnership starts to operate.

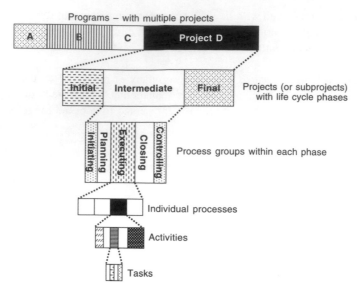

FIGURE 6.1 PMBOK project management terminology.

Where a project scope is very broad or project components are distinct, *sub-projects* are appropriate. An example of a "distinct" subproject could be a piece of the project that is farmed out to a third party.

Returning to Figure 6.1, the next level shows how a project decomposes into product life cycle *phases*. Figure 6.1 shows three generic time-based phases — *initial*, *intermediate* and *final*. The names and number of phases will depend on the type of project. Building construction may have life cycle phases like feasibility, planning and design, construction and turnover and startup. Feasibility and planning and design are part of the initial phase. Construction is an intermediate phase. Turnover and startup is the final phase. Product development might use a stage gate vocabulary with stages being the phases. Examples are idea development, preliminary investigation, development and launch.

A Level 3 PMMM organization would have guidelines for naming these life cycle phases. Actual names would vary with the type of project. In Chapter 11, as an example, we recommend the following life cycle phases for SCM improvement projects:

1. Supply Chain Strategy
2. Internal Alignment
3. Short Term Improvement
4. Long Term Improvement

Returning to Figure 6.1, each life cycle phase contains *processes* that are divided into five *process groups*. Project management process groups (1, 2, 4, and 5 in the list of process groups below) control the project. The product-related process group (#3 below) produces the output of the project. The project management body of

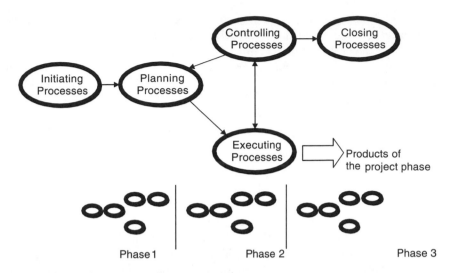

FIGURE 6.2 Links among process groups in a life cycle phase.

knowledge is the domain of the project management groups, while the "application area," SCM in our case, is the domain of the product-related group. SCM is such an application area. In Section III, we describe SCM processes in all five process groups.

Chapter 7 describes the groups and related processes in greater detail. Figure 6.2 shows information flow among the process groups. Here are short descriptions of each process group:

1. **Initiating** processes authorize the phase.
2. **Planning** processes define and refine objectives and chart the path toward those objectives.
3. **Executing** processes coordinate resources to carry out the plan.
4. **Controlling** processes monitor and measure progress to promote corrective action.
5. **Closing** processes formalize acceptance of the phase or project, bringing it to an end.

The bottom of Figure 6.2 symbolizes the presence of each process group within each life cycle phase of the project. Each *process* has inputs, outputs, tools and techniques that are described in the PMBOK.

Processes consist of multiple *activities*. Each activity has duration, cost and resource requirements. Activities may be further broken down into *tasks* and, if desired, *subtasks*. The processes are the core of project management's body of knowledge and are the subject of Chapter 7. In Chapters 12–15 we endeavor to do for SCM what the PMBOK does for project management. This is to describe the project processes needed to execute an SCM project.

A *work breakdown structure* (WBS) is a product-oriented view of the program and defines all of its outputs, or scope. This presentation is particularly helpful because deliverables are tangible outputs, useful for getting agreement on the scope, communicating products and identifying resource requirements. For Event A in Table 6.1, the WBS might list *communications links, redesigned transportation network, subassembly design facility* and *inventory policies* as project deliverables. This will help the partners in defining requirements, making sure nothing needed to make the partnership work is missing.

6.2.2 PROGRAMS, PROJECTS AND WBS APPLICATION

PMI acknowledges that the project management discipline is new. As mentioned above, it is also a discipline with a great potential for proliferation of terminology from one organization to another. The PMBOK seeks to bring consistency to the application of project management terms.

A company improving its supply chain must make choices. Is a supply chain improvement initiative a "program" or a "project?" Should supply chain improvement be coupled with other initiatives like strategic planning? Does it make any difference? As we go forward, we'll follow the terminology guidelines in the following paragraphs. The reader should be aware that there are viable alternatives.

As we proceed, we'll characterize our programs and projects as producing *results*, not products or services. We will also refer to the process that produced this result as a project, not a program, even though it could have a continuous improvement and operating stage after the initial project. However, readers should use the nomenclature that fits their situation best, with the earlier warning from Chris Christensen in mind.

Flexibility exists in terms of organizing a program or project. In some cases, it may make sense to use a deliverable-oriented decomposition. For example, an aircraft design program might be broken into WBS components like the wing, fuselage, engines and so forth. In other situations, particularly where deliverables are highly interdependent, decomposition based on time-based phases fits best. This is the case in supply chain development. SCM is a great example of "progressive elaboration," where general goals are articulated at the beginning of the project and refined as the project proceeds.

Figure 6.3 illustrates a time-phased WBS for a supply chain improvement program. The project's ultimate product, shown in Figure 6.3, is an *implemented SCM* strategy. The figure uses the five SCM tasks, which also represent our SCM knowledge areas, to assign deliverables associated tasks shown at the upper right corner of each WBS element. The five tasks are:

1. Designing supply chains for strategic advantage.
2. Implementing collaborative relationships within the organization
3. Forging supply chain partnerships
4. Managing supply chain information
5. Removing cost from the supply chain

Section III describes how to develop these deliverables. They require project processes described in Chapters 12–15 that rely on SCM knowledge and practice.

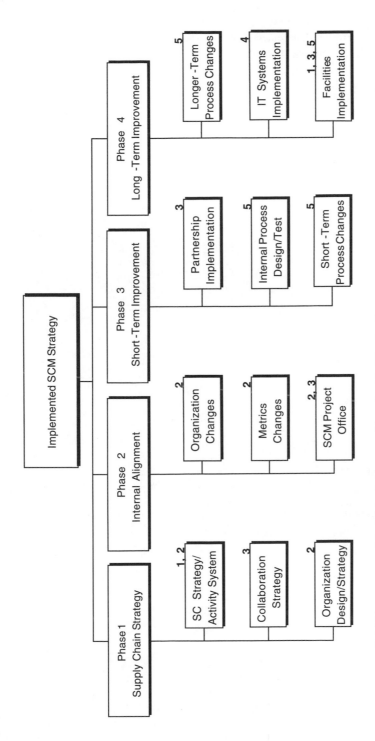

FIGURE 6.3 WBS, or deliverable, view — supply chain improvement project.

ENDNOTE

1. A Guide to the Project Management Body of Knowledge (PMBOK Guide®), New-town Square: Project Management Institute, 2000.

7 Project Management Knowledge Areas

This chapter describes project management knowledge areas and related processes needed to execute projects. It also evaluates the need for supplementing project management knowledge area processes with SCM knowledge. Section III details the supplemental processes that incorporate this knowledge.

In Chapter 6, we introduced the project management body of knowledge, or PMBOK, process groups — initiating, planning, executing, controlling and closing. The PMBOK also defines nine knowledge areas for classifying these processes. Each project management process will belong to a knowledge area and a process group, as shown in Figure 7.1. Section III will identify SCM project processes and assign them to our SCM knowledge areas and the five PMBOK process groups.

This chapter summarizes the PMBOK know-how needed to execute project management processes effectively. Readers should view this as a summary only and no substitute for having the PMBOK Guide close at hand. In some knowledge areas, the PMBOK level of expertise is sufficient for a supply chain project. In other knowledge areas, SCM know-how should supplement pure project management knowledge.

Figure 7.1 lists the nine project management knowledge areas down the left column. Along the top are the five process groups: initiating, planning, executing, controlling and closing. Related processes lie at the intersection of these groups and the knowledge areas. PMBOK describes 39 processes for effective project management, recognizing that the role and intensity of each will vary from project to project.

7.1 NEED FOR SUPPLEMENTAL SCM KNOWLEDGE

A supply chain project, or indeed any project in an application area, cannot be successful without application area knowledge. Figure 7.2 illustrates a central reason for supplemental SCM knowledge for supply chain improvement projects. (This figure was first discussed in Chapter 4 and was presented there as Figure 4.4.)

"Levels of Implementation" in Figure 7.2 refers to the breadth of the project in terms of participation by different organization levels. Level 1 involves a single function, often a department. Level 2 broadens the involvement from the department to the business unit level. A business unit might be a division of large corporation or a standalone company. Level 3 is the supply chain level, where more than one company or business unit participates in the project.

Process Groups

Knowledge Areas	Initiating	Planning	Executing	Controlling	Closing
Integration		Plan Development	Plan Execution	Plan Change Control	
Scope Management	Initiation	Scope Planning Scope Definition		Scope Verification Scope Change Control	
Time Management		Activity Definition Activity Sequencing Duration Estimation Schedule Development		Schedule Control	
Cost Management		Resource Planning Cost Estimating Cost Budgeting		Cost Control	
Quality Management		Quality Planning	Quality Assurance	Quality Control	
Human Resources		Organization Planning Staff Acquisition	Team Development		
Communications		Communications Planning	Information Distribution	Performance Reporting	Administrative Closure
Risk Management		Risk Planning Risk Identification Qualitative Analysis Quantitative Analysis Response Planning		Risk Monitoring & Control	
Procurement		Procurement Planning Solicitation Planning	Solicitation Source Selection Contract Administration		Contract Closeout

FIGURE 7.1 Project management processes by knowledge area and process group.

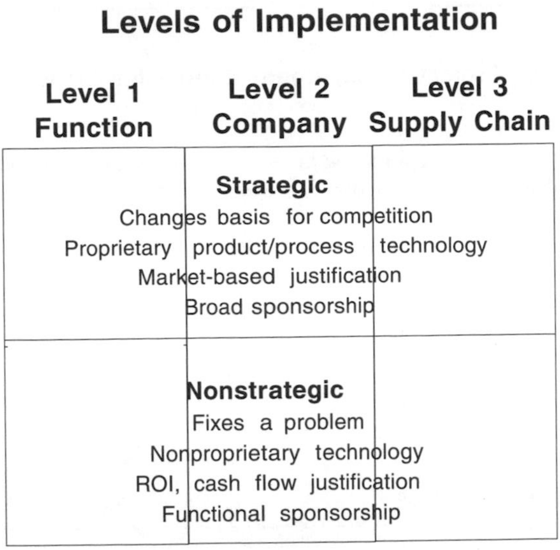

Levels of Implementation

Level 1 Function	Level 2 Company	Level 3 Supply Chain
Strategic Changes basis for competition Proprietary product/process technology Market-based justification Broad sponsorship		
Nonstrategic Fixes a problem Nonproprietary technology ROI, cash flow justification Functional sponsorship		

FIGURE 7.2 Model for competing through SCM.

Increasing implementation levels makes formal project management even more critical to successful supply chain change. Most projects in an organization happen at Level 1 — the departmental level. This is where sponsorship resides and where clear accountabilities and budget authority help get things done. Control of projects is easier. An individual company will likely increasingly need to pursue a portfolio of business unit (Level 2) and supply chain (Level 3) projects. For projects that extend to supply chain partners, coordination must cross company boundaries, demanding new integration skills and knowledge, taxing the resources and capabilities of many.

7.2 SCM KNOWLEDGE REQUIREMENT BY KNOWLEDGE AREA

Table 7.1 lists the nine PMBOK knowledge areas and an estimate of the need for supplemental SCM knowledge for each. This is the need an experienced project manager would have for assistance by someone versed in SCM knowledge areas. The table summarizes — by a High, Medium or Low ranking — the need in the knowledge area for specialized SCM knowledge and processes. Definitions of high, medium and low are the following:

- **High**: Major need for tailored SCM-specific processes to support PMBOK processes for demanding projects.
- **Medium**: Moderate need for tailored SCM-specific processes to support PMBOK processes for demanding projects.
- **Low**: PMBOK processes are sufficient for demanding SCM projects.

TABLE 7.1
Impact of SCM on Project Management Knowledge Areas

		SCM Considerations			
PMBOK Knowledge Area	**Need for SCM Expertise**	**Strategic**	**Multi-Company**	**Paradigm Shift**	**Ambiguous Deliverables**
Integration Management	High	X	X		X
Scope Management	High	X	X		X
Time Management	Low				
Cost Management	Medium	X	X		X
Quality Management	Medium	X			X
Human Resources	High		X	X	
Communications Management	Medium		X		X
Risk Management	High	X	X	X	X
Procurement Management	High		X	X	

If a project is a demanding one in terms of complexity, issues addressed or the needs for supply chain expertise, then a "high" rating is warranted. A "low" rating is given where PMBOK processes should be sufficient for most project managers. Table 7.1 calls attention to "considerations" because a project is in the SCM domain. SCM project management considerations stem from one or more of the following factors:

1. Aggressive SCM projects are *strategic*, elevating visibility and increasing the criticality of the project to the future of the business.
2. Projects are Level 3, or *multicompany* (from Figure 7.2). This requires project management coordination across company boundaries. Participants are more likely to be described as "partners," not uninvolved buyers and sellers.
3. A *paradigm shift* from functional to supply chain thinking is necessary. This is a shift from viewing other departments, customers and suppliers as adversaries to viewing them as project stakeholders.
4. *Ambiguous deliverables* require SCM knowledge-based judgment to evaluate the deliverables for completion and to develop proper control responses.

In this chapter, we'll identify sources of complexity and the resulting need for supplemental processes. Our Section II reviewers, project management experts Chris Christensen and Lars Rosqvist, provided their reactions to the initial expertise evaluations; their input has been considered and, in some cases, incorporated.

Section III is a step, hopefully for the reader a significant step, toward providing the supplemental processes needed to complete demanding SCM projects. Anyone undertaking an important SCM project should keep both this book and the PMBOK close at hand.

7.3 KNOWLEDGE AREAS AND SCM

This section describes each of the nine knowledge areas and related knowledge requirements for implementing supply chain improvements. Accompanying tables list the PMBOK processes for each knowledge area along with the process group to which the process is assigned. The high, medium or low rating for required SCM knowledge is at the top of the table.

7.3.1 KNOWLEDGE AREA: PROJECT INTEGRATION MANAGEMENT

High SCM Knowledge Required

Project Integration Management Processes	Process Group
Plan Development	Planning
Plan Execution	Execution
Integrated Change Control	Controlling

Processes in this knowledge area hold the project together and produce most of its products. As the requirements of a project become increasingly complex, so do the tools and knowledge required. The need for "high" SCM knowledge is inherent because this knowledge area, under the plan execution process, is assigned all work specific to the knowledge area.

Plan Development takes other planning inputs and produces a project plan that is modified as the project proceeds. The PMBOK assumes projects have their genesis from other planning processes, like strategic planning. Chapter 12 in Section III describes a process for supply chain strategy development that takes this input and develops a supply chain design.

The PMBOK lists the following elements for the project plan:

1. Project charter
2. The strategy for completing the project, including individual plans from other knowledge areas like SCM
3. Scope including objectives and deliverables
4. A preliminary work breakdown structure (WBS) to the level of control desired plus responsibility for deliverables
5. Cost and schedule estimates
5. Staff required and cost
6. Risks, constraints, contingencies and responses
7. Subsidiary plans for scope, schedule, cost, quality, staffing, communications, risk and procurement
8. Issues faced by the product and required decisions

The world would likely be a better place if all projects had this documentation before they kicked off. When several organizations must contribute, as is the case in supply chain projects, a complete plan is even more important.

Plan Execution oversees performance of the plan and provides needed feedback to change it. Most of the project budget will fund these product-producing processes that create "work results," the project outcomes. Section III describes needed execution processes for supply chain projects. According to the PMBOK, both Plan Development and Plan Execution rely on organizational policies as inputs. Cross-organization participation in Level 3 projects raises the issue of integrating these policies.

Integrated Change Control is responsible for assuring that work results meet requirements and adjusting the plan accordingly. Change control produces corrective actions that have to be incorporated into project plans. The initial plan provides the baseline for comparing revisions with planning parameters like cost, schedule and objectives. Chapter 9 examines root causes for project failures. One culprit identified in that chapter that highlights the importance of this process is inflexibility in projects.

7.3.2 KNOWLEDGE AREA: PROJECT SCOPE MANAGEMENT

High SCM Knowledge Required

Project Scope Management Processes	Process Group
Initiation	Initiation
Scope Planning	Planning
Scope Definition	Planning
Scope Verification	Controlling

The need for additional SCM knowledge for scope management is ranked "high." Scope decisions set the level of the project — whether it's departmental, business unit, or supply chain. Processes in this knowledge area address how to divide programs into projects or projects into phases. This answers questions like, "Do planning and control considerations require us to have five projects in our program, or will three do?" Or, "How many project phases, which are often separated by major deliverables, do we need to control the effort without bogging down in paperwork?"

Second, and of particular importance in supply chain management, are issues regarding what supply chain level (function, business unit, or supply chain) should the project pursue. Should it pursue limited scope and implement only at Level 1 or 2, confining the project to one's own company? This strategy may produce faster results, but will it sacrifice greater benefits? Or should we move faster, but take higher project management risks, by implementing across our supply chain? Such a decision is usually input to the initiation process group. However, in many situations, it is likely to become a real issue requiring ongoing decisions by executive level steering committees. Chapter 9 also documents project failures associated with poor scope planning.

Initiation requires a description of the project's "product." In PMBOK terminology, this can be a physical *product*, a *service*, or a *result*. SCM is about designing processes for delivering physical products. So a supply chain improvement product will likely be framed as a service or a result. A typical SCM project "product" could be "extend distribution into China" (a service) or "reduce inventory by 30%" (a result).

The product description defining the project comes from company strategic planning or a management steering committee. Examples of drivers for a project, according to the PMBOK, can include any of the following categories:

1. Market demand either on a one-time or ongoing basis, such as demand for a new product
2. Business need to increase revenues and profits or improve productivity
3. Customer requests often in the normal course of business like a security alarm company installing a new customer's system
4. Technology advances, driving the need for upgraded or new products or processes
5. Legal requirements such as environmental compliance
6. Social needs like civil infrastructure or fund raising

The first four of these drivers could all involve supply chain change, with the supply chain component an adjunct to another driver. So that effort, development of a new product for example, might become the "program" as defined in Chapter 6. The supply chain effort can be a project, or a group of projects, within that program.

In category 1 above, market demand on a one-time basis might involve a supply chain design to support a construction project in some remote area. In another example, the product life cycle, described in Chapter 4, brings different missions for the supply chain at different stages in a product's evolution.

In category 2 above, many companies pursue ongoing continuous improvement programs. These take the title of Six Sigma, total quality management, process reengineering and many local adaptations. Supply chain improvement may have its own continuous improvement effort or it may support other initiatives.

With regard to category 3, many companies build design-to-order or configure-to-order products in addition to the more common make-to-stock model. Supply chain design must support these alternatives. This support involves front-end ordering processes, engineering design for easy assembly and backend material requirements, pricing and fulfillment.

Technology advances, category 4 above, include new product technology, new processes for manufacturing or distribution, or advances in supply chain software tools — of which there are many. The supply chain space is fertile ground for new and improved software marketed by a multitude of providers. An integrated supply chain project should define supply chain process requirements and match those to the universe of candidate solutions.

Perhaps a supply chain project is attached to a new product introduction or seeks to improve the market penetration of an existing product. In this case, it is appropriate to take the view, described in Chapter 3, that supply chains encompass both base product and "extended product" components. For a personal computer, the base product is what you carry out of the store. The extended product includes availability, options, financing, after-sale service and warranty and repair access.[1] In this case, the supply chain initiative may produce all three project result types— a product, a service and a result.

Scope Planning is an ongoing process to keep the scope definition current with the progress of the project. Beginning with the project plan developed by the *Project Plan Development* process, it involves ongoing analysis of the project along with identifying alternatives and deciding whether to modify the scope. In a complex multicompany supply chain project, there are likely to be a number of triggers for reevaluating scope. An obvious one is the failure of a supply chain partner to uphold its commitments to provide deliverables on time or at all.

Scope Definition subdivides the project. Among the inputs is the project plan that should include a preliminary WBS. Among the outputs is a refined work breakdown structure (WBS). The WBS divides the project into manageable "chunks" or phases, as shown in Figure 6.3. Each phase produces major deliverables, corresponding to the WBS view. *Scope Verification* confirms with the executive authority like a steering committee the scope. Scope Verification is formal acceptance of the product of the project.

Scope Change Control is the ongoing process of reviewing and changing the scope. An SCM challenge may be gaining agreement from partners to changes in scope. These changes can require added staff or funding.

7.3.3 KNOWLEDGE AREA: PROJECT TIME MANAGEMENT

Low SCM Knowledge Required

Project Time Management Processes	Process Group
Activity Definition	Planning
Activity Sequencing	Planning
Activity Duration Estimating	Planning
Schedule Development	Planning
Schedule Control	Controlling

The need for supplemental SCM knowledge for this additional knowledge is ranked "low." This by no means diminishes the importance of time management in projects. Certainly, poor estimating can sink any project. For example, time may have to be added to supply chain projects to account for complications in coordinating across participating companies.

However, time management approaches for SCM projects will be similar to those needed for other types of projects. Figure 7.3 shows the relationship between processes for a systematic approach to time management, along with principal inputs and outputs for each process.

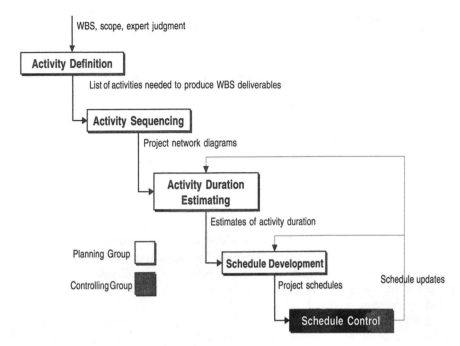

FIGURE 7.3 Processes for time management.

Activity Definition requires an understanding of the steps needed to complete a deliverable, as defined in the WBS. The WBS is an output of the scope planning process. An input to the task is expert judgment, which is likely to be drawn from multiple companies in a supply chain project.

Once activities are listed, the *Activity Sequencing* process puts them in the order in which they are performed. This encompasses development of milestones and dependencies. An output is often in the form of a project network diagram. Some companies, at Level 2 or 3 of the PMMM, may develop templates with activities and associated networks. These templates come in handy when project types repeat. Sequencing becomes critical when different organizations in Level 2 and Level 3 projects are dependent on others for input to their tasks.

Following sequencing is *Activity Duration Estimating*. The duration depends on scope, resources, approvals required, logistics, dependence on other activities and many other factors. Contingencies can also be applied if estimates or their underlying assumptions are uncertain. There are many tools available, some of which are listed in the PMBOK, for displaying duration and testing schedules for ways to reduce overall duration.

Schedule Development anchors activities to specific start and stop dates. As a project proceeds, the *Schedule Control* process updates the schedule based on actual performance. A schedule baseline, developed during *Project Plan Development* is the standard against which actual progress is marked.

7.3.4 KNOWLEDGE AREA: PROJECT COST MANAGEMENT

Medium SCM Knowledge Required

Project Cost Management Processes	Process Group
Resource Planning	Planning
Cost Estimating	Planning
Cost Budgeting	Planning
Cost Control	Controlling

The need for supplemental SCM knowledge by cost management is rated "medium." This is not because the PMBOK doesn't present a complete methodology for cost management of conventional projects. The changes lie in the nature of supply chain projects — particularly multicompany participation. Multicompany participation raises the prospect of joint decisions about conducting the supply chain project, including the costs involved.

Above, we said that a project, by PMBOK definition, produces a product, a service or a result. Most supply chain projects, we observed, will have products in the last two categories — services and results. Also, many supply chain projects have no neat end when the product of the project might be handed over to a user and considered complete.

A dot-com like Amazon is more a *service* company than a product company. Its innovations are in the realm of distribution services, marketing the products of others that are widely available through other channels. In another example, a product company may partner with a local distributor to expand into an untapped market. The outcome is a *result* — penetrating a new market with an existing product. In both examples, the project that set up the businesses can continue for many years after inception, evolving from "set-up" into a "sustaining" mode.

Supply chain projects can also be give-and-take affairs with multicompany funding and active participation in the projects. There is less of the buyer–seller role in the traditional sense. An analogy in traditional project management is construction. But even the construction project involves a buyer–seller relationship. The buyer owns the asset after the project is completed while the sellers — the designer, suppliers, the project financers, the contractor and the project manager — reach closure of the project when they turn the building over to the owner. A supply chain project will likely involve partnerships where participants expect long-range benefits. The partners are, in effect, both buyers and sellers.

Some nontraditional cost management arrangements that may come to play in the supply chain project could include:

- Long term contracting, committing to a supplier or customer
- Tracking cost using innovations like activity-based costing, a version of what Harold Kerzner refers to in Chapter 5 as "horizontal accounting"

- Balancing up-front partner capital investments with future profit splits
- Joint investments in systems to run the supply chain
- New product development — the contribution of intellectual property (IP), manufacturing capacity, or cash
- New services or processes — IP and cash contributions
- Penalties for departing from approved practices that add cost
- Penalties for abandoning the effort
- Fixed prices for certain project products
- Innovations in incentives for exceeding plan
- Methods for handling changes in scope or products that affect costs and investments

The cost management planning processes described in the following paragraphs may be done separately or as a continuous process.

Resource Planning turns WBS and the related activities into resource requirements. The type of resource and quantity for each WBS element defines requirements. Key resources are likely to include expertise, staff for accomplishing work, facilities, systems and materials.

Identification of resources is also a helpful input. Some sources will reside within the participating supply chain organizations; others must be procured from outside the partnership. In planning a supply chain project, partners may or may not have their own resources. On the other hand, one partner can claim to have the resource, but other partners may be happier with an alternative outside source.

Cost Estimating converts resources, resource unit cost and duration into project costs. Risks should be evaluated for each cost component. Risk arises from uncertainty in any component of cost — resource identification, resource cost and duration. Contingency estimates can be added to compensate for risk. The PMBOK describes cost estimating techniques including the following:

- Analogous estimating. A top-down estimate using actual cost experience from other projects and/or from expert inputs.
- Parametric modeling. Turning project-related parameters into costs, like using the cost per square foot for estimating home construction cost.
- Bottom-up estimating. Rolling up individual, lower level components, such as activity-level estimates.

With cost estimates, the *Cost Budgeting* process creates the cost baseline necessary to monitor project costs. Ideally, budgeting is done after estimating. However, projects may be budgeted before formal estimates are ready. *Cost Control*, like other control processes, uses actual experience to update estimates. It also produces an "estimate at completion" to alert managers to the likelihood of final actual cost. In cases of major cost shifts, a "rebaselining" of the project budget may be necessary.

7.3.5 KNOWLEDGE AREA: PROJECT QUALITY MANAGEMENT

Medium SCM Knowledge Required

Project Quality Management Processes	Process Group
Quality Planning	Planning
Quality Assurance	Executing
Quality Control	Controlling

As in the Project Time Management knowledge area, the impact of SCM on Project Quality Management is rated "medium." The outputs of a supply chain project will be services and results, not physical products. So supply chain projects are less amenable to objective measurement against product specifications or drawings. For this reason, quality management of SCM projects is not necessarily easy.

Quality Planning establishes standards relevant to the project and a plan for applying them. The tools vary widely depending on the needs of the project. Since supply chains are essentially collections of business processes, process performance standards will apply to many processes under development. Examples include defect rates, first time capability, fill rates for orders and so forth.

In the area of forecasting and inventory control, we suggest using the percentage of planning decisions based on actual demand vs. forecasts of that demand. The higher a supply chain ranks on this measure, the more "demand-driven" it is. Chapter 15 describes the approach. The technique is useful for planning in that it produces an estimate of how demand-driven a supply chain might be. Later, the quality assessment should use the same methodology to measure progress toward the potential.

Quality Assurance is the process that measures quality levels as the project proceeds. It is part of the executing process group and incorporates execution of the Quality Plan along with periodic audits to assure that the plan is adequate and is being followed.

Examining project results is the role of the *Quality Control* process. Quality control, according to the PMBOK, includes not only project products but also the project management outcomes, such as cost and schedule performance.

7.3.6 KNOWLEDGE AREA: PROJECT HUMAN RESOURCE MANAGEMENT

High SCM Knowledge Required

Project Human Resource Management	Process Group
Organizational Planning	Planning
Staff Acquisition	Planning
Team Development	Executing

Our assessment need for SCM knowledge is "high." In Chapter 4, we described two tasks for effective supply chain management that centered on organization issues.

Multicompany supply chain efforts may require shared resources. Also, many supply chain projects will require different mindsets. While it may be possible to get "bodies" to support a project, integrating these bodies into effective teams can be difficult. This is also true in the usual host of projects requiring teams but can be even truer when cross-functional and multicompany teams are involved. The term "collaboration" describes processes to overcome these differences.

Organization Planning establishes roles and responsibilities, an organization structure and a staff management plan for the project. The management plan profiles requirements as the project proceeds. The format and formality of the plan are flexible, depending on the needs of the project. In cases when partners must help staff the project, added detail is justified. The plan should also address what team members will do once they are released from the project.

Roles and responsibilities might be displayed in matrix form. PMBOK refers to this as a RAM, or responsibility assignment matrix. With phases on one side and participants on the other, the intersection shows the level of participation. These levels can include categories that meet the needs of the project. One supply chain project approach uses *responsible, accountable, consulted* and *informed (RACI)* as categories. The PMBOK suggests *participant, accountable, review required, input required* and *sign-off required.*

Confusion regarding terms is easy. Harold Kerzner clarifies the obligations that go with different roles.[2] *Authority* is granted to those "who make final decisions for others to follow." *Responsibility* goes with roles in the project as they are assigned to people or groups. *Accountability* is the "state of being answerable for completion" of the project. Accountability comes when the responsible party has both authority and responsibility.

Appendix B2 lists roles and responsibilities for the supply chain project detailed in Section III. There can be many variations on RAMs in a project. For example, there may be a RAM assigning communications responsibilities or a RAM delegating responsibilities in the project procurement process.

After requirements are defined, the *Staff Acquisition* process obtains the identified skills and numbers. Of course, many projects founder for lack of skills, numbers or both. Even if commitments are made, the need may not be filled in a timely way. This is particularly true when the project is a second priority or regular nonproject work is "urgent and unimportant" even though the project work is "nonurgent and very important." It is all too likely that the regular work will take priority over the project work.

Team Development is part of project execution. The PMBOK cites tools for team building. Examples are the rewards and recognition from team participation plus collocation of the team. Increasingly, with new technology, teams are able to work at a distance. This is likely for many supply chain projects since supply chains tend to spread out over the planet. Training is another tool for team building. It is especially important for teams where individuals represent many disciplines.

7.3.7 Knowledge Area: Project Communications Management

Medium SCM Knowledge Required

Project Communications Management Processes	Process Group
Communications Planning	Planning
Information Distribution	Executing
Performance Reporting	Controlling
Administrative Closure	Closure

Communications call for a "medium" level of specialized SCM knowledge. Multicompany participation is the principal reason for the added impact. Security arising from the potential transfer of proprietary information is an additional factor. This is somewhat mitigated by the fact that supply chain efforts are difficult to "hide" from an industry's community. Despite efforts to keep it quiet, others may learn of an initiative. Also, building a new capability for a supplier or customer unlocks the possibility that the supplier or customer will pass on the innovation to others.

Communications Planning transforms communications requirements into a Communications Management Plan. The PMBOK recommends a "stakeholder analysis" as the basis for the plan. This analysis addresses information user needs in terms of content, method of delivery, frequency and support systems. Care should be taken to avoid unnecessary communication. To facilitate, process templates in Chapters 12–15 identify stakeholders.

The Communications Management Plan, according to the PMBOK, should cover the following:

- Methods of gathering and storing various types of information
- Information distribution and method (report, data, meeting, etc.) that is coordinated with the organization structure
- Production schedules for each type of communication
- Updating and refinement of the plan

We at CGR Management Consultants have also helped clients in project environments implement "proactive" systems for project communication. These are a form of "workflow" where rules provide for automatically forwarding information to designated decision-makers.

The process for *Information Distribution* executes the communications plan. Another process, *Performance Reporting,* describes what is happening in the project. These reports include both current status and forecasts of future performance based on those results. Performance reporting includes performance review meetings, variance analysis, trends and earned value analysis.

Earned value analysis has created a vocabulary for reporting progress. Table 7.2 summarizes a few of the newer measures used for project performance reporting. Again, supply chain projects often produce services or results. So there are challenges in measuring progress in producing deliverables. In fact, the actual result

---

TABLE 7.2
Earned Value Analysis Terms For Project
Performance Reporting

Abbreviation	Term	Related Calculation
AC	Actual cost	
PV	Planned value	
CPI	Cost performance index	= EV/AC
CV	Cost variance	= EV-AC
EV	Earned value	
SV	Schedule variance	= EV-PV

---

may not be apparent until the project is over. What is measurable is accomplishment of activities delineated in the project plan.

Administrative Closure formalizes acceptance of the product of the project or its termination. Deliverables include acceptance of the product using project records, archives of the project, and project closure.

7.3.8 KNOWLEDGE AREA: PROJECT RISK MANAGEMENT

High SCM Knowledge Required

Risk Management Project Processes	Process Group
Risk Management Planning	Planning
Risk Identification	Planning
Qualitative Risk Analysis	Planning
Quantitative Risk Analysis	Planning
Risk Response Planning	Planning
Risk Monitoring and Control	Controlling

The PMBOK guide devotes considerable attention to risk, or uncertainty, associated with project outcomes. In fact, if there is any rationale at all for the project management discipline, it is as a tool for mitigating risk. One could argue that the absence of risk equates to no need at all for PMBOK's disciplined processes.

Chris Christensen, a Section II reviewer, observes that there are many additional reasons for project management, including communications and increased efficiency in using resources. To a degree, risk is like the flexibility imperative described in Chapter 3. That chapter described how many of the other drivers of supply chain change pointed toward the need to provide supply chain flexibility. Likewise, better communications and use of resources reduce the risk that somebody doesn't do his or her job or that the project doesn't overrun its budget. This applies particularly to supply chain projects that produce "results," not hard-to-verify physical products. Supply chain projects also rely on strategic decisions and the enthusiastic participation of many players — both risky areas fraught with uncertainty.

Risk management, according to PMBOK, maximizes the probability and consequences of positive events and minimizes the probability and consequences of negative ones. Note that risk is not limited to a negative outcome. Risk management includes capitalizing on good outcomes as well as protecting against poor ones. An example is a supply chain cost reduction project. If a company expects a $50 million annual saving from its effort, each week of delay cost a little less than $1 million. Such a number is useful in making decisions on schedule and making resources available for the project. One might readily add $10,000 in weekly expense to a 6-month project, an added cost of about $260,000, to bring the project in 2 months early and save $2 million.

The risk impact from SCM over a conventional project arises from all four risky considerations inherent in supply chain projects: strategic goals for the project, multicompany participation, the need for paradigm shifts and ambiguous deliverables. So the risk management knowledge area is ranked "high" in terms of the need for SCM knowledge and processes.

Risks due to strategic projects lie not just in execution, internal risk factors like cost and schedule, or doing things right. They also lie in doing the right thing or external factors beyond the project's control like sales levels. This means the strategies on which projects are based must be sound. These strategies are themselves a product of a supply chain project, Phase 1 in Figure 6.3. Multicompany risk has been addressed in discussions of other knowledge areas. In particular, the executing group of processes may be awkwardly coordinated and performed. The same is true for paradigm shifts where participants come from several companies and departments within those companies, each with a different culture and values. Ambiguous deliverables apply when the results of the project may not be known for some time.

7.3.8.1 Risk Planning and Identification

The *Risk Management Planning* process also must consider risk tolerances of management. In fact, these risk tolerances will drive the architecture of the supply chain program itself. A risk-intolerant management may limit the program to Level 1 or 2 projects because of perceived difficulties in pursuing Level 3 projects. The risk-averse managers may also require more reporting and narrower projects done on a slower sequential schedule.

The PMBOK guide recommends the following outputs from the risk planning process:

- How risk is to be measured, the tools required and the type of assessment to use. This includes both quantitative and qualitative risk assessment.
- Roles and responsibilities for risk management, including who is to perform risk-related activities. The PMBOK notes that a third party outside the project office may be best for this role.
- The timing of risk assessment during the project life cycle.

- Scoring and interpretation methods for qualitative and quantitative risk analysis.
- Risk thresholds including criteria for action, who should act and what response is appropriate.

Risk Identification draws in stakeholders to list areas of uncertainty. Risk categories include technical, quality and performance risk. We have mentioned four areas inherent in supply chain projects (strategic projects, multicompany, paradigm shift and ambiguous deliverables). Additional technical risk comes with dependence on unproven or complex technology. Quality standards and performance goals can also be ambitious, if not totally unrealistic. Environmental risks include political-, economic- and weather-related uncertainties. PMBOK also recommends developing "triggers" that provide an early warning that a risk event has or might occur.

7.3.8.2 Qualitative Risk Analysis

Supply chain projects will depend heavily on *Qualitative Risk Analysis*. Many risk factors will be such that a quantitative approach is not feasible. To score a risk, PMBOK recommends an approach that multiplies the *impact* of an event by the *probability* that event will occur. The scores are displayed in a probability-impact matrix. The procedure for constructing a matrix, which we use in an example later in this section, is the following:

1. Prepare a list of objectives for the project. A PMBOK example consists of internal project performance measures: *cost, schedule* and *quality.* Such a list should also include external factors.
2. Prepare descriptions of each outcome classified by the impact of that outcome from best to worst.
3. Use tolerance for risk to set a scale for each level of impact. Such a scale can be linear or nonlinear. Nonlinear scales reflect risk aversion because the worst outcomes are heavily penalized.
4. Prepare a table of risk scores that multiply the risk for probabilities of occurrence by the impact of the result. Designate which areas of qualitative risk will be *low, medium* and *high.*
5. Provide relative risk factors for each outcome using the risk score table. Use the scores to set priorities for risk reduction efforts.

A risk-associated issue with supply chain projects arises from the nature of the product. In many cases, we observed earlier, the product is a service or a result. So one can have a successful project from the viewpoint of internal project measures, but fail because the environment needed for success did not materialize. Also, success can't be measured until results are known. This can be later in the project life cycle, after the solution is installed and has operated long enough to measure results.

As an example, consider a project whose mission is "to extend distribution into China." The project team may be successful in setting up the supply chain. The cost, schedule and quality goals were met. However, the strategy that set our sights on China was flawed. The Chinese hate our product; returns are flooding in and retailers won't pay.

Is such a project a failure? In a construction project, an analogy would be the office tower built on speculation that there was a market for the space. But, the market didn't materialize, causing the project to go into bankruptcy. These are examples where "the operation was a success but the patient died."

Ambitious supply chain projects will challenge managers to decide where risk should be assessed and accounted for. In Tables 7.3 and 7.4, we've adapted the five-step approach to the risk assessment example described above to include both external (strategy-related) and internal (cost, schedule, quality) risk factors for a project. We next apply the procedure above to develop qualitative risk scoring for the supply chain project.

TABLE 7.3
Impact of Risks On Project Objectives

	Project Objectives	Impact			
		Favorable −1	Low 3	Medium 5	High 9
Internal risk factors	Implementation project cost	Below budget	<10% over budget	10–30% over budget	>30%over budget
	Implementation project schedule	>1 mo. ahead of schedule	<1 month late	1–3 months late	>3 months late
External risk factors	Unit sales	>10% over plan	>90% of plan	70–90% of plan	<70% of plan
	Operating profit	>10% over plan	>90% of plan	70–90% of plan	<70% of plan

TABLE 7.4
Scoring a Risk: Impact Multiplied By Probability

	Outcomes and Their Impact (from Table 7.3)			
Probability	Favorable −1	Low 3	Medium 5	High 9
80–100%	−1.0[a]	3.0[b]	5.0[c]	9.0[c]
60–80%	−0.8[a]	2.4[b]	4.0[c]	7.2[c]
40–60%	−0.6[a]	1.8[a]	3.0[b]	5.4[c]
20–40%	−0.4[a]	1.2[a]	2.0[b]	3.6[b]
0–20%	−0.2[a]	0.6[a]	1.0[a]	1.8[a]

[a] Low risk.
[b] Medium risk.
[c] High risk.

1. **Prepare a list of project objectives**. Table 7.3 lists four objectives. Two are "internal" traditional project performance measures. The other two are "external," measuring the business result the project seeks to accomplish. These are goals for units sold, prices and operating profit.
2. **Prepare descriptions of potential outcomes from best to worst**. These outcomes populate Table 7.3. The organization believes that project expectations can be exceeded if things go well. This can bring the benefit of early implementation, increasing sales and profits plus beating the competition into a new market. These outcomes are shown in the "Favorable" column. The "High" impact column contains outcomes that are the most negative in their impact.
3. **Use tolerance for risk to set a scale for each level of impact**. The scores (–1, 3, 5, 9) are a nonlinear scale, meaning higher-impact penalties for really awful outcomes. So, being more than 30% over budget earns a "9" impact. A "–1" is used for favorable outcomes so that poorer outcomes produce higher risk scores.
4. **Score the risk for probabilities of occurrence resulting in a matrix of risk scores**. Table 7.4 is a "look-up" table that shows risk scoring. The table is a tool for classifying specific risks contained in Table 7.3. Scores are the product of the Impact rating and the Probability shown in the left-hand column of Table 7.4. The probability used is at the high end of the range (e.g., the probabilities in the 60–80% range use 80%).
5. **Designate which areas of qualitative risk will be *low, medium* and *high***. Estimating the probabilities of outcomes in Table 7.3 does this. Table 7.4 shows, by a, b and c superscripts, areas of risk. Outcomes with scores of "4.0" or greater are high risk. Medium-risk scores are between 2.0 and 3.9. Low-risk scores are 1.9 or below.

If the probability of being greater than 30% over budget is 40%, reference to Table 7.4 produces a risk score of 5.4. Of course, the probabilities of outcomes for any risk factor cannot exceed 100%.

The PMBOK notes that qualitative risk assessment can be adapted to the needs of any project. Most supply chain projects will likely need both internal and external risk measures, and measures will extend past initial implementation into the operating period of the project life cycle.

In application, project risks are identified through interviewing, brainstorming and analysis of the project activities. If our program is to extend distribution into China, an important project or subproject could be to establish a transportation network. If this is a critical path item, lateness in this project can make our project late.

Suppose we have allowed 6 months for setting up the network but think it could easily take 10 months because we don't know much about the problems we might encounter. Then we might assume there is a probability of 50% of taking 10 months, to which we assign a "9" score for impact. Our risk score, taken from Table 7.4, is 5.4, a high-risk project component due to schedule uncertainty.

Once risks are collected and scored, according to the PMBOK, the outputs of the task should include the following:

- Overall risk of the project. A project risk profile can be based on the highest risk score for each project objective.
- List of risks grouped in different ways. Examples include risk scores, priorities for addressing the risks, time-phased risks and related objectives.
- Risks requiring further analysis. High and medium risks may be served with a quantitative risk analysis.
- Trends in qualitative risk analysis. The trend in risk can be tracked over time as the project proceeds.

7.3.8.3 Quantitative Risk Analysis

The *Quantitative Risk Analysis* process often follows qualitative analysis when identified risks are screened qualitatively and deemed to merit further analysis. Quantitative analysis can take several forms, which are mentioned briefly here.

- **Interviewing** to develop ranges for outcomes instead of single, most likely planning outcomes.
- **Sensitivity analysis** to understand the impact of a risk item on the overall project. For example, scheduling uncertainty for an activity not on the project's critical path may not present that much risk to the project. The analysis will vary the outcome of the risk under examination, while holding all other factors at their baseline levels.
- **Decision trees**, described below, structure anticipated outcomes to lead to a decision that reduces overall risk.
- **Simulation** uses computer models to translate uncertainties from multiple factors into expected outcomes. The display shows the range and distribution of outcomes.

Figure 7.4 illustrates the use of a decision tree. It assumes that, in conjunction with our move into the Chinese market, we have a choice of using the existing transportation network or developing our own new network. Logistics are problematic in China, so we believe having our own network will lead to increased sales.[3] However, a proprietary network increases costs — to $10 million from the $5 million for using the existing network.

On the left, we begin with the decision required, whether to develop or outsource our transportation requirements. At the next level are our two alternatives: to develop our own network or use the existing one. The Probability/Payoff level captures assumptions about demand and profit. It shows the units sold and profit, assumed to be $2 per unit sold. Different sales levels reflect uncertainties about the market plus the capabilities of the resulting transportation network to get our products to those markets.

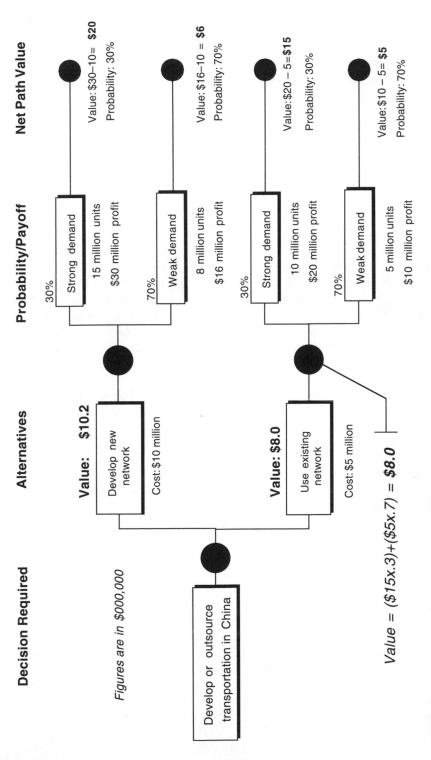

FIGURE 7.4 Use of a decision tree to analyze risk.

So, in the case of strong demand, our dedicated network would deliver 15 million units into the market. Using the existing network, with all its limitations, would enable us to sell only 10 million units, despite strong demand from the market.

"Net Path Value" captures the profit from each outcome. So the new network, with strong demand, produces the best outcome — a profit of $20 million. This includes the profit less the cost to set up the network.

Weak demand, with the existing network, means a profit of only $5 million. Applying the probabilities of each outcome, we value the new network at $10.2 million and use of the existing network at $8.0. Assuming we have access to the additional capital and trust our analysis, we should develop the transportation network.

The PMBOK recommends as outputs of *Quantitative Risk Analysis* a prioritized list of quantified risks, forecast distributions of cost and schedule, probabilities of achieving objectives and trends as quantitative analysis is repeated throughout the project.

7.3.8.4 Risk Response and Control

Risk Response Planning devises options for responses to identified risk events. This is a planning process, not a reaction to an actual outcome. Of course, the level of advanced planning should be in proportion to the risk involved. A feature of the PMBOK recommended approach, one that has excellent potential in SCM projects, is selection of "risk owners." These are the responsible stakeholders to be involved in developing risk responses. Measures recommended by the PMBOK include the following:

- **Avoidance** of the risk by changing the project plan. This could eliminate the risk by reducing the project scope, adding resources, extending the schedule or using more tried and true approaches.
- **Transference** involves shifting risk consequences to third parties. Such a move may not eliminate the risk but could reduce the consequences. An example is an insurance policy, where the issuer of the policy is paid for assuming risk. Another transference device is the fixed-price contract.
- **Mitigation** reduces the probability of suffering the consequences of the risk. This is a prevention measure where extra effort is justified before the event occurs rather than afterward. From our China case, this might involve more market research to determine whether demand will be strong or weak.
- **Acceptance** means that no preventive action will be taken. A contingency plan plots what will happen if the risk event occurs. For a high-impact event, a fallback plan may be prepared to reset direction of the project. A contingency allowance is a frequent acceptance response — this is addition of resources or time over what is thought to be sufficient to compensate for the uncertainty.

The principal output is a Risk Response Plan specifying what risks remain after the plan is in place. Secondary risks may exist. These are new risks that arise as a result of having a risk response. Other outputs include needed contractual arrangements and contingency reserves.

Risk Monitoring and Control is a process for monitoring known risks and identifying new ones. Part of this process is developing earned value, a measure of progress in executing the project plan. Table 7.2 contains a vocabulary for earned value. Another output is the "workaround plan." These are responses to emerging risks that should be incorporated into the project plan.

7.3.9 KNOWLEDGE AREA: PROJECT PROCUREMENT MANAGEMENT

High SCM Knowledge Required

Project Procurement Management Processes	Product Group
Procurement Planning	Planning
Solicitation Planning	Planning
Solicitation	Executing
Source Selection	Executing
Contract Administration	Executing
Contract Closeout	Closing

Because supply chain efforts will be multicompany, and partnerships with suppliers and customers will require new ways of thinking, the need for SCM knowledge is ranked "high." There are two contexts for project procurement management when it comes to supply chain projects.

The first context is the procurement of goods and services for the project itself. The contractor you chose for building your new house is an illustration. Your criteria are probably price, delivery and reputation for quality. However, you are not likely to build a house more than once or twice in your lifetime, so your criteria are straightforward.

However, if you are a developer who plans to build many houses, you'll look at the contractor decision differently. Certainly you will want to be an important customer to your contractor. You will want financial stability in the organization you select. You will also likely seek consideration for the volume of business you'll give your selection.

SCM procurement is often performed in an environment like the developer's. In a supply chain effort, a frequent project activity is selecting partners or being selected as a partner. If you are doing the procuring, those who are selected will be those you must work with after the supply chain is established and operating. In this case, the provider of project management services and the provider of materials for running your business are the same entity.

Procurement responsibilities in supply chain projects may reside with a single party or they may be shared. To the extent several companies will use the procured product or service, there is need for collaboration and joint decision-making in supplier selection.

Partnerships in many companies are "unnatural" acts. This is particularly true if the pathway to partnerships goes through the purchasing function. Transforming one's mindset from a "buyer" to a "collaborator" can be difficult. This is especially true because few partnerships are truly developed among equals. One partner is often dominant. Slipping back into the arm's-length paradigm is all too easy.

Procurement in a supply chain context is a two-step process. The first step is often referred to as "strategic sourcing." If you provide major components to your customers, you want to be a partner to your customers. The second step is "procurement," day-to-day purchases of goods from the suppliers selected in the sourcing process.

Because so many supply chain projects depend on collaboration with suppliers, procurement processes are key to a successful effort. Likewise, customers may seek out one's company as a partner. Not being selected because you are an unattractive partner jeopardizes your future.

Procurement Planning begins with deciding what to buy and when during the project. The process includes deciding whether to make or buy the purchased product or service. It also requires a decision on the type of contract needed. Options include fixed price, cost-reimbursable and time and material contracts. The risk analysis may assist in contract type decisions. The result is a procurement management plan. The procurement planning process also includes what won't be purchased by the organization. Responsibility for procuring some items can be assigned to suppliers.

Another output is the statement of work (SOW). At the outset, these should be as complete as possible. The SOW can be revised as needed throughout the project. A Statement of Objectives (SOO) covers procurement items where specific products or services are difficult to define.

The next process, *Solicitation Planning,* develops procurement documents and evaluation criteria. Actual *Solicitation* gathers responses, often through bidders conferences and advertising. A formal solicitation process makes sense to solidify a partnership arrangement. *Source Selection* processes review supplier responses and select the supplier, resulting in a contract for the goods and services.

Ongoing *Contract Administration* is needed to see that contract terms are fulfilled and to administer changes to the contract. *Contract Closeout* brings a formal close to the procurement.

ENDNOTES

1. *Handbook of Supply Chain Management*, page 6.
2. Kerzner, Harold, *Project Management: A Systems Approach to Planning, Scheduling and Controlling*, 7th edition, New York: John Wiley & Sons, 2001. pp. 100 and 243.
3. For more reading on this topic, refer to Red Tape, an article on logistics in China by Russell Flannery, in *Forbes*, March 3, 2000. pp. 97–100.

8 SCOR and SCM Project Management

The SCOR model provides structure for designing or improving a supply chain. It supports the project management approach with a supply chain vocabulary and a process model that facilitates scope setting and completeness of design. Related SCOR technical committee work adds insights on the importance and format of collaboration among supply chain partners.

The mission of this book is to help readers achieve a *structured, collaborative* and *measurable* approach to supply chain management. Chapter 5 described Kerzner's Project Management Maturity Model (PMMM). Level 1 of that model is a "common language" for project management; Level 2 is "common processes," which evolves to Level 3, "a singular process." Chapters 6 and 7 described project management approaches for achieving this objective using the Project Management Body of Knowledge (PMBOK), published by the Project Management Institute.[1]

The Supply-Chain Operations Reference Model (SCOR) can also play an important role in achieving structure in project management and moving toward higher levels of maturity in managing projects. Members of the Supply-Chain Council (SCC) maintain the SCOR model. (The SCC uses the hyphenated form of "supply chain" in its name.) In this chapter, we describe the model and how practitioners might apply it in supply chain projects.

SCOR incorporates supply chain architectures, performance measures and best practices for a wide range of supply chain activities. The model is intended to apply across industries. It is flexible enough to be used in any company that is part of a supply chain, including those that deliver services. An obstacle to the success of multicompany efforts can be the lack of a common vocabulary to facilitate communications among companies linked in the chain. SCOR addresses that obstacle, as the following description from the model explains:

> Process reference models integrate the well-known concepts of business process reengineering, benchmarking and process measurement into a cross-functional framework.[2]

The model in effect at the time of writing, Version 5.0, charts processes commonly associated with the logistics of making products. This focus is reflected in the Level 1 SCOR processes: PLAN, SOURCE, MAKE, DELIVER and RETURN.[3] Notice of exceptions to SCOR's scope is also in order. At the time of writing, SCOR did not address sales and marketing, RandD and product development processes. However, activities in these categories can be linked to SCOR processes.

TABLE 8.1
Applying SCOR to Supply Chain
Project Phases

SCOR Level	Type of Process
1	Core processes
2	Configuration
	• Planning
	• Execution
	• Enable
3	Process element
4	Company-specific processes

We begin with the SCOR structure, highlighting important features. These highlights, based on Version 5.0, should help readers evaluate SCOR's potential for a role in their own improvement efforts. The model undergoes continuous review, so new features will be forthcoming. The descriptions in this chapter related to collaboration were not officially part of SCOR at the time of writing. We cover them because they are an important contribution to understanding barriers to internal and external cooperation, as described in Chapter 4. The council's Web site provides access to background papers on collaboration.

Supply chain design is intrinsically a complex process. So, it is no accident that navigation through SCOR is not particularly easy for the neophyte. The SCOR vocabulary takes getting used to and many may wonder whether the price is worth it. However, those that stick with it report good success from applying SCOR. In addition to this chapter, the Glossary in this book also contains common SCOR terms. Project templates in Chapters 12–15 also indicate how SCOR might support elements of a supply chain project.

SCOR is constructed from the top down, starting with the five broad processes at Level 1 listed previously. These are broken down into smaller pieces at Levels 2 and 3. The top three SCOR levels portray processes that are common across industries. Level 4 is company-specific, to be designed by individual companies to fulfill their strategies. So Level 4 is not covered by SCOR.

Therefore, the first three levels provide a "skeleton" on which to build proprietary Level 4 processes. SCOR users generally work across the levels starting with Level 1 and then progress to lower levels defining supply chain components in greater levels of detail.

How does this structure enable better supply chain project management? Table 8.1 lists the SCOR levels, while Figure 8.1 shows how they fit in terms of producing project deliverables. These deliverables were introduced in Figure 6.4, which depicts a WBS for a supply chain improvement project. As we describe SCOR in the following sections, we'll refer to the linkages shown in Figure 8.1.

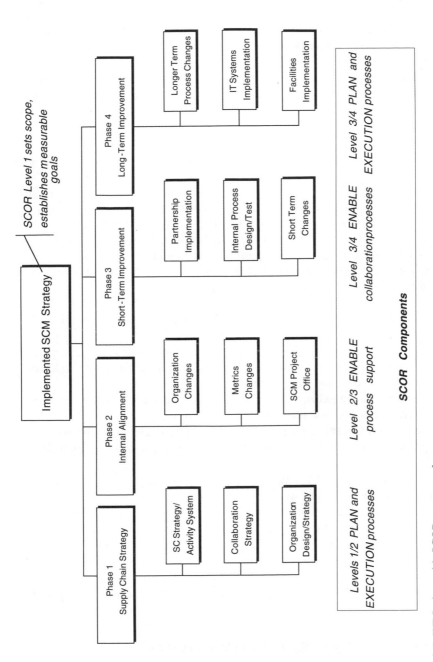

FIGURE 8.1 WBS view with SCOR support roles.

8.1   LEVEL 1: CORE MANAGEMENT PROCESSES

The scope and content of the supply chain are defined in five processes at Level 1. The five are described by SCOR as "core management processes." As mentioned above, these are PLAN, SOURCE, MAKE, DELIVER and RETURN. These processes link one's own company with suppliers and customers, as shown in Figure 8.2, the council's graphic that illustrates the SCOR view of the supply chain.

The five Level 1 processes reflect the flow of goods and the way many companies are organized. In fact, until early 2002, SCOR upgrades were assigned to separate teams for each of the Level 1 processes. More recently, a model-changing effort can range over all of SCOR. This should produce simultaneous integrated changes across processes.

Level 1 performance metrics include both "customer-facing" (or "external-facing") and "internal-facing" elements, listed in Table 8.2. These are in the categories of *reliability, responsiveness* and *flexibility* for customer-facing metrics. Internal-facing metrics cover cost and assets. The customer-facing and internal-facing categories in the table also identify performance metrics for lower-level process elements.

Senior management presenters at the Supply-Chain Council's 2003 Executive Retreat stressed trends in supply chain performance measurement emphasizing financial measures. This is likely a byproduct of ebbing business levels and falling stock prices. Related observations include the following:

- Cash flow and cash-to-cash cycle times are, in an adverse business climate, prevailing over expense and service measures.
- Supply chain cost can no longer omit the working and fixed asset capital needed to operate the supply chain. This requirement requires residual income or economic value-added measures.
- Time to volume (when the new product produces cash flow) trumps time to market as a metric for supply chain performance.
- Investors are increasingly awarding higher price-to-earnings multiples for SCM competence. Companies with good stories to tell should tell them.

Practitioners use Level 1 to align their supply chains and their business strategies with specific performance measures for a new or upgraded chain. This conveys to a project team an understanding of what is sought from the project. For the team following the PMBOK processes described in Chapters 6 and 7, work at Level 1 should produce a Project Plan. The plan includes the project charter, the scope, a work breakdown structure of the deliverables and targets for cost and delivery. These targets can rely on the SCOR performance measures for all or some of the targets. In Figure 8.1, this Level 1 contribution is at the top level of the WBS, *Implemented SCM Strategy.*

8.2   LEVEL 2: CONFIGURATION LEVEL/THREADS

At Level 2, SCOR moves to process groups that remain generic but allow for dividing a supply chain improvement project into logical chunks. Figure 8.3 shows

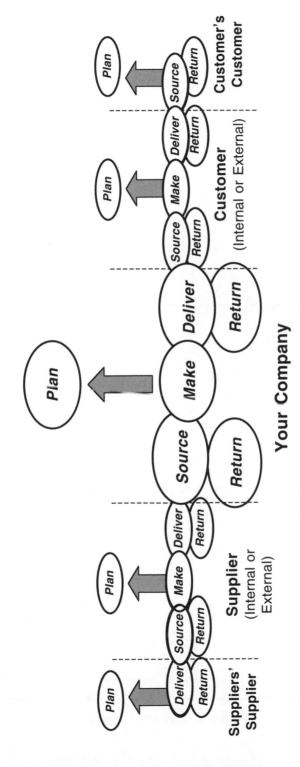

FIGURE 8.2 Supply with Level 1 processes. *Source:* Supply-Chain Council. With permission.

TABLE 8.2
Level 1 Performance Metrics

	Customer-Facing			Internal-Facing	
Attribute	Reliability	Responsiveness	Flexibility	Cost	Assets
Delivery	X				
Fill rate	X				
Order fulfillment (perfect order)	X				
Order lead-time		X			
Supply chain response time			X		
Production flexibility			X		
Supply chain management cost				X	
Cost of goods sold				X	
Value-added productivity				X	
Warranty/returns processing cost				X	
Cash-to-cash cycle time					X
Inventory days of supply					X
Asset turns					X

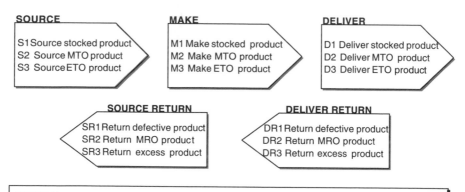

PLAN

P1/PP* Plan supply chain
P2/PS Plan SOURCE
P3/PM Plan MAKE
P4/PD Plan DELIVER
P5/PR Plan RETURN

*P1 is the nomenclature in the official SCOR model. PP is used elsewhere.

SOURCE

S1 Source stocked product
S2 Source MTO product
S3 Source ETO product

MAKE

M1 Make stocked product
M2 Make MTO product
M3 Make ETO product

DELIVER

D1 Deliver stocked product
D2 Deliver MTO product
D3 Deliver ETO product

SOURCE RETURN

SR1 Return defective product
SR2 Return MRO product
SR3 Return excess product

DELIVER RETURN

DR1 Return defective product
DR2 Return MRO product
DR3 Return excess product

ENABLE

EP.1 Manage business rules
EP.2 Manage performance
EP.3 Manage data collection
EP.4 Manage inventory
EP.5 Manage capital assets
EP.6 Manage transportation
EP.7 Manage network
EP.8 Manage regulatory requirements/compliance
EP.9 Manage other items (financial plan, agreements)

FIGURE 8.3 SCOR level 2 toolkit. *Source*: Supply-Chain Council. With permission.

the Level 2 SCOR processes. The council refers to these Level 2 processes as a "toolkit." It is quite useful for flowcharting purposes and conveying high-level supply chain relationships.

There are three types of Level 2 processes: PLANNING, EXECUTION and ENABLE. Logically, those in the PLAN category are planning processes, those in ENABLE are enabling processes; and those in SOURCE, MAKE, DELIVER and RETURN are executing processes. In Version 5.0 there are nine Level 2 ENABLE processes. All ENABLE processes are Level 2 and Level 3; there are no Level 1 ENABLE processes. The following sections describe PLANNING, EXECUTION and ENABLE Level 2 process categories.

8.2.1 PLANNING Processes

Level 2 planning processes are intended to balance supply and demand. Two formats exist for designating planning processes and are shown in Figure 8.3. For example, *P1* is used to describe the process "Plan Supply Chain." PLAN processes guide both long-term and short-term planning to match supply and demand. For example, they include setting up supply chain capabilities like factories, production lines and other assets. PLAN processes also include short-term planning and scheduling of execution tasks — SOURCE, MAKE, DELIVER and RETURN.

Level 3 process elements in PLAN follow a four-step algorithm:

1. Gather requirements in terms of delivered product
2. Gather resources to bring delivered product to market
3. Balance requirements and resources
4. Produce a plan to provide those resources

Each resource category would be guided by an appropriate methodology and time interval for updating the plan. Physical assets, for example, might be replanned at yearly intervals while production plans are replanned hourly, daily or weekly. The planning horizon, the time period covered by the plan, should also be consistent from plan to plan. For example, the horizon for physical assets might be 5 years, with annual replanning intervals.

PLAN processes have an operational focus, like generating production schedules. They also cover periodic replanning project efforts, like evaluating assets and supply chain partners. These are neglected in many companies, with replanning done only in response to a crisis of some kind. The effectiveness of PLAN processes is measured by supply chain response time and flexibility to react to changes in supply and demand.

8.2.2 EXECUTION Processes

Execution processes recognize three supply chain business models: make-to-stock (MTS), make-to-order (MTO) and engineer-to-order (ETO). In the MTS company, forecasts drive production requirements. Customer shipments are made from a finished goods inventory. An MTO company has an order in hand before it produces.

Boeing's commercial aircraft business and Dell computers are examples. An ETO company must design parts of the product for customer requirements. Each delivered product to a customer can be unique. A configure-to-order company, not specifically addressed in SCOR, is a hybrid of the MTO and the ETO models.

A company with multiple supply chains can use one model in one supply chain and a different model in another. In Section I, we saw that this is justified by competitive strategies tailored to different product-market combinations.

A company can also use different models in its own SOURCE, MAKE and DELIVER links. For example, it can follow an MTO model in its MAKE link, while its raw materials link follows a source-stocked-product model. The make-to-order sandwich shop does just this, replenishing components to forecasts of daily volume while "manufacturing" each sandwich in response to customer orders.

Linked supply chain companies may also have varied models within their networks. For example, an MTS company may sell components to an MTO company. This would likely be the case with Dell component suppliers. The suppliers use the MTS model, while Dell uses the MTO model.

"Threads" is the SCOR term that characterizes a supply chain configuration. Referring to the Level 2 execution steps in Figure 8.3, a thread of three companies might use the following models:

1. An S1, M1, D1 manufacturer (Company 1 in the supply chain) has a ready inventory for shipping ...
2. to an S2, M2, D2 manufacturer (Company 2 in the chain) who supplies ...
3. an S1, D3 distributor (Company 3 in the chain) who assembles one-of-a-kind configured products for its customers.

Company 1 above is a traditional BTS manufacturer. It serves its customers by forecasting and producing to these forecasts for finished goods inventory. One of its customers, Company 2, is a specialized firm that only builds to order (M2, D2). Company 2 also orders stock only when it has such an order (S2). The final link in the supply chain is Company 3, a distributor who does light assembly, including the addition of customized software to the product. So it must do some engineering (D3) to deliver its products. It does maintain a components inventory (S1) to meet its customer service goals. Because its "manufacturing" is limited to assembly, its modeling team takes the option of excluding the MAKE component.

The presence of multicompany threads in the supply chain evokes the need for collaboration to set them up. This set-up process is what SCOR calls "configuring" the supply chain. A description follows of plans for including collaboration in configuring supply chains. In Section 4.4.1, we described "spheres" as a tool for dissecting the supply chain. For terminology clarification, the two terms *spheres* and *threads* are not synonymous. Spheres are broader definitions covering customer–product–operation combinations. A sphere could utilize one or several threads.

Spheres and related threads can be a product of planning and process design in a supply chain project. Figure 8.1 points to their role. SCOR Levels 1 and 2 support Phase 1 conceptual design, which includes strategy, activity systems, collaboration and organization design. SCOR Levels 3 and 4 support detail design of new processes in Phases 3 and 4.

8.2.3 ENABLE PROCESSES

Enable processes may be the most important of the SCOR processes. Many supply chain failures can be traced to the absence of one or more of these processes, often "controlling" processes as identified in the PMBOK. ENABLE processes are the backbone of any supply chain. Without an adequate backbone, supply chain performance can go only so far.

ENABLE processes are ongoing, providing a platform for supply chain projects. They address resources that can be shared among multiple supply chain spheres, as defined in Section 4.4.1. Examples are facilities, the transportation network, distribution centers, contracted service providers, metrics, information systems and preferred suppliers.

ENABLE processes are good candidates for oversight by the SCM Project Office, shown as a Phase 2 deliverable in Figure 8.1. The other alternative is to assign enabling work to functional departments, like distribution, transportation or facilities. However, functional groups may lack visibility over all supply chain requirements.

In Version 5.0, there are nine enabling processes, spanning the five Level 1 processes of PLAN, MAKE, SOURCE, DELIVER and RETURN. Also included is a category for "other" process specific elements. SCOR users should decide as they proceed whether a particular activity is part of an EXECUTION process or is part of an ENABLE process. For example, inventory levels are a product of SOURCE, MAKE and DELIVER execution process. So they can be managed as part of those processes. The enabling process for inventory (EP.4) could provide the facilities for storing the inventory, general inventory business rules, or the capital for financing it.

Our recommendation is that planners create an "Enable Sphere," as described in Section 4.4.1. This sphere would include activities supporting product-producing spheres. In short, if multiple spheres rely on common business rules, systems and other supply chain components, they should be included in the Enable Sphere. Here we describe and comment on each ENABLE process.

8.2.3.1 Establish and Manage Business Rules

The rules align supply chain policies with business strategy, goals and objectives. These include service standards and other objectives for the supply chains serving the customer base. These requirements can also be determinants of the replanning cycle. Faster shifts in underlying market conditions should activate more frequent supply chain replanning projects.

The approach to strategic planning described in Section I promotes the idea that supply chain design is a strategy component. SCM should be incorporated into strategic planning and should not simply respond to it. An output of supply chain strategy making should be the business rules for this ENABLE process.

8.2.3.2 Manage Performance of the Supply Chain

This enabler puts into place supply chain performance measures. Often, objectives are set, but systems don't exist to measure performance against those objectives. This can be especially true when the source of the data is a supplier or a customer. Another problem occurs when measurement cycles are out of sync with the action cycle. The information may be too late to make timely decisions.

8.2.3.3 Manage Data Collection

Data collection is the process of managing, collecting, maintaining and communicating information to support EXECUTION process planning and execution. An example is product-related data. Keeping this data current is an important contribution to supply chain operations. There are many solutions in the form of supply chain software for doing this. It is often difficult to avoid making implementation of software the ends rather than the means. Care should be taken to assure that systems support planning and execution processes. This will avoid wasting time and money on unneeded technology.

8.2.3.4 Manage Inventory

This enabling process should fill gaps in PLANNING and EXECUTION processes needed to satisfy inventory requirements. As mentioned above, however, inventory is a consequence of these processes. This ENABLE process addresses general policies and facilities. General policies include ownership, preferred service providers, ridding inventory of slow-moving items and corporate constraints on inventory levels. Inventory facilities include the physical infrastructure and associated information systems.

8.2.3.5 Manage Supply Chain Capital Assets

This category of decisions can address whether the company will invest in facilities to provide capacity or will purchase those capabilities from a supply chain partner. Related support includes decisions regarding additions and deletions of capital assets and related justification processes.

8.2.3.6 Manage Transportation

Like facilities and inventory, there can be benefits in having common resources for transportation. These include both internal, or intra-company, and external (intercompany) transportation requirements. This enabling process can include selection of a transportation service provider and the mix of internal and purchased resources. Effectiveness here should be measured in terms of service, not cost. Minimizing transportation cost at the price of poor service can be expensive in terms of customer satisfaction.

8.2.3.7 Manage Supply Chain Configuration

This is an important process for ongoing integration of supply chain design with the rest of the business. The following is a list of configuration design components from PLAN, SOURCE, MAKE, DELIVER and RETURN.

- Information about products including life cycle position including new products
- Sales promotion planning and integration
- Product structure, bill of materials and routing embedded in planning systems
- Support tools like inventory usage analysis and selection criteria for product discontinuation
- Supplier management including qualification, logistics and business arrangements
- Production facility missions, roles and product assignments
- Channel maintenance for products

This enabler can be the source of "trigger events" that call for updating supply chains. For example, new products, product discontinuation, opening or closing a facility and channel design changes corresponding to changes in a product's life cycle, described in Section 4.2.1, can be triggers.

8.2.3.8 Manage Regulatory Requirements and Compliance

These requirements involve government and trade requirements. Related issues have increasing importance in global supply chains. Topics include taxes and tariffs, efforts to combat terrorism, environmental regulation, social policy, religious customs and liability law. An important consideration can be RETURN-related issues in areas where the company sells, makes, or sources materials for its products.

8.2.3.9 Process Specific Compliance

This category covers processes that center on single process elements. In SCOR Version 5.0 there are three of these supporting PLAN, SOURCE and RETURN. The first, "Align Supply Chain Unit Plan with Financial Plan," assures that the supply chain plan uses the same assumptions as company financial plans. The alignment includes the numbers generated by the plan as well as the related assumptions. "Manage Supplier Agreements," the second, oversees existing purchase orders or supplier contracts. The third, "Manage Customer Returns," defines and maintains the business rules, data, information systems, procedures and transportation for returned products.

8.3 LEVEL 3: DETAILED PROCESS ELEMENTS

In SCOR, Level 2 processes decompose into Level 3 "process elements." Level 3 makes up most of the SCOR model, since there are several process elements for each Level 2 process. Level 3 details remain generic, applicable across industries. Level 3 provides a structure for company-specific detail design at Level 4, which is Phase 3 of a supply chain project. ENABLE processes are also broken into Level 3 process elements for each of the Level 2 processes.

Documentation of process elements includes the following items. Some of these elements are not included in SCOR templates for particular process elements, depending on appropriateness.

1. Process definition
2. Performance metrics by attribute (Reliability, Responsiveness, Flexibility, Cost and Assets)
3. Best practices and features (including technology), a list of suggestions for implementation
4. Inputs from other SCOR Level 3 process elements
5. Outputs to other SCOR Level 3 process elements

Tables 8.3 and 8.4 are examples of process element documentation. Most users will view element documents as "guidance" rather than mandatory for adaptation to their organizations. Another area of user discretion is the level of detail for flowcharting process elements at Levels 3 and 4. This should be based on business needs and defined in the Project Plan.

8.4 COLLABORATION

At the time of writing, the Supply-Chain Council was considering incorporating collaboration into SCOR. The proposals, described here, had been 2 years in the making by a Technical Committee composed of Council members.

A need to address collaboration grew from a perceived void in SCOR, namely that SCOR has a single company focus. That is, its structure and presentation are oriented toward individual companies thinking and working at arm's length with suppliers and customers. Also, many feel that collaboration between departments is not all that strong inside company walls. For these reasons, the greatest gains from SCM are likely to involve effective collaboration, and SCOR should provide more direction to help its users achieve this end.

The products of the committee defined collaboration, forms of collaboration and the environments where collaboration is needed. What follows is the author's interpretation of the proposals and their implications for supply chain project management.

Table 8.3
Example Level 3 Execution Process Element Documentation
(SCOR Version 5.0)

Process Element: Schedule Product Deliveries   **Process Element Number: S2.1**

S2.1 Schedule Product Deliveries

Process Element Definition
Scheduling and managing the execution of the individual deliveries of product against the contract. The requirements for product deliveries are determined based on the detailed sourcing plan. This includes all aspects of managing the contract schedule including prototypes, qualifications or service deployment.

Performance Attributes	Metric
Reliability	% Schedules generated within Supplier's Lead Time
	% Schedules changed within Supplier's Lead Time
Responsiveness	Average Release Cycle of Changes
Flexibility	Average days per Schedule Change
	Average days per Engineering Change
Cost	Product Management and Planning Costs as a % of Product Acquisition Costs
Assets	None Identified

Best Practices	Features
Use EDI transactions to reduce cycle time/ costs	EDI interface for 830, 850, 856 and 862 transactions
VMI agreements allow suppliers to manage (replenish) inventory	Supplier managed inventories with scheduling interfaces to external supplier systems
Mechanical (Kanban) pull signals are used to notify suppliers of the need to deliver product	Electronic Kanban support
Consignment agreements are used to reduce assets and cycle time while increasing the availability of critical items	Consignment inventory management
Advanced ship notices allow for tight synchronization between SOURCE and MAKE processes	Blanket order support with scheduling interfaces to external supplier systems

Inputs	Plan	Source	Make	Deliver
Sourcing Plans	P1.4, P2.4			
Source Execution Data		ES.2	M2.2	
Logistics Selection			ES.6	
Replenishment Signals			M1.2, M2.2, M3.3	D2.3
Production Schedule			M1.1, M2.1, M3.2	
Outputs	**Plan**	**Source**	**Make**	**Deliver**
Procurement Signal (Supplier)				
Sourced Product on Order	P2.2	ES.9		
Scheduled Receipts			M1.1, M2.1, M3.2	
Product on Order				D

TABLE 8.4

Example Level 3 Enable Process Element Documentation (SCOR Version 5.0)

Enable Process: Manage Business Rules for PLAN Processes   **Process Number: EP.1**

Enable Process Definition

The process of establishing, maintaining and enforcing decision support criteria for Supply Chain Planning which translate to rules for conducting business, i.e., developing and maintaining customer and channel performance standards of an entire supply chain such as service levels, given service requirements by supply chain stakeholders/trading partners. Business rules align PLAN process policies with business strategy, goals and objectives.

Performance Attributes	Metric
Reliability	None Identified
Responsiveness	None Identified
Flexibility	None Identified
Cost	Total Supply Chain Costs
Assets	None Identified

Best Practices	Features
Integrated business and supply chain planning processes where cross-functional input is leveraged to set business rules.	Supply Chain performance dashboard capability.

Inputs	Plan	Source	Make	Deliver
Business Plan				
Strategic Plan				
Service Requirements				

Outputs	Plan	Source	Make	Deliver
Planning Decision Policies	P1.3, P2.3, P3.3, P4.3			
Service Levels	P4.1			

8.4.1 COLLABORATION DEFINED

The technical committee defined *collaboration* as follows:

> A relationship built on trust that is benchmarked by the commitment to the team objective and where consensus may not always be achievable but where nothing takes place without the commitment of all involved.

Some could argue that unanimous commitment may be difficult to achieve. In Section 4.4.2, we described different types of partnerships and a way of classifying them. The classification scheme includes the balance of power in the relationship. If a strong customer or partner dictates new terms to its partners or suppliers, commitment will follow because it is mandatory. This is certainly a linkage, but it might not fit the "warm and fuzzy" definition above.

The collaboration technical committee defined motivations for collaboration in terms of a "hierarchy of business needs." The levels are comparable to Maslow's familiar hierarchy: survival, safety, social and belonging, esteem and aesthetic and self-actualization. The collaboration hierarchy is the following:

1. Business survival
2. Sustained business activity
3. Sustained growth and market recognition
4. Channel master control
5. Value chain leadership

If your customer dictates to you, your choices are limited. Your motivating force is likely to be Level 1 or 2 in the hierarchy. On the other hand, levels 3, 4 and 5 might drive the carving out of new space on the competitive landscape as described in Section 4.4.2.1. At this point, the supply chain project moves beyond cost reduction to expanding market share and revenues.

The committee defined three levels of collaboration. Ranging from lower to higher levels, these were:

1. Data exchange collaboration where partners (internal or external) exchange information as required, principally to complete day-to-day transactions. Data exchange can be one way or two way.
2. Cooperative collaboration where partners (internal or external) share systems and tools so that all have access to information simultaneously.
3. Cognitive collaboration is the highest level requiring "joint, concurrent intellectual and cognitive activity between partners." This level embraces information sharing to reach joint decisions.

The committee originated the term *collaboratory* to define a partnership between parties. A collaboratory includes the business, cultural and system environment needed to build and operate a linkage between partners. The collaboratory is intangible, based on trust and predictability and involves work requiring intellectual skills to set it up. Collaboratories include the first two levels above while the third level, the "cognitive" collaboratory, is the highest level.

Figure 8.4 provides a roadmap for identifying the collaboration type that best fits a particular business situation. On the vertical axis is uncertainty, which could also be *risk,* according to the PMBOK.

The horizontal axis in Figure 8.4 measures "mutual adjustment." Low levels mean that, even if a transaction has a wide range of potential outcomes, these outcomes will bring little disruption to either party's operation. Business will "go on as usual" under most scenarios. Higher levels of mutual adjustment drive the need for more collaboration.

Intensity of information exchange is measured by volume, frequency and complexity. As mutual adjustment and uncertainty increase, so does the need for increasing intensity of information exchange.

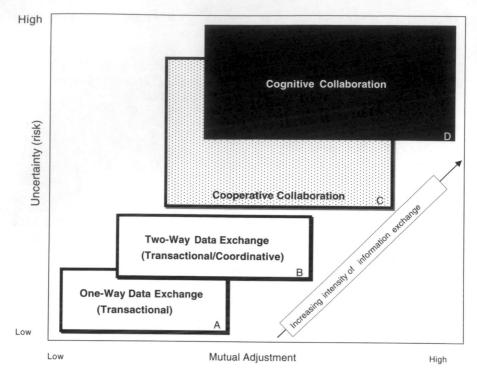

FIGURE 8.4 Collaborative roadmap.

In transaction settings, low intensity is associated with readily available commodity products at widely known market prices. It is likely such a transaction can be completed by a simple one-way information transaction as in box A in Figure 8.4. For example, a buyer goes to the bookstore for a book. The book is in stock; the buyer buys the book and leaves the store. Communication is one-way from the book buyer to the bookstore.

To the extent that any of these three conditions grows more uncertain, the need for communication increases. In box B, the book buyer goes on line and sends an order for a book. The seller confirms the order by e-mail and notifies the buyer when the book is shipped. In this setting, there is two-way communication between buyer and seller.

High levels of mutual adjustment go with potentially disruptive outcomes. So the cognitive collaboratory in box D needs to anticipate these outcomes and possible reactions. As an example, the auto assembly plant receiving just-in-time components shuts down if a single part is missing. The resulting "cognitive collaboratory" assures capacity at the supplier, qualifies new parts, puts supplier plants close to assembly plants, requires buffer stocks, sets up real-time communications and continuously monitors the financial and operating health of the supplier.

An article in the *Wall Street Journal* illustrates the need for cooperative forms of collaboration in box C.[4] The article tells the story of the Grant J. Hunt Co., a distributor of potatoes and the experience of its president, Grant Hunt, in evaluating

TABLE 8.5
BTB Exchange Transactions — Promises and Realities

The Promise	The Reality
Joining an exchange would bring new customers.	The exchanges were seen to attract customers with marginal credit ratings.
	A Net-posted offer to sell cherries produced no bidders in four days.
The exchange would streamline transactions bringing "incalculable efficiencies."	The existing infrastructure (faxes, phones, etc.) is not that inefficient.
	The exchange systems wouldn't link to home grown systems. The result was duplication.
The Web would increase business.	The best way to get business was to hit the phones and call suppliers and customers. The Net alone wouldn't attract incremental business.
	Much of the service consists of advising suppliers and customers on market conditions. It is difficult to automate this function and it wasn't covered by the exchange.
Big customers would require Web-based transactions.	The large customers said they wanted to shift business to the exchanges but weren't able — as of the date of the article — to follow through.
The Web would improve visibility along the supply chain.	It was important to keep some prices and transactions confidential; the Web opened the terms of these transactions to too many parties.
The exchange fee was competitive.	The fee of 1-2% was a steep price in a narrow margin business like distribution.
The software would work.	The software wasn't read for use.
	Several of the early providers that Hunt encountered left the business.
The software was flexible.	The systems wouldn't allow Hunt to change prices quickly in response to market conditions.
	The software had difficulty processing abnormal transactions like returns. It failed on four of nine transactions selected for a test.
	The software had difficulty classifying different types of potatoes. Different distributors used different codes for the same potato.
The Hunt systems were outmoded.	They worked, however, and supply chain partners had grown accustomed to using them.

business-to-business (BTB) exchanges. The Hunt company buys from potato farmers and sells their products to supermarket chains, wholesalers and restaurant-supply companies. Many might view potatoes as the "ultimate" commodity — one readily adaptable to online trading, characteristic of boxes A or B.

However, Mr. Grant's experience showed there is more to the buying and selling of potatoes than meets the eye. Table 8.5 summarizes the result of trial implementation of the exchange.[5] Selling potatoes turned out not to be like selling books. In fact, much of the over-the-phone collaboration centered on advising customers about market conditions, not completing transactions. Also, potatoes, as it turns out, have many variations; and the type the buyer wanted wasn't always available. Mr. Hunt's staff had to work out alternatives with customers.

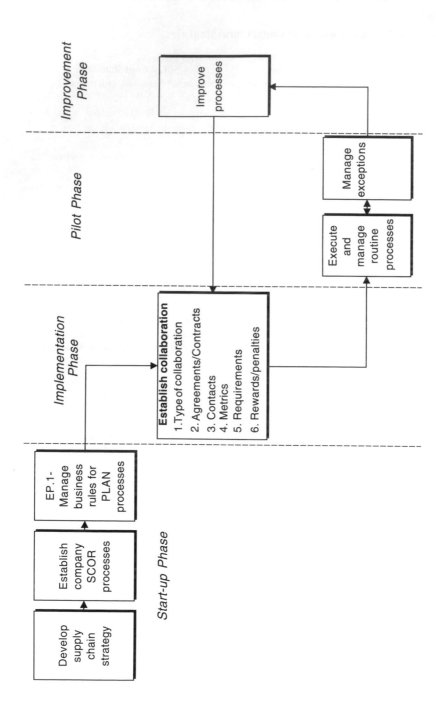

FIGURE 8.5 Project life cycle for a collaboration.

TABLE 8.6
Using SCOR in Supply Chain Improvement Projects

PMBOK Knowledge Area	Need for SCM Expertise	SCOR Contribution
Integration Management	High	SCOR covers most of the activities involved in a supply chain, making it an important integration tool.
Scope Management	High	SCOR contains several types of activities: planning, executing and enabling. This is a checklist of items that might be included in any supply chain improvement project.
Time Management	Low	The metrics of SCOR and the company's performance relative to industry standards can aid priority setting.
Cost Management	Medium	SCOR and its performance measurements can justify or not justify expenditure for supply chain improvements. An enabling process seeks coordination of supply chain and company financial goals.
Quality Management	Medium	SCOR contains many metrics at Level 3 process elements for measuring supply chain service and cost performance.
Human Resources	High	By defining activities an organization should undertake, that organization can better identify the skills it needs. Threads will identify the capabilities needed in partner organizations.
Communications Management	Medium	SCOR provides a vocabulary for better communications between supply chain partners. New collaboration approaches also provide a framework for ongoingprocesses.
Risk Management	High	SCOR enabling processes should lower the risk in planning and execution on a variety of fronts. Model content should reduce the risk that a technology or approach to operating a supply chain is not overlooked in the design process.
Procurement Management	High	SCOR covers many SOURCE, DELIVER and RETURN process elements, providing metrics and best practice in each. It will aid suppplier selection by defining what is needed in a partner. The collaboratory includes a high-level framework for partnership agreements.

Using a box A business exchange model failed. Cooperative collaboration, in box C of Figure 8.4, was the best model for Mr. Hunt. The lesson of the Hunt case is that one has to examine buyer–seller relationships in the supply chain in some detail to establish the real needs for collaboration.

8.4.2 COLLABORATORY LIFE CYCLE

Figure 8.5 shows a project life cycle for establishing a collaboratory. In the figure, there are four phases for the project. The *Start-up Phase* contains internal activities that establish the strategic need for the collaboratory. EP.1 is an ENABLE PLAN process described in Table 8.4, establishing the business rules for collaboration. The figure contains possible elements of the collaboratory. Of course, these will vary depending on the collaboratory's mission. The *Implementation Phase* sets up the collaboration linkages. The *Pilot Phase* tests the linkages in operation. In the *Improvement Phase*, collaboration processes are upgraded.

8.5 SHORTCUT TO BETTER PROJECT MANAGEMENT

SCOR is an important component of supply chain practice, as shown in Figure 1.1. SCOR helps an organization "jump start" its supply chain improvement projects. There is no reason to duplicate what others have already done. To illustrate, Table 8.6 contains examples of how SCOR supplements each of the PMBOK knowledge areas that were described in Chapter 7. The table repeats the need for supplemental SCM knowledge in each area — high, medium, or low.

ENDNOTES

1. Thanks to Katie Kasper for her review of parts of this chapter.
2. Supply-Chain Operations Reference-model: Overview of SCOR Version 5.0 Supply-Chain Council, 2001, p. 1.
3. To avoid confusion, when referring to SCOR processes, we use capital letters.
4. Gomes, Lee, How lower tech gear beat web "exchange" at their own game, *The Wall Street Journal*, March 16, 2001, p. A1.
5. A copy of this table appeared in *Supply Chain Myths and Realities* by James B. Ayers published by Auerbach Publishers, #41-50-50, 2001, p. 10.

9 Information Technology Projects — Lessons for SCM

Information technology projects are important enablers of supply chain change. Their successes and failures are also better documented than the successes and failures of other types of supply chain projects. Lessons learned from supply chain Information Technology (IT) projects alert us to potential failures in project management.

9.1 WHY LOOK AT INFORMATION TECHNOLOGY PROJECTS

There is little doubt that IT is an important and frequently vital enabler of supply chain improvement. By looking at these projects, we hope to draw broader lessons on the subject of supply chain project management. And there is certainly a great deal written on the subject of IT project management, much of it describing project failures and other shortcomings.

A survey by the Standish Group International, Inc. is cited in *Project Management*, a book about implementing technology.[1] The survey reports that 31% of IT projects aren't completed, only 16% are completed on time and within budget and 52% post cost overruns by 189%. This is not an admirable record.

Our proposition is that root causes for IT failures provide "lessons learned" for supply chain projects in general. In this chapter, we'll take reports of IT project failures and trace their root causes. With the insights gained, our project management templates in Chapters 12–15 will be all the stronger. Each template will describe which root causes are addressed by the recommended project process.

Prior chapters contain a foundation of knowledge and practice applicable to SCM projects. Figure 1.3 is an overview of knowledge and practice categories. We define the term *knowledge* as what is known about the field. *Practice* refers to actions that result from experience gained through application of that knowledge. Chapters 2–4 summarized SCM knowledge areas and practice for SCM. Chapters 5–8 covered both SCM and project management knowledge and practice. These include the Project Management Maturity Model (PMMM), the Supply-Chain Council's SCOR model and project management knowledge areas (PMBOK) from the Project Management Institute (PMI).

Sources in this chapter report shortfalls in IT projects that relied on technology that is closely associated with supply chain operations. This chapter will link the root causes reported in these cases with the four categories of supply chain project management. This is a worthy exercise for two reasons. First, the reported experiences tell us the types of project failures. This allows us to tailor our project templates to focus on the root causes of failures. Second, the findings provide solid guidance to those setting up their own projects. They may be overlooking an area of real vulnerability.

Each of the following five sections describes a project failure root cause. At the risk of oversimplifying root causes, the five should take in most of the obstacles to effective supply chain project management. A summary at the end of the chapter describes the conclusions we reach from this process. Our five root causes are the following:

1. Rigidity, insufficient flexibility
2. Organization roadblocks
3. Top management abrogation
4. Inadequate technical capability
5. Misunderstood technology

9.2 RIGIDITY, OR INSUFFICIENT FLEXIBILITY

Chapter 3 describes the need for flexibility in our supply chain designs. Such flexibility enables the supply chain to better match supply and demand in spite of fluctuations in either. Flexibility is also needed in our project management approach to avoid big dollar write-offs.[2] Robert Austin and Richard Nolan of the Harvard Business School conducted the study of Enterprise Resource Planning (ERP) projects that led to this conclusion. They report that 65% of executives surveyed said that ERP systems have at least a moderate chance of hurting their businesses because of implementation problems.

9.2.1 RIGIDITY ROOT CAUSE

Austin and Nolan observe that most ERP systems as they are ultimately implemented look different from what was envisioned in their original requirements. They reach a counterintuitive conclusion. They recommend that ERP implementation should not be considered a "project" governed by traditional project management paradigms.

Instead of a project model, they recommend a new business venture model. The venture model is preferable because the venture continually adjusts its plan as the business changes due to unforeseen requirements or changes in the business situation. The authors conclude that the same kinds of changes are likely during an ERP implementation.

Specific recommendations include the following:

- Divide the effort into stages and invest accordingly. Change plans frequently; don't be "locked in" on requirements and priorities throughout the project. It's the planning that's important, not the plan.
- Appoint an executive leader who is not easily influenced to screen proposals made by vendors and team members. (This person obviously has to know his stuff and people of this caliber are in short supply.)

- Assign strong, solidly qualified team members. The authors note that most investors in new enterprises base their investment choices on the executives running the company, not the plan.
- Use incremental funding to trigger periodic reviews and adjustments to the plan.
- Share risks for success, including outside vendors who have to make complex decisions during the project.
- Big projects are risky; pay for information that lowers risk, even though it doesn't produce a deliverable.

The PMBOK describes the "progressive elaboration" property of projects. This root cause calls on project managers to build appropriate responses into project plans.

9.2.2 RIGIDITY — LINKS WITH KNOWLEDGE AND PRACTICE AREAS

While the authors examined ERP projects, the lessons cited apply as well to the technology and nontechnology components of large-scale SCM projects. In particular, correction will be facilitated by attention to the following knowledge and practice areas.

Project management knowledge	Both *Project Integration* and *Scope Management* will be challenged by the need to change frequently. This is counter to the idea that project plans should be unchanging through the product life cycle. Sophistication is required to incorporate this flexibility. A company should consider the supply chain improvement as a major project with a series of short subprojects.
	Procurement Management will require risk-sharing contracts with suppliers for both IT and supply chain services. *Risk Management* encourages the use of project phasing to reduce risk as well as information gathering, where justified.
Project management practice	At level 3 of Kerzner's PMMM, Singular Methodology, the company has a singular approach for project management. But that approach is broad enough to accommodate a number of project types. A feature of Level 3 is "informal project management," a flexible approach requiring trust in the project team.
SCM knowledge	Execution of **Task 1. Designing supply chains for strategic advantage** will design the new supply chain. Little advanced planning means more changes during the project; more planning results in fewer changes.
	Work associated with **Task 3. Forging Supply Chain Partnerships** will spin off supplier and customer agreements. These agreements produce a systems design to support interconnections with suppliers and customers.
SCM practice	**Task 2. Implementing collaborative relationships** requires assignment of high caliber staff to projects. This includes both team members and project leadership. The task must also address which functional departments, suppliers and customers that should be on the team.

9.3 ORGANIZATION ROADBLOCKS

One of our SCM tasks, described in Section 4.3, is to align internal departments to supply chain design. John Bermudez of AMR Research reinforces this need.[3] His firm also researched success rates for companies implementing supply chain software. The success rate was less than 15% in terms of implementing more than a few of the applications they had purchased. Bermudez doesn't fault the software companies but blames organization complexity and lack of understanding of how supply chains actually work.

9.3.1 ORGANIZATION ROADBLOCKS — ROOT CAUSE

Bermudez cites the problem of department-sponsored software projects. But supply chain processes are expected to involve many functional departments in the organization. Each department has its own procedures and makeshift systems using tools like Excel spreadsheets and faxes. Goals vary across departments and often conflict. For example, the customer service department's objectives for taking care of customers may conflict with the distribution department's objective for low inventory. If the distribution center is the function charged with implementing supply chain software, it has three basic choices:

1. Tailor the application to the interaction between distribution and customer service — an added expense that will preserve existing organization conflicts.
2. Implement the application within its own function, which limits its potential.
3. Fight for changing processes, including measures, in both departments.

Which option would you, the reader, take if you were running the distribution center? Neither of the first two approaches will produce the desired "bang for the buck" from the software promised by the vendor. The best option for the company is 3, moving to a "real supply chain management process" before implementing new technology. However, too often this is not politically feasible or is not high enough on the company's list of priorities.

9.3.2 ORGANIZATION ROADBLOCKS — LINKS WITH KNOWLEDGE AND PRACTICE AREAS

The problems raised are the result of sponsorship of projects at the departmental level. This idea was first introduced in the Chapter 4 discussion of Figure 4.4, Types of SCM Improvement Projects. That figure shows three levels of supply chain project — department, business unit and supply chain. Companies faced with this situation require raising the level of project planning at least to the business unit level. This would sidestep the problem of conflicting goals between the distribution and customer service functions cited above.

| Project management knowledge | *Project Scope Management* is challenged by organization boundaries. As the example above demonstrates, boundaries are an obstacle to changing cross-department processes. Awareness of the consequences is often the barrier. |

Project management practice	A situation like that described would be typical of a Level 1 company on the PMMM. It demonstrates that project management thinking hasn't permeated the organization. The company isn't capable of effectively implementing a multidepartment change.
SCM knowledge	*Task 1. Designing supply chains for strategic advantage* calls for identifying "spheres" before designing supply chains. This tool aligns the organization before designing systems and procedures. *Task 2. Implementing collaborative relationships* calls for elevating measures to the company or supply chain levels and away from parochial departments.
SCM practice	The SCOR model uses the term "threads" to define supply chain configurations for different products or markets. The tool communicates the shape of different types of supply chain. Classifying projects as shown in Figure 4.4 will identify the types of projects an organization is pursuing. The presence of too few company or supply chain projects (Levels 2 and 3) signals that the efforts aren't broad enough.

9.4 TOP MANAGEMENT ABROGATION

Management support from the top is a requisite for success for any change endeavor. This is no less important for supply chain and IT efforts, which are often wrapped together. This is not a problem in itself. However, too often management classifies the overall effort as a "systems" initiative and then relegates critical decisions that should be retained to IT professionals.

9.4.1 TOP MANAGEMENT ABROGATION — ROOT CAUSES

Jeanne Ross and Pete Weill, affiliated with MIT's Center for Information Systems Research, identify six decisions that fall into the category of those *not* to be delegated.[4] Their research shows that companies that retain these decisions achieve returns 40% higher than in companies that do not. The six, divided into *strategy* and *execution* categories, include the following:

- Strategy
  1. How much to spend overall on IT.
  2. What business processes should receive IT funds.
  3. What companywide IT capabilities are required to be competitive.
- Execution
  1. Required information systems service levels.
  2. Acceptable security and privacy risks.
  3. Who should be held responsible for IT failures.

Their message was reinforced by a report by Forrester Research Inc.[5] The report covered 291 companies and compared financial performance with IT spending expressed as a percentage of revenue. Financial performance measures were growth in cash flow and sales as well as return on assets. Forrester compared companies with others within their industry group.

The result showed that throwing money at technology is not the road to financial success. Top-quartile companies spent 3.3% of revenue on IT; second- and third-quartile companies spend 4.5% and 4.2%, respectively, while the fourth quartile spend 2.6%. The authors concluded that getting a return on investment requires strategic alignment, process alignment and change management. Sometimes less is more.

All these issues are the purview of top management. The study leads to another question any company might ask of itself. If our management abrogates decisions in important areas related to IT, what other important decisions are relegated to functional managers?

9.4.2 Top Management Abrogation — Links with Knowledge and Practice Areas

So much here depends on the abilities and willingness of managers to be involved in "nuts and bolts" issues inside their organizations. Project management and SCM disciplines assure that the right organization level addresses the right issues. Project templates in Chapters 12–15 define these roles for different project processes.

Project management knowledge	*Scope Management* is challenged by the need to draw the line between projects that are properly the purview of functional management and those that are the purview of senior management. A determining issue could be the risk exposure from the project. This calls for use of *Risk Management* knowledge to identify and analyze these risks.
Project management practice	The behavior noted here, abrogation of decisions, is typical of a Level 1 PMMM organization. A motivation for a company's moving to Level 2 of the PMMM is the survival stake the company has in its major projects — IT and others. Components at Level 2 include financial accountability in projects and disciplined project management project policies and procedures.
SCM knowledge	A company will need a tool like spheres to develop customer-focused processes to which top management should direct improvement efforts. Each of these spheres will have different process requirements. Funding should go to the most attractive spheres.
SCM practice	SCOR Level 3 processes are useful for process characterization to support planning for projects. Also, SCOR lists collaboration and other best practices to assist design. Companies should review their enabling processes to determine whether they have the infrastructure for new processes. Better metrics, along the lines of those in SCOR (Table 8.2), aid measurement of process performance.

9.5 INADEQUATE TECHNICAL CAPABILITY

A company should not pursue technology for its own operations without necessary technical talents. Supply chain systems raise the bar even further. Not only must one's own company possess needed capabilities, but its trading partners may also have to match it. So risks rising from weak technical capabilities apply to both our own and our partners' competence.

9.5.1 OUR OWN CAPABILITY

Key to this is an effective IT function — whether it is represented by internal staff or acquired through a contracted external capability. Two resources identify questions to ask and issues to address regarding the readiness of the IT function. Tinnirello,[6] cited above, recommends asking the following questions about the company's development function before launching a new project:

- Is the development organization aligned to company business needs?
- Are users satisfied with current products of the developers?
- Are managers and users satisfied with the development organization's schedule and cost performance?
- Are development processes adequate to the task?
- Are development people's skills, training and morale adequate to the task at hand?

If the answer to any of these is "no," the company should correct the shortcoming before beginning — an example of project risk mitigation.

However, many companies cannot pick and choose when they must move ahead with change. David Ritter, of the Boston Consulting Group, is our second reference.[7] He encourages IT managers to "be prepared" for the call to implement new systems. His 12-step process, summarized below, specifically addresses processes and systems for material acquisition that are an important supply chain element.

1. Understand your existing process. Don't automate it if it's a mess. Reengineer it first.
2. Coordinate with suppliers. Make sure your solution will fit.
3. Examine your internal network. If you need to change, consider moving from electronic data interchange (EDI) to the Internet. Also consider a virtual private network (VPN).
4. Understand technical challenges for extracting data from legacy systems. ERP system data to support forecasting is a good example of a supply chain application.
5. Adopt existing standards where possible. Examples include XML and data exchange initiatives in your industry. (CPFR, described in Section 3.7.2, is also an example.)
6. Survey application vendors. Understand what different applications can or cannot do.

7. Determine what product information you must pass on to suppliers; identify the form it's in and its accessibility. Is it accurate, are formats appropriate and is it accessible to suppliers?
8. Survey electronic markets. Understand what role they should play, if any.
9. Automate processes with workflow (what we refer to as "proactive" systems). Consider using software to integrate applications.
10. Consider the needs for different kinds of tendering, particularly short-term spot buying vs. long-term contracts. What is being done now? What should the future look like?
11. Reevaluate current legacy systems. Should they be extended? What has to be done to get ready for the new technology?
12. Have your purchasing manager select suppliers who have appropriate SCM capabilities.

These steps provide a blueprint for early project stages before committing to a course of action for process improvement. Another consideration is the ability of partners along the chain to respond technically to your initiatives. In particular, actions resulting from step 1 in the list above will call for a joint supply chain and IT effort.

9.5.2 PARTNER CAPABILITIES

"A chain is as strong as its weakest link" is a saying that applies to real chains — the kind attached to anchors. To a degree, the saying is also true of supply chains. Certainly an important element in SCM is reducing risk in the supply chain. Figure 9.1 illustrates the nature of the risks.

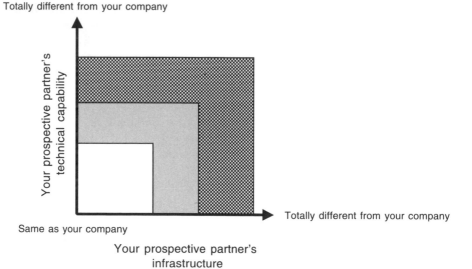

FIGURE 11.1 Capability and infrastructure disparities.

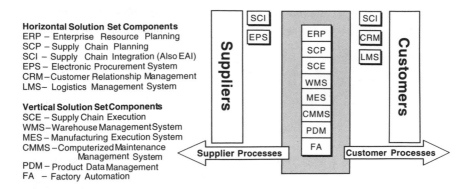

FIGURE 11.2 Supply chain applications.

With respect to IT, there are two types of partner limitations to what a company leading an initiative can accomplish. The first limitation is differences between partners in technical capability. A common complaint is this disparity, particularly when the initiating company is much more sophisticated than its trading partner. Figure 9.1shows this separation on the vertical axis with the difference between capabilities increasing further up the vertical axis. A wide gulf in capabilities is likely to increase project risk.

The second limitation is differences due mostly to geography and takes the form of "infrastructure" disparities. Infrastructure is the network capability, along with logistics capabilities, in the regions where the companies are located. In this context, a company in a country with a strong infrastructure must deal with partners in "have-not" areas with weak infrastructures.

Infrastructure differences lie along the horizontal axis in Figure 9.1. Steven Morris and Denise Johnson McManus describe this situation as a barrier to constructing the virtual enterprise — one that's a network of companies brought together quickly in response to a business opportunity.[8] In particular, they warn that development of internal technology reliant on a first world infrastructure may limit options for expansion to places where that infrastructure doesn't exist.

Figure 9.2 illustrates the problem. The figure shows various types of supply chain applications that can lie within an organization. These are the "vertical solutions set components." One way partners can gain links is with SCI (Supply Chain Integration) applications, shown at the intersection of the companies. These enable disparate systems to interact with each other.

In each case, a company may want to temper its choice of supply chain design, particularly its IT capability. This would provide needed flexibility to take on less capable partners.

9.5.3 INADEQUATE TECHNOLOGY CAPABILITY — LINKS WITH KNOWLEDGE AND PRACTICE AREAS

Most of the previous root causes of project failure have focused on "management" not "technical" issues. This root cause encompasses risk due to technical limitations.

The risks involved are compounded by the need to work with trading partners and in parts of the world with undeveloped or unfamiliar enabling infrastructure.

Project management knowledge	Addressing the cited issues lies in *Risk Management* knowledge area. Risk can be mitigated through application of *Procurement Management* knowledge. *Mindsets for Implementing IT* (Table 4.7) are also important in formulating projects. The proper mindsets put process improvement ahead of technology "elegance."
Project management practice	A Level 2 company in the PMMM may be reluctant to move from its disciplined processes at that level to informal processes at Level 3. And maybe it shouldn't. It is likely that a company must reach Level 2 before they can seriously consider complex supply chain projects.
SCM knowledge	**Task 3. Forging supply chain partnerships** uses frameworks for characterizing partnerships. **Task 4. Managing supply chain information** addresses the needs for internal competence in supply chain technology tools. The idea that the enterprise has multiple supply chains centered in sphere will also lead system developers away from enterprise-wide (one-size-fits-all) solutions. Messed up existing processes should be reinvented before undertaking automation.
SCM practice	Process mapping tools, described in Chapter 15, for both cost and cycle time will also prove useful, particularly if they track information and material movement in the entire supply chain. They can be used to search out weak links for strengthening with appropriate technology tools.

9.6 MISUNDERSTOOD TECHNOLOGY

Figure 9.2, introduced in the previous section, depicts the potential for confusion that is symptomatic of a dilemma faced by most managers. The application types referred to would confuse even the most sophisticated. What does each application do? When should it be used? How much effort is involved in implementing the application? Do I need it?

These and other questions are natural. A trap is trying to correct basic process flaws with complex software. The consequences of the confusion can be seen in the implementation of one popular application — customer relationship management (CRM). It is a certainly a supply chain application, located in Figure 9.2 at the interface between the company and its customers.

9.6.1 CRM PERILS — ROOT CAUSES

In the late 1990s in the U.S., many companies rushed to implement CRM applications. Three consultants from the consulting firm Bain and Company describe their research into outcomes from these efforts.[9] Their decision to pursue this line of research came from CRM's low ratings in Bain's 2001 survey of management tools.

CRM was third from the bottom of 25 tools evaluated. As an example, they note one manufacturer who scrapped a $30 million investment in the technology.

The researchers attribute the failure of CRM installations to one central factor — *the assumption on the part of management that the software would manage the customer relationship.*

The reality is that CRM is a "bundling of customer strategy and processes," supported by software. The authors recommend avoiding the four perils in implementing CRM in the following sections. The reader should note that the advice applies to any supply chain project.

9.6.1.1 No Customer Strategy

According to the Bain Consultants, strategy starts with identifying attractive customer segments and determining what it takes to acquire and retain customers in those segments. Less attractive segments will have alternative strategies, depending on the prospects for making them profitable to serve. At this point, it is possible that a company will conclude that it doesn't need a CRM effort to woo the attractive segments. They should pursue other measures like reducing cost, building a focused supply chain, or tailoring the product line.

9.6.1.2 Implementing CRM Without the Environment Needed To Make It Work

Noting that this may be the most dangerous pitfall, the survey authors draw on a survey by CRM Forum that attributed 87% of CRM failures to inadequate change management. New organization structures, metrics and processes — oriented to attractive segments — should be instituted before the technology.

9.6.1.3 Assuming More Technology Is Better

CRM, in its management context, doesn't require technology. Proper responses can range from low tech to high tech depending on the needs and wants of the targeted segment. One can also ramp technology use as it proceeds, starting with low-tech, easy-to-implement CRM measures for short-term gains and proceeding to hard-to-implement, higher-technology solutions.

9.6.1.4 Stalking Customers

"Just because managers can contact a customer doesn't mean they should." This quote from the authors demonstrates the fine line between customer care and heckling. Any investment in CRM techniques should reflect what that customer would like to see and that may not be — and most likely will not be — what the technology is capable of, including pestering from salespeople.

CRM, as a solution, is a technology that has been pursued for the wrong reasons. In the supply chain technology space, there are many other examples where the promise fell short of the reality. A key is a requirement for purchasers to know their business need well enough to evaluate a solution. If the solution still looks attractive, the next step is to prepare the organization for the technology. This is the strategy of the Web site managers described in Section 4.5.

9.6.2 MISUNDERSTOOD SOFTWARE — LINKS WITH KNOWLEDGE AND PRACTICE AREAS

Many organizations place huge bets on technology and other supply chain projects with little understanding of the payoff and the risks. The software supply is abundant and vendors constantly produce new products. The manager is on his own in evaluating a solution in the form of software or technique in terms of its fit with company needs.

Project management knowledge	Overcoming this root cause requires competencies in structuring programs and then phasing the projects that make up those programs. This, as do others, challenges the *Scope Management* process.
Project management practice	Level 2 and 3 organizations in the PMMM will be leery of "quick fix" technology solutions. They will understand the large stakes involved in expensive software efforts.
SCM knowledge	General business knowledge and its implications for SCM are essential building blocks. Chapter 4 mentioned the product life cycle, functional or innovative products and differing customer requirements. Awareness of all is needed to understand how a technology will support your business.
	Task 4. Managing supply chain information includes the need to stay current with technology advances and retaining the practical know-how to apply technology to business requirements. **Task 5. Removing cost from the supply chain** may bring nontechnical process change that is better than an ambitious system effort like CRM. At a minimum, existing processes should be redesigned to satisfy the strategy as much as possible before automating.
SCM practice	A principal theme of Chapter 4 is that supply chain and customer strategies should be aligned. Tools like activity systems directed for spheres make this possible. This will produce finely tuned rifle shot requirements for supply chain processes.

9.7 CONCLUSIONS — LESSONS LEARNED

All SCM and project management knowledge and practice components are necessary to complete a project, just like having all the parts of a car — the engine, the screws, the steering wheel and so forth — must be present to drive that car. However, that doesn't mean that some knowledge and practice components shouldn't receive special attention. Table 9.1 summarizes what the five project shortcomings described in this chapter suggest for special attention. The bold items are those that appear to be the most important in reducing risk in our projects.

9.7.1 PROJECT MANAGEMENT KNOWLEDGE

Of the nine project management knowledge areas, just three are mentioned more than once as corrections for project shortcomings. *Project Scope Management* is

**TABLE 11.1
Summary of IT Project Shortcomings**

	Rigidity	Organization Roadblocks	Management Abrogation	Technical Capability	Misunderstood Technology
Project Management Knowledge	Integration Scope Cost **Human resources** Risk	Scope	Scope Cost Risk	Human resources Risk	Scope
Project Management Practice	PMMM Level 3 **Project structure (phasing)**		**PMMM Level 2**	PMMM Level 2	PMMM Levels 2 and 3
SCM Knowledge	Task 1. Strategy Task 2. Collaborative relationships Task 3. Partnerships	Task 1. Strategy **Task 2. Collaborative relationships**	**Task 1. Strategy**	Task 3. Partnerships **Task 4. Information** Task 5. Cost removal	**Task 1. Strategy** Task 4. Information Task 5. Cost removal
SCM Practice		SCOR threads SCOR metrics Types of SCM projects	SCOR Level 3 processes, metrics, collaboration		

Note: The bold items are particularly important in addressing the identified project shortcoming.

mentioned four out of five times. *Project Risk Management* is mentioned in three. *Project Cost Management* and *Project Human Resource Management* are mentioned in two. A reasonable conclusion is, that if an organization gets these three project processes right, chances for success increase significantly.

9.7.2 PROJECT MANAGEMENT PRACTICE

Many project shortcomings would likely be addressed by moving the organization to higher levels of the PMMM. This requires a level of awareness that's absent in many organizations. At least Level 2 maturity is required in four out of five short-comings. Level 3 is likely to be required to avoid rigidity since Level 3 calls for an "informal process" that is flexible enough for a variety of projects.

Structuring phases of a project into shorter periods will also increase agility in adjusting to change. These changes are likely in increasingly dynamic business environments.

9.7.3 SCM KNOWLEDGE

All five SCM tasks are represented in Table 9.1. *Task 1. Designing Supply Chains for Strategic Advantage* is mentioned as a solution four times. Not having a strategy is a frequent complaint when projects go bad. Kerzner's PMMM is designed to provide a competitive advantage from better project management. Tasks 2 and 3, internal and external collaboration, are mentioned twice. Our observation is that companies still struggle with internal alignment. Aligning several companies in a supply chain is a relatively new challenge.

Task 4. Managing Supply Chain Information also appears twice. The lesson to draw is that shortcomings in IT projects are less about technology and more about management. *Task 5. Removing Cost from the Supply Chain* appears twice, as the knowledge area contains tools for analyzing operations. However, few processes should be automated without improvement in the current system environment. Perhaps the automation won't be needed at all. So this task will likely accompany any major system improvement.

9.7.4 SCM PRACTICE

Knowledge of several SCOR elements will help address risk areas. The idea of "threads" that cross organization boundaries communicates supply chain missions to departments and partners. Metrics play a role in preventing conflicts between functions. All the SCOR elements — processes, metrics and collaboration — provide decision tool to enable top management to define which responsibilities to delegate and which to retain.

NDNOTES

1. Tinnirello, Paul C., *Project Management*, Boca Raton: Auerbach Publications, 2000, p. 391.

2. Cliffe, Sarah, ERP implementation; How to avoid $100 million write-offs, *Harvard Business Review,* January–February 1999, pp. 16–17.

3. Bermudez, John, Supply chain management: More than just technology, *Supply Chain Management Review,* March–April 2002, pp. 15–16.

4. Ross, Jeanne W. and Weill, Peter, Six IT decisions your IT people shouldn't make, *Harvard Business Review,* November 2002, pp. 85–91.

5. Technology spending offers no guarantee of better performance, *Wall Street Journal,* November 1, 2002, p. B2.

6. Tinnirello, Paul C., *Project Management,* Boca Raton: Auerbach Publications, 2000, p. 464.

7. Ritter, David, We must never break the chain, from *The Supply Chain Yearbook, 2001 Edition,* New York: McGraw-Hill, 2001, pp. 199–200.

8. Morris, Steven A. and McManus, Denise Johnson, Information infrastructure centrality in the agile organization, *Information Systems Management,* Fall 2002, pp. 8–12.

9. Rigby, Darrell K., Reichheld, Frederick F. and Schefter, Phil, Avoid the four perils of CRM, *Harvard Business Review,* February 2002, pp. 101–109.

Section III

Supply Chain Management Project Processes

10 SCM Maturity Model

A maturity model for SCM enables tracking progress in the capability to improve supply chains. It is a qualitative methodology to be supplemented by quantitative measures for customer service and financial performance.

This book includes the term "measurable" in its title. A methodology for measurable SCM improvement requires a map defining levels of performance. The map enables readers to define Point A, where they are now and track their progress to Point B, where they want to be. Having the map is useful because two organizations will neither start from the same place nor will they necessarily have the same destination.

This chapter develops a maturity model for progress in an organization's capability to use SCM to improve their businesses. This is a role similar to that of the Project Management Maturity Model (PMMM) introduced in Chapter 5, which measures proficiency in project management. Any such model should be adaptable to individual company needs and useful for justifying and measuring the benefits of implemented projects. Note that the maturity model describes maturity stages and doesn't directly measure the results from supply chain projects. These quantitative measures show up in company market share and its bottom line.

As might be expected, consultants have already fashioned several maturity models. All have value, so in the interest of "full disclosure" we describe several of these models here and propose our own version, using the supply chain knowledge areas described in this book. also, there is no use reinventing useful approaches, so our model adopts selected features of the other models.

10.1 WHERE ARE WE? WHERE DO WE WANT TO GO?

Supply chain maturity models are designed to answer these two questions. Most well publicized models have either four or five levels. In the first two models described here, Levels I and II reflect an internal focus, while Levels III and IV move outside the company. For example, Charles Poirier, a consultant with Computer Sciences Corporation (CSC), has recommended the following four levels as a maturity model:[1]

1. Sourcing and logistics — characterized by functional excellence and programs like supplier reduction, inventory reduction, cost reduction.
2. Internal excellence — use of activity-based costing and process management.
3. Network construction — development of differentiated processes across the enterprise and cooperative planning with partners.

4. Industry leader — wide use of technology tools, demand–supply linkages and a global perspective.

For these four levels, Poirer's model has nine factors that help its user define a particular level. These include executive sponsorship, benefits, types of projects, tools used, financial targets and alliances.

Poirer's model is a good representation of how a company might develop excellence within its departments and then move outward, using its "network," or supply chain, to achieve industry leadership. At Level 4, the model argues for wide use of information technology to tie the supply chain together.

More recently, Poirier has proposed a five-level model.[2] A summary of the levels in this model, which is similar to his four-level model, is shown below.

I. Enterprise integration focused on functional processes
II. Corporate excellence at the intraenterprise level
III. Partner collaboration that begins the process of working with selected suppliers and customers
IV. Value chain collaboration through e-commerce, the Internet and other cyber technologies
V. Full network connectivity through integrating systems to the benefit of all partners

The second model is somewhat similar. The consulting firms PRTM and the Performance Measurement Group (PMG), both of which are active in the Supply-Chain Council, have also developed another four-stage model.[3] Its stages are the following:

1. Functional focus — department level activity with functional measurement. Discrete supply chain processes are well understood and documented.
2. Internal integration — resource management at functional and enterprise levels. There is a companywide process and data model.
3. External integration — partners along the supply chain collaborate on objectives and action plans. Common processes and data sharing occur along the chain. Management reacts to performance metrics.
4. Cross-enterprise collaboration — enabled by IT and e-Business[4] solutions. Real-time planning, decision-making and execution to customer requirements mark this level. Multicompany business process alignment including objectives has been achieved.

This maturity model has parallels to those from CSC, proceeding from a functional, or departmental, to a company focus and then to partners in the supply chain. At advanced level stages (4 and 5) in all these models, information technology plays an important role. PRTM and PMG also rely heavily on benchmarking competitor performance to gage progress. The implied goal is to reach or exceed competitors in the metrics of importance to customers. This is a laudable objective, but often a "necessary but not sufficient" goal for creating strategic advantage. This is particularly true when that advantage requires being different from competitors.

10.2 THE SUPPLY CHAIN SPECTRUM

Joseph L. Cavinato represents the Center for Strategic Supply Leadership at the Institute for Supply Management, and teaches SCM courses at Arizona State University. The Institute is the former National Association of Purchasing Management.

Cavinato maintains that there is no one-size-fits-all supply chain design.[5] In fact, because of current fashion, many refer to their operations as a supply chain. Yet these companies have no supply chain at all. In reality, they are a loose-knit group of departments, perhaps like Level 1 in the models described above. Cavinato notes that there are many types of supply chain and that the supply chain must be aligned with company goals for competing. Also, under scrutiny, most companies have multiple, not just one, supply chain.

This supports the idea that all companies need not pursue the same destination. Based on strategy, a company may choose any number of levels of integration internally or with its partners. After a 2-year study completed in late 2001, Cavinato's organization identified 16 supply chain types — a spectrum of possible models. Table 10.1 contains summary descriptions of each type. The table has a column describing the complexity of operating a supply chain of a particular type.

Also shown is the contribution to competitive advantage and profit using four levels like those described above.

At the first level — the traditional supply chains — Chains 1–3 have a negative impact on the company's fortunes. Their chains are "anchors" holding the company back. Chains 4–8 are neutral with regard to longer-term strategic benefits. However, their implementation produces one-time benefits in cost savings.

Chains 9 and 10 begin to produce not only savings but also competitive advantage on the supplier and customer side. Chains 11 (which may be illegal in some places) through 16 offer increasing long-term benefits in terms of market share and revenue. Chain 11 is understandably the least complex to implement while chain 16, Information Networks, is the most complex. Chain 16 most closely matches the highest levels in the Poirier and PRTM/PMG maturity models.

These 16 models capture the realities that go with different industries and the relationships that exist in those industries. Auto manufacturing is a much different environment from that in a high-technology industry or in food distribution. These environments place constraints on how far one should or can go in implementing technology or other supply chain solutions. A solution that we use later is to reframe the maturity model in terms of the five competencies that compose our SCM knowledge areas, not what kinds of technologies a company employs.

Another reality in Cavinato's model is that, while supply chains can be a source of operating efficiencies and competitive advantage, they can also hold a company back. That is, they can be "dysfunctional" when it comes to reaching goals for growth and profits. We will also build the dysfunctional level into our model since we have observed it often.

TABLE 10.1
Supply Chain Types

#	Type of Chain/Network	Description/Characteristics	Relative Complexity	Maturity Model Stage
1	No chain	Functions act freely, no strategic advantage from supply chain.	Low	1
2	Don't know	Mostly outsourced supply chain operations. No strategic advantage. "Blank check to outsiders," like 3rd party logistics providers.	Low	1
3	Chains that tie down the firm	Internally focused. Lagging competitors, catch-up mode. Logistics-centered with measures focused on warehousing and transportation cost.	High	1
4	Nano-chain	Internally focused. Focused on manufacturing efficiencies in plants requiring high utilization. Inbound and outbound processes are secondary. Examples include autos and aircraft manufacturing.	Low	2
5	Micro-chain	Logistics model with integrated physical and information flows. Balances inbound, production and outbound distribution.	Low	2
6	Project logistics chain	Efficient at project supply and execution. Integrates multiple suppliers to the project. Like the nano-chain except it's a project environment.	Medium	2
7	Cash-to-cash cycle chain	Focused on cash flow, perhaps to detriment of suppliers. The starting point is a cash flow goal, with operations structured accordingly.	High	2
8	Synergistic chain	Eliminates duplication. No competitive advantage. Seeks to leverage buying power. Common in large companies with multiple independent divisions. Focus on common commodity purchases.	High	2
9	Demand chain	High collaboration often dictated by dominant customers like Wal-Mart. Interdisciplinary with sales and operations. Tailored arrangements by customer. Flexible company. Uses technology.	Medium	2
10	Extended supply chain	Has a supply chain mindset. Managers developed in the supply chain role. Good processes for new products and production of existing ones.	Medium	2
11	Market dominance and blocking	Enjoys a monopoly with control over market and pricing. Often illegal in developed countries.	Low	3

TABLE 10.1 (Continued)
Supply Chain Types

	Type of Chain/Network	Description/Characteristics	Relative Complexity	Maturity Model Stage
12	Supply integration	Highly interdisciplinary, evolving from process-oriented cost reduction efforts. Complete supply chain view, platform for competitive initiatives.	Medium	3
13	Speed-to-market	Emphasizes new product development. Flexible. Uses time as a metric. Seeks to tap unused capacity in the supply chain to speed roll-outs.	Medium	3
14	Innovation	Network of manufacturing and logistics suppliers for flexibility. Focuses on product creation, launch and growth phases of product life cycle. Examples are high technology electronics and seasonal toys.	Medium	4
15	Value chain	Chain-to-chain competition, seeking innovation throughout the chain. Shared outcome arrangements are common. Procurement coordinates. Partners invest to develop capabilities needed for their part of the chain.	High	4
16	Information networks	Flexible networks with few physical assets processing a flow of innovations. Supply chain managers are network creators and leaders. Data is accessed and converted into information, knowledge, and intelligence.	High	4

10.3 A MATURITY MODEL FOR SCM PROJECTS

The CSC and PRTM/PMG maturity models start, at Level 1, with an implied mastery of department-level processes. Level 1 companies, in this view, really have their acts together — at least at the department level. Having achieved excellence in departmental functions, they are ready to work cross-functionally. Our view is that this is overoptimistic. In fact, many organizations are like Chains 1, 2 and 3 in Cavinato's model. They are in a "deep hole," with a need to overhaul both processes and organizations, including those inside department boundaries, before they can inch forward.

As an example, departments may do well against the traditional functional measures by which they are evaluated. But these are outmoded or, even worse, downright counter-productive where supply chain, not departmental, excellence is required. For example, many companies expect their transportation managers to minimize transportation costs. But a tight-fisted policy to squeeze transportation costs can hurt customer service. The functional measures produce unintended circumstances and present a barrier to moving to the next SCM level.

End points in both the CSC and PRTM/PMG models point to technology as a mark for reaching the highest level of maturity. These models, in our view, don't sufficiently consider the need for strategies that differentiate a company. They better fit strategies for battling head-to-head in price-based competition. They are too silent on using SCM in business strategies that set companies apart from competitors. Cavinato, on the other hand, provides several different versions of Level 4 supply chains, notably Chains 12 through 16.

Table 10.2 is the SCM maturity model we will employ for design of SCM project processes. Down the left two columns are our five SCM tasks described as knowledge areas in Chapter 4. Along the top are maturity Stages I through V. At each stage for each task, there is a short description of what it takes to achieve that stage. These descriptions are framed in terms of management's use of SCM knowledge and practice.

We use Stage I to account for the unfortunate, but all too common, "dysfunctional" organization. Stage I organizations really struggle with basic processes. A number of factors, including high turnover, poor leadership, fast-changing markets and products, misguided functional measures, unabsorbed acquisitions or lack of basic information technology cause this. Such companies are often a "mess," and working in one is chaotic.

A company at Stage I needs to get its own house in order. It must cease counterproductive practices to be ready for Stage II. Having the sharpest, most finely tuned departmental functions, which could be the case in Cavinato's 1–3 supply chain types, may make you a flop as a company since your measures are too narrow and ambitions too limited.

At Stage II, called "Infrastructure" in Table 10.2, the company remains functionally focused. Internal efforts concentrate on department budgets, squeezing the organization for cost reduction. The Stage II company is in a position, however, to put together basic systems and procedures, talent, organization and measures. A Stage II company should be at Level 1 in Kerzner's PMMM described in Chapter 5, as indicated at the bottom of Table 10.2. This means managers are at least talking about project management.

Stage III is labeled Cost Reduction. At this level, the company optimizes its own cost and profits. It does so with both internally and externally directed cross-functional efforts. Six Sigma process improvement initiatives for internal process improvement would be a typical Stage III activity. In terms of the PMMM, the Stage III company might be at Level 2, using disciplined project management tools.

Cross-functional cost reduction efforts are under way in a Stage III company, likely targeting bill-of-material and service-provider costs. Supplier cost reduction at Stage III usually focuses on price negotiations of a "zero-sum game" nature. This is often the case when the company has power over its suppliers and is able to dictate the terms of engagement. Supply chain types 4–10 in Table 10.1 would be typical of this stage. Able competitors can readily copy most initiatives, so little in the way of sustainable advantage is produced by the effort.

TABLE 10.2
Stages of SCM Maturity

		Stages of Supply Chain Management Maturity				
Task	Name	I. Dysfunctional	II. Infrastructure	III. Cost Reduction	IV. Collaboration	V. Strategic Contribution
1	Strategic supply chain planning projects	No strategy exists to guide supply chain design.	Supply chain awareness takes hold. However, managers still view the company as standalone.	Supply chain is viewed as a nonstrategic "cost center" for internal cost reduction.	Joint strategic initiatives are pursued on a limited basis with suppliers and customers.	Activity systems are implemented for strategic advantage.
2	Internal collaborative relationships projects	Internal department measures, goals and objectives conflict with supply chain excellence.	The organization is functionally focused. Initiatives are departmental.	Cross-functional initiatives begin, limited to the company and focused on cost reduction.	Supply chain has moved into a single function, which manages multicompany relationships.	The organization has established multicompany infrastructure for important chains.
3	Forging supply chain partnerships projects	Relationships with suppliers and customers are arm's length at best, antagonistic at worst.	Collaboration up and down the supply chain is limited to transaction data.	Efforts are limited to supplier initiatives focused on cost reduction, not revenue increases.	Partners collaborate but roles are static. Partners pursue sphere strategies.	Members of the supply chain expand their value contributions.
4	Managing supply chain information projects	Basic information needed for decision-making is missing.	Technology improvements focus on individual departments and maintenance.	Systems efforts support cost reduction within the organization. May or may not be process justified.	Two-way information exchange supports transactions and mutual decision-making.	Technology is a key element integrated into supply chain activity systems
5	Making money from supply chain projects	Cost reduction and process improvement is a "hit-and-miss affair. Efforts often hurt more than they help.	Reductions are internal and measured through department budgets. Service is not an issue.	Cost-reduction efforts cross departments but are limited to internal efforts.	Supply chain cost reduction is limited to logistics and other operating costs.	Cost reduction across the supply chain is the target. Benefits are shared among partners.
PMMM (Chapter 5):	0	1	2	3	4	5

Stage IV, in Table 10.2 is Collaboration. Supply chain partners adopt collaboration models appropriate to process needs. In Chapter 8, the SCOR model defined several modes of collaboration. These included the following:

- **Data exchange collaboration** where partners (internal or external) exchange information for transactions as required. Data exchange can be one-way or two-way.
- **Cooperative collaboration** where partners (internal or external) share systems and tools so that partners have access to information simultaneously.
- **Cognitive collaboration** is the highest level requiring "joint, concurrent intellectual and cognitive activity between partners." This includes information sharing of all types leading to mutual decisions.

Collaboration at Stage IV is shaped by efforts to reduce cost and speed supply chain processes. This is admirable. However, the overriding collaboration goal is improvement in operating effectiveness. It takes forms like sharing end-sales data, working together on new products, optimizing competencies with outsourcing and rationalization of products and production resources. Chain types 12 and 13 in Cavinato's array closely fit Stage IV.

With regard to technology deployment, our maturity model's Stage IV would be like Level 4 in the CSC and PRTM/PMG models described at the beginning of the chapter. A maturity model shouldn't view deployment of technology solutions as the end game. Of course, technology can be an important enabler; but the company that measures progress in terms of the technology it installs runs the risk of missing the mark competitively — an important lesson from Chapter 9.

Michael Porter supported this view in an award-winning article.[6] Our update in Chapter 4 described his thinking on the role of the technology and the Internet in strategy setting. His view is that the Internet and related technology should complement the strategy. Your strategy defines what provides your company's competitive advantage, which arises because somehow you are different from your competitors. And that difference makes you the logical choice by the customer segments you have targeted. Technology alone doesn't bestow this difference, but it can be an important element in its delivery.

Porter also notes that the Internet will change the structure of many industries. This will make some industries more attractive and some less so. An example lies in the openness of the Internet. This openness means that the technology is available to all competitors, perhaps wiping out an industry leader's advantage. The Internet also enables companies to bypass traditional channels and appeal directly to end-users.

For these reasons, we define our Stage V as Strategic Contribution. At this stage, the outputs of our tasks are measured not by technology but by their support of plans for improving competitiveness. These plans derive from the business model, strategy and the activity system that makes the organization different from competitors. In the Stage V company, the supply chain is no longer a "cost" of doing business, but a clear component in its strategy to survive and prosper. Cavinato's chain types 14–16, in particular, correspond to this stage.

Across the bottom of Table 10.2, we show the likely match of our supply chain stages with Kerzner's PMMM. The assumption is that pursuing ever more expansive and complex SCM projects requires ever greater maturity in applying project management knowledge and practice.

The discussion in this chapter is intended to help readers establish their current position as well as select a model that best fits their destination. In Chapter 11, we will describe a process template for moving from one stage of SCM maturity to another.

ENDNOTES

1. Poirier, Charles C., The path to supply chain leadership, *Supply Chain Management Review*, (2/3), Fall, 1998. pp. 16–26.
2. Poirier, Charles, Achieving supply chain connectivity, *Supply Chain Management Review (6/6), November/December 2002*, pp. 16–22.
3. Montcrief, Bob and Stonich, Mark, Supply-chain practice maturity model and performance assessment, a presentation by the Performance Management Group (PMG) and Pittiglio Rabin Todd and McGrath (PRTM), November 6, 2001.
4. The term *eBusiness* stands for electronic business, usually associated with Internet-connected supply chain partners.
5. Cavinato, Joseph L., What's your supply chain type? *Supply Chain Management Review*, pp. 60–66, May/June 2002.
6. Porter, Michael E., Strategy and the Internet, *Harvard Business Review*, pp. 62–78, March 2001.

11 Introduction to SCM Executing Processes

Here we describe the process for transferring SCM knowledge into processes for executing supply chain projects. Supply chain project processes in Chapter 12–15 use the template introduced in this chapter.

A review of prior sections will set the stage for introducing recommended SCM process processes. Section II describes best practices in project management from the Project Management Body of Knowledge (PMBOK) Guide from the Project Management Institute. In Chapter 7, our recap included descriptions of PMBOK's project management processes. As shown in Figure 7.1, these were sorted into nine project management knowledge areas and five process groups, listed here for reference.

PMBOK Knowledge Areas	PMBOK Process Groups
Integration Management (H)	Initiating
Project Scope Management (H)	Planning
Project Time Management (L)	Executing
Project Cost Management (M)	Controlling
Project Quality Management (M)	Closing
Project Human Resource Management (H)	
Project Communication Management (M)	
Risk Project Management (H)	
Project Procurement Management (H)	

(H,L,M) — Indicates the relative need (low, medium, or high) for SCM expertise, as described in Chapter 7.

The "executing" process group, third down the right-hand list of process groups, is the domain of application areas like SCM. In the remaining chapters, we provide PMBOK-style descriptions of these executing processes, plus a few in other process groups, for supply chain improvement projects.

In addition, we also must address project management processes requiring "supplemental" SCM expertise to perform them effectively. The table above indicates our Chapter 7 rating for each knowledge area in terms of its SCM domain expertise.

Our purpose is to fill a gap in the project management practices of most companies — that is, the gap between planning and execution, between strategy setting and implementing that strategy. Figure 11.1, using a format introduced in Chapter 4, illustrates the gap. Most supply chain projects are functional and nonstrategic, as shown by the shape in the lower left-hand corner of the figure. If SCM is to be

155

Levels of Implementation

	Level 1 Function	Level 2 Company	Level 3 Supply Chain

Strategic Projects
Changes basis for competition
Proprietary product/process
technology
Market-based justification
Broad sponsorship

Nonstrategic Projects
Fixes a problem
Nonproprietary technology
ROI, cash flow justification
Functional sponsorship

FIGURE 11.1 Gap between supply chain planning and execution.

performed effectively, as measured by our SCM maturity matrix (Table 10.2), the project portfolio must migrate to the upper right-hand corner of the figure, the domain of strategic, enterprisewide and supply chain-level projects. Herein lies a challenge for any company, even those who have mastered function-level project management.

In Chapter 9, we traced root causes of project failures by examining reported shortcomings in projects that are closely related to SCM. Our list of root causes includes the following:

1. Rigidity, insufficient flexibility — project management straitjackets and an inability to adapt to external changes during the project
2. Organization roadblocks — goal conflicts between departments
3. Top management abrogation — over-delegation to lower levels of what should be executive decisions
4. Inadequate technical capability — inside the organization and at supply chain partners
5. Misunderstood technology — what the technique would and would not accomplish and whether it was the right solution

To be complete, our SCM processes must address these shortcomings.

Concepts from Kerzner, SCOR and the PMBOK Guide facilitate the effort. Kerzner, at Level 3 of his PMMM, recommends a "singular methodology" for managing projects, so our processes represent a single, but flexible, structure, despite the fact that programs and projects covered can differ substantially. We hope many will find value in adapting these elements as their own singular methodologies. Or, if they have such a singular methodology, they can use the ideas here as part of a continuous improvement effort, reflective of Levels 4 and 5 management maturity.

SCOR contains structures and best practices for supply chain configuration that aid the implementation of our processes. These include both supply chain operating processes and enabling processes that ensure that an organization has its infrastructure in order. SCOR is a top-down model. This means it can only go so far — in SCOR's case, Level 3 — in recommending processes. Beyond that, Level 4, processes are tailored to the organization. We will point to areas of SCOR support for our supply chain processes.

PMBOK uses its nine knowledge areas to organize project management processes. This book's Chapter 4 describes five knowledge areas for SCM, which we can also use for our SCM project process descriptions. The chapter listing below summarizes how each chapter addresses its knowledge area or areas.

Chapter		**Description**
12	SCM Task 1. Developing a Supply Chain Strategy	Covers strategies to achieve supply chain excellence. Includes the strategy and supporting organization.
13	SCM Task 2. Implementing Collaborative Relationships	Develops internal collaboration among departments and dedicates staff to improvement efforts.
14	SCM Task 3. Forging Supply Chain Partnerships	Develops relationships up and down the chain with outside suppliers and customers.
15	SCM Tasks 4 and 5. Improving Supply Chain Processes and Systems	These tasks are managing supply chain information and removing cost from the supply chain.

Table 11.1 is the process template employed in Chapters 12–15. Inputs, outputs and tools and techniques are also included in PMBOK's process descriptions. Where appropriate, we provide additional elements — process definition, project management shortcomings addressed, PMMM level, SCM maturity stage, terminology, stakeholders and SCOR support — as shown in Table 11.1. In some cases, a template element is not included because it does not apply or has been covered elsewhere.

Table 11.2 lists the 26 processes we cover. They represent all the PMBOK process groups, but are naturally weighted to the executing processes in the SCM application area. There are two processes in the Initiating group, four in the Planning group, 15 in the Executing group, four in the Controlling group and one in the Closing group. .

Chapters 12–15 are organized by SCM task and their related processes. The process-numbering approach shown in Table 11.2 will be carried through Chapters 12–15. So 1.1, *Chartering the Supply Chain Effort* is the first process covered in Chapter 12. *Inputs* for the process are 1.1.1; *process elements* are 1.1.2 and *outputs* are 1.1.3. These appear in Sections 12.1.1, 12.1.2 and 12.1.3 respectively.

Users have flexibility in determining which components they want in which project phases. We suggest beginning with the arrangement shown in Figure 11.2. Figure 11.2 shows four generic life cycle phases for a supply chain improvement project. These are the following:

TABLE 11.1
Process Template

| Inputs | Process Name (Process Number from Table 11.2) | Process Group |
	Process Elements (Appropriate Items Only)	Outputs
Inputs to the process from other processes or external sources. (Source of the input*)	**Process definition** — Includes scope and objectives of the process.	Outputs from the process to other processes or external users.
	Approaches and techniques — Concepts and tools useful in executing the process.	
	PM shortcomings addressed — Shortcomings in project management addressed. (Chapter 9) PMMM level. (Chapter 5) Project management knowledge areas and processes	
	SCM maturity — Relevant stages in the supply chain maturity model. (Chapter 10)	
	Terminology — Supply chain terms applicable to the process. (Glossary)	
	Stakeholders — Those who execute the process, influence its outcome, or are affected by its outcome.	
	SCOR support — Supportive SCOR model elements. (Chapter 8)	

* For documents generated inside the project, the source is the process that generated it. "External" refers to company documents generated outside the project.

TABLE 11.2
Mapping of SCM Processes to Process Groups and Knowledge Areas

SCM Knowledge Area	Initiating	Planning	Executing	Controlling	Closing
			Process Groups		
1. Developing a supply chain strategy	1.1 Chartering the supply chain effort	1.2 Supply chain scope planning	1.3 Sphere definition 1.4 Activity system design 1.5 Organization alignment 1.6 Collaboration strategy	1.7 Integrated change control	1.8 Phase closure
2. Implementing collaborative relationships		2.1 Organization planning 2.2 Staff acquisition	2.3 Organizing for activity system implementation 2.4 Supply chain metrics	2.5 Schedule control	
3. Forging supply chain partnerships		3.1 Communications planning	3.2 Supplier base 3.3 Customer base 3.4 Stage 3 organization 3.5 Risk sharing	3.6 Project staffing 3.7 Partner scope verification	
4. Managing supply chain information			4.1 Defining linkages		
5. Removing cost from the supply chain	5.1 Process improvement initiation		5.2 Supply chain mapping 5.3 Identifying root causes 5.4 Reducing material cost 5.5 Demand-driven supply chain		

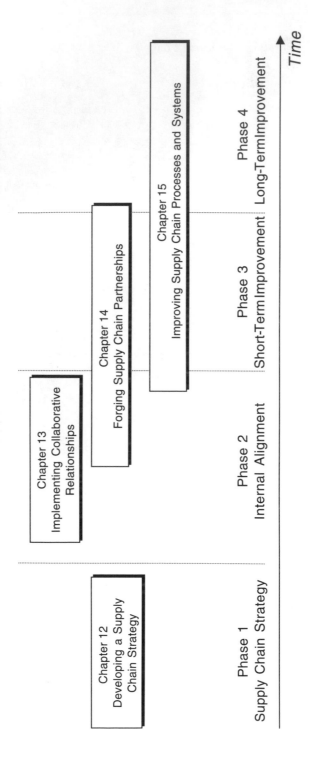

FIGURE 11.2 Interrelationships between SCM project life cycle phases.

TABLE 11.3
Descriptions of SCM Project Life Cycle Phases

	Life Cycle Phase	Start	End
1	Supply chain strategy	Upon initiation.	When the strategy is accepted and implementation plans are developed. Includes conceptual design for organization.
2	Internal alignment	On completion of strategy and related organization design.	When the organization design is implemented and defined improvement projects are staffed and funded.
3	Short term improvement	When service and cost improvement projects are started.	When short-term projects (those that require no large systems and/or facility changes) are completed.
4	Long term improvement	When long-term projects are started. (Not just approved or funded)	When long-term projects (those requiring major systems and/or facilities) are completed.

1. Supply chain strategy
2. Internal alignment
3. Short-term improvement
4. Long-term improvement

Table 11.3 describes when each life cycle phase starts and ends. Note that SCM knowledge area processes can occur in more than one phase. This is due to the nature of the work involved. For example, *Forging Supply Chain Partnerships* can begin in Phase 2 and carry over to Stages 3 and 4.

An important element in keeping the "players" straight is a responsibility assignment matrix, or RAM. The RAM is a project management tool that summarizes who is accountable for the success of the project, who is for responsible for producing work products, who participates or is consulted, or who is informed. Appendix B2 is a RAM for supply chain project processes. The labels use the RACI (responsible, accountable, consulted, informed) format for the responsibility assignment categories. The roles of various "stakeholders" are also described throughout the process descriptions. Participants identified in Appendix B2 include the following:

Company Steering Committee	A single group of senior managers in our company. Accountable for the overall project.
Multicompany Steering Committee	One or more senior-level groups convened as needed to oversee collaboration between our company and one or more partners. There could be several of these to fit the type of collaboration undertaken.

Project Manager or Project Office	The person or group responsible for executing the project. The project could proceed through phase 1 with a manager and be expanded to a project office depending on the strategy developed.
Supply Chain Design Team	A single group from supply chain and related functions responsible for supply chain design including spheres, activity systems and organizations.
Sphere Design Team	Multiple teams who design supply chains in each sphere.
Process Design Team	Multiple teams selected to improve an assigned process or multiple processes.
Company Internal Departments	The supply chain and supporting functions within our organization.
Partner Internal Departments	The supply chain and supporting functions in our partners' organizations.
	A single participant can serve on multiple teams.

12 Developing a Supply Chain Strategy

This chapter describes processes for creating a supply chain strategy, referred to here as the HOW, that is consistent with the company's strategic direction, the WHAT. Two cases in Appendix A describe real-life strategic situations. These are A3, Lessons from a Failed Supply Chain Initiative and A4, Adapting to a New Supply Chain Role.

The supply chain strategy defines how operations in the supply chain will support overall corporate strategies. Section 4.2 described tools and techniques for developing the supply chain strategy, which should make objectives for supply chain operations clear.

However, in many organizations, the strategy needed to guide supply chain design may not be defined. The lack of formal strategy need not impede a supply chain effort if managers choose to move ahead. However, prudence demands that the project team gather as much information on company direction as possible.

Figure 12.1 is a flowchart for *Task 1: Developing a Supply Chain Strategy*, showing the project processes for developing the strategy. This chapter describes the inputs, process elements and outputs for those processes. The list below names each process by section number. The number in parenthesis is the process number using our numbering convention described in Table 11.2. Appendix B contains summaries of all SCM project processes with their outputs (Appendix B1) and a recommendation for assignments of responsibility for each project process (Appendix B2).

12.1 Chartering the Supply Chain Effort (1.1)
12.2 Project Plan Development (1.2)
12.3 Sphere Definition (1.3)
12.4 Activity System Design (1.4)
12.5 Organization Alignment (1.5)
12.6 Collaboration Strategy (1.6)
12.7 Integrated Change Control (1.7)
12.8 Phase Closure (1.8)

Processes 1.1 through 1.6 lie in the domain of SCM knowledge and practice. Integrated Change Control (1.7) is a PMBOK controlling process. Phase Closure (1.8) is in PMBOK's closing process group. Because they are logically associated with strategy setting, and the strategy guides the total project, these change control and closing processes are placed in this chapter.

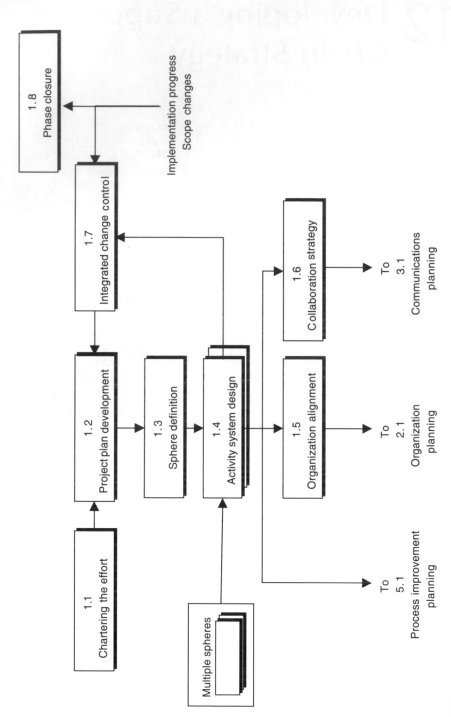

FIGURE 15.1 Developing a supply chain strategy.

12.1 CHARTERING THE SUPPLY CHAIN EFFORT (1.1)

Table 12.1 summarizes the chartering process, an important initiating process that sets expectations for the entire supply chain project. Table 12.1 under Inputs lists the documents that might be available for chartering at the outset of the project. Understanding these documents or equivalent information best assures alignment of the supply chain project with the organization's strategic initiatives. Our process definition also includes gathering the inputs needed to define the issues that the project should address. A running list of project issues is very useful for establishing project scope and keeping track of progress. Such progress is measured in terms of addressing these issues.

12.1.1 INPUTS TO CHARTERING THE SUPPLY CHAIN EFFORT (1.1.1)

The purpose of inputs is to understand what strategic planning (the WHAT) requires of supply chain features (the HOW). If documentation is lacking, ideas representing a number of functions may be lodged in the minds of managers. Examples include executive management (CEO, COO), marketing and sales, engineering and operations.

A company is smart if it elicits as much participation as possible in chartering the project. The following inputs are suggestions that may be delivered in document, presentation, or brainstorming formats. The fastest way, in the absence of formal documents, is often an off-site session that meets to surface issues addressed by the strategy.

12.1.1.1 Customer and Product Briefing

This input defines for planners what customer and product combinations are in the project scope. Section 4.2.1, The Nature of Markets and Products, describes ways to portray these combinations. These ways include the position of the product within its life cycle — inception, growth, maturity or decline. Each phase makes different demands on supply chain design. Another concept described in Section 4.2.1 is the idea of innovative and functional products. Innovative products require a responsive supply chain. Functional products require a cost effective one. Mismatching the type of supply chain with the type of product is a common mistake.

Also, the customers and products in the project scope need not be limited to the current ones. New products and targeted segments that aren't currently served should also be included.

Desired information includes sales by major product or product group to each identified market segment. Ideally, it should also include relative market share, key success factors in the market and strengths and weaknesses of competitors. In the descriptions that follow, "External" indicates that the input comes from documentation outside the supply chain project.

12.1.1.2 Strategy (External)

The external strategy covers formal or informal plans for becoming a more effective competitor. "External" refers to the company's intended measures to improve its

TABLE 15.1
Chartering the Supply Chain Effort (1.1)

1.1 Chartering the Supply Chain Effort

Initiating Process

1.1.1 Inputs	1.1.2 Process Elements	1.1.3 Outputs
Customer and Product Briefing (External) Business forecasts Customer requirements Profitability Relative competitive performance ***Strategy (External)*** New product plans Product sought/desired deliverables Strategic plan and objectives (the "what") ***Environmental Briefing (External)*** Change drivers Governance structure Historical perspective Product/process technology background ***Issues*** Initial list of issues	Process definition Approaches and techniques PM shortcomings addressed SCM maturity	Authorizes the project. Links the supply chain project with other efforts. Starts the process of listing issues. Group meetings to discuss the potential role SCM (the "how") can play in strategy (the "what") execution. Well-designed charters should mitigate the consequences of rigidity, organization roadblocks and top management abrogation. Linkage of projects to strategy is key to higher levels on the PMMM. In particular, Level 3 calls for reliance on project management to implement strategy. Chartering addresses the Initiation process in PMBOK's Project Scope Management knowledge area. Narrow charters lead to Stages II or III. Broader charters lead to Stages IV or V.	***SCM Charter Elements*** Assumptions Change management considerations Constraints Project authorization Updated issues list ***Project Management Charter Elements*** Project management assignments (project management, PMO, project team members) Project change procedures Decision making authority Deliverables required Responsibilities Schedule objectives Steering Committee assignments

Terminology
- Business Model
- Economic Value Added
- Issue, Issues List
- Steering Committee
- Trigger Events
- Voice of the Customer
- Charter
- Manufacturing Strategy
- Target Costing
- Value Chain

Stakeholders

Senior management, through the company steering committee, should be responsible for the charter. A project manager could be assigned to speed the process. Functional managers or department heads should provide viewpoints on the charter.

SCOR support

The following SCOR processes are relevant to chartering:
- P1 Plan supply chain
- EP.1 Manage business rules for PLAN processes
- EP.9 Align supply chain unit plan with financial plan

competitive position, not necessarily how it plans to do it. The list of measures should go a long way toward identifying initiatives that can be supported by better supply chains.

To the extent the current strategy requires supply chain-related projects, these should also be listed and, to the extent possible, documented according to the model described in Section 4.2.2 and shown in Figure 4.4. That figure shows six types of projects based on whether they are strategic or nonstrategic and at what level they are. The three levels are functional, business unit and supply chain. Of course, it is quite possible that there is no mention of the supply chain in the company strategy. This is not an unusual situation and missions for the supply chain must be developed.

12.1.1.3 Environmental Briefing (External)

The environmental briefing should define other outside issues. These can be functional. For example, an engineering vice president can address technology. A marketing vice president can address plans for penetrating a new overseas market. Driving forces for supply chain change, described in Chapter 3, should also be addressed in this category. This input might come from the CEO or COO.

12.1.1.4 Issues

An effective way to define the project's scope is to maintain a running list of issues. Issues are defined by questions that arise at any point in the project from this process forward. The list can grow to dozens, even hundreds, of issues. Theoretically, when all the scope questions posed in the issues have been addressed, planning of the supply chain project is done. By selecting or rejecting questions as "in scope" or "out of scope," the project team, particularly the project manager and the company steering committee, is expanding or shrinking the project boundary.

For organizing the issue list, each entry should receive a name and include three parts: (1) the issue stated as a question or questions, (2) background on the issue needed to explain how it surfaced and (3) any decisions related to the issue as they are made. Those decisions can resolve the issue or identify further steps to achieve resolution. The example below, introduced in Section 7.3.8.3, illustrates.

> **Issue Name:** Transportation Network in China
> **Question(s):** Is the existing network suitable for distributing our products? Should we develop a new network? How much would developing a new network cost?
> **Background:** Profitability of our products in the Chinese market will depend on our effectiveness in reaching targeted customers. Existing transportation is problematic in China for our type of product. A risk analysis shows that developing a new network is attractive, but our board of directors will be reluctant to make the required investment.
> **Decision:** We need to strengthen the case for investing in the transportation network by doing further studies of the market potential and identifying supply chain partners that can provide the needed transportation services.

Because the issues list can be a long one, issue categories are useful for better organization. The following is an alphabetical list of candidate categories an organization might consider:

Customers/markets: Customer requirements that affect product and supply chain design

Decision-making: Availability and accuracy of information

External constraints: Conditions that limit supply chain options for the company

Finance: Financing and cash flow considerations. Includes justification processe.

Infrastructure/capacity: Physical plant — buildings and equipment, locations

Internal relations: The role of the organization with regard to other company divisions

Organization: Operating functions performed by the organization and its business partners and their assignment

Processes: Supply chain processes required to provide products

Staff: Questions regarding the number or skill levels of staff members

Technology: Product and process technology and its capability, cost and reliability in service

Supply chain planners should choose categories that fit their situations and then add others as needed. A database tool is useful for updating issues, making changes and issuing reports that communicate status. Periodically during the project the project manager should update the issues list. This will close some issues that have been resolved and will open others for creation of project tasks.

12.1.2 Process Elements for Chartering the Supply Chain Effort (1.1.2)

This section describes aspects of chartering that recognize the special characteristics of a supply chain improvement project. Section 7.3.1 identified the Integration project management knowledge area as being one requiring high levels of supplemental SCM knowledge and practice. This is due to the strategic nature of SCM projects and the fact that supply chain projects can cross company boundaries.

12.1.2.1 Process Definition for Chartering the Supply Chain Effort

The chartering process, as shown in Table 12.1, should gain approval of the project, link the supply chain project with other projects and define initial issues for project coverage. Sections 7.3.1 and 7.3.2 in our chapter describing PMBOK knowledge areas list integration and planning elements. Project drivers listed in Section 7.3.2 include market demand, an internal requirement to improve performance, a specific customer request or a product or process technology advance.

The charter should document the motivators for the project. The list in 7.3.2 and the supply chain driving forces described in Chapter 3 support this documentation.

12.1.2.2 Approaches and Techniques for Chartering the Supply Chain Effort

The charter is an essential first step. Gaining such a charter can be painful or relatively easy, often depending on the level of management issuing the charter. A group meeting of key stakeholders is sometimes sufficient to start a project. At other times, getting off the ground can take many months. The charter is complete when the planning team that includes the steering committee and the project manager or office has the input needed to plan the project (Process 1.2).

12.1.2.3 Project Management Shortcomings Addressed by Chartering the Supply Chain Effort

A strong charter decreases the chances of encountering "showstoppers" like those listed in Chapter 9 that jeopardize project success. These include lack of flexibility in changing the direction of the project, organization roadblocks, top management abrogation, inadequate technical capability and misunderstood technology.

Flexibility is introduced if the charter calls for periodically synchronizing the project with changes in the environment. Organization clout counts; the charter from an executive in a strong position will reduce the chances of organization roadblocks. Of course, not getting a charter from that level is a signal that the project has a narrow focus or does not have executive backing.

12.1.2.4 SCM Maturity for Chartering the Supply Chain Effort

The charter should be explicit regarding the reach of the supply chain project. Section 4.2.2 described the three possible levels: functional, business unit and supply chain. The broader the project, the more complex it becomes. Counteracting that, there may be an advantage in pursuing a broader project as long as the scope doesn't exceed project team capabilities. Broader scopes correspond with higher levels, Stage III and above, of SCM maturity as defined in Section 10.3 and shown in Table 10.2.

12.1.2.5 Terminology for Chartering the Supply Chain Effort

Glossary terms for the chartering process focus on strategic planning. The supply chain project is an extension of the organization's overall strategy. In fact, it may be the centerpiece of that strategy if the company depends on operational excellence to be competitive.

12.1.2.6 Stakeholders for Chartering the Supply Chain Effort

Chartering should involve top management in the sponsoring organization, the project manager, the project team if assigned and functional managers. The charter is an announcement of the project. Internal stakeholders and involved partners should comprehend and identify with the charter. Appendix B2 recommends that the company steering committee be the ultimate approver of the charter; the project manager should supervise its development.

12.1.2.7   SCOR Support for Chartering the Supply Chain Effort

A supply chain project charter can include implementing processes for long-term operation. Three, in particular, merit attention in chartering. SCOR PLANNING processes (P1 in SCOR) focus on planning as matching supply and demand in the supply chain. Reference to the Level 1 PLAN process elements may be valuable at the chartering stage if this function is important to the supply chain project's mission.

ENABLE PLAN processes, particularly EP.1 and EP.3, which address business rules and financial plan alignment, should also be reviewed in the chartering process. EP.1 calls for aligning business rules with strategy. EP.9 is the SCOR element that couples the strategic plan with the supply chain plan. This matching generates supply chain capacity and other resource requirements to meet the plan.

12.1.3   OUTPUTS FROM CHARTERING THE SUPPLY CHAIN EFFORT (1.1.3)

The charter should include two deliverables. The first deals with the supply chain aspects of the project; the second with the project management elements. Table 12.1 lists components of the deliverables. These two deliverables need not be separate documents. However, they might be coordinated by different people in the project office — those with supply chain expertise and those with project management expertise.

12.1.3.1   SCM Charter Elements

Suggestions for the supply chain portion of the charter include assumptions, change management considerations, constraints, an updated issues list and the project charter. This package should contain any inputs to the project management team that the authorizing authority wants conveyed. Changes to SCM Charter Elements may occur during the course of the project.

Change management considerations contain guidance regarding anticipated ways of communicating and gaining acceptance of changes from the internal organization and supply chain partners.

12.1.3.2   Project Management Charter Elements

The listing of project management charter elements in Table 12.1 should signal management expectations for the project. This includes assignment of a company steering committee to oversee progress, be responsible for key decisions and retain responsibility for project success. At the strategy-setting stage, this steering committee is internal. Later, a multicompany steering committee may be needed to address cross-company issues. If it hasn't been decided, another important structural output is identification of the project manager or the project office.

12.2 PROJECT PLAN DEVELOPMENT (1.2)

Table 12.2 summarizes the project plan development processes. This process takes chartering inputs (Process 1.1) and converts them into concrete plans for proceeding. This process corresponds with PMBOK's Project Plan Development process in the Project Integration Management knowledge area. To avoid duplication of PMBOK knowledge area process descriptions, we use the Project Plan as the document containing both project scope and needed resources. As such, it draws on several project management knowledge areas, including the following:

- **Project Scope Management** including Scope Planning, Scope Definition, Scope Verification and Scope Change Control. Scope Change Control is addressed in 1.7, Integrated Change Control.
- **Project Time Management** including the processes of Activity Definition, Activity Sequencing, Activity Duration Estimating and Schedule Development. We develop Schedule Control in another process, 1.7 Integrated Change Control.
- **Project Cost Management** including Resource Planning, Cost Estimating and Cost Budgeting. Cost control is part of 1.7 Integrated Change Control.
- **Project Quality Management** including Quality Planning and Quality Assurance. Quality Control is part of 1.7 Integrated Change Control.
- **Project Human Resource Management** including Organizational Planning, Staff Acquisition and Team Development. The process templates suggest roles for SCM management and project teams throughout the processes.
- **Project Communications Management** including Communications Planning, Information Distribution and Performance Reporting. Administrative Closure is part of 1.8 Phase Closure.
- **Project Risk Management** including Risk Management Planning, Risk Identification, Qualitative Risk Analysis, Quantitative Risk Analysis, Risk Response Planning and Risk Monitoring and Control.
- **Project Procurement Management** including Procurement Planning, Solicitation Planning, Solicitation, Source Selection, Contract Administration and Contract Closeout.

The reader who wants to supplement the SCM executing process described in this chapter and Chapters 13–15 should draw on the PMBOK and Chapters 6 and 7 for more information on approaches to the processes listed above. Of course, the PMBOK contains useful additions in each of the knowledge areas listed above.

12.2.1 INPUTS FOR PROJECT PLAN DEVELOPMENT (1.2.1)

The outputs of Process 1.1, Chartering the Effort, are the inputs for this process. These include the SCM and Project Management Charter Elements described in the last section. These documents are primarily views external to the project, taking

TABLE 15.2
Supply Chain Project Plan Development (1.2)

	Planning Process	
1.2.1 Inputs	**1.2.2 Process Elements**	**1.2.3 Outputs**
SCM Charter Elements (1.1) Project Management Charter Elements (1.1)		
Process definition	Develop operations and WBS to be included in the supply chain project. Produce activities, budgets, schedules and assignments. Create additional issues. Develop a project vocabulary.	**_SCM Plan_** Benefits expected Enabling process evaluation Functions covered Partner policies Project vocabulary Updated issues list
Approaches and techniques	Alternatives identification Communications with supply chain partners Cost benefit and risk analysis Decomposition Modeling of supply chain operations Project selection and justification processes Work Breakdown Structure (WBS)	**_Project Management Plan_** Activity list Activity sequencing Approval to proceed Cost baseline Design Team assignments Network diagrams Project execution plan
PM shortcomings addressed	Rigidity, organization roadblocks are targets of better planning. Project plan development is fundamental to achieving Level 1 of the PMMM. No Project plan development is indicative of Level 0 maturity.	Resource requirements Project phasing Project schedule Scope management plan WBS
SCM maturity	Willingness to define supply chain project broadly will lead to higher levels (IV and V) of the maturity model.	

TABLE 12.2 (Continued)
Supply Chain Project Plan Development (1.2)

	Planning Process
	1.2 Supply Chain Project Plan Development
Terminology	– Activity – Cost baseline – Critical path – Decomposition – Design Team – IDEF – Network diagram – Partner – Phase – Program – Progressive elaboration– Project – Project life cycle – Project office – Scope – Subproject – Task – Work Breakdown – Structure (WBS)
Stakeholders	The company steering committee should oversee project plan development. Candidates for the supply chain design team can support the effort. Users of supply chain processes and key operating managers should be consulted.
SCOR support	Enabling process descriptions can be used as a basis for evaluation of readiness for improved supply chains. Process elements can serve as a checklist to assure plans are complete.

into account the organization's goals for success in its markets with the products it delivers.

Careful scope planning should match the needs presented in the external view with a view of the company's supply chain. This supply chain view should include an honest assessment of how well one's supply chains are doing the job they need to do. The gap between these views defines the SCM project's scope.

12.2.2 PROCESS ELEMENTS FOR PROJECT PLAN DEVELOPMENT (1.2.2)

In this section, we assume that our effort is a single SCM "project." We did mention earlier that the SCM effort could be a "program" instead of a project. This is best if SCM is expected to go on for a long time with intermittent projects. Alternatively, a project with several components may use "subprojects" to make the job more manageable. This process should address this structural issue — whether SCM is a "program" or a "project." As we proceed, we assume it will be a "project."

The core of our Project Plan is scope definition. PMBOK makes two distinctions regarding the definition of "scope." *Product* Scope constitutes the products, services, or results produced by the project. A work breakdown structure (WBS) is a way of displaying the product of the project. *Project* Scope is the work to be done to produce the products. The term scope includes both components.

12.2.2.1 Process Definition for Project Plan Development

Many paths are possible when defining the scope and content of a supply chain project. Supply chain projects can be defined in terms of any of the three definitions for the output of a project, a product, a service or a result. The same SCM project can be defined as a *product* (implement a distribution system in China) or as a *service* (make sure our retail outlets in China have our product) or as a *result* (maximize our profitability in China). Note that each level is broader in terms of scope and produces a product that will take longer to evaluate in terms of success or failure.

This idea reinforces the one first presented in Section 9.2.1. This section pointed to lack of flexibility as a principal reason for project failures. The proposed solution was to treat a project like a new business venture rather than as a traditional project. Supporting recommendations, listed in Section 9.2.1, include dividing the project into short phases, providing incremental funding, making sure your best people are on the project, sharing risk and reward with partners and paying for more information if it will be useful in lowering risk.

12.2.2.2 Approaches and Techniques for Project Plan Development

Project plan development should consider the organization's level of maturity in terms of the PMMM. It should also understand its business plan and the importance of the supply chain in fulfilling that plan. If SCM is vital and needs are urgent, the organization may have no choice but to pursue broader supply chain programs, Stage

III and above. Often, a wide range of choices is available. In these cases, the tools described here will be useful.

A good start is identifying alternatives, as described above. How do we frame the project — as a product, a service, or a result? How much discretion do we give to the project team? What phasing do we see? This will determine how frequently the project team returns for progress reviews and renewal of their charter.

A WBS, like that in Figure 6.3, can represent different product alternatives. This defines the deliverables of the project and can reflect major phases. Operations coverage could rely on SCOR process elements including planning, execution and enable processes. Threads can tie these processes together in high-level flow charts. Because scoping is top-down, decomposition can provide added levels of detail as necessary.

Talking to partners is a way of communicating your intent and gaining commitments to broader scope projects. If partners are unable or unwilling to work with you, your scope will necessarily be limited to your own organization.

Modeling, cost–benefit analysis and risk analysis are other tools to analyze alternatives. Section 7.3.8 provided an example of risk analysis. Activity-based costs can be quickly constructed for the purpose of scope planning and project justification.

12.2.2.3 Project Management Shortcomings Addressed by Project Plan Development

Project management failures due to rigidity and organization roadblocks can be anticipated by project plan development. Too broad a scope may exceed the organization's capability to implement the project. The fact that project scope is planned at all is indicative of Level 1 in the PMMM, shown in Table 5.1. If the project is to go beyond the organization's boundary, Level 3, a singular methodology is likely to be necessary.

12.2.2.4 SCM Maturity for Project Plan Development

The scope definition directly reflects the maturity level reached by the organization, as shown in Table 10.2. Stage III is indicative of a company ready to undertake cross-functional projects inside their own walls, even if those projects are limited in scope. At Stages IV and V, a multicompany group might make, review or approve scope decisions.

12.2.2.5 Terminology for Project Plan Development

Terms listed in Table 12.2 describe project management terms that may be encountered in project plan development. The scope will also indicate how the project might be completed, what it will take in resources and how ambitious its effort will be.

12.2.2.6 Stakeholders for Project Plan Development

Senior management, represented by the company steering committee, has an important stake in scope development. As the example of China distribution in Section

12.2.2.1 indicates, alternative scope definitions will produce vastly different projects. Different scenarios call for a wide range of staff resources, technical skills, money for the project and time to complete the effort.

The company steering committee should also include key operating function managers who will operate the redesigned processes. Those charged with carrying out the project are, of course, also key stakeholders. The project manager or office will be charged with executing the project. A supply chain design team from inside the company will be in charge of designing new supply chain processes.

Scope definition may be an appropriate time to enlist partners in the project. This interaction will likely provide important insights on how to proceed and how far you can go.

12.2.2.7 SCOR Support for Project Plan Development

SCOR supports scope setting since it is essentially a list of processes. One way to define the scope of a supply chain project is by listing corresponding SCOR processes. Another use of SCOR is as a self-assessment tool. This self-assessment can point to areas of needed improvement. ENABLE processes are particularly important. Effective ENABLE processes provide the environment in which planning and executing processes can flourish.

Figure 12.2 illustrates such an evaluation. It shows the nine ENABLE processes across the top. Six responders were asked to make their evaluation in two steps. The first step is to evaluate whether the organization has the ENABLE process at all. This is shown by the results of the "yes/no/unsure" responses at the top. For example, one responder said that "Assess performance" is not done at all. Those who responded that the processes are performed evaluated effectiveness on a four-point scale. A "4" is the most effective evaluation. Scores below 2.0 are in bold because they highlight problem areas. For example, ENABLE RETURN processes scored lowest in several categories.

12.2.3 OUTPUTS FROM PROJECT PLAN DEVELOPMENT (1.2.3)

The outputs, SCM and project management scope plans correspond to the input charters, as shown in Table 12.2. An essential element is whether the project will be functional, business unit or supply chain in scope.

From the project management point of view, the output should define the products and, to the extent possible, the traditional project planning and control elements that are common to any project. This includes phasing, participation and governance. These will call on the project management knowledge areas listed at the beginning of this process description. Examples are Project Time Management for the Project Schedule and Project Cost Control for the Resource Requirements section of the Project Management Plan.

The process of project plan development should raise more issues to be covered by the project. The running list should document these. In the cases of issues that have been resolved in the process, project planners should document the resolution.

		1	2	3	4	5	6	7	8	9	
		Maintain business rules	Assess performance	Manage data	Manage inventory	Manage capital assets	Manage transportation	Manage supply chain configuration	Manage regulatory compliance	Align supply chain & financials	
Performed?	Yes	5	5	6	6	4	6	5	5	4	
	No	1	1		1					1	
	Unsure	1			1			1	1	1	
PLAN		2.0	1.4	1.6	2.6	2.5	3.3	1.4	3.0	1.8	2.2
SOURCE		2.2	2.4	1.5	1.8	2.5	3.5	2.4	2.8	1.5	2.3
MAKE		2.0	2.3	2.6	2.0	2.0	3.0	1.7	2.3	2.0	2.2
DELIVER		2.6	3.0	2.3	2.3	3.5	2.8	2.4	3.2	2.8	2.8
RETURN		2.6	2.4	2.0	1.8	2.0	3.3	1.0	2.3	1.5	2.1
		2.3	2.3	2.0	2.1	2.5	3.2	1.8	2.7	1.9	

FIGURE 15.2 Self-assessment of ENABLE processes.

12.3 SPHERE DEFINITION (1.3)

Table 12.3 summarizes the Sphere Definition process. The rationale for spheres was described in Section 4.4.1. In summary, most organizations operate a "one-size-fits-all" supply chain. Supply chain design takes the form of functions like procurement, manufacturing and distribution working in departmental silos. The design is seldom the result of a conscious decision, but one born of long-time habits.

If the supply chain designer took a "clean sheet" approach, it is doubtful that the present supply chain structure, including processes and organization, would be the result. Except in the smallest organizations, it is unlikely the ideal would be a single supply chain for all the company's product–market combinations. This process, sphere definition, is necessary to either validate the current single supply chain or identify the need for multiple supply chains, each with a separate design including activities, processes, organization, systems and measures.

A "sphere" is a three-dimensional market–product–operations combination. The *market* can be specific customers or, more likely, a customer segment. A segment, for our purposes, is a group of customers with the same preferences and buying behavior. The *product* is a single product category or a group of products consumed by the market. *Operations* include the factories, suppliers, distributors, retail outlets, warehouses and transportation links needed to produce the product or products for the markets.

Sphere design entails making choices about serving customer segments. A company that pursues too many spheres (more than 4–6) is spread too thin. That company should combine the spheres or drop some low profit customer segments, reducing the number of spheres. This is often a difficult choice in a company driven by sales growth. A sphere can also be defined with internal customers. This is an *enable sphere* of activities used by *product-producing spheres* that have external customers. Figure 12.3 shows the relationships between these two types of spheres.

12.3.1 INPUTS FOR SPHERE DEFINITION (1.3.1)

Table 12.3 shows the inputs for sphere definition. These should identify segments served and provide an understanding of their needs. The SCM Scope Plan from Process 1.2 is also important to this process. It provides a mission statement for the project and defines what parts of the supply chain are in scope or out of scope. Also important is an understanding of market position and needs for improvement in supply chain operations. Documents developed for chartering the project (Process 1.1) are useful here. The running list of issues will also help in defining spheres.

12.3.2 PROCESS ELEMENTS FOR SPHERE DEFINITION (1.3.2)

Consulting experience indicates that this process, or its equivalent, is seldom performed. This is a direct result of a Stage I and Stage II SCM maturity. Companies make major investments in facilities, systems, new businesses and equipment, with little attention to their fit in the overall supply chain. Also absent is any thought that the SCM project might change the organization's structure. The consequence is an

TABLE 15.3
Sphere Definition (1.3)

	1.3 Sphere Definition	Executing Process
	1.3.2 Process Elements	**1.3.3 Outputs**
1.3.1 Inputs		***Enabling Process Definition***
Customers and Products Briefing	Process definition	Enabling processes needed
Strategy	Define spheres, market-product-operations combinations, which warrant separate supply chain designs. Determine the enabling processes needed to support product-producing spheres.	***Supply Chain Sphere Definition***
Environmental Briefing		Sphere definition
Issues		Nomination of sphere design teams for activity system development
SCM Plan (1.2)		Updated issues by enabling and product-producing sphere
	Approaches and techniques	
	Market segmentation. Functional (sales, marketing, manufacturing, procurement, distribution) expertise. Group meetings.	
	PM shortcomings addressed	
	The use of spheres targets rigidity, organization conflicts, inadequate technical capability and misunderstood technology.	
	Spheres break down an overall supply chain project into "subprojects" where different designs suited to the sphere's business needs are implemented. A singular methodology (Level 3) supports multiple efforts.	
	SCM maturity	
	Using spheres as a basis for strategy moves the organization to Stage IV for Task 1 in the supply chain maturity model.	

Terminology	– Branding – Channel – Customer-centric supply chain – Enable sphere – Focused factory – Innovative product – Kano Model – Partnering – Product-centric supply chain – Project life cycle – Segmentation – Supply chain	– Business Model – Collaboration – Early manufacturing/ supplier involvement – Extended product – Functional product – Integration – Manufacturing strategy – Postponement – Product-producing sphere – Representative product – Sphere
Stakeholders	The supply chain design team should be responsible. The company steering committee should approve the choices. Users of supply chain processes and key operating managers can support the definition. Support functions like IT, finance, and facilities should also provide guidance.	
SCOR support	SCOR threads, metrics and process element descriptions support sphere development.	

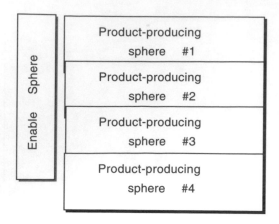

FIGURE 15.3 Relationship between product-producing and enable spheres.

effort that fails for lack of support from people. So this process is vital in creating a new way of thinking about the business that will lead to better decisions and avoid project disappointment, if not catastrophe.

12.3.2.1 Process Definition for Sphere Definition

The process takes what is probably a single supply chain and divides it into customer-centric, product-centric, or enable spheres. These spheres are distinct enough to warrant customized activity systems developed in the next process. A likely outcome is definition of two to seven product-delivery spheres and a single enable sphere. The enable sphere contains activities that are shared among the product-delivery spheres. Table 12.4 provides examples of spheres. Note that operations aren't limited to those inside the organization. Upstream and downstream partners' operations can also be included in the definitions.

12.3.2.2 Approaches and Techniques for Sphere Definition

Developing spheres is an art. A team process, in Appendix B2 identified as a supply chain design team, is often best when team members have an understanding of the markets, products and operations within the project's scope. Asking a series of questions about the company's business is a logical approach. In addition to knowledge of the business, access to data on operations and profitability will be helpful.

The following is an example of questions that might be asked in the process of defining spheres.

Markets:
1. Does your company serve different market segments? If "yes," list the segments. (If "no," then the supply chain design will not depend on segmentation. Skip to question #4.)
2. Do the segments make different demands on supply chain design? (If "yes," then your segments require different supply chain designs.)

TABLE 15.4
Sphere Definition Examples

Company	Markets	Products	Operations
Car company	Affluent customers	SUV's, luxury sedans	Flexible plants for SUV's and large cars, high end dealers
Contract machine shop	Customers desiring one day lead times.	High volume products	Short cycle manufacturing cell, finished goods, WIP buffer inventory, customer service center
Personal computer products firm	Customers desiring the latest technology	Stage 2 life cycle products (new microprocessor, premium price, latest features)	Flexible manufacturing cells designed to be responsive to changes in demand, lots of inventory in the distribution network, and supplier contracts calling for fast response
	Customers wanting a "capable" machine at a discounted price	Stage 3 life cycle products (older technology, heavily discounted price, value-seeking customers)	Functional manufacturing cells focused on efficiency, low cost distribution network, supplier contracts emphasizing cost
Capital equipment aftermarket parts distributor	All markets and customers	All products supported	Selection and business arrangement negotiation with suppliers for high value commodity groups, supplier certification and supplier performance measurement

3. Do segments differ in profitability? (If some aren't profitable or produce very little profit, they might be dropped entirely. The needs of the most profitable segments should be a priority in supply chain design.)

4. In general, a segment has to pass two tests: have different needs (#2) and be profitable (#3) to justify a supply chain design. An exception would be the case of a project mission to turn an unprofitable product into a profitable one.

Products:

4. Do products or product lines differ in terms of profitability? If so, why is one product more profitable? Note that question 3 assesses market, not product profitability. Group products by profitability. Profitability is measured by either gross margin per unit sold or by total gross margin.

5. Do products or product lines require different production capabilities? If so, group the products by the production capabilities they require.

The questions yield four categories of products based on high or low profit and unique or common processes. A product or product group must be either more profitable or have different production requirements to be considered for a distinct sphere.

Operations:
6. Do different operations (including key suppliers and distribution channels as well as your own operations) specialize in producing specific products? (If so, group the operations by the products they produce.)
7. What is the capacity and current utilization of each of the operations? (Allocate the utilized capacity to the product groups.)

To consider dedicating an operation (e.g., facility, work cell, distribution channel or supplier capability) to a sphere, operations must be specialized; capacity considerations must make it attractive and market segment or product requirements must make it necessary.

Sphere definition for product-producing spheres will likely reflect one of three themes. The resulting spheres will be functional, product-centric or customer-centric, depending on the answers to questions like those posed above. An enable sphere should capture activities like ENABLE process elements in SCOR. These are listed in Section 8.2.3.

12.3.2.3 Project Management Shortcomings Addressed by Sphere Definition

Sphere definition adds flexibility to the project. Supply chain solutions are to be tailored to segments with different needs. This should reduce the risk of being whipsawed by changing requirements during the project because a sphere acts as a firewall. Problems in one sphere need not affect progress in another. All the company's chips aren't riding on one solution. A program for enabling elements also assures that the backbone structure is available to serve product-producing spheres.

Organization design is a byproduct of sphere definition. The sphere approach to organization substitutes the sphere's goals for those of functional departments. One of the lessons of failed projects, described in Section 9.3, is that organization-goal misalignment is a major pitfall.

Technology solutions can also match a particular sphere's requirements. The whole supply chain project need not be held hostage to a technology needed only in one sphere. One basis for sphere identification can even center on a technology capability. Thus, one sphere might encompass Internet channels where fulfillment is essentially on line. Another sphere might employ traditional channels.

Breaking the supply chain into spheres does increase project complexity. In a way, if there are three spheres, there may be triple the amount of project management activity and other work required. However, although spheres help assure that the right things are being done, there will be more project activity to manage doing them right. At this stage, project managers may want to set up subprojects to control implementation in individual spheres.

12.3.2.4 SCM Maturity for Sphere Definition

Differentiating one's supply chain to achieve competitive advantage is characteristic of Stages IV and V of SCM maturity for Task 1, Building Strategic Supply Chains. The spheres are also the foundation for the execution of the other tasks. Namely, Organization Alignment Through Internal Collaborative Relationships (Task 2) is based on the demands of specific spheres. Collaboration with Partners (Task 3) follows as well; suppliers and customers may be engaged for overall improvement. The activity systems designed for each sphere will define processes that need to be done well, efficiently and effectively making proper use of technology (Tasks 4 and 5).

12.3.2.5 Terminology for Sphere Definition

Terms shown in Table 12.3 refer to different ways to create spheres. For example, separate spheres might be created for innovative and functional products (Section 4.2.1). This is consistent with the idea that innovative products require responsive supply chains while functional products require cost effective ones. Another basis for spheres is making splits based on the life cycle of products. New products might have one sphere, growth another and mature products another still. Material sources and internal operations are also possible foundations for spheres.

12.2.2.6 Stakeholders for Sphere Definition

Since spheres are likely to be the basis for reorganizing the reporting structure, all managers have an interest in the outcome of the sphere-definition process. A common result is the broadening of responsibilities for some and narrowing of responsibilities for others. The company steering committee, which is ultimately responsible, will have to reassign people and perhaps their own members based on sphere decisions.

The supply chain design team is also an important stakeholder and would probably develop the sphere design for approval by the company steering committee. Creation of spheres raises project management complexity and may force the company steering committee to make choices for moving ahead, focusing on high-priority efforts and delaying those that are low priority.

Support functions that provide enabling services will also see their roles change. This is due to different demands from managers in product-producing spheres resulting from different needs. In essence, support activities that catered to functional departments will now provide services to managers in spheres that look at the world differently and have different needs.

12.2.2.7 SCOR Support for Sphere Definition

The SCOR model threads tool can be used to flowchart processes in a sphere. Also, a test of sphere design is the suitability of different SCOR metrics for each of the spheres. For example, metrics for a sphere delivering innovative products will stress external measures of service; those for functional products will stress internal measures like cost. The design team should develop measures of performance for each sphere as they are developed and SCOR provides a good source. Table 8.2 lists the SCOR metrics.

12.3.3 OUTPUTS FROM SPHERE DEFINITION (1.3.3)

Outputs consist of sphere definitions for both enabling and product-producing spheres. Table 12.4 provides examples of the format. The top four spheres are for product-producing spheres. The last is an enabling sphere. In this case, the enabling sphere is a central sourcing function that identifies and negotiates agreements with top tier suppliers. The activity focuses on top commodities where such arrangements have the greatest impact on the company's material expenditures.

Another deliverable of the process should be an update of the issues list. The update should show the resolution of issues as they occur and the addition of others that have emerged from sphere definition.

12.4 ACTIVITY SYSTEM DESIGN (1.4)

Section 4.2.3.2 provided background on activity systems and how a design team develops them. Summarizing that section, activity systems are "networks" of operating processes, including those we associate with the supply chain. Competitiveness comes when multiple activities and their supporting processes support each other. For example, in Figure 4.5, an Expert Scheduling application supports a Build-to-Order activity. While a competitor might attempt to replicate individual activities, the linked combination of activities, because it is much more difficult to copy, is greater than the sum of the parts.

Activity systems for each sphere (identified in Process 1.3 above) will enhance the job of project planning for implementation. Enhancement comes because, through spheres, the total SCM effort splinters into smaller pieces that are more easily prioritized for funding. The organization is less likely to be pulled into a major, "world peace"-type project, one of the root causes for project failure described in Chapter 9. Activity System Design may also produce changes in SCM project scope.

The activity system tool is particularly amenable to group design. The concepts behind the tool are easy to understand and "experts" in a sphere can translate needs into requirements for activities in that sphere. We also use the term "design team" to designate a team specifically chartered with design of an activity system in a sphere. In Appendix B2, this is referred to as the "sphere design team." These teams are distinguished from the supply chain design team. Sphere design teams will require special expertise related to the sphere.

12.4.1 INPUTS FOR ACTIVITY SYSTEM DESIGN (1.4.1)

The principal input for Activity System Design is the sphere definition from Process 1.3. There will be two types of spheres: product-producing and enabling. Product-producing spheres have external customers. Enabling processes have internal customers, the product-producing spheres. Enabling processes provide supply chain infrastructure for ENABLE.

12.4.2 PROCESS ELEMENTS FOR ACTIVITY SYSTEM DESIGN (1.4.2)

Activity systems developed in this process constitute a vision for future operations. There should be a design team for each sphere. The teams should ignore any perceived constraints like political acceptability, the cost that might be quite high and the need for special skills. A good model is the "greenfield" vision unconstrained by existing operations. Also, activity systems — in the supply chain spirit — should not be confined to one's own company. Encompassing the supply chain, not just the business unit or single department, should release creative juices. Consultation with partners is appropriate as well.

12.4.2.1 Process Definition for Activity System Design

Activity System Design should cover all the spheres produced in Process 1.3. A project team may be tempted to pick only one or two of these spheres for initial design, believing that the company can't handle all the spheres at once. This should be discouraged. Designing the requirements for all the spheres provides a complete vision of what needs to be done. With all the requirements assembled, priorities can then be set for subprojects or activities to move ahead; scope changes may be required, as indicated in Figure 12.1. After that, the company steering committee could decide to implement in selected spheres.

12.4.2.2 Approaches and Techniques for Activity System Design

The process for developing activity systems, first listed in Section 4.3.2.3, is straightforward. The following are the steps:

- Pick attractive market segments for your products. This is done in 1.3 Sphere Definition.
- Make choices on how to compete for attractive segments. For Enable spheres, consider the customer to be the product-producing spheres.
- Develop themes to support each choice. The themes are foundations for the activity system.
- Design activities to support each theme. Activities define the supply chain processes, which should also be listed. These will be the basis for process development or improvement.
- Link the activities into the activity system. The links provide a difficult-to-duplicate barrier to competitors.

Supporting tools for the process include an understanding of customer requirements. The Quality Function Deployment (QFD) tool can capture and display
this information. Benchmarking one's own processes against best-practice companies or competitors is also helpful. Section 4.2.3.1 described how SCOR
metrics also support this approach by showing gaps in company performance
that need to be filled.

12.4.2.3 Project Management Shortcomings Addressed by Activity System Design

An important byproduct of defining spheres and developing activity systems is
identification of gaps and the efforts required to fill those gaps. This enables priority
setting for implementing those projects where resources are limited. Table 12.6 is a
simple example of how project selection is facilitated where it is impossible to do
all the things required by the activity system design. The table shows four projects,
one for each of three product-producing spheres and one enabling project that applies
to all three.

If the organization can do only two of the four projects in the near term, the
two most viable alternatives appear to be the following:

1. Project #1 and Project #4
2. Project #1 and Project #2

Selection of option #1 over option #2 would depend on the benefits expected
for Project #4 in all three spheres compared with the benefits from #2 in one sphere.
Also to be considered is the cost of the projects, the timing of benefits and the
availability of resources. However, without spheres and the ability to define focused
projects, the company might over-commit to too many projects.

The ability to make choices addresses the flexibility shortcoming described in
Section 9.2. The recommended solution calls for project managers and steering
committees to be "fast on their feet" by funding incremental improvements with
measurable benefits.

12.4.2.4 SCM Maturity for Activity System Design

A focused project portfolio will move the organization to higher levels of SCM
maturity. By definition, efforts to fill gaps in activity system processes should move
process improvement out of the functional level (Stage II) into, at a minimum, the
business unit level (Stage III).

12.4.2.5 Terminology for Activity System Design

Terms listed in Table 12.5 are likely to arise in Activity System Design.

TABLE 15.5
Activity System Design (1.4)

1.4 Activity System Design	Executing Process
1.4.1 Inputs	
	1.4.3 Outputs
Supply Chain Sphere Definition (1.3)	*Activity System Designs*
Enabling Process Definition (1.3)	Activity diagram
Environmental Briefing	As-is understanding
Issues	Conceptual designs
	• Processes
	• Organization
1.4.2 Process Elements	Strategic themes/choices
Process definition	Develop a vision for operations to be conducted in each sphere. This involves choices on ways to compete and identifying relationships between activities.	Operational gaps
		Processes related to activities
		Subproject definition and priority
Approaches and techniques	Use of customer requirements in design. Activity systems. Benchmarking.	Sphere measures
		Collaboration points
PM shortcomings addressed	Activity systems enable closer control of project scope (Level 2 in the PMMM) through the ability to set implementation priorities in spheres. They also enable short-cycle project implementation tasks that can be sequenced to produce fast results.	SCM Change Requests
SCM maturity	Activity systems that produce cross-functional projects and closer bonds with partners lead to higher levels of SCM maturity.	

TABLE 12.6 (Continued)
Activity System Design (1.4)

	1.4 Activity System Design		Executing
Terminology	– Benchmarking	– Category management	
– Activity System	– Channel	– Channel Master	
– Cellular manufacturing	– Customer	– Demand-driven supply chain	
– Collaborative Execution Systems	– End-user	– Flexibility	
– Echelon	– Greenfield vision	– Order penetration point	
– Functional organization	– Performance-based pricing	– Price-taker	
– Partnership classification	– Quality Function Deployment	– Reengineering	
– Product tree	– Strategic sourcing	– Supply chain strategy	
– Reverse logistics			
– Virtual value chain			
Stakeholders	Design teams for each sphere should develop activity systems. Support functions needed to implement the activity systems should be represented on the design teams.		
SCOR support	SCOR process element descriptions provide "best practices" and metrics for reference.		

TABLE 15.6
Example Project Portfolio

Projects	High Priority Sphere	Medium Priority Sphere	Low Priority Sphere
#1	X		
#2		X	
#3			X
#4 (Enabling)	X	X	X

12.4.2.6 Stakeholders for Activity System Design

The supply chain design team that defined the spheres should add to its ranks in developing the activity systems. The purpose is to gather the expertise needed in what goes on in a sphere. In Appendix B2, we refer to these as sphere design teams.

If resources are limited, the company steering committee may have to choose which projects it wants to pursue. Its job is more complex since the total supply chain effort has more components. Moving ahead isn't a "one-shot" chunk of work. Top management must stay involved since the total supply chain effort is more "granular," with many options available for picking and choosing projects.

Since the activity system defines how the organization intends to operate, the work of most employees in those processes will change, often significantly.

12.4.2.7 SCOR Support for Activity System Design

SCOR threads and process element descriptions are useful in translating activities into processes.

12.4.3 Outputs from Activity System Design (1.4.3)

The principal outputs are activity systems designs. These should contain the items listed in Table 12.5.

1. Strategic themes and choices. The foundations for the activity system design and why they were selected.
2. As-is understanding. How and how well current processes affect sphere operations.
3. Activity diagrams. Activities supporting the themes and their interrelationships. Figure 4.5 is an example. A list of existing or needed processes that support performance of an activity.
4. "Greenfield" conceptual (high-level) designs for processes and organization. What's expected of the processes and their inputs and outputs. Conceptual (high-level) organization design to manage processes.
5. Sphere measures. Measures of performance that should improve by implementing the projects.

6. Operational gaps. Differences between where we are and where we want to be. A recommended format lists processes that are in place and operating satisfactorily, processes that are in place that aren't operating satisfactorily and processes that need to be added.
7. Project definition and priority. Initiatives in the form of separate projects or subprojects needed to close the gaps.

These outputs are the basis for all the subsequent SCM tasks. Figure 12.1 reflects this by showing the flow of outputs to process improvement planning, organization planning and communications planning. Communications planning addresses the information needs of partners who are required to support the strategy.

In addition, Activity System Design is likely to produce scope changes for the overall supply chain project. This output will return Process 1.7 Integrated Change Control.

12.5 ORGANIZATION ALIGNMENT (1.5)

Organization Alignment, summarized in Table 12.7, requires decisions to implement the conceptual organization design from Activity System Design (Process 1.4). Organization Alignment's purpose is to weigh alternatives, evaluate the current organization's capability and produce a deliverable, Organization Design. This is a plan to be implemented as part of *Task 2, Implementing Collaborative Relationships*.

12.5.1 INPUTS FOR ORGANIZATION ALIGNMENT (1.5.1)

The principal input is Activity System Design, which contains high-level conceptual designs of sphere processes and organizations. These cover both product-producing and enable spheres. The activity system will be accompanied by as much information as the sphere design teams are capable of producing. Items listed in Table 12.5 include processes, organization, metrics, gaps between the need and the current reality and a tentative definition of subprojects needed to develop the capability.

This process is not part of Activity System Design because it requires decisions from the senior management steering committee. These decisions address people-sensitive issues and require many trade-offs.

12.5.2 PROCESS ELEMENTS FOR ORGANIZATION ALIGNMENT (1.5.2)

The Organization Design process is crucial to the success of the project. Should the organization structure be lacking or the people in it not committed, successfully implementing new processes is not possible. To address this reality, in Process 2.1 Organization Planning we recommend implementing organization changes before proceeding with process changes. This sequencing gives managers who must run the new processes a role in their design and implementation. This process sets the stage.

TABLE 15.7
Organization Alignment (1.5)

1.5 Organization Alignment

1.5.1 Inputs		1.5.2 Process Elements	1.5.3 Outputs
			Executing Process
Organization Design			
Activity System Design (including organization conceptual design) (1.4) Issues	Process definition	Define the organization structure to support sphere activity systems. This includes both supply chain and supply chain enabling process execution. Confirm the metrics to measure performance in each sphere.	**Organization Design** Activity responsibilities — planning, execution, and enable processes from SCOR Metrics Skills needed Structure
	Approaches and techniques	Organization design. Use of functional, product-centric, or customer-centric structure. Measurement approaches such as the Balanced Scorecard. Benchmarking	
	PM shortcomings addressed	Assigning implementation tasks to those who will run the processes leads to at least PMMM Level 1 in which the organization is aware of the need for project management. A new organization structure should remove organization roadblocks. Also, focused efforts to develop enabling processes should address shortcomings in technical capability and misunderstanding technology.	
	SCM maturity	This process will enable the organization to move to Stage III (cross-functional projects) and beyond to Stages IV or V.	

TABLE 2.7
Organization Alignment (1.5) (Continued)

1.5.1 Inputs		1.5 Organization Alignment	Executing Process
		1.5.2 Process Elements	**1.5.3 Outputs**
Terminology		Balanced ScorecardCustomer-centric organization Enable processFunctional organization Focused factoryProduct-centric organization SCO, supply chain orientation	
Stakeholders		This is a senior management process, executed by the supply chain design team under direction from the company steering committee. Most employees will be affected if the strategy changes roles and reporting relationships.	
SCOR support		SCOR provides a comprehensive list of measures for processes that can be applied to organization units. SCOR process elements can also serve as a checklist for responsibility assignment.	

12.5.2.1   Process Definition for Organization Alignment

The process produces a long-term organization structure designed around the activity systems and their related processes. Each of those activity systems will contain one or more processes that need people to make it work. These people will man product-producing sphere activities and processes. They may staff enable sphere processes serving the product-producing spheres. The company may also decide to outsource the staff capabilities. Confirmation of metrics, done in this process, will define organization roles more clearly.

Since organization design in this process is a long-term "end-state" structure, it is unlikely to be implemented all at once. Deciding just how implementation is phased in is done in 2.1 Organization Planning.

12.5.2.2   Approaches and Techniques for Organization Alignment

The Sphere Definition process (1.3) produces conceptual designs for both future processes in the form of activity descriptions and organizations to support those processes. There will be different organizations and employee functions in each product-producing and enable sphere depending on the needs of the processes. The design, at this stage, is a "clean sheet," or greenfield vision, including both structure and performance measures.

Perhaps the most difficult aspect is deciding whether processes will be in the product-producing sphere, an enable support organization, or outsourced. Those functions in enable organizations will serve all product-producing spheres, as shown in Figure 12.3.

The decision where to place a responsibility is driven by an assessment of how unique a requirement is to a product-producing sphere. Uniqueness argues for assigning the function to the product-producing sphere. Commonality argues for a support enable function. Supply chain capabilities available from third parties are candidates for outsourcing.

An example illustrates. An organization providing aftermarket support for capital equipment chose the following as enable functions. These supported the product-producing spheres serving different channels for aftermarket parts.

Enable Function	Reason
Continuous improvement/six sigma	A consistent process for the group was desired.
Customer interfacing systems	A common interface solution for part ordering was seen as efficient regardless of the channel.
Human resources	The parent corporation required standard practices.
Organization planning	This resided with the business unit executive.
Product configuration	All product spheres relied on similar configuration data. Product-producing spheres set priorities for documentation.
Replenishment order processing	A common system covered ordering of replacement parts from suppliers.
Return part refurbishment	Used parts for recycling from any sphere were handled by a common supply chain.

Sourcing/key supplier interface	All product spheres used common sources of supply.
Supplier quality	Material for all product-producing spheres came into the same facility where it was inspected and supplier performance (quality, delivery) was recorded.
Warehousing for incoming material	Central warehousing was more economical. The product-producing spheres did not have the volume to justify separate facilities. This was also considered an outsourcing candidate.

The same organization chose to assign the following functions to the product-producing spheres' delivery functions.

Product Delivery Function	Reason
Common parts requisitioning	The functions were in direct touch with customers. Equipment needs and country languages varied from customer to customer.
Custom parts purchasing	Items, unique to a sphere, were sourced and procured in the sphere.
Customer logistics	Part replenishment triggers and delivery service expectations varied among spheres.
Customer service warehousing	Each customer contract had tailored requirements for staging parts for consumption.
Project management	Specialists were required to serve customer technical needs and maintenance needs.
Sales, customer requirements definition, bidding	Each service product provided by the organization required different customer logistics.
Warehousing for outgoing material	Each large contract had unique requirements with regard to location, parts carried and service level requirements.

The two lists illustrate the thinking that must go into organization design. The most important point is to start with processes and activities and then build the organization chart. With basic decisions on where a function is to be performed, measures developed in Sphere Definition (1.3) should be confirmed.

12.5.2.3   Project Management Shortcomings Addressed by Organization Alignment

Translating strategy into organization responsibilities will energize those who will play important roles in new supply chains. This "wake-up call" should be an incentive to turn to formal project management techniques if not yet used. This is a criterion for PMMM Level 1.

This process addresses several of the project shortcomings described in Chapter 9. Aligning the organization with supply chain designs is fundamental to removing misaligned departmental goals. The need for enabling technologies like information systems are likely to be better understood by defining what the enabling processes must accomplish. This could result in going outside for skills or altering plans or priorities to fit the skills available.

Finally, because top management must be involved in organization alignment decisions, members of the steering committee will likely have personal stakes in supply chain project outcomes.

12.5.2.4 SCM Maturity for Organization Alignment

Alignment of the organization, particularly into product-producing spheres, enables cross-functional efforts. It also creates a climate for exploring outside partnerships to implement strategy. This is characteristic of at least Stage III SCM maturity, establishing a basis for partnerships and multicompany process improvement initiatives.

12.5.2.5 Terminology for Organization Alignment

Terms for this process characterize different ways of thinking about and structuring an organization.

12.5.2.6 Stakeholders for Organization Alignment

The steering committee and the human resources function will actively perform this process, assisted by the supply chain design team. Most employees will be affected by an aggressive reorganization. At this stage, the most important stakeholders are those who will lead the "businesses within the business" or the spheres. They will have to assemble teams from inside and outside the organization to staff their functions.

12.5.2.7 SCOR Support for Organization Alignment

SCOR performance measures at the process element level (level 3) offer candidates for aligned organization metrics. The same process elements may be useful in assembling a list of processes for both enable and product-producing activities.

12.5.3 OUTPUTS FROM ORGANIZATION ALIGNMENT (1.5.3)

The principal output, Organization Design, advances the conceptual design developed in Activity System Design (1.4). The product should be sufficient to draw an organization chart and table mapping activities to these organization entities. Metrics will confirm objectives for the organization functions.

This product will be handed off to the Organization Planning (2.1) process to begin the transition in organization structure.

12.6 COLLABORATION STRATEGY (1.6)

Table 12.8 summarizes this process. A plan for implementing collaboration relies on Activity System Design (1.4). The strategy also calls for identifying a role for a multicompany, or stage 3, steering committees. Multicompany steering committees are separate from the company steering committee that oversees the supply chain project inside the company. These steering committees are formed with senior management at one or more of our partners to facilitate joint collaborative decision-making.

12.6.1 INPUTS FOR COLLABORATION STRATEGY (1.6.1)

Sphere definition and activity system designs are the principal input to this process. There are likely to be several of collaboration strategies, one for each sphere. Candidates for internal and external collaboration will be identified by the design.

12.6.2 PROCESS ELEMENTS FOR COLLABORATION STRATEGY (1.6.2)

This process engages top management in the process of partnership development. To the extent the organization will rely on partnerships for successful implementation of its strategy, it will need the output of this process to guide its efforts. The supply chain design team will consult with sphere design teams in the preparation of the strategy.

12.6.2.1 Process Definition for Collaboration Strategy

Like Organization Design (1.5) this process defines the "rules for engagement" during the supply chain project. Elements include both necessary internal collaboration and collaboration with partners. Internal collaboration covers department-to-department efforts as well as collaboration with other business units in the same corporation. Upstream partnerships are with suppliers; downstream partnerships are with distribution partners, customers and end-users.

The basics of the collaboration strategy include the following:

What. Where is internal and external collaboration authorized, based on needs from the activity system designs?

Who. Which partners or partner groups — internal or external — require a collaborative effort? Is a multicompany steering committee needed? If so, how many — one for each partner or only one with several partners?

When. What are the priorities for collaboration and expectations for completing arrangements? Should there be both short- and long-term plans for collaboration efforts?

Where. Which internal organizations are responsible for executing the collaborations?

How. What is the shape of the collaborative effort in each case where collaboration is needed? This includes technology requirements, collaborations, business arrangements and products and services covered.

12.6.2.2 Approaches and Techniques for Collaboration Strategy

Two approaches have been described that address the "how" on the list above. Section 4.3 describes a partnership classification methodology. This "vocabulary" characterizes a partnership in terms of its purpose, direction and choice. **Purpose** asks whether the partnership creates new "space" in the supply chain. If the answer is "yes," roles along the supply chain will change. Bypassing a level of distribution is an example.

Direction is either horizontal or vertical, or both. Vertical is a partnership in the direction of product flow — upstream or downstream. For a typical manufacturer, these partnerships are usually with suppliers, distributors, or customers. A horizontal partnership is with like functions. A consolidating industry "rollup" of organizations with like products and services is an example.

Choice reflects relative power in the partnership. A "one-to-many" choice reflects a strong partner, the "one," making a relationship where "many" choices were available. Figure 4.12 illustrates the concept.

The form of interaction in the partnership can utilize recent Supply-Chain Council efforts to characterize four types of "collaboratory." These range from simple exchanges of information to joint decision-making, as shown in Figure 8.4 and described in Section 8.4.

12.6.2.3 Project Management Shortcomings Addressed by Collaboration Strategy

Definition of collaboration measures is a vehicle for organization communication. Complex collaboration efforts, pulling in multiple departments and partners, will build the case for formal project management. A strategy for a multicompany steering committee captures the need for formal oversight beyond company boundaries.

The process addresses all five of the project management shortcomings described in Chapter 9. Top management, represented by the company steering committee, must ratify the strategy, so it has their stamp of approval. Early development of the strategy should help remove organization roadblocks. A well developed strategy includes consideration of alternatives, identification of appropriate technology and time phasing for implementing links. Communication with partners provides an early start in making sure the technology used matches process needs and partner technical capabilities.

12.6.2.4 SCM Maturity for Collaboration Strategy

The collaboration strategy bridges the space between the strategy, a Task 1 product and Tasks 2 and 3 covering internal collaboration and external partnerships. For Task 2, this corresponds to Stage III maturity. For Task 3, the strategy is likely to contain a range of collaborative links best described as either Stage II, III, IV, or V depending on the individual link.

12.6.2.5 Terminology for Collaboration Strategy

Terms are those that might arise in developing and communicating the strategy internally and externally.

12.6.2.6 Stakeholders for Collaboration Strategy

The company steering committee will ratify the collaboration strategy. It need not develop it, however. This can be the role of the supply chain design team, assisted by the sphere design teams that developed the activity systems.

12.6.2.7 SCOR Support for Collaboration Strategy

SCOR, through Version 5.0, did not explicitly address collaboration. Many process elements, however, have collaboration components. Updating, along the lines described in Section 8.4, is planned. The working documents generated by the collaboration effort are useful references for this process and are available through the Supply-Chain Council's website.

12.6.3 OUTPUTS FROM COLLABORATION STRATEGY (1.6.3)

The strategy should communicate as much of the organization's collaboration intent as possible. Characterization of the supply and customer bases will frame types of collaboration recommended both upstream and downstream. New roles may be planned for one's own company with or without the support of partners. Organization of the strategy report should be by activity system. If two or more activity systems have similar collaboration needs, the strategy should integrate these.

Linkages should recognize the information requirements of processes served by the collaborative arrangement. Much money is spent on collaboration technology tools. Some, if not most, as described in Chapter 9, is wasted. The strategy should address risk reduction in the development of these technology links. The best approach is to define closely the technology needs for these links.

12.6.3.1 Characterization of the Supply and Customer Base

This portion of the collaboration strategy defines the "as-is" of the upstream and downstream components of the supply chain. The characterization should include summary information like the following:

- Flowcharts of the supply chain within the sphere
- Numbers of suppliers/customers; amount of business done with each
- Type of current partnership using the framework described in Section 4.4.2
- Profitability of products and downstream markets
- Supplier ratings
- Constraints and issues

12.6.3.2 Information Requirements

This component should describe requirements up or down the supply chain. The format should describe the data, not the applications for delivering it. Examples of data requirements include the following:

- Actual sales to end-users
- Forecasts
- Product technical information
- Customer complaints/suggestions for improvement
- Financial information including cost and investment data
- Suggestions for improvement (those received to date/possibilities)
- Test data and other quality information
- Performance targets (cost, quality, delivery, flexibility)
- New or modified business rules

12.6.3.3   New Upstream and Downstream Roles

Activity system designs should produce ideas for new "space" in the supply chain. New space means new roles in the chain. The new roles may be assumed by one's own company, by an upstream or downstream partner or a combination.

12.6.3.4   Technology

Technology refers to both product and process and includes information technology. Process technology could point to the need for investment by one's own company or a partner. Process technology can include manual or automated linkages. To the extent there are alternatives, like a more sophisticated technology vs. a simpler way, these alternatives should be identified.

12.7   INTEGRATED CHANGE CONTROL (1.7)

Table 12.9 describes this process. It corresponds with PMBOK's Integrated change control process. PMBOK, in its integration knowledge area, pulls together all reporting and change management processes from other knowledge areas. These include scope, schedule, cost, quality, risk change and contract administration. This process takes change requests of any of these types from many sources and translates them into changes to the SCM and project plans developed in Process 1.2.

Readers wanting to supplement the control elements in this description should refer to the PMBOK and other project management literature.

12.7.1   INPUTS FOR INTEGRATED CHANGE CONTROL (1.7.1)

Many circumstances in a supply chain project will generate a change request. For example, progress tracking and review meetings can show when the project is falling behind or moving ahead in terms of planned schedule or cost. Such a situation can generate a change in scope or schedule or both. A change in the environment, or external situation, can also generate a need for change.

Another source of change can be actual supply chain operating performance, a factor outside the execution of the project. An example is a quality problem at a supplier or a competitor's announcement of a new product or service. The situation may indicate a need to do something different, bolster an area of attention or change deliverables in the work breakdown structure.

Partners can also produce suggestions for scope changes. These can be explicit or implicit. Explicit changes take the form of written or spoken requests. Implicit changes lie in the ability of a partner to support a supply chain design. For example, if our own company seeks an elaborate technology solution but the partner can't support that technology, then a change is called for. The change can take the form of switching partners — if possible — or switching the technology called for in the plan.

12.7.2 Process Elements for Integrated Change Control (1.7.2)

This process sits at a major "crossroads" in the flow of project control information. It receives inputs from a variety of sources, generated for many reasons. Changes that are generated affect many elements of the project, including scope, schedule, cost and quality of project work.

12.7.2.1 Process Definition for Integrated Change Control

In these templates, changes can occur to either of two documents, the SCM Plan or the Project Management Plan. Both are generated in process 1.2 and rely on many SCM and project management knowledge areas. Change requests can deal with one or more of the project's aspects, including all SCM technical areas and project management concerns like schedule and cost.

12.7.2.2 Approaches and Techniques for Integrated Change Control

Integrated Change Control, as defined in this process, makes use of PMBOK Integrated Change Control tools and techniques. These include a change control system, configuration management, performance measurement and project management information systems. The need for formality will depend on the organization and its project management practices. The broad scope for most SCM projects points to a need for more formal processes, characteristic of Level 3 maturity as defined in the PMMM (Chapter 5).

12.7.2.3 Project Management Shortcomings Addressed by Integrated Change Control

In Chapter 9, lessons learned pointed to rigidity in projects as a root cause for failure. The recommended solution is to be ready to change frequently. A company can't launch a project and then forget it. A well-oiled change control process is needed to make ongoing adjustments. Such a process requires at least Level 2 maturity on the PMMM. Supply chain projects, where many spheres have been identified, also calls for fast ways of processing changes. This is a strong motivation for Level 3 informal processes common to all projects.

12.7.2.4 SCM Maturity for Integrated Change Control

Supply chain partners will have valuable inputs for project changes. This requires enhanced collaboration along the chain, characterized as Stage IV and V for *Task 3, Forging Supply Chain Partnerships*.

12.7.2.5 Terminology for Integrated Change Control

Terms listed in Table 12.8 are related to areas where project changes are likely to occur.

12.7.2.6 Stakeholders for Integrated Change Control

A project manager or the project office should administer this process. The company steering committee should ratify important changes. Project planning should identify authority for making changes. Project participants — internal and external — will generate the change requests.

12.7.2.7 SCOR Support for Integrated Change Control

The SCOR framework for collaboration described in Section 8.4 describes different levels of collaboration. Even if two partners plan to collaborate through a low level of data exchange collaboration, they will likely need to collaborate at higher levels to successfully implement the data exchange. Figure 8.4 is a collaboration roadmap that illustrates these different levels. Guiding such a project through integrated change control is an example of higher-level collaboration.

SCOR addresses supply chain configuration in EP.7 Manage Supply Chain Configuration. SCOR describes components of the configuration in each of its level 1 processes, PLAN, SOURCE, MAKE, DELIVER and RETURN.

12.7.3 Outputs from Integrated Change Control (1.7.3)

The output of the process is changes to the Project Management and SCM Plans developed in Process 1.2. Likely updates to other documents encompass the WBS, supply chain configuration, other project documents and corrective actions. The latter are measures that will prevent a recurrence of a problem to assure that future actions will be in line with project plan. Corrective actions should aid in avoiding future variations from project plans.

12.8 PHASE CLOSURE (1.8)

Project discipline calls for formal closure of a phase of the project or the entire project when all phases are completed or the project shuts down. Table 12.10 summarizes the process involved in closing a phase or the project itself. This process corresponds to Administrative Closure in the PMBOK.

TABLE 15.8
Collaboration Strategy (1.6)

		1.6 Collaboration Strategy	Executing
		1.6.2 Process Elements	**1.6.3 Outputs**
1.6.1 Inputs			*Collaboration Strategy*
Activity System Design (1.4) Issues	Process definition	Develop the goals and objectives for collaborating with upstream and downstream partners. Define "space" to be created, process needs and technology requirements.	Characterization of the supply and customer base
	Approaches and techniques	Partnership classification (Section 4.3) and SCOR collaboration approaches (Section 8.4).	Information requirements New upstream and downstream roles
	PM shortcomings addressed	The strategy defines expectations for partner technical capability. It also develops "how's" for consideration in making supply chain links, reducing the risk of ineffective links.	Technology requirements Multicompany steering committee plan.
	SCM maturity	The strategy will identify Stage III, IV, and V efforts involving partners. It communicates the need for outside-the-organization projects.	

TABLE 12.8 (Continued)
Collaboration Strategy (1.6)

	1.6 Collaboration Strategy		Executing
Terminology	Collaboration	Collaboration execution systems	
	Core competence	Customer	
	Demand chain	Downstream	
	Early manufacturing and supplier involvement	Echelon	
	Extended product	Independent, dependent demand	
	Integrated supply	Lean enterprise	
	Partnering	Partnership classification	
	Price-taker	Product-centric supply chain	
	Stage 3 supply chain organization	Strategic sourcing	
	Supplier clustering	Synchronized supply chain	
	Target costing	Upstream	
	Virtual enterprise		
Stakeholders	This is a senior management process, executed by the supply chain design team under direction from the company steering committee. Major players in the supply chain will be affected. Those not chosen for partnerships will likely not receive long term commitments.		
SCOR support	SCOR best practices embedded in process elements provide ideas for the strategy. SCOR-related white papers covering collaboration define forms of collaboration further.		

TABLE 15.9
Integrated Change Control (1.7)

	1.7 Integrated Change Control	Controlling Process

1.7.1 Inputs

Change requests (1.4, 2.5 3.5, 3.7)   Process definition
Environmental Updates
Implementation Progress
Partner Inputs
Performance reports
Project Management Plan (1.2)
Review Meetings   Approaches and techniques
SCM Plan (1.2)
Supply chain performance
measures

PM shortcomings addressed

SCM maturity

1.7.2 Process Elements

The process incorporates both internally and externally generated changes. The changes can be to project products or the project work needed to produce them. SCM projects are expected to be dynamic with "progressive elaboration" causing ongoing changes in scope, phasing and schedules.

Performance reporting using project management reporting techniques will indicate when the project is off plan. Special studies into root cause of variances may also accompany changes.

The process specifically addresses rigidity in project management. Integrated Change Control is necessary at Level 2 of the PMMM.

To the extent partner inputs of project changes are considered, Stages IV and V are achieved.

1.7.3 Outputs

Project Management and SCM Changes
Corrective actions
Project planning document updates
Supply chain configuration changes
WBS changes

Terminology	Cause and effect diagram	Certified supplier
	Charter	Cost baseline
	CPIO	Critical path
	Design Team	Driving force
	Milestone	Optimization
	Process owner	Progressive elaboration
	Project life cycle	Project office
	Schedule baseline	Specification
	Steering Committee	Template
	Work package	

Stakeholders   The project manager or office oversees this process. All participants (internal and external) should be able to contribute to project modifications.

SCOR support   SCOR may offer direction as problems requiring change are encountered in the project. Changes call for more collaboration as measured by collaboration frameworks. SCOR process element EP.7 Manage Supply Chain Configuration calls for documentation of supply chain processes.

**TABLE 15.10
Phase Closure (1.8)**

	1.8 Phase Closure		**Closing Process**
1.6.1 Inputs	**1.6.2 Process Elements**		**1.6.3 Outputs**
Deliverables	Process definition	Each project phase is formally closed. This involves confirmation that deliverables for that phase are complete.	Phase Closure
Project Management Plan (1.2)	Approaches and techniques	Deliverable review.	
	PM shortcomings addressed	Formal reviews of deliverables address top management abrogation. Phases and reviews are also a fundamental building block of a Singular Process, Level 3 of the PMMM.	
	SCM maturity	This process facilitates internal and external communication of progress, needed for Stage I and above.	
	Stakeholders	The project manager or office oversees this process. Any participant, particularly those who are responsible for completing a phase, will be a stakeholder. Top management in the company, the company steering committee, and multicompany steering committees that review progress, should review and confirm phase closures.	

12.8.1 INPUTS FOR PHASE CLOSURE

There is great flexibility in deciding what phases are appropriate for a supply chain project. The Project Management Plan process 1.2 defines project phasing. Chapter 11 recommended the following phasing for initial consideration:

- Supply chain strategy
- Internal alignment
- Short term improvement
- Long term improvement

The milestones for this phasing arrangement are in Table 11.3.

12.8.2 PROCESS ELEMENTS FOR PHASE CLOSURE

The company steering committee should monitor deliverables and progress toward completion of phases. This is one way to communicate and obtain stakeholder agreement that deliverables are complete. The project manager or office should administer the process and assure compliance with the project plan.

12.8.3 OUTPUTS FROM PHASE CLOSURE

Phase closure is the principal output. This includes the last phase when the project is declared at an end. It also includes shutdown of the project in progress for whatever circumstance warrants it. The PMBOK Guide calls for archiving documentation and cataloging lessons learned from the project experience.

13 Implementing Collaborative Relationships

This chapter describes processes to achieve alignment of functions inside the company with the supply chain strategy. Because management must capture employee hearts and minds, implementing collaborative relationships is a high-risk endeavor. The processes in this chapter focus on gaining internal cooperation and staffing improvement efforts. Two cases describe how others have dealt with similar situations successfully and not so successfully. These are A2, Change Management in Complex Supply Chain Configuration Project and A3, Lessons from a Failed Supply Chain Initiative.

The critical factor in project implementation is the people available to do the job — their numbers, their skills and their motivation. Therefore, filling both organization and project roles is the critical factor. As people take up their roles, efforts to make short- and long-term improvements can begin. Figure 13.1 is a flowchart of the required processes.

Harold Kerzner points out that the likelihood of success will depend on the organization's comfort level in working on projects.[1] If people have been accustomed to working autonomously, they will have difficulty with the project environment, particularly broad projects using market-product-operations combinations or spheres, as domains for improvement rather than their traditional departments. Lars Rosqvist, who reviewed Section II, also warns that many employees don't view their organizations as project-delivering organizations. They do not want to be involved because they are most comfortable with running an ongoing stable operation.

13.1 ORGANIZATION PLANNING (2.1)

This process takes the Organization Design, which is a long-term vision produced by the company steering committee, and converts that vision into a short-term "pathway" transition plan. Table 13.1 is a summary of the process.

13.1.1 INPUTS TO ORGANIZATION PLANNING (2.1.1)

The principal input to this process is the *Organization Design*, a product of Process 1.5 described in Section 12.5, which shows how activities and processes are to be assigned to organization units. These reflect the needs of spheres, or businesses within the business, that have unique activity systems. The activity systems, prepared

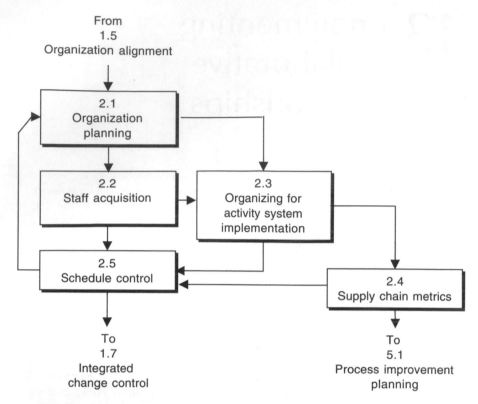

FIGURE 13.1 Implementing collaborative relationships.

by sphere design teams, reflect management decisions on how to compete. Skill requirements are a derivative of the activity structure.

As time passes, updates in the form of *Organization Changes* from process 2.5 should modify the *Organization Implementation Plan,* the output of this process. These changes will reflect actual progress made in finding people and integrating them into the organization.

13.1.2   PROCESS ELEMENTS FOR ORGANIZATION PLANNING (2.1.2)

The process converts a long-term vision for the organization into a time-phased plan. The Organization Design from process 1.5 is the "end game," while the organization plan from this process charts the "pathway" to that vision. This plan reflects constraints and other realities like current capabilities and priorities for implementing the supply chain strategy.

13.1.2.1   Process Definition for Organization Planning

The process is a foundation for moving ahead with strategy implementation. The skills component is particularly critical. A company can take different approaches to implementing a strategic activity. For example, in implementing links with sup-

TABLE 13.1
Organization Planning (2.1)

		2.1 Organization Planning	**Planning Process**
2.1.1 Inputs		**2.1.2 Process Elements**	**2.1.3 Outputs**
Organization Design (1.5)			*Organization Implementation Plan*
Organization Changes (2.5)			Detailed, time-phased organization structure
			Justification for choices
			Required documentation (e.g. titles, position descriptions, compensation, etc.)
			Source of people for identified positions
			Timing of implementation
	Process definition	Use the Organization Design to plan implementation of organization changes. Implementation encompasses the skills, numbers, structure and metrics needed to effect activity systems. The plan reflects staff availability and project priorities.	
	Approaches and techniques	Sequencing organization and process change. Portfolio management.	
	PM shortcomings	The planned organization seeks to minimize conflicts between functions. This process requires top management participation to authorize staff additions and organization changes, so it counters abrogation by senior managers. The process supports organization awareness and management support elements on the PMMM. Changing one's title or position gets attention.	
	SCM maturity	Task 2 maturity, at least at Stage III, is supported. This process responds to the strategy and the organization structure needed to implement it.	
	Terminology	– Activity system – Core competence – Product-centric organization – Customer-centric organization – Customer-centric supply chain – Portfolio – Demand-driven supply chain – Functional organization – Greenfield vision	
	Stakeholders	Internal, including those in supply chain positions or functions whose mission and structure will change. Steering committee will have provided its vision in Organization Design. Supply chain design team can complete this process with assistance from human resource function.	
	SCOR support	SCOR process elements can guide selection of people for roles in the organization by serving as input for position descriptions and organization roles.	

pliers, it could rely on pull signals methods, like kanban, that require little in the way of automation. An alternative would be to pursue information technology to meet the same end. Each of these two alternatives demands different skill sets to implement. A decision on which path to take has broad ramifications.

13.1.2.2 Approaches and Techniques for Organization Planning

The organization planning process must juggle priorities and constraints. Appendix B2 recommends that the assignment be given to the supply chain design team. An example of a constraint is the availability of needed skills. A big hurdle is passed if the skills are already on board and need only be deployed to improvement projects or subprojects. If the skills are not present, they must be acquired. Priorities are related to the urgency for improving operations. Greater urgency, particularly where added skills are needed, also makes skills and numbers a constraint. Consultants or temporary employees are often the best solution.

To justify added expense, the company steering committee should weigh the benefits and costs. A sound approach is to estimate the monthly benefits as measured by increased profits and cost savings. This monthly benefits figure puts a value on timely implementation. For example, if full implementation is worth $1,000,000 monthly, planners can gauge the value of speeding up the process. Too often, only costs are considered when making decisions that lead to added short-term cost.

Ideally, the people who will run a new process should supervise its implementation. Figure 13.2 illustrates the ideal sequence for implementing organization and process changes. The strategy produces conceptual long-term designs for both processes and the organization needed to support those processes. This is item #1 in Figure 13.2. The conceptual organization design follows the process conceptual design — item #2. For implementation (items #3 and #4), the sequence should be reversed. To assure the involvement and commitment of people in the organization, organization implementation precedes process change implementation.

Constraints from limitations on staff additions require portfolio management decisions. This means that the lack of staff will produce changes to the Project

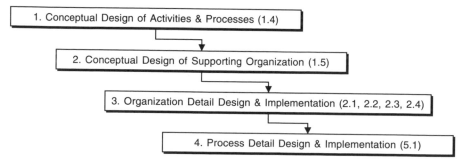

FIGURE 13.2 Sequencing organization and process change.

Management Plan. Figure 13.1 shows the flow of these updates from the Schedule Control process (2.5).

13.1.2.3 Project Management Shortcomings Addressed by Organization Planning

There is nothing like organization restructuring to engage people whose jobs and responsibilities are likely to change. Top management involvement is inevitable if organization changes range over multiple functions, which is likely. Top management, represented by the company steering committee, will necessarily make trade-offs regarding elements of the plan. This requires using available resources for the highest-priority strategy elements. The resulting structures should be more closely aligned with the strategy, addressing project failures due to unaligned objectives.

With respect to the PMMM, organization shifts reinforce the reality of top management support for the program. If the strategy leads to organization shifts, the "corner office" must be serious. This is a planning process so it disciplines downstream processes setting goals and enabling measurement of progress.

13.1.2.4 SCM Maturity for Organization Planning

The organization changes facilitate cross-functional initiatives. This is characteristic of Stage III of SCM maturity for Task 2 Implementing Collaborative Relationships. In the recommended phasing of the supply chain project introduced in Chapter 11 and documented in Table 11.3, internal alignment is shown as a precursor to broader collaboration with partners and multicompany process improvements.

13.1.2.5 Terminology for Organization Planning

The terms listed in Table 13.1 relate to the issues described in this process and are likely to arise in its execution. They include the types of organization and supply chains that might result from the strategy. This process requires "hard-nosed" tradeoffs in terms of implementing parts of the supply chain project and subproject portfolio.

13.1.2.6 Stakeholders for Organization Planning

The project management function, whether it is a single project manager or a project office, should oversee the organization transition. Assistance from the human resource staff should support the effort. The supply chain design team is a good candidate to execute the process. The company steering committee should ratify the plan. Functional departments inside the company and at partner organizations should be consulted. The consultation can include availability of skills, priorities and preferred technical approaches. Comprehensive programs will touch many employees through changes in assignments, shifts in their responsibilities or new methods for doing their work.

13.1.2.7 SCOR Support for Organization Planning

SCOR executing processes are benchmarks for process design. They include both an inventory of these processes and ideas for their execution in the form of "Best Practices." The latter should indicate what skills are needed.

13.1.3 Outputs from Organization Planning (2.1.3)

The Organization Implementation Plan is the principal output. The plan includes a time-phased organization structure, a roadmap for moving from where the organization is to where it needs to be. The plan's format can include 6-month "slices" showing where the organization expects to be at the end of each period. Justification for choices should contain analysis needed to authenticate decisions. Supporting information includes required documentation matching the organization's policies for defining employee positions. It should also identify sources of people that are internal or recruited from outside the company. Timing of implementation summarizes milestones in the implementation for easy reporting of progress.

13.2 STAFF ACQUISITION (2.2)

Acquisition of staff can easily be a critical path activity in project implementation. The plan developed in process 2.1 guides the effort. Table 13.2 summarizes the staff acquisition process.

13.2.1 Inputs to Staff Acquisition (2.2.1)

The Organization Implementation Plan (from 2.1) to change the organization through additions, reductions or transfers should be backed by the resources to implement that plan. Staff Acquisition Resources include internal personnel staff, budgets for recruiting and dedication of employee time to the recruiting process.

13.2.2 Process Elements for Staff Acquisition (2.2.2)

The process includes traditional ways to obtain, retain and manage staff resources. Employee evaluations can help decide whether to transfer an existing employee to a new role or to recruit a new employee. Supply chain project success is limited by the capabilities of people executing the plan. These include people who both implement and run new processes.

Building the organization will engage many stakeholders, as shown in Table 13.2. Knowledge of supply chain technology, including SCOR, can be a positive factor in staff selection.

13.2.3 Outputs from Staff Acquisition (2.2.3)

The Implemented Organization Plan process output takes several forms. Internal transfers, new recruits and temporary resources are all sources of specified skills.

TABLE 13.2
Staff Acquisition (2.2)

2.2.1 Inputs	2.2 Staff Acquisition 2.2.2 Process Elements		Executing Process 2.2.3 Outputs
Organization Implementation Plan (2.1) *Staff Acquisition Resources*	Process definition	This process is central to success at implementing supply chain change. It populates the organization with those who must execute the supply chain strategy.	*Staff Resources* Internal transfers New recruits Temporary resources
	Approaches and techniques PM shortcomings addressed SCM maturity	Employee evaluation. Staff identification and recruiting. Excellence in this process is central to execution of the overall plan. Placing the right people in the right slots in a timely way improves the chances of having an organization aligned to the strategy. This would correspond to Task 2 Stage IV and V of SCM maturity.	
	Stakeholders	Managers of departments undergoing change are stakeholders as are managers with new assignments. The human resource staff, assisted by recruiters, will pursue the plan. The project manager/office should track progress.	
	SCOR support	Awareness of SCOR and supply chain technology can be a criterion for staff selection.	

13.3 ORGANIZING FOR ACTIVITY SYSTEM IMPLEMENTATION (2.3)

Having a great plan and great people is insufficient for successful implementation. The two must be meshed in a way that implements the intent of the supply chain strategy and, where necessary, generates changes to the strategy. So this process is a "make or break" one for the supply chain project.

People in the project management and operating roles are the source of the progressive-elaboration characteristic of the project environment. This property of projects means that the "car must be steered," not left to find its own course.

13.3.1 INPUTS TO ORGANIZING FOR ACTIVITY SYSTEM IMPLEMENTATION (2.3.1)

This process matches people with positions. The people come from the staff acquisition process (2.2). The positions are output from the organization planning process (2.1). This process, summarized in Table 13.3, integrates the staff plan with the strategy, creating an environment for success. The structure is aligned with the needs of the business. Measures are consistent. Skills match the demands of new processes.

The implementation plan and staff resources are the central inputs. However, many other documents like the Strategy Issues List and the Environmental Briefing will find use in mobilizing people.

13.3.2 PROCESS ELEMENTS FOR ORGANIZING FOR ACTIVITY SYSTEM IMPLEMENTATION (2.3.2)

Table 13.3 lists approaches and techniques for the process. The process covers an extended time and requires attention to countless details. Employee-oriented approaches and techniques list ways to communicate to operating and project employees about the project. Other techniques, including teams and roles in process change, are structural in nature.

Many companies enjoy the process of planning much more than the job of implementing. Ease of implementation will depend on whether the roles designed for an individual are operating or project management — or both. The following are questions about the realism of implementation plans.

Will a new person assigned to an operating role design the new job or the process? Or will design be the responsibility of a dedicated project team? Can dedicated people be made available?

How much time will operating managers have for the project? How much is sufficient to gain their commitment?

Is implementation of new supply chain processes a "bootstrap" operation? That is, will operating managers have to design and make changes to the process at the same time they operate them? Many organizations do just this.

The "right" answers depend on the amount of change, the degree of difficulty, requirements for specialist knowledge and available funds for dedicated project staff.

TABLE 13.3
Organizing for Activity System Implementation (2.3)

2.3 Organizing for Activity System Implementation

2.3.1 Inputs		2.3.2 Process Elements	2.3.3 Outputs *Executing*
Organization Implementation Plan (2.1)	Process definition	This process integrates people and a time-phased organization plan. It implements the new internal organization over time.	*Implemented Organization Plan*
Staff Resources (2.2)	Approaches and techniques	**Employee oriented:** Orientation. Team building. Process design training (e.g., six sigma). Technical skills development. Leadership skills training. Process owners. Design Teams. Front line teams. Chief Process Improvement Officer. Facilitation.	*Organization Plan Implementation Progress Reports*
		Structural: Recognition and reward systems. Design Teams. Front line teams. Chief Process Improvement Officer. Facilitation.	
	PM shortcomings addressed	The process addresses top management abrogation, organization roadblocks and internal technical capability. In terms of the PMMM, the process is essential to organization awareness, management support and process discipline.	
	SCM maturity	The process moves the organization to higher levels of Task 2 maturity (Stages III, IV, and V) and sets the stage for higher levels of Task 3 maturity.	

TABLE 13.3 (Continued)
Organizing for Activity System Implementation (2.3)

	2.3 Organizing for Activity System Implementation		Executing
Terminology	Center of Excellence	Channel	
	Channel master	CPIO	
	Design Team	Process owner	
	Project office	Sponsor	
	Steering Committee	Third party logistics provider	
Stakeholders	Internally senior managers are involved, particularly those responsible for coordination with supply chain partners like procurement, sales and distribution. The project management function, a manager or project office, should implement the process in a coordinated effort with the human resource function.		
SCOR support	SCOR can serve as a training tool on SCM for employees whose roles are changing.		

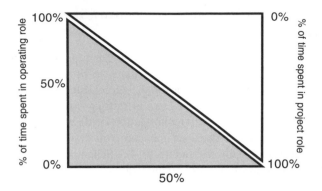

FIGURE 13.3 Split responsibility for implementation.

Project implementation often calls for people in the organization to take on roles described above and illustrated in Figure 13.3. The first role is the operating role, gray in the figure. If one spends 100% of his or her time running the business, there is no time for the project role to change the business. On the other hand, a dedicated project person will spend 100% of his or her time on a project role shown as the white triangle in Figure 13.3. If so, will that person have sufficient input and acceptance by operating people?

The author's experience is that split roles don't work. In general the operating role dominates. The reason is that most operating jobs create necessary, urgent tasks. There is no time to focus on the longer-term changes that are needed. Therefore, dedicated people are needed for the project. However, operating people have to have a role. A practical limit to the amount of time spent by operating managers is about 20%.

A possible solution is to add facilitation skills to the project team. This makes it possible for operating managers to spend nondisruptive time on the project. Facilitation may be from process improvement staff, consultants or the project management team.

Many supply chain initiatives unravel at this point in the project. Putting resources to work on implementation is confirmation that the project is real. A company that forsakes bootlegging implementation is at least demonstrating Level 2 maturity as measured by the PMMM.

With regard to SCM maturity, failure at this process is likely to cause a regression back to Stage II from the intent to be a Stage III company. This is akin to the rubber band that, after stretching, returns to its natural state. The use of spheres and their related activity systems is a risk-mitigating approach. Failure to find staff or implement change in one part of the business need not slow implementation in another where the people are available to implement the strategy.

The project management team should oversee this process. However, it requires close coordination with operating managers, particularly those in key new roles. The company steering committee should monitor the process continuously.

13.3.3 OUTPUTS FROM ORGANIZING FOR ACTIVITY SYSTEM IMPLEMENTATION (2.3.3)

The output is an Implemented Organization Plan. The plan will call for staffing the organization over time. Needed skills aren't likely to be available at once. So the deliverable unfolds as the process proceeds. Organization plan implementation progress reports will communicate progress in staffing positions.

Implementation progress will, whether faster or slower than called for in the Organization Implementation Plan, set the pace for strategy implementation. For this reason, Figure 13.1 calls for inputs to 2.5 Schedule Control. This process, described below, generates scope and organization changes.

13.4 SUPPLY CHAIN METRICS (2.4)

This process, described in Table 13.4, takes earlier inputs and solidifies measures for both project and supply chain performance. Placing this process at this point in the overall project gives the employees responsible for the process the opportunity to set goals for process measurements.

13.4.1 INPUTS TO SUPPLY CHAIN METRICS (2.4.2)

Candidate measures for new supply chain processes are developed along with the process. Activity System Design (from 1.4) contains sphere measures developed by the sphere design team. These transmit the sense of design teams regarding the rationale for their designs. Organization Design (1.5) goes one step further. It makes assignments of metrics to specific organizations or functions. The Collaboration Strategy (1.6) should signal opportunities and constraints for dealing with partners. There is no reason that internal metrics shouldn't be considered for use outside our organization up and down the supply chain.

Organization plan implementation progress reports from process 2.3 reflect the pace of metrics confirmation and development. At a minimum, new functions should reaffirm metrics proposed earlier in the project. If employees taking up roles need new metrics, these should be added.

13.4.2 PROCESS ELEMENTS FOR SUPPLY CHAIN METRICS (2.4.2)

The process doesn't start from scratch. Metrics development has been a part of prior processes, particularly Activity Systems Design (1.4) and Organization Design (1.5). This process confirms some metrics, deletes some and adds some. In measurement, more is not necessarily better. So pruning metrics is perfectly acceptable. The metrics address two needs. The first is measuring performance for the balance of the project; the second is performance measurement for supply chain operations in the future.

The project-related metrics will result in changes to the project's scope and schedule. These are handled through process 2.5 Schedule Control. The supply chain metrics will confirm or modify metrics for supply chain performance. They are an input to process 5.1 Process Improvement Planning. Supply chain scope

TABLE 13.4
Supply Chain Metrics (2.4)

2.4 Supply Chain Metrics

2.4.1 Inputs	2.4.2 Process Elements	Executing Process
		2.4.3 Outputs
Activity System Design (1.4)	**Process definition**	*Project Control Metrics*
Collaboration Strategy (1.6)	Develop or confirm metrics for supply chain operations tailored to each key position as it is filled, including those that supply chain partners can use in monitoring their own supply chain performance.	*Supply Chain Metrics*
Organization Design (1.5)		
Organization Plan	**Approaches and techniques**	
Implementation Progress	Balanced Scorecard. SCOR metrics (Please refer to Section 4.2.3.1 and Table 4.2.).	
Reports (2.3)	**PM shortcomings addressed**	
	Project Control Metrics measure the effectiveness of the implementation effort. In fact, the PMMM is itself one such metric. With respect to the root causes for project failure, metrics alert us when plans go awry.	
	SCM maturity	
	Metrics measure the ability of the organization to execute in all the SCM knowledge areas. The SCM maturity matrix is a metric measuring internal capabilities to use the supply chain to improve competitiveness. Supply Chain Metrics will monitor the health of new processes.	

TABLE 13.4 (Continued)
Supply Chain Metrics (2.4)

Executing

2.4 Supply Chain Metrics

Terminology
- Activity based costing
- Business model
- Cost of quality
- Discounted cash flow
- Key characteristic
- P:D ratio
- Statistical Process Control
- Total Cost of Ownership

- Balanced Scorecard
- Cash-to-cash cycle time
- C_p, C_{pk}
- Economic Value Added
- Mean absolute deviation
- Quality threshold
- Synchronized supply chain
- Velocity

- Benchmarking
- Cost baseline
- Cycle time
- Forecast error
- Mixed-model production
- Six sigma
- Target costing
- Yield management

Stakeholders

All supply chain members will be measured and guided by selected metrics. Initial stakeholders will be those in the organization responsible for operations in various spheres. The project manager/office should oversee execution by the supply chain design team.

SCOR support

SCOR in its process elements has many metrics for consideration. SCOR enabling process EP.2 is Assess Performance. SCOR contains descriptions of these for PLAN, SOURCE, MAKE, DELIVER and RETURN.

Note: Terminology refers to Glossary terms relating to supply chain performance.

should not be limited to one's own organization but should also include upstream and downstream partners.

The Balanced Scorecard and SCOR provide approaches useful for this process. Table 13.4 points out that the PMMM and SCM Maturity Model are essentially ways to measure the effectiveness of the process of creating more-competitive supply chains. Embracing higher levels of maturity does not guarantee success in creating a high-performance supply chain. It is, however, necessary to achieve that end.

Managers, as they take up new operating or project management roles, should confirm the metrics on which they will be measured. Those filling only operating roles should be responsible for supply chain metrics. They can develop these with the assistance of project staff. Project managers will address project control metrics. Those with split responsibility, as illustrated in Figure 13.3, should produce both.

13.4.3 OUTPUTS FROM SUPPLY CHAIN METRICS (2.4.3)

Project Control Metrics are those to be used to complete the process implementation phase of the project. Using the phasing suggested in Chapter 11 and summarized in Table 11.3, these can be for both short-term and long-term efforts. These are inputs into Schedule Control (2.5). Supply Chain Metrics are those that measure expected performance of the supply chain once new processes are implemented. To the extent possible, managers should document current performance.

13.5 SCHEDULE CONTROL (2.5)

A schedule control process, described in Table 13.5, is inserted here to transmit change requests to process 1.7 Integrated Change Control. These change requests result in modifications to the project plan. Changes arise from variations in the plan for finding staff (process 2.2), variations in integrating people into project management and operation functions (2.3) and changes generated by the need to move people into new positions (2.4).

13.5.1 INPUTS TO SCHEDULE CONTROL (2.5.1)

The inputs to the process, listed in Table 13.5, are outputs of other tasks described in this chapter.

13.5.2 PROCESS ELEMENTS FOR SCHEDULE CONTROL (2.5.2)

Table 13.5 describes project elements. The project management staff should manage the process. The environment is likely to be complex, particularly in larger organizations. There can be several "spheres" in some phase of the development process. Places where there is activity can be scattered geographically. There may also be language barriers in companies operating in several countries. The pace of change may vary from sphere to sphere. The project management team will have to be proactive in soliciting change and assuring that the project plan is up to date.

TABLE 13.5
Schedule Control (2.5)

		2.5 Schedule control	Controlling
2.5.1 Inputs		**2.5.2 Process Elements**	**2.5.3 Outputs**
Organization Plan	Process definition	Responsibility for implementation will reside inside the organization. So a control	*Organization Changes*
Implementation Progress		process is placed here that recognizes that the addition of people and their inputs	*SCM Change Requests*
Reports (2.3)		will produce modifications to the supply chain design and the schedule.	*Project Change Requests*
Project Control Metrics			
(2.4)	Approaches and techniques	Time estimating. Project network diagrams. Project management software.	
Supply Chain Metrics (2.4)			
	PM shortcomings addressed	Control of scope, time and cost elements is fundamental to project success.	
		Placed here it is tied to responsibility centers in the initiating organization.	
		Rigidity was also a root cause of poor project outcomes described in Chapter	
		9. This process provides for making adjustments to the project as it proceeds.	
	SCM maturity	Metrics that control multicompany efforts characterize Stage III and IV	
		organizations.	
	Terminology	– Activity – Cost baseline	
		– Critical path – Decomposition	
		– Deliverable – Level of effort	
		– Network diagram – Phase	
		– Process, process group – Program	
		– Progressive elaboration – Project	
		– Project life cycle – Project office	
		– Risk – Schedule baseline	
		– Subproject – Task	
		– Template – Work package	
	Stakeholders	Internal functions must react to needs for changes. Company steering committee	
		should ratify changes; project manager/office should execute the process.	

13.5.3 OUTPUTS FROM SCHEDULE CONTROL (2.5.3)

The process produces organization changes and change requests. These can be changes to the project plan (1.7) that is the overall plan for the strategy or Organization Planning (2.1), which sets the timing of staff changes. SCM change requests recommend modification to the design of the supply chain. Project change requests recommend changes to the project management plan.

ENDNOTE

1. Kerzner, Harold, Marketing the project-driven organization, in *Project Management: A Systems Approach to Planning, Scheduling and Controlling, Seventh Edition*, New York: John Wiley & Sons, Inc., 2001, pp. 26–32.

14 Forging Supply Chain Partnerships

A supply chain project won't fulfill the promise implicit in its label until the project involves upstream and downstream partners. This chapter describes project processes to plan multicompany efforts For further reading, please read the case study A1. Change Management in Complex Supply Chain Configuration Project.

Figure 14.1 is a flowchart of processes associated with our SCM *Task 3. Forging Supply Chain Partnerships*. Chapter 13 described Task 2 processes for internal alignment that focus on cross-functional cooperation inside the organization.

The project property, "progressive elaboration," works with a vengeance in the processes covered in this chapter. Arguably, one has greater control over its own operations. However, it may have little or no influence over what partners will do. A lot depends on the supply chain orientation, or SCO, of those partners. Described in Section 2.1, SCO is a gauge of their willingness to collaborate. Until the company presents its partners with a plan, it will not know for sure what it can or cannot accomplish with their cooperation.

So, Figure 14.1 recommends two control processes. The first, Project Staffing (3.5), occurs when the partnership calls for a multicompany staff to man projects. The second, Scope Verification (3.7), calls for feedback that results in changes to the project plan. Performance at these control points will expand or limit the scope of the supply chain project.

Principal features of the processes include the following:

- A communications process (3.1) to elicit participation from partners.
- Separate branches for upstream and downstream partners. These include two executing processes (3.2 for the upstream supplier base and 3.3 for the downstream customer base) tailored to individual partners or partner groups.
- The use of a "Level 3" or multicompany organization to guide collaborations and staff improvement efforts. (3.4)
- Risk sharing through win-win arrangements. (3.5)
- A process for partner verification of our scope. (3.7)

The importance of these processes to a company's supply chain effort will vary enormously among those pursuing supply chain improvements. Variables depend on the number of partners, location of the company in the chain, relative power and

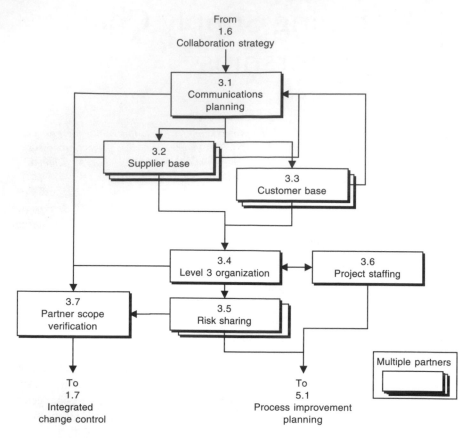

FIGURE 17.1 Forging supply chain relationships.

influence of the company and supply chain complexity as measured by the number of spheres, or "businesses within the business."

The project team has great flexibility in applying these processes. For example, the processes here treat upstream and downstream partners separately. However, in Chapter 4, we described "vertical" spheres that include our company, upstream and downstream partners. In this case, the planning may include both types of partner.

14.1 COMMUNICATIONS PLANNING (3.1)

This process translates outputs of strategy processes into a plan or plans for communicating the organization's intent for modifying its existing relationships with partners. The process takes what are essentially internal planning documents and turns them into instruments for communications.

14.1.1 INPUTS TO COMMUNICATIONS PLANNING (3.1.1)

The collaboration strategy (described in Section 12.6.3) defines what the project plan is seeking in the way of strategy fulfillment. This input is an internal document developed in process 1.6 Collaboration Strategy that serves as a basis for the output of this process. Elements described in Chapter 12 (Section 12.6.3) include the following:

- Characterization of the supply and customer base
- Information requirements
- New upstream and downstream roles
- Technology

Another input to the process is collaboration plan change suggestions from upstream suppliers and downstream customers. These result from dialog during processes 3.2 and 3.3. Partner suggestions lead to changes in the external communications plan.

14.1.2 PROCESS ELEMENTS FOR COMMUNICATIONS PLANNING (3.1.2)

Communications planning, summarized in Table 14.1, launches collaboration initiatives along the supply chain. It is a "selling" document, or a series of documents, in many ways. If it is not persuasive to partners, those elements of the strategy are in jeopardy. In cases where partners cannot be compelled to collaborate by virtue of the organization's position in the chain, the planning must address the "what's in it for me" question.

14.1.2.1 Process Definition for Communications Planning

Table 14.1 includes a definition of the process. The process should screen the inputs provided by the collaboration strategy to determine what is available for "public consumption." Also, the plan can have separate parts for each partner or group of partners. For example, on the upstream side, one part may address smaller suppliers of commodities. Another may address large suppliers of components engineered for the company. On the downstream side, separate communications may be tailored to the needs of a few large customers or major distribution channels.

Of course, multiple tailored communications will take longer to produce. So, priorities for releasing communications documents should guide the schedule for their preparation.

14.1.2.2 Approaches and Techniques for Communications Planning

Collaboration covers a broad range of issues and topics. Examples include negotiation of prices, service levels, risk distribution, extended product features and investments for mutual benefit. The document should recognize the industry drivers behind the need for collaboration. Chapter 3 listed six, which were:

1. New product or process technology
2. The need for extended products with additional services accompanying the physical product

TABLE 17.1
Communications Planning (3.1)

3.1 Communications Planning

3.1.1 Inputs	3.1.2 Process Elements	Planning Process — 3.1.3 Outputs
Collaboration Strategy (1.6)		**External Communications Plan**
Collaboration Plan Change Suggestions (3.2, 3.3)		Objectives
Process definition	Develop a plan addressing goals, staffing, oversight, projects, contracting and process integration. Include all spheres. The process provides external communications to upstream and downstream partners. It also communicates company direction for collaboration to internal stakeholders.	Description and scope
		Timetable
		Technology
Approaches and techniques	Drivers of supply chain change (Chapter 3). Cross-company process documentation. External stakeholder needs analysis. Contracting. Activity-based costing. Risk analysis techniques.	Business rules
		Risk sharing
PM shortcomings addressed	Since several companies who may have bargained at arm's length must support the broadest implementations, this is especially challenging. Success requires Level 3 PMMM performance for multiple organizations. This requires a "supply chain orientation" among these parties. (Refer to Section 2.1)	Enabling processes
		Participation
	The resulting plan should address senior management abrogation, technology and organization roadblocks.	
SCM maturity	The willingness to communicate externally implies at least a Stage II organization with regard to Task 3. The depth of collaboration will determine whether a company is reaching Stage III, IV, or V.	

Terminology
- Activity Based Costing
- Collaboratory
- Customer
- E-commerce
- Flexibility
- Independent, dependent demand
- Kanban
- Milk run
- Postponement
- Push and pull systems
- Risk pooling

- APS
- CRM
- Disintermediation
- Electronic Data Interchange
- Glass pipeline
- Just in Time
- Lean enterprise
- PDCA
- Process owner
- Replenishment cycle time
- Safety stock

- Certified supplier
- Target costing
- Echelon
- Extended product
- Target Costing
- Kaizen
- Mass customization
- Point of Sale
- Product pipeline, product funnel
- Reverse logistics
- Steering Committee

Stakeholders

The company steering committee should be accountable; the supply chain design team should execute the process. Any upstream or downstream contact person, important supply chain partner and internal functions that must collaborate are stakeholders.

SCOR support

SCOR process collaboration frameworks will assist in shaping the message to partners. SCOR vocabulary may also standardize term definition and process descriptions.

3. Globalization of markets and sources of supply
4. The flexibility imperative to ensure survival in dynamic environments
5. Process-centered management that addresses process rather than functional improvement
6. Collaboration results that generate further supply chain improvements

The communication plan should translate these drivers into requirements for supply chain process changes. The plan might use the many process documentation tools available, including several covered in Chapter 15. Activity-based costing is also useful for establishing a cost model to facilitate communications and provide a tool for negotiations.

Risk analysis, a topic introduced in Section 7.3.8, can add structure to conversations about the assumption of risk along the chain. An example is responsibility for carrying inventory to ensure against disruptions, to provide flexibility to respond to changing demands and to respond quickly to changes in end-user demand.

14.1.2.3 Project Management Shortcomings Addressed by Communications Planning

The external communications plan, because it goes outside the company to important partners, should be subject to top management approval. The company steering committee is the logical forum. This approval is also a signal of commitment to the project's direction to partners.

The plan calls for a section on technology requirements. This should trigger a dialog with partners regarding their readiness to participate at the plan-defined technology level.

Organization roadblocks inside the company and in partner organizations should be addressed by the plan. Communication through the plan should raise partner comments and feedback that the company steering committee and supply chain design team should address.

14.1.2.4 SCM Maturity for Communications Planning

Maturity in Task 3, Forging Supply Chain Partnerships, depends on the type of collaboration planned. Stage II in the SCM maturity model (Figure 10.2) is simple data exchange. Stage III is characterized by cost reduction with suppliers where the organization has most of its leverage. Stage IV begins upstream and downstream partnerships, but roles of partners in the supply chain remain static. This is typical of incremental efforts addressing cost and perhaps service. No new space is created by the planned partnerships. Stage V brings role changes and characterizes major change in the chain.

14.1.2.5 Terminology for Communications Planning

Terms in Table 14.1 are examples of the vocabulary for multicompany interaction. The company steering committee is responsible for oversight of the project internally. A multicompany steering committee is an additional governance group to coordinate the effort among partners. Multicompany steering committees, formulated in process 3.4, are needed for higher levels of maturity, particularly Stages IV or V.

There may be several multicompany steering committees. Some will have just two members, your own company and your partner. An example would be the case of a major supplier who works with our company to develop a key technology. Others may have more than two members, with representatives from a group of customers. Many companies now have "supplier conferences" and "user groups." The multicompany steering committee will have a more intense agenda than that typical of these forums.

14.1.2.6 Stakeholders for Communications Planning

The process is intended to draw key partners into the project. The ones selected will be those most important to the company's future, those partners one wants to transform from an arm's-length negotiating stance into a collaborative effort. This will not be all suppliers or all customers. Appendix B2 recommends that the supply chain design team should execute the process under close monitoring from the company steering committee. If they exist at this point, multicompany steering committees along with internal and partner functions should be consulted.

14.1.2.7 SCOR Support for Communications Planning

Section 8.4 describes the direction of the effort to incorporate collaboration into SCOR. This direction recognizes that different supply chain processes, PLANNING, EXECUTING and ENABLING, require different forms of collaboration. These range from forms of data exchange (Stage II in SCM maturity) to collaboration decision-making (Stages IV and V). The term *collaboratory* is used to define the act of collaborating between partners.

14.1.3 OUTPUTS FROM COMMUNICATIONS PLANNING (3.1.3)

The external communications plan should, at a minimum, have the following components:

- **Objectives** — including financial objectives for customer service, market share and cost reduction
- **Description and scope** — products and processes included
- **Timetable** — desired implementation schedule
- **Technology** — process requirements, including information technology, facilities and equipment
- **Business rules** — guidelines for the partnership. Rules cover operations, planning and contributions by partners
- **Risk sharing** — how risks and rewards might be distributed. How such risks and rewards will be measured
- **Enabling processes** — SCOR and other processes on both sides of the partnership needed to make the collaborative processes work
- **Participation** — anticipated contributions to a multicompany steering committee and desired project staff contributions

14.2 SUPPLIER BASE (3.2)

This executing process, shown in Table 14.2, takes the collaboration plan and turns it, through a joint effort with a partner or several partners, into an organization design for supplier and company implementation. One result is the identification of a process design team. A similar process takes place with the downstream side in process 3.3 Customer Base.

The organization, once the design developed in this process is implemented, will prepare partners for improvements to supply chain processes covered in Chapter 15. The sequence is also consistent with Figure 13.2 in that the organization goes into place before the processes.

The process is limited to upstream partners where collaboratories are desired. These are expected to be the few largest suppliers, probably the 20% of suppliers that account for 80% of what is spent for materials and services. Priorities for spheres as well as resources from both one's company and the suppliers' organizations will dictate the order of process design development with suppliers.

14.2.1 INPUTS TO SUPPLIER BASE (14.2.1)

The principal inputs are the activity system design, collaboration strategy and the external communications plan. The project team, assisted by functional staff, should coordinate partnership design with the supplier, including the organization to support it. Organization requirements may entail new staff and functions for one's own company and the supplier. However, it may be possible to execute the plan without such additions. This process is an important first action of that partnership.

14.2.2 PROCESS ELEMENTS FOR SUPPLIER BASE (14.2.2)

Table 14.2 lists the process elements producing an organization design based on input planning documents. It is an example of "cognitive collaboration," as described by the Supply-Chain Council's collaboration effort. This involves joint decision-making with each supplier or supplier group. It is the point in the process where suppliers provide input regarding what they can or cannot do.

This interaction will be a test of the willingness and ability to collaborate with the company. Suppliers will be different in their capability. Reactions can vary from complete willingness to support the partnership to downright hostility. Much will depend on our own company's "heritage" with regard to supplier relations. If our company has been antagonistic and a "price taker," suppliers will likely be wary of any new initiative.

Also not resolved at this time is risk sharing in the partnership. The supplier has a right to ask, " What's in it for me if I collaborate?" The going-forward plan should list the alternatives and plan negotiation of risks and rewards.

14.2.3 OUTPUTS FROM SUPPLIER BASE (14.2.3)

The design will reflect the upstream supplier's commitment to the company's supply chain initiative. The deliverable is the plan for placement of functions within its

TABLE 17.2
Supplier Base (3.2)

3.2 Supplier Base

3.2.1 Inputs

Activity System Design (1.4)
Collaboration Strategy (1.6)
External Communications
Plan (3.1)

3.2.2 Process Elements

Process definition	Execute the plan for upstream (supplier-side) collaboration. Include all spheres. Address goals, staffing, oversight, projects, contracting and process integration.
Approaches and techniques	Regular meetings. Feedback from partners.
PM shortcomings	The process engages upstream partners. It is facilitated by Level 3 singular processes in the PMMM, particularly if several suppliers are engaged in the effort.
	A well-executed process will reduce risks from mismatched technical capability and misunderstood technology. It also engages top management across the companies involved.
SCM maturity	Such a plan is needed for moving beyond Stage I of SCM maturity. Initiatives in the plan will determine which level (II, III, IV, or V).
Stakeholders	Internal functions facing upstream in the supply chain. These include commodity managers, buyers, quality engineering, warehousing, engineers and sourcing managers.
	Principal upstream supply chain partners, of course, are also key stakeholders. The company steering committee is accountable for the process; the supply chain design team should execute the process.
SCOR support	SCOR processes SOURCE and SOURCE RETURN will assist definition of needed processes.

Executing Process

3.2.3 Outputs

Level 3 (multicompany)
Organization Design—
Supplier Base
Implementation

organization. It is unlikely that both parties will get all they want. So changes will have to made to the project plan. These change are funneled through process 1.7 Integrated Change Control.

There are many examples of supplier organization responses to a supply chain initiative:

- Providing engineering support for new products or value engineering for existing products.
- Establishing manufacturing cells dedicated to our product to support a sphere strategy.
- Establishing a customer service function tailored to our organization's need.
- Agreeing to just-in-time deliveries, tailored packaging or buffer inventories.
- Adding capacity through purchases of equipment or facilities.
- Commitment to linkages and production control approaches. Agreeing to consider information technology investments to support collaboration.
- Sharing of quality data. Joint efforts to improve quality. These can include changes to our part or subsystem specifications.
- Selection of second-tier suppliers.
- Changes to return processes.

Commitments made in this process pave the way for process improvements. Chapter 15 covers these; they include service improvements, cost reductions and changes that introduce flexibility to the supply chain.

14.3   CUSTOMER BASE (3.3)

This executing process, shown in Table 14.3, takes the collaboration plan and turns it into a design for downstream implementation. This includes channels from our own company to end-users. These channels cover downstream manufacturers, distributors, retail outlets, buyers of our product and end-users. Note that buyers may not be end-users.

A similar process takes place with the upstream side in process 3.2 Supplier Base. The organization, once the design developed in this process is implemented, will prepare partners for improvements to supply chain processes covered in Chapter 15. The sequence is also consistent with Figure 13.2 with organization commitments made before embarking on process improvements.

The process is limited to downstream partners where collaboratories are desired. These are expected to be the few largest distributors or customers, probably the 20% of downstream partners that buy 80% of one's own company's sales. Priorities for spheres, as well as resources from both one's company and the downstream partner, should dictate the sequence of design development.

14.3.1   INPUTS TO CUSTOMER BASE (3.3.1)

The principal inputs are the activity system design, collaboration strategy and the external communications plan. The project team, assisted by functional staff, should

TABLE 17.3
Customer Base (3.3)

	3.3 Customer Base	Executing Process
3.3.1 Inputs	**3.3.2 Process Elements**	**3.3.3 Outputs**
Activity System Design (1.4) Collaboration Strategy (1.6) External Communications Plan (3.1)		*Level 3 (multicompany) Organization Design— Customer Base Implementation*
Process definition	Execute the plan for downstream (customer-side) collaboration. Include all spheres. Address goals, staffing, oversight, projects, contracting and process integration.	
Approaches and techniques	Regular meetings. Feedback from partners.	
PM shortcomings	The process engages downstream partners. It is facilitated by Level 3 singular processes in the PMMM. A well-executed process will reduce risks from mismatched technical capability and misunderstood technology. It also engages top management across the companies involved.	
SCM maturity	Such a plan is needed for moving beyond Stage I of SCM maturity. Initiatives in the plan will determine which level (II, III, IV, or V).	
Stakeholders	Internal functions facing downstream in the supply chain and principal downstream supply chain partners are stakeholders. The company steering committee is accountable; the supply chain design team should execute the process.	
SCOR support	SCOR processes DELIVER and DELIVER RETURN will assist definition of needed processes.	

coordinate the design of the partnership with the downstream partner, including the organization to support it. This process is an important first action of that partnership.

14.3.2 PROCESS ELEMENTS FOR CUSTOMER BASE (3.3.2)

Table 14.3 lists the process elements. It produces an organization design for downstream operations based on the input planning documents. It is an example of "cognitive collaboration" as described by the Supply-Chain Council's collaboration effort. This involves joint decision-making with each partner. It is the point in the process where the downstream partners provide input regarding what they can or can't do.

This interaction is a test of the willingness and ability to collaborate with the company. Downstream companies with whom we deal will be different in their willingness and ability to enter into a new relationship. Reactions will vary from complete willingness to downright hostility to one's company's overtures. Much will depend on our own company's "heritage" with regard to the targeted partners. If our company has been antagonistic and hard to work with, potential partners will likely be wary of a new initiative.

Also not resolved at this time is risk sharing in the partnership. The partner has a right to ask, " What's in it for me if I collaborate?" The going forward plan should list the alternatives and plan negotiation of risks and rewards.

14.3.3 OUTPUTS FROM CUSTOMER BASE (3.3.3)

The design will reflect the downstream partner's commitment to the company's supply chain initiative. The deliverable is the plan for placement of functions within its organization. It is unlikely that both parties will get all they want, so changes will have to made to the project plan. These change are funneled through process 1.7 Integrated Change Control.

There are many examples of downstream organization responses to a supply chain initiative. Examples include the following:

- Shifting assembly operations to a downstream partner as part of a postponement plan.
- Providing information on consumption of end product to assist our planning.
- Establishing a liaison function to facilitate supply chain operations and performance information.
- Adding capacity through purchases of equipment or facilities.
- Commitment to linkages and production control approaches. Agreeing to consider information technology investments to support collaboration.
- Sharing of quality data and joint efforts to improve quality. These can include changes to downstream partner specifications.
- Changes in our supply base imposed by our downstream customer.
- Changes to return processes.

Commitments made in this process pave the way for process improvements. Chapter 15 covers these; they include service improvements, cost reductions and changes that introduce flexibility to the supply chain.

14.4 LEVEL 3 (MULTICOMPANY) ORGANIZATION (3.4)

This executing process takes upstream and downstream plans and builds the corresponding multicompany infrastructure for process improvements. Table 14.4 summarizes the process. As shown in Figure 4.4, Level 3 refers to multicompany efforts; Level 1 is departmental; Level 2 is the business unit level.

An earlier article described the characteristics of Level 3 supply chain project management.[*] Key features include the following:

- A focused goal for the effort including strategic positioning, increased revenue and profit improvement.
- Multicompany groups supporting and funding the effort.
- If needed, a third-party "honest broker" to facilitate the effort.
- A steering committee, manned by senior managers, to guide the effort.
- A project or group of projects that create returns to all the partners.
- Contracting that distributes costs and rewards based on achieving measures of performance.
- Balanced deployment of technology with judicious use of legacy systems, new technology or "low-tech" linkages.

This process integrates plans from processes 3.2 and 3.3 to put these elements into place. One can't ignore the timing issue with this process. An aggressive supply chain plan will cover many partners. Not all can be done at once. So the multicompany organization will have evolving membership, reflecting the partner involved at any point. Also, multiple multicompany steering committees can execcute different parts of the strategy.

14.4.1 INPUTS TO LEVEL 3 (MULTICOMPANY) ORGANIZATION (3.4.1)

The activity system design (1.4) and the collaboration strategy (1.6) are internal documents. Multicompany plans from processes 3.3 and 3.4 are the result of partner collaboration. This process takes these inputs from paper to reality.

14.4.2 PROCESS ELEMENTS FOR LEVEL 3 (MULTICOMPANY) ORGANIZATION (3.4.2)

Table 14.4 lists the process elements. The goal is to staff project positions then identify and possibly fill operating positions needed to start process improvements. As mentioned above, this corresponds to the sequence of implementation described in Figure 13.2. It assigns design responsibility to people who will operate the process.

In Table 5.1, project management maturity is measured by organization awareness, management support and process discipline. This process requires partner

---

[*] Ayers, James B., Gustin, Craig and Stephens, Scott, Reengineering the supply chain, *Information Strategy: The Executive's Journal*, Fall, 1997 (14/1).

TABLE 17.4
Level 3 (Multicompany) Organization (3.4)

3.4 Level 3 (Multicompany) Organization

		Executing Process
3.4.1 Inputs	**3.4.2 Process Elements**	**3.4.3 Outputs**
Activity System Design (1.4) Collaboration Strategy (1.6) Level 3 (multicompany) Organization Design — Supplier Base Implementation (3.3) Level 3 (multicompany) Organization Design — Customer Base Implementation (3.4)	Process definition: The process puts in place the logistics required to maintain communications links and decision-making procedures for ongoing collaboration. Elements include project staff leadership at partners and appointments to steering committees.	*SCM Subprojects* *Multicompany Project* *Staffing Requirements* *Multicompany Risk* *Sharing Plan*
	Approaches and techniques: Organization meetings. Joint decision making in activity system implementation. Partnership classification.	
	PM shortcomings: A continuing organization will provide ongoing multicompany awareness, management support and process discipline.	
	SCM maturity: Forums are needed for reaching Stage IV and V levels of SCM maturity.	
	Stakeholders: Important upstream and downstream partners are key stakeholders. So are company employees in functions that must support the plans. The company's supply chain project team should be responsible for executing the process. The multicompany steering committee should be accountable.	
	SCOR support: Process element definition and collaboration methods can reinforce initiatives. SCOR metrics can serve as a basis for risk sharing discussions.	

commitments, which are confirmed by their assigning staff to the project. An output is SCM subprojects or, if it's the preference of the project team, separate projects for implementation.

Higher levels of SCM maturity are hampered by the lack of a "governance" structure beyond the immediate company's boundaries. This is a major obstacle in achieving supply chain improvements. The structure put in place in this process will promote communications and formal decision-making. Again, partners will vary in the level of their SCO, or supply chain orientation. An organization should be prepared for varying levels of cooperation. This will lead to decisions to change partners or to modifications in project goals or plans.

14.4.3 Outputs from Level 3 (Multicompany) Organization (3.4.3)

The process has three principal outputs. *SCM Subprojects* represents efforts that the multicompany steering committee has ratified. The term "subprojects" is used since these are components of the overall supply chain project. One has choices in nomenclature. These efforts can be "activities" within the supply chain project, a project extension or separate standalone projects. The choice will depend on the effort's scope and relationship with parallel efforts. This deliverable is used in process 3.5 Project Staffing, 3.6 Risk Sharing and 3.7 Scope Verification.

Multicompany project staffing requirements are needs for project and operating staff to support the plan approved by the multicompany steering committee. The output is to a control process, 3.5 Project Staffing. The plan should include positions, numbers, skills and timing for each staffing requirement.

A multicompany risk sharing plan sets the ground rules for business arrangements between the partners regarding assumption of risk for supply chain performance. This plan might be considered a memorandum of understanding, or MOU, to be later supplanted by formal contracts, if necessary. Figure 8.5 from Chapter 8, our description of the Supply-Chain Council's SCOR model, describes the life cycle of a collaboratory. This includes the following six elements that a collaborative relationship might address:

1. Type of collaboratory as characterized by the framework in Section 8.4.1.
2. Agreements or contracts needed to solidify the relationship.
3. Contacts between the collaborating companies. These can include a variety of functions (engineering, tech support and so forth) beyond procurement staff.
4. Metrics for service and cost.
5. Requirements including service guarantees, staffing and investments.
6. Rewards or penalties for meeting or not meeting requirements.

SCOR Level 1 metrics, listed in Table 8.2, for customer-facing and internal-facing metrics provide examples of risks to be addressed. The multicompany risk sharing plan should identify which risks are important in each partner relationship. It should then define expectations for each party. For example, delivery performance and cost might be an important metric for a particular supplier. The plan should define expectations for performance and the premiums and penalties that might go with exception or substandard performance.

14.5 RISK SHARING (3.5)

This executing process, summarized in Table 14.5, formalizes collaborative agreement to share risk in the supply chain relationship. Risk sharing defines the rewards and liabilities when things go right or things go wrong in a supply chain process. Collaboration in process 3.4 Stage 3 Organization has produced a "handshake" agreement to risk sharing. However, this is a signal of overall intent worked out at a high level. This process formalizes it with agreements, as detailed as necessary, with each supplier. The agreement is a necessary step to planning and designing supply chain processes.

14.5.1 INPUTS TO RISK SHARING (3.5.1)

The multicompany risk sharing plan is the principal input. This executing process turns the plan into reality. It involves negotiations with each major partner within the framework provided by the plan.

14.5.2 PROCESS ELEMENTS FOR RISK SHARING (3.5.2)

Table 14.5 lists process elements. In addition to metrics, the SCOR model provides ideas for inclusion in the resulting agreements. These take the form of enabling processes for PLAN processes. Table 14.6 summarizes ENABLE PLAN processes that could apply to particular partnerships.

Of course, the need will vary from partner to partner. For example, an agreement with an upstream manufacturing supplier may not require EP.6 Manage Transportation elements. However, working with a third-party transportation company for downstream distribution of products certainly would require it.

14.5.3 OUTPUTS FROM RISK SHARING (3.5.3)

Partner business arrangements are the resulting deliverable. The business arrangement goes beyond the normal arm's-length transaction. In fact, it may not even specify normal purchase order terms like price and delivery terms if these are spelled out in alternative documents. A principal goal is to gain agreements to pursue supply chain level process improvements and define participation in those efforts.

14.6 PROJECT STAFFING (3.6)

This controlling process, summarized in Table 14.7, monitors the readiness of partners and the company to make supply chain process improvements. Methods to implement these improvements constitute Chapter 15. This process is considered a controlling, not an execution, process. This is because it tracks "compliance" with agreed-upon staffing plans. The staffing plans encompass needs for both project and

TABLE 17.5
Risk Sharing (3.5)

3.5 Risk Sharing

3.5.1 Inputs Multicompany Risk Sharing Plan (3.4)	3.5.2 Process Elements	Executing Process 3.5.3 Outputs *Partner Business Arrangements*
Process definition	Collaboration between upstream and downstream partners leads to formal and understood arrangements for operating supply chain processes. Risks can be external (such as natural disasters) and internal (related to partner performance).	
Approaches and techniques	Contingency planning. Risk identification and analysis. Financial analysis. Capital investment analysis.	
PM shortcomings	Most agreements to share risk will require top management participation. Larger risks will involve correspondingly higher levels of approval.	
SCM maturity	Risk sharing will likely be key in Achieving Stage V of SCM maturity for Task 3. Sharing is also a component of aggressive (Stages IV and V) supply chain process improvements described in (Chapter 15).	
Stakeholders	The process is the responsibility of the multicompany steering committee. All participating companies are stakeholders. However, normal partner contacts — procurement on the upstream side and sales/customer service on the downstream side — are stakeholders as well.	
SCOR support	SCOR metrics can serve as measures for inter-company process effectiveness. Risk sharing can be shaped around achieving or not achieving levels of performance. Several SCOR ENABLE processes serve as references for the process. These include 1. Establish and Manage Rules, 2. Assess Performance and 7. Manage Supply Chain Configuration.	

TABLE 17.6
Business Arrangements and SCOR ENABLE PLAN Processes

Process #	Process Name	Summary
EP.1	Manage business rules	Define decision support criteria for customer service based on strategy.
EP.2	Assess performance	Establish which performance measures will govern the collaborative arrangement.
EP.3	Manage data	Define what data will be exchanged and the level of detail needed.
EP.4	Manage inventory	Define inventory needs including replenishment rules, ownership, products and location.
EP.5	Manage capital assets	Define capacity strategy and responsibility for providing that capacity.
EP.6	Manage transportation	Develop plan for transportation at the supply chain level and identify needed resources.
EP.7	Manage supply chain configuration	Agreement developed in this process should be an element in the configuration.
EP.8	Manage regulatory compliance	Identify and assure compliance with rules set by regulatory bodies.
EP.9	Align supply chain plan with financial plan	Assure that agreement aligns with business assumptions like sales and capacity requirements.

operating staff. Project staff includes people assigned for the duration of the sub-project or project extension. Operating staff is likely to be for new functions identified as part of the supply chain strategy and process improvement.

14.6.1 INPUTS TO PROJECT STAFFING (3.6.1)

Multicompany project staffing requirements from process 3.4 are the principal input. The requirements, as described in the previous process, include the position, number of people, the skills needed for the position and the timing of the requirement.

14.6.2 PROCESS ELEMENTS FOR PROJECT STAFFING (3.6.2)

The process is not complicated in concept. However, if staffing requirements are ambitious and complicated, acquiring staff will be difficult. It is assumed this is to be done outside the project by partner human resource function. Often, a person nominated for a project or operating position is a "near fit." In these cases, the process should include confirmation of the near-fit selections by examining what risks might be involved in the selection.

The arrow between processes 3.4 and 3.5 in Figure 14.1 is two-headed. This reflects the need for the multicompany steering committee to deal with variances to the plan.

TABLE 17.7
Project Staffing (3.6)

3.6 Project Staffing

3.6.1 Inputs	3.6.2 Process Elements	Controlling Process
Multicompany Project Staffing Requirements (3.4)		**3.6.3 Outputs** *Staffed SCM Projects, Subprojects, or Project Extensions* *Staff Plan Exceptions*
	Process definition — This process monitors partner company commitments of staff to multicompany SCM projects on both the upstream and downstream sides. It includes activities to confirm the suitability of people nominated for certain positions. Exception reporting causes modifications to project plans.	
	Approaches and techniques — Planning for scope changes, subprojects or new standalone SCM projects. Reporting of readiness to proceed on process improvements.	
	PM shortcomings — Staffing is a sign of commitment from top management (to counter abrogation) and should include the skills necessary to make new processes work. Process methodology at Level 3 of the PMMM will communicate project needs to partners.	
	SCM maturity — Staff commitments reflect willingness to commit to process improvements that cross company boundaries — Stages IV and V of the SCM maturity model for Tasks 4 and 5.	
	Stakeholders — All participating companies and, particularly, the assigned employees are stakeholders. The project management staff should monitor the process.	
	SCOR support — SCOR can assist in educating assigned project staff.	

14.6.3 Outputs from Project Staffing (3.6.3)

Outputs include exception tracking of the pace of staffing based on the plan. The output is reported as staffed SCM projects, subprojects, or project extensions. Staff plan exceptions are reported to 1.7 Integrated Change Control; the exceptions could cause changes to the project plan. Such changes might affect only the timing of implementation. If the changes reflect a serious shortcoming in finding people to get the work done, then the scope of the supply chain project will have to change.

14.7 SCOPE VERIFICATION (3.7)

This control process, summarized in Table 14.8, takes various change suggestions and processes them into change requests. These are of two types: changes in the SCM elements and changes in the project management element of the overall supply chain project plan.

TABLE 17.8
Scope Verification (3.7)

3.7.1 Inputs		3.7 Partner Scope Verification 3.7.2 Process Elements	Controlling 3.7.3 Outputs
Changes (3.1, 3.2, 3.3, 3.4, 3.5, 3.6)	Process definition	Collaboration with partners is likely to produce many changes to the project plan.	SCM and Project Management Change Requests
SCM Subprojects (3.4)	Approaches and techniques	Project and scope plan reviews	
	PM shortcomings	Scope changes formalize an important project management element.	
	SCM maturity	Scope changes formalize an important SCM collaboration element.	
	Stakeholders	Project Office. Project Steering Committee.	

14.7.1 Inputs to Scope Verification (3.7.1)

Table 14.9 lists examples of the types of changes that arise in the process of developing partnerships with other companies.

TABLE 17.9
Typical Changes Associated With Partnership Formulation

Process #	Process Name	Examples
3.1	Communications Planning	Development of the external communications plan turns up the need for changes. An example is disclosure of company-confidential information.
3.2	Supplier Base	Feedback from suppliers reflecting their willingness to participate and suggestions for the shape of the partnership.
3.3	Customer Base	Feedback from downstream partners reflecting their willingness to participate and suggestions for the shape of the partnership.
3.4	Level 3 Organization	Meetings with partner executives and staff will lead to more suggestions for changing the project plan.
3.6	Risk Sharing	The actual shape of partner business agreements may differ from the original collaboration plan's intent.

14.7.2 PROCESS ELEMENTS FOR SCOPE VERIFICATION (3.7.2)

The naming of the process reflects the need in a supply chain project to get partner "buy in." An organization can conceive of a plan to suit its need. But, to the extent the organization depends on its partners, they must come aboard as well.

14.7.3 OUTPUTS FROM SCOPE VERIFICATION (3.7.3)

Outputs from the process are inputs to process 1.7 Integrated Change Control. Accepted changes will make their way into project planning documents.

15 Improving Supply Chain Processes and Systems

Most supply chain project efforts develop and improve processes. These efforts support the supply chain strategy that identifies needs to improve one or more performance metrics. The most effective process improvements will involve partners, take a process-centered approach and address root causes, not symptoms. Three case studies describe process improvements in supply chains: A2. Supply Chain Facility Network Design, A5. Chasing Low Labor Production — Words of Warning, and A6. Cost Analysis — A Case of Unintended Consequences

Many, if not most companies pursuing supply chain improvement make a huge mistake. That is, they start their efforts at this point in the overall process, omitting the processes described in Chapters 12, 13 and 14. They have ignored, explicitly or out of sheer ignorance, several important questions. What is our strategy? Does what we plan for a supply chain process affect our ability to compete? Is our organization aligned across its departments to make changes? Can "lowly vendors" help the effort? Why involve customers when they just want to beat us up?

In these companies, SCM consists of appeals to cut costs to improve profits. However, without executing preparatory processes from earlier chapters, disappointment should be expected. That said, a quick payback — even a local one — could spark and sustain interest in a longer project. However, preparatory work need not take forever. To move the process forward quickly, conceptual design in Chapter 12, internal alignment in Chapter 13 and enlistment of partners in Chapter 14 can proceed on a fast track for high-priority or obviously broken processes.

Figure 15.1 is a flowchart of the processes covered in this chapter. The processes cover two of our five SCM management tasks. These are *Task 4. Managing Supply Chain Information* and *Task 5. Removing Cost from the Supply Chain*. The rationale for the combination is that information exchange through links between partners is integral to process design. Putting information technology together with process improvement is consistent with the "process-centered" management described in Chapter 3.

SCM Task 5's label "removing cost" should not be misinterpreted. The intent is not just to remove cost but also to make more money from operations by achieving other measures related to delivery and quality specified in the strategy. There is no intent to cut cost, inventory and other expenses if the result is a process that can't meet its quality and delivery targets.

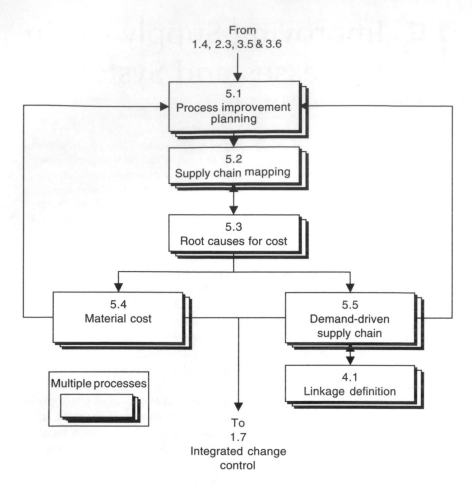

FIGURE 15.1 Improving supply chain processes and systems.

Section 4.2.1 described the market and product nuances that need to be considered. Considerations include the position of the product in its life cycle and whether the product is *innovative*, requiring a responsive supply chain, or *functional*, requiring a cost-effective supply chain.

Also, as we proceed, the reader should note that we emphasize identification and elimination of root causes for cost. With the root cause gone, the costs also vanish. Not addressing root causes brings on unintended consequences. An example is hard negotiations with suppliers to lower prices, when actions from our own company, like changing a design or specification, is the best route to lower both supplier costs and our prices.

Another common mistake is using "benchmarking" to set budgets. A typical method is ratio comparison, like so many dollars of procurement cost per dollar of material spending. This approach is generally too broad-brush to account for differences among companies and among our own company's "businesses within the business" or spheres.

The processes described here apply both to establishing new processes and improving existing ones. In many cases, the strategy for a sphere calls for brand-new processes — activities that aren't now performed in the organization or elsewhere in the supply chain. In other cases, a process may be in place but is deemed wanting in light of the supply chain strategy. Also, some processes are acknowledged by all to be broken and in need of repair. The motivators for new or improved processes can be higher performance in any measure — service, cost, quality, flexibility or a combination thereof.

Process improvement is an expansive topic. Many management and software tools are available to conduct needed analysis of the process and implement improvements. As an example, the Supply-Chain Council's SCOR reference model, described in Chapter 8, documents in great detail basic supply chain processes. SCOR also includes many best practices for employment in these processes.

Within the constraints of this book, we'll describe what we believe to be the most fundamental and indispensable approaches to improve supply chain performance. As mentioned just above, when it comes to process improvement, the greatest errors are those of omission, because Chapter 12, 13 and 14 processes are ignored, not because of an absence of motivation, analytical tools or software.

Process-improvement efforts are likely to be "subprojects" within the overall supply chain project. Referring to Figure 15.1, 5.1 Process Improvement Initiation launches individual process improvement efforts, which can focus on improving an existing process or creating a new one. Supply Chain Mapping (5.2) follows this process, collecting information that puts the process under a microscope.

Process 5.3 Root Causes for Cost seeks out the real cost drivers based on information from the mapping exercise. This approach is advanced to the reader because too few efforts really address root causes. Too many companies pursue "results," not causes. Examples of pursuing results include reduction in cost categories like inventory or labor. Such fixes become band-aids, effective for only a short time. Failure to address root causes results in long-term futility.

From root causes the processes then branch into 5.4 Material Cost and 5.5 Demand-Driven Supply Chain. These processes implement actions that evolve from root cause identification. Process 5.4, as the name implies, looks for solutions related to material cost like design specification, material used, lack of commonality in components and tolerances. These interventions require support from our own company's engineering function.

The "demand-driven supply chain" is a label originated by the author's company, CGR, and applies to operations associated with the supply chain and captured in tools like SCOR. Process 5.5, addressing the demand-driven supply chain, covers operating activities including manufacturing, distribution, production control, procurement and inventory management. The "demand-driven" name embodies what is most likely a universal vision — to make supply chain decisions with "perfect" information being available in the form of actual end-user consumption.

The demand-driven supply chain is the tightly linked chain where demand signals from end-users are instantly transmitted throughout the chain. Of course, this is an ideal. Many fall far short of the ideal, as related by Dr. Hau Lee of Stanford. He uses the term "bullwhip effect" to describe situations where level end-user demand, when translated by upstream human or automated decisions, produces wide swings in production.

However, we give our process the "demand-driven" label since such a chain should be the goal of supply chain designers. Other labels applied that have the same or similar meanings include "synchronized" and "lean." The supply chain process design teams should examine the potential of each supply chain to be demand-driven, determining the gap in the current operations and then systematically closing the gap.

Abetting the demand-driven supply chain are links among partners along the chain. Process 4.1 Linkage Definition defines those links for any particular supply chain. The "4" indicates this process is tied to our SCM *Task 4. Managing Supply Chain Information.* The links invariably involve the passing of data, so linkage definition is an important competency for handling information flow. However, other features of the linkage could be captured in the process. Examples include transportation, forms of collaboration, face-to-face meetings and planning for supply chain exceptions called "events."

Supply chain practitioners are awash in sales pitches for "linkage solutions." They exist for both material improvements and for implementing the demand-driven supply chain. Section 4.5 describes how three large e-commerce companies cope with the deluge. Their method, making a list of process requirements as a screen, is consistent with the philosophy used here.

The tables in this chapter and the glossary also list many terms that have proliferated around information technology links. Most of these solutions are expensive. More perniciously, however, they can bring on complacency through the illusion that something is being done to improve the process. But, without a strategy or knowledge of root causes, that something may not be the right thing. Chapter 9 recounted the root causes for technology failures. It is fervently hoped that those who use the disciplines in this book will sidestep the potential disasters that might lurk.

Chapter 11, as illustrated in Figure 11.2, described four phases for an SCM project. Process improvements covered by this process fall chiefly into the last two of four phases — short term improvement and long term improvement. Processes described in this chapter will note this division in anticipation that some process improvements will be achieved in the short term while some will require more time. It is often the short-term improvements that managements look to for financing the longer-term ones. In applying the concept of process-centered management, cleaning up the existing process and organization can be a short-term measure. A system to further enhance the processes might be a long-term initiative.

15.1 PROCESS IMPROVEMENT INITIATION (5.1)

Table 15.1 summarizes this process. There will likely be multiple process improvements in a single supply chain effort. Many will justify the *project* or *subproject* label. That is, they are significant enough to warrant being managed as independent efforts using project management knowledge and practice. Since we are considering our overall supply chain effort to be a project, we will refer to each separate process improvement effort as a subproject.

TABLE 15.1
Process Improvement Initiation (5.1)

5.1.1 Inputs	5.1 Process Improvement Initiation — 5.1.2 Process Elements		Initiating/Planning/Controlling Process — 5.1.3 Outputs
Activity System Design (1.4)	Process definition	Initiate and plan supply chain processes implementation and improvements by sphere. Set priorities for implementation. Confirm staff deployment for improvement projects. Coordinate efforts with project phasing from the Project Plan (Table 12.2).	**Process Improvement Initiation** Charter Elements (Table 12.1) Project Plan Elements (Table 12.2)
Implemented Organization Plan (2.3)			
Multicompany Project Staffing Requirements (3.4)			
Partner Business Arrangements (3.5)	Approaches and techniques	Cost analysis. Customer priorities. Competitive analysis. Project management knowledge and practice. Project progress reporting. Earned value measures (See Section 7.3.7 and Table 7.2).	Subproject plan changes Change requests
Staffed SCM Projects, Subprojects, or Project Extensions (3.6)	PM shortcomings addressed	This multicompany commitment requires top management support for the effort. It will also deploy needed skills to projects, reducing the cost of failure. Process improvement planning will test the "process discipline" component of project management maturity. Multiple projects must be coordinated across companies.	
	SCM maturity	Broader scope process projects are indicative of Stages IV and V of the SCM maturity model.	

(continued)

TABLE 15.1 (Continued)
Process Improvement Initiation (5.1)

		5.1 Process Improvement Initiation			Initiating/Planning/ Controlling Process
Progress Reports from Process Improvement Subprojects (5.4 and 5.5)	Terminology	– Business process reengineering	– Category management		
		– Chief process improvement officer (CPIO)	– Discounted cash flow		
		– Portfolio, project portfolio management (PPM)	– Quality function deployment		
		– Quality threshold	– Specification		
		– Target costing	– Yield management		
	Stakeholders	Participating internal functions and partners are stakeholders. Any function can participate in multiple projects. The ability of partnerships to implement may be the limiting factor in the improvement achieved.			
		The supply chain project management should administer the process. The company steering committee should have the ultimate responsibility for process success.			
	SCOR support	SCOR provides a common vocabulary for multicompany efforts. Process improvement teams use SCOR process elements to define project scope and SCOR metrics to quantify objectives. Depicting processes as threads is also a potential communication device.			

Departing from PMBOK conventions, we identify this process with three project management process groups: initiating, controlling and planning. In other words, it is an "integrated" process incorporating several elements.

Process 5.1 plays the role of "traffic cop" at a busy intersection when the traffic lights don't work. The traffic cop must decide when to initiate, or turn on traffic movement in any particular direction. He or she must also decide when to stop flow in that direction or divert the flow, being mindful of the buildup in traffic at the intersection. This requires decisions in all three areas, initiating, controlling and planning, to balance the workload with the organization's ability to handle it. This is an important function, needed to avoid taking on too many projects or the wrong projects.

Appendix B2 recommends assigning it to the project manager or project office.

15.1.1 INPUTS TO PROCESS IMPROVEMENT INITIATION (5.1.1)

This process assures that the company manages process improvement in a disciplined way. The approach urges project managers to make no distinction between an IT project and any other operational improvement initiative. This philosophy was introduced in Section 3.6, describing process-centered management, and reinforced in Chapter 9. Inputs to the process, as shown in Table 15.1, should provide the following needs for a go-ahead:

- *Activity System Design (1.4)* identifies conceptual designs of needed processes.
- *Implemented Organization Plan (2.3)* puts key people in place who will operate the new process. Sponsors for the effort and the process design team should come from this group.
- *Multicompany Project Staffing Requirements (3.4)* brings needed resources from outside the company. In particular, this assures there is assigned partner staff, where needed, to support the process improvment effort.
- *Partner Business Arrangements (3.5)* define business rules for the partnership. Agreements should be in place to govern the process improvement.
- *Staffed SCM Projects, Subprojects, or Project Extensions (3.6)* is a control process that tracks progress in making assignments. Its outputs signal when partners are ready to proceed.

The process synthesizes these inputs into a process improvement initiation document that charters and plans the effort. The process also takes feedback from ongoing process improvement subprojects. This input will cause adjustments in plans for the portfolio of process development and improvement subprojects.

15.1.2 PROCESS ELEMENTS FOR PROCESS IMPROVEMENT INITIATION (5.1.2)

The process will be continuous while process improvements continue, tracking the portfolio of ongoing subprojects. It will also have an intermittent element each time a process improvement is kicked off. Each supply chain project will be different. The number of discrete subprojects will depend on the number of spheres, requirement for enabling processes and management's desire for overall control. An organization desiring close control would tend to have many smaller, narrower subprojects. Looser control would produce fewer, larger projects.

15.1.2.1   Process Definition for Process Improvement Initiation

Principal responsibilities for executing the process include the following:

- Track progress made in developing deliverables, inputs in Table 15.1, needed to charter the improvement subproject.
- Monitor the workload generated by subprojects and their progress. Avoid overloading the company and their partners. Don't "under-load" them either.
- When incoming deliverable "packages" for a process are complete, develop the charter and project plan for the subproject. Cluster like projects together.
- Launch projects at the appropriate time. This time will avoid conflicts between projects for staff, budgets and management attention.
- Provide inputs to process *1.7 Integrated Change Control* regarding needed changes.
- Confirm budgets for implementation. Use the company approval process to gain budget approvals. Budgets can be quite large if major expenditures for information technology are contemplated.

15.1.2.2   Approaches and Techniques for Process Improvement Initiation

Techniques listed in Table 15.1 address the need to coordinate several subprojects and play the role of "dispatcher" for a complex undertaking. Work described in prior chapters should assure that resources are available. However, plan changes are inevitable. Cost and benefit analysis will help set priorities. Similarly, customer priorities may make a project that saves less more important. Intelligence on competitors' initiatives may also cause a shifting of priorities.

Feedback of progress toward milestones and achievement of results will also lead to changes in plans. Project management measurements, such as earned value, may quantify progress measures.

15.1.2.3   Project Management Shortcomings Addressed by Process Improvement Initiation

Initiation of each subproject should reflect the intent of the multicompany steering committee. So any project that reaches this stage should have internal senior management support and, to the extent partners are involved, multicompany support.

Combining IT and process improvement should also address both misunderstood technology and technology capabilities of partners, as described in Chapter 9. The first downfall can be sidestepped by closely weaving the technology requirement into the process improvement. By signing off on the project, one's own company and its partners are confirming that the technology choices match their capabilities.

Project management maturity is advanced by the process discipline provided by this step. To the extent there are many subprojects, central control enforces a singular methodology. In fact, without such a singular methodology, it may be impossible to manage the complexity involved in executing the subproject portfolio.

15.1.2.4 SCM Maturity for Process Improvement Initiation

Achieving Stages IV and V SCM maturity for Tasks 4 and 5, as described in Table 10.2, requires multicompany efforts. In particular, working jointly to reduce material costs is a signal of Stage V maturity. The presence of several multicompany subprojects signals achievement of this level.

15.1.2.5 Terminology for Process Improvement Initiation

Terms in Table 15.1 relate to methods for sorting and selecting subprojects for implementation. The chief process improvement officer (CPIO) term is relatively new. If there were ever a roadmap for such a position, the processes described in this book would be a good place to start.

15.1.2.6 Stakeholders for Process Improvement Initiation

The supply chain project manager or project office should administer the process. Any function involved in the project — whether in your company or a partner's — is a stakeholder. Other stakeholders include outsiders like software vendors, system integrators and consultants. These parties may constitute the process design team. The company steering committee should retain ultimate responsibility for the process. Some processes may involve outsourcing supply chain activities to service provider companies.

15.1.2.7 SCOR Support for Process Improvement Initiation

The SCOR model was originated to facilitate communications among supply chain partners, so providing a common vocabulary of supply chain terms is a natural role for SCOR when partners are involved. The SCOR structure also identifies supply chain process elements and related metrics. These are useful for defining process boundaries, as-is performance and to-be objectives.

15.1.3 OUTPUTS FROM PROCESS IMPROVEMENT INITIATION (5.1.3)

The output includes a charter and subproject plan to move ahead. This plan, like the supply chain project plan developed in process 1.2, should include both supply chain and project management elements. The following is a list of project management elements, including several from Table 12.2:

- Role of the subproject within the overall supply chain project
- Approval to proceed with the subproject
- Work breakdown structure describing deliverables
- Activities that must be done in the project and their sequencing
- Subproject phasing and schedule — a particularly important component when large expenditures are required
- Network diagrams showing interrelationships of activities
- Cost baseline for project budgeting
- Process Design Team assignments from one's own company and participating partners
- Scope management plan including controlling processes

Two control outputs from this process are changes to the overall supply chain project and to process improvement subprojects that are already under way. The former goes back to process 1.7 Integrated Change Control.

15.2 SUPPLY CHAIN MAPPING (5.2)

After initiation, a logical first step is to "map" the process. We've said that the process under consideration can be either new or one that's already in place. Mapping in the first case is a design effort, describing in detail how the process should operate. In the case of an existing process, presumably we seek process changes to meet new requirements or to improve on old ones to be more competitive. In either case, mapping provides the detail needed to make design decisions.

Mapping, summarized in Table 15.2, documents the process and focuses attention on areas for further action. In the context used here, mapping is broadly defined. We include documentation of customer requirements, product structure and all elements of outbound and return flow, including the physical, information and financial components.

The deliverables for process mapping described here are not exhaustive. Practitioners should add or subtract items as needed for a particular effort. Also, many of the suggested flowcharting components do assume some degree of partner cooperation. In the event that cooperation isn't forthcoming, it may be impossible to gather needed information. However, if the information is important, one shouldn't hesitate to make estimates of partner costs, technology employed, lead-times, or quality parameters as warranted.

In Figure 15.1, the link between the mapping and root cause identification is two-headed. This means the project team should augment initial documentation if initial mapping uncovered only symptoms, not root causes.

15.2.1 INPUTS TO SUPPLY CHAIN MAPPING (5.2.1)

The charter and project plan from process 5.1 define the scope of the process for mapping and lay down goals for completing the mapping. Each process will support

TABLE 15.2
Supply Chain Mapping (5.2)

5.2.1 Inputs		5.2 Supply Chain Mapping 5.2.2 Process Elements	ExecutingProcess 5.2.3 Outputs
Process Improvement Initiation (5.1)	Process definition	Characterize each authorized process as defined in the process improvement initiation documentation.	*Process Analysis* *Markets:* Customers served Distribution channels Customer requirements/ performance gaps *Products:* Product descriptions/ structure Product profitability
	Approaches and techniques	Cost and lead-time tracking. Functional flowcharts ("swim lane" format). Activity-based costing. Constraint analysis. Product structure (VAT). Supply chain surveys. Benchmarking.	
	PM shortcomings addressed	Developing a standard for characterizing a process and its effectiveness should be a component of Level 3 singular methodology for project management.	
	SCM maturity	Skill in assessing processes is fundamental to success in creating new value (SCM Task 1) and reducing supply chain cost (SCM Tasks 4 and 5)	

(continued)

**TABLE 15.2 (Continued)
Supply Chain Mapping (5.2)**

5.2 Supply Chain Mapping

			Executing Process
Terminology		– Batch-and-queue system	Materials consumed
– Activity Based Costing	– Assemble-to-order	– Cellular manufacturing	SKU ABC analysis
– Capacity strategy	– Cash-to-cash cycle time	– Constraint	*Operations:*
– Channel	– Configuration	– Cost of quality (COQ)	Flowcharts
– Control points	– Cost driver	– Cycle time	Cost/cycle time map
– C_p, C_{pk}	– Customer service ratio	– Engineer-to-order	Cost categories
– Deficiency, discrepancy	– Drumbeat	– IDEF	Quality performance
– Extended product	– Five focusing steps	– Just in Time (JIT)	Facilities/assets employed
– Implosion	– Inventory turns	– Make-to-order	Information systems support
– Key process parameter	– Lead-time	– Order penetration point	
– Make-to-stock	– MRP, MRP II	– Representative product	
– Process owner	– Quality standard	– Six sigma	
– Reverse logistics	– Seven wastes	– Statistical Process Control	
– SKU (Stockkeeping unit)	– Specification	– Transfer pricing	
– Theory of Constraints	– Throughput	– Wall-to-wall inventory	
– VAT analysis	– Velocity		
– Work in progress (WIP)			

Stakeholders   Process design teams for each process from functions and companies involved in the process map the supply chain. Employees who contribute to the assessment of the process are also stakeholders.

SCOR support   Process element descriptions in SCOR provide best practice suggestions. Both executing and enable processes should be evaluated.

an activity that in turn supports a sphere-centered strategy for competing. Section 4.2.3.2 describes the approach to developing these strategies.

15.2.2 PROCESS ELEMENTS FOR SUPPLY CHAIN MAPPING (5.2.2)

This process gathers information about the process. As much as possible, it should rely on existing documentation. The elements suggested here enable an organization to identify the process improvements available by applying a number of technical approaches. These include process streamlining by removing low-value activities, value engineering, changes in product specifications and design, information links between partners, new performance metrics and organization changes.

15.2.2.1 Process Definition for Supply Chain Mapping

This process sets the vision for new or reengineered processes based on information gained through mapping. Its purpose is to gather sufficient information to determine root causes for potential deficiencies in an existing process or new process design. This work doesn't design the solution; that is done in downstream project processes. However, the ability to come up with the best solution will depend on the understanding gained here.

An important element is multicompany participation. Too often, a company pursues its initiatives with blinders on. Perspectives are limited to what's going on inside, not what is happening elsewhere in the supply chain. In the case of nonexistent processes, partner participation is even more vital, providing technical support to the team. For a new complex manufacturing process, equipment suppliers will be important contributors.

15.2.2.2 Approaches and Techniques for Supply Chain Mapping

The following tools will document the processes and analyze their potential for improvement. As stated above, a project team should add to this list or delete approaches based on the issues they face.

15.2.2.2.1 Activity-Based Costing (abc[1])

This tool is particularly useful for multicompany process analysis. It moves away from compliance-driven accounting systems that vary from partner to partner and aren't particularly helpful for process design. The technique captures all the resources required by a process, whether they are represented by traditional "direct" or "indirect" cost. The former includes items like labor and material, the latter items like capital recovery, maintenance, engineering, support, scrap and rework and administrative cost.

---

[1] Doug Hicks, one of our case-study writers, adopted the convention of using "abc" rather than ABC to describe focused use of activity-based costing for decision making. This avoids building expensive, but seldom used, activity-based accounting systems, which he calls ABC.

In essence, abc turns as many indirect and overhead costs created by a process into direct costs that vary with changes in the activity volume. The volume variable is called a *cost driver*. Examples include labor or machine hours, number of transactions or cost per time period (hour, day, month).

15.2.2.2.2 Constraint Analysis

In the theory of constraints (TOC), bottleneck operations determine the capacity of the process of which they are a part, in this case, the supply chain. A bottleneck operation warrants special attention. Expanding capacity there raises the capacity of the whole chain to produce profits for its partners. So the potential benefits, assuming the products produced by the added capacity can be sold, are magnified. This is because the operation itself may not only be more efficient but the added capacity also produces more profitable revenue. Increasing capacity elsewhere will have little effect, since these operations are not bottlenecks. Improving them produces no more supply chain capacity.

At this point, the process team should identify supply chain bottlenecks, which may be in one's own company or at a partner's operation. A good indicator is to look at lead times throughout the process. Long lead time for a component is indicative of a bottleneck in the production of that component.

15.2.2.2.3 Cost Improvement Categories

Different cost categories are amenable to different techniques for performance improvement, including cost reduction. Table 15.3 lists categories for cataloging activity-based costs. The broad categories include labor, capital and material components. Labor comes in four forms, as shown in the table. Each requires a different approach for improvement. However, without knowing how much activity cost there is in each category, it will be difficult to set priorities and identify root causes in the next process.

Fixed costs include both real life depreciation and required return on investment. "Real life" is not the accounting life span of the asset but the period that the asset will be productive. This is often much shorter than the physical life due to obsolescence of the asset. Even though your 3-year-old computer still works as well as it did when purchased, it's obsolete because it's too slow.

Purchased material items are another example where approaches must differ. We have much more control over subcontracted material that we design ourselves or with a partner than we do over commodity material that is widely available. We might turn to bidding in exchanges for commodities. On the other hand, we may want to limit the number of suppliers for subcontracted material in order to collaborate closely to reduce cost.

15.2.2.2.4 Flowcharts

Flowcharts are always useful for displaying a process. Figure 15.2 is an example. The figure uses a "swim lane" format, familiar to many practitioners. This format shows the path of a component or product along a supply chain with four companies and seven work centers. At the top of the flowchart is the cycle time in weeks, with individual work center and cumulative figures. Along the bottom is similar information for costs.

TABLE 15.3
Cost Improvement Categories

Work Force Costs

Factory direct labor	Labor that "touches" the product. Often has assigned work measurement standards.
Factory indirect labor	Labor that doesn't have a work measurement standard but supports the direct labor component.
Clerical/administrative/sales	Secretaries, accounting staff, receptionists, clerks and sales administration.
Technical/professional	Design engineers, system engineers, procurement staff and white collar functions.
Fixed Costs	Annualized costs of capacity including depreciation and capital cost — generally plant and equipment. Other fixed expenses, including inventory.

Purchased Item costs:

Services	Accounting, consulting and engineering support.
Subcontracted material	Material made to the company's specification. This category is normally susceptible to cost reduction.
Commodity material	Material bought by many companies. There is normally a "market" price for commodity material. Not considered susceptible to cost reduction.

Time (wks)	5	10	5	2	13	15	15	10
	5	15	20	22	35	50	65	75

Company 1
Work center A
Work center B
Work center C

Company 2

Company 3
Work center A
Work center B

Company 4
Work center A
Work center B

Cost (%)	20	5	5	10	5	10	15	30
	20	25	30	40	45	55	70	100

FIGURE 15.2 Flowcharting the supply chain.

Such a display focuses attention on high cost and long cycle time steps. Can the side trip to Company 2 be avoided? Why is Company 3 taking so long to process our work? Do we really need 10 weeks to get the product to the customer? Why is that customer delivery process, at 30% of cost, so expensive? Can we reduce the cost of Company 1's Work Center A? This was the kind of analysis Herman Miller used to design its supply chain, as described in Section 4.2.3.2.

A process design team may face a decision regarding the level of detail required to document its processes. A process that produces more than 100 components using a common process does not require 100 flowcharts. The use of a representative part chosen from the 100 will be sufficient.

15.2.2.2.5   Product Structures (VAT)

The product structure is also important to the analysis of root causes for cost. Another model from the theory of constraints, called VAT analysis, reflects how materials are transformed into final products. A "V" product has a few component materials (at the bottom of the V) that can be turned into many end products (at the top of the V). A pharmaceutical company manufacturing a pill could have multiple end-item SKUs. For a single tablet, these SKUs could include different bottle sizes and country-specific labeling for global distribution. Some companies also incorporate storage locations into their SKU numbering, leading to even more numbers for the same physical product.

An "A" structure is the opposite of the "V" structure. With the A structure, many components are assembled into a single product. An aircraft is a good example; thousands of part numbers and millions of individual parts make up one deliverable product. The "T" product line uses common components or assemblies to make a few finished products. A Mexican restaurant is an example. Beans, rice, tacos, chicken, pork and beef combine to make many menu items.

The VAT approach should cause the process design team to look downstream for "V" product improvements and upstream for "A" and "T" products. For example, product structure is at the heart of postponement strategies. Postponement, for a "V" structure, delays production commitments to more closely track production to actual demand, a goal of the demand-driven supply chain. A company may also have products with "A" structures that can be turned into "T" products through a part commonality strategy.

15.2.2.2.6   Surveys and Benchmarking

Surveys and benchmarking are also ways to assess supply chain process effectiveness. Surveys can target respondents upstream or downstream in the chain. If partner participation has not been sought or has not been forthcoming after requests, there may be no choice but to use surveys outside the partner base to gather needed information. Benchmarking looks for best practices for targeted operations from companies in any industry. Insights provided include the following:

- What you do and don't do well as a supplier or a customer
- How you stack up to your peers or competitors
- Where you might add more value for your customers

		Suppliers		
		A	B	C
Products/SKUs	A	Develop partnerships *Negotiate consigned/ demand-driven supply chain (synchronized)* *Reduce lead-times Cost reduction,incentives*	Add business *Negotiate consigned/ demand-driven supply chain* *Reduce lead times*	Focus on "A" SKUs Move B and C items to other suppliers *Reduce lead times*
	B	Develop partnerships *Pursue supplier- managed inventory*	Add business Move to distributor	Find A or B supplier Eliminate SKU
	C	Consolidate demand *Apply activity costing Give more"C" SKUs*	Eliminate SKU Consolidate demand Substitute SKUs Move to distributor	Eliminate SKU Consolidate demand Substitute SKUs Move to distributor

FIGURE 15.3 Supplier/SKU analysis.

- Methods your partners are using for collaboration
- Actions you should take to make your suppliers' lives easier and lower your cost
- "Best practice" objectives for process performance that you might adopt

15.2.2.2.7 Supplier/SKU ABC Analysis

We talked about activity-based costing, or abc, above. This acronym is popular; ABC is also a term, defined further in the glossary, used in inventory analysis. "A" inventory items, or SKUs, are the top few (10–20%) that make up the largest share of material spending (in the range of 50–70%). "C" items are reversed — the many items that account for a small share of material spending. "B" items are in between.

Dave Malmberg of CGR Management Consultants recommends applying ABC simultaneously to both SKUs and suppliers. Figure 15.3 illustrates the approach and suggests strategies for different categories. For example, for "A" suppliers providing A SKUs, the figure first suggests partnering. This recommendation is in plain type, indicating it is a supplier strategy that would apply to all the SKUs provided by that supplier. The three other recommendations — instituting a demand-driven supply chain, lead-time reduction and cost reduction with incentives — are in italics to indicate they are SKU strategies to be applied on an item-by-item basis. These actions could follow an agreement to work together.

At the other end of the spectrum, the box for "C" suppliers and SKUs, an SKU strategy might seek elimination of the SKU. A corresponding supplier strategy could shift that business to a distributor who supplies many purchased items, in effect outsourcing the costs of administering and stocking these SKUs.

15.2.2.3 Project Management Shortcomings Addressed by
Supply Chain Mapping

In the event of multiple processes for development or improvement over multiple companies, using common methods of process documentation is consistent with a singular methodology for project management. "Erratic" and inconsistent methods will create confusion, blunting the ability to achieve objectives.

15.2.2.4 SCM Maturity for Supply Chain Mapping

With regard to SCM maturity, mapping is an important opportunity to test the strength of collaborative relationships, described in Chapter 10. Such relationships represent Stage III and above for *Task 3. Forging Supply Chain Partnerships*. For *Task 5. Making Money from the Supply Chain*, such collaboration is indicative of Stage 5.

15.2.2.5 Terminology for Supply Chain Mapping

Terms selected for the process, defined in the glossary, are useful for process documentation. They include measures, techniques for documentation and common features found in supply chain processes.

15.2.2.6 Stakeholders for Supply Chain Mapping

A process design team should map the processes under the direction of the multi-company or company steering committee. Stakeholders in the process include any involved function. These stakeholders, to the degree it is possible, should contribute to mapping and review its results. Stakeholders are also a rich source of commentary on the effectiveness of processes.

15.2.2.7 SCOR Support for Supply Chain Mapping

SCOR provides a format for mapping in the form of threads. The thread technique, described in Section 8.2.2, is an additional way, beyond the swim lane format, to depict supply chain process steps.

15.2.3 OUTPUTS FROM SUPPLY CHAIN MAPPING (5.2.3)

The output format, it is suggested here, can follow the markets-products-operations standard used to define spheres. This is a useful way to collect and present a large amount of information to be used to determine root causes for cost — whether the process is an existing one or a new one.

15.2.3.1 Customer Documentation

A beginning should include the customers or customer segments served. This should indicate the distribution of sales by customer or segment. This level should be expressed in terms of revenue and unit volume. Documentation should also identify end-user distribution channels. From documentation gathered earlier in the project, customer requirements should be documented and performance gaps estimated. The format choice should consider the SCOR approach (Section 4.2.3.1) or Quality Function Deployment (QFD). A complete description of QFD is available in *The QFD Handbook*.[2]

15.2.3.2   Product Documentation

Each sphere represents a product, several products, or one or more product groups. These products include both the physical and extended product. For cost reduction, the information gathered about products will yield opportunities related to the design of the physical product, potential postponement strategies and other measures like material substitution.

Product Descriptions/Structure. This deliverable should describe products in the sphere's portfolio. That description should include the VAT structure.

Product Profitability. This information identifies priorities for improvement. "Profitability" is the product of unit margin and volume. High profitability products might be high priority for implementing new capabilities; low profitability might indicate the need for operating improvements or dropping the product. Profitability data also indicates whether the product is *innovative* or *functional*, using terms introduced in Chapter 4.

Materials Consumed. Material documentation should include the ABC analysis. Surveys may also have uncovered other opportunities to reduce cost in the bill of materials purchased by the company.

15.2.3.3   Operations Documentation

Table 15.2 lists some deliverables in this category. Flowcharts, a cost/cycle time map and cost categories are described above. *Quality performance* can include the cost of quality, first pass yields on processes and individual yields along the supply chain. Low yields at a bottleneck deserve special attention. Also, an upstream process may be a bottleneck by virtue of low yields downstream. In other words, to produce 1 pound of product for sale, we have to launch 2 pounds at the front end of the supply chain. The root cause for a bottleneck at the front end is not necessarily lack of capacity but poor yields downstream. Perhaps the problem can be solved by improving those yields, reducing capital investment for more equipment and saving money for materials lost to scrap.

Facilities and *assets* employed is an inventory of investments supporting the process. Information *systems support* should list the hardware and software in use by the process. Particularly germane to this process are the computerized links between partners.

15.3   ROOT CAUSES FOR COST (5.3)

This process, summarized in Table 15.4, is separated from the collection of data about the process (5.2) and execution of changes to the process (5.4 and 5.5). The reason for this separation is to stress the value in agreeing to root causes for process shortfalls. As Chapter 9 indicated, things are not always what they seem and we have to dig deep to get to root causes. This may require people to work differently.

TABLE 15.4
Root Causes For Cost (5.3)

		5.3 Root Causes for Cost	Executing Process
5.3.1 Inputs		**5.3.1 Process Elements**	**5.3.3 Outputs**
Process Analysis (5.2)	Process definition	Identify the root cause for costs inherent in each process examined. "Cost" here is interpreted broadly. Reducing cost by diminishing service to uncompetitive levels doesn't count as a legitimate cost reduction.	*Process Root Cause Identification and To-Be Process Design*
		Root causes, listed in Section 4.6, include lack of clarity over costs, process variability, product design, poorly executed or nonexistent information sharing, weak links and unintended circumstances.	Root causes addressed
	Approaches and techniques	Ask "why" five times. Spend analysis. Partner meeting/task forces. Gap analysis. Demand-driven potential assessment.	To-Be (short-term)
	PM shortcomings addressed	Analysis of root causes will reduce the risk of applying the wrong solution to improve the process.	To-Be (long-term)
	SCM maturity	Understanding root causes will help preserve the collaborative relationship in the supply chain. This is particularly important if one's own company holds economic power over the partner.	Action Steps
	Terminology	– 5S – Cause and effect diagram – Operational excellence (OE) – Safety factor, safety stock – Total Productive Maintenance – Toyota Production System – ABCD analysis – Economic Order Quantity – Optimization – Total Cost of Ownership (TCO) – Total Quality Management – Variable costing	
	Stakeholders	A process design team should identify root causes. Process improvements involve considerable investments in time and money. Executives approving these efforts will need assurances that the correct solution is being proposed. The multicompany steering committee should agree to the identified root causes and the to-be design.	
	SCOR support	Once a root cause is identified, SCOR lists best practices that might address those causes.	

The process uses documentation from process 5.2 Supply Chain Mapping. The two-headed arrow in Figure 15.1 symbolizes the potential for back-and-forth movement of information between the processes. If initial mapping data isn't sufficient to identify root causes, then more mapping-type investigation may be necessary.

The process output is root cause identification and a to-be design. This may not be a perfect, ultimate design — a version we call the greenfield vision. However, it will be something capable of achievement and it will address root causes. The to-be, as explained later, can have two forms — a short-term version without major systems and facility changes and a long-term version with those system and facility features included. These correspond to Phases 3 and 4 in our generic phases for the supply chain project.

15.3.1 INPUTS TO ROOT CAUSES FOR COST (5.3.1)

The *Process Analysis* from process 5.2 is the principal input. An exhaustive documentation like that recommended should contain plenty of clues identifying root causes. However, it is important to get agreement from supply chain partners that these are problems worth solving. The approach is just as applicable to new processes as it is to processes that are not in place. For processes that are totally new to the company or supply chain, the organization must understand the critical drivers for a successful process.

15.3.2 PROCESS ELEMENTS FOR ROOT CAUSES FOR COST (5.3.2)

Identifying root causes and getting agreement is a mixture of art and science. It requires analytical skills, process design ability and persuasion. Analytical skills are needed to dissect the process mapping information. The design skills are needed to translate specifications into short-term and long-term process designs. Persuasion is required to enlist stakeholders so that recommended changes will work.

15.3.2.1 Process Definition for Root Causes for Cost

The process begins with data on the process from the Process Analysis. The same people, presumably in the process design team, who collect the information can also flesh out the root causes. Once root causes are identified and agreed to, a "specification" should set criteria for the new process design. There are two downstream processes: 5.4 Material Cost and 5.5 Demand-Driven Supply Chain. There are two processes identified because the nature of change efforts for the two categories is different.

15.3.2.2 Approaches and Techniques for Root Causes for Cost

Approaches and techniques are geared to getting approval for moving ahead with implementation. This requires laying out the path to realization of the process changes.

15.3.2.2.1 Gap Analysis[2]

Figure 15.4 shows the relationship between elements in a gap analysis. The gap referred to is between today's existing situation and where one would ideally like

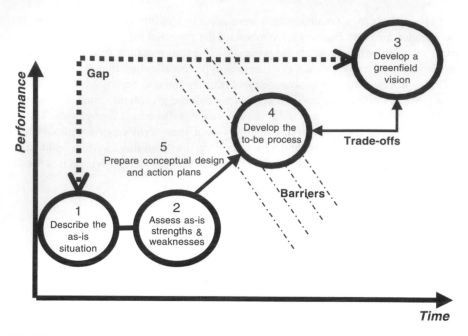

FIGURE 15.4 Gap analysis.

the process to be. This is called a "greenfield" vision and is what you would do if you could start from scratch. If you really are starting from scratch, steps 1 and 2 in Figure 15.4 can be skipped. Elements of the greenfield vision include the following:

- A revised process flow
- Organization structure to support the process
- Required systems changes
- Other infrastructure support (facilities, equipment)
- Measures for the redesigned process
- Implementation cost and benefit estimates

15.3.2.2.2 Demand-Driven Supply Chain Assessment

This assessment tool was developed by CGR Management Consultants and reported in late 2002.[3] The technique establishes the design team's assessment of the potential for a supply chain to be demand-driven. Figure 15.5 and Table 15.5 illustrate the technique. Figure 15.5 shows points along the supply chain where decisions are made regarding replenishment of end-user stock, manufacturing of the product and ordering of raw materials. Table 15.5 documents the basis for each decision, identifying whether the basis is actual demand or a forecast of demand. For the example in Table 15.5, there are eight decisions points. Only two are demand-driven, making the existing demand-driven percentage 25%.

A second step is to assess whether a decision based on forecasts can be converted to a decision based on actual demand. Once this is done we know the potential for our supply chain to be demand-driven. This implies action plans to convert forecast-

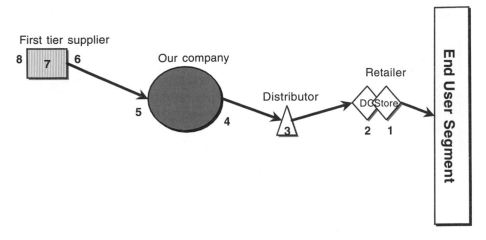

FIGURE 15.5 Demand-driven assessment.

driven steps to demand-driven ones. In Table 15.5, the process design team would have to look at each decision point and assess how it might be converted. The analysis might decide to start at the end-user and convert decision points 6, 7 and 8. This would raise the demand-driven percentage in the supply chain to 62%, the potential for the chain to be demand-driven.

15.3.2.2.3 Spend Analysis

This name pretty much explains what has to be done. The spend analysis should profile spending by both supplier and commodity or SKU. Other categories might include country, lead-time information, a measure of engineering content and a history of prices paid. It should include the purchased item categories shown in Table 15.3.

15.3.2.3 Project Management Shortcomings Addressed by Root Causes for Cost

Misunderstood technology, as described in Chapter 9, is the most important project management shortcoming addressed. Unless the entire project team, including key partners, accurately identifies root causes, the wrong problem may be solved.

15.3.2.4 SCM Maturity for Root Causes for Cost

Identifying root cause is an important step to achieving Stage II maturity. Organization communication that seeks employee support is more credible if the audience believes that the homework has been done. Few want to expend precious time and other resources on a wild goose chase. Such efforts sap an organization's ability to respond to real threats and opportunities.

TABLE 15.5
Assessing Demand-Driven Potential

1	2	3	4	5	6	7	8
Level	Entities	Step	Decision(s) Required	Frequency	Basis of Decision	Responsibility	Forecast or Demand-Driven
1	Retail chain	Order: Store level replenishment	Refill stock to target levels	Daily	Point of sale system data	Automatic. Set by chain replenishment system.	Demand-Driven
2		Order: Chain distribution center replenishment	Reorder predetermined batch quantity	Weekly	Reorder point set in system by line item	Automated system. Buyer reviews by exception.	Demand-Driven
3	Distributor	Order: Manufacturer warehouse replenishment	Order predetermined batch quantity	Bi-weekly	Reorder point and forecast	Demand manager using forecast. Review by exception.	Forecast
4	Manufacturer	Produce: Manufacturer	To make or not to make a batch on fixed schedule	Monthly	Orders from warehouse	Factory production planner Manufacturing manager	Forecast
5		Order: Manufacturer raw material	Order predetermined batch quantity	Quarterly	Sales forecast	Commodity manager/buyer Sales department	Forecast
6	Manufacturer's supplier	Order: Supplier warehouse replenishment	Batch size based on forecast	Quarterly	Manufacturer forecast	Commodity planner	Forecast
7		Produce: Supplier	Batch size based on forecast	Quarterly	Sales forecast and production plan	Factory production planner Manufacturing manager	Forecast
8		Order: Supplier material replenishment	Batch size based on forecast	Quarterly	Sales forecast	Commodity manager	Forecast

15.3.2.5 Terminology for Root Causes for Cost

The terms listed in Table 15.4 point to methodologies for performing the analysis.

15.3.2.6 Stakeholders for Root Causes for Cost

Few executives on the company and multicompany steering committees will authorize an effort unless they are confident that the solutions proposed are correct. The design team assigned to the process should identify the root causes and present the case to the multicompany steering committee.

15.3.2.7 SCOR Support for Root Causes for Cost

The process design team can use SCOR process elements to identify and isolate root causes. The elements have best processes that might be root cause solutions. At the time of writing, SCOR had some limitations. Notably, SCOR did not include design processes, and many root causes do lie in product design.

15.3.3 OUTPUTS FROM ROOT CAUSES FOR COST (5.3.3)

The output is called *Process Root Cause Identification and To-Be Process Design.* That documentation provides a going-forward plan for implementation. Elements include the following:

- Root causes addressed. These will likely fall in the categories identified in Section 4.6. Those related to processes are lack of clarity over costs, process variability, poorly executed or nonexistent information sharing, weak links and unintended circumstances. Product design is related to design and material acquisition.
- "To-be" scenarios for the short and long term. Short-term improvements are implemented in whatever time horizon, probably less than 2 years, has been defined as short term. These are improvements that can be achieved inside the current systems environment and facilities configuration. Long-term changes require systems and facilities changes. Product design changes may be either short- or long-term.
- Action steps answer what's next for implementation. Measures related to material constitute work done in Process 5.4 Material Cost. Measure for process improvements constitute work for Process 5.5 Demand-Driven Supply Chain.

15.4 MATERIAL COST (5.4)

This process focuses on work with upstream partners to improve service and quality and, if possible, lower costs. Table 15.6 summarizes the process. In many companies, such activity requires a radical change in mindset. Many people are not at all willing or even able to work in cooperative fashion with suppliers. An article in the Council of Logistics Management's *Journal of Business Logistics* describes two models attributed to Sam Walton, founder of Wal-Mart, for collaboration between supply chain partners.[4] In a "diamond" relationship, partners are connected across a broad front. The interface is at the middle of the diamond where the bases of two triangles meet. The broad front includes not just procurement but also engineering, finance, marketing, production and other functions. The reverse is the "bowtie." In this model, partners are connected at a point; there is only one connection, probably purchasing, that links partners.

Relative power between partners is another factor setting the stage for partner collaboration. If one partner is vastly more powerful than the other, collaboration turns to dictation. Relatively equal partners may find collaboration an economic necessity and probably much easier. Our following process description assumes that both sides of the link are motivated toward mutual benefits and are willing to pursue the diamond model.

15.4.1 INPUTS TO MATERIAL COST (5.4.1)

Process 5.3 produces a deliverable, *Process Root Cause Identification and To-Be Process Design*, which includes deliverable Action Items for implementation. The short- and long-term to-be describe what is hoped for in terms of improvement. Identified root causes will shape the implementation. Table 15.7 lists some examples of symptoms, root causes and their indicated actions. Symptoms become apparent in Process 5.3 Supply Chain Mapping; root causes are identified in Process 5.4 Root Cause for Cost.

15.4.2 PROCESS ELEMENTS FOR MATERIAL COST (5.4.2)

This process reserves a window in the supply chain project for a broad range of measures. As the examples in Table 15.7 illustrate, a number of different measures could be brought to the table with a supplier. This is particularly true if the company buys or makes engineered products.

15.4.2.1 Process Definition for Material Cost

Table 15.6, under Process Definition, lists some of the solutions that might be pursued to reduce material cost. Solution selection will depend on accurate identification of root causes for cost. That is abetted by supplier cooperation in mapping processes and identifying root causes.

15.4.2.2 Approaches and Techniques for Material Cost

The choice of technique will likely depend on relative partner power. For equal partners, joint teams, SCOR-type collaboration and cost–benefit sharing are more likely. Unilateral actions include eliminating a supplier through supplier base consolidation and dropping unprofitable products to avoid the related headaches.

Engineering changes address key characteristics, value engineering and DFA. If the supplier is responsible for design, then an inducement may be needed to affect

TABLE 15.6
Material Cost (5.4)

	5.4 Material Cost	Executing Process
5.4.1 Inputs	**5.4.2 Process Elements**	**5.4.3 Outputs**
Process Root Cause Identification and To-Be Process Design (5.3)		*Reduced Material Costs* *Project Plan Change Requests*
Process definition	Pursue improvement efforts to reduce material costs over the product's life cycle. These include design changes, quality control, value engineering, altering specified materials, standardization of components, supplier base changes, product rationalization and other measures.	
Approaches and techniques	Joint teams representing engineering, marketing and operations. Design for assembly (DFA). Key characteristic analysis. Capital investment analysis. Cost/benefit sharing. Supplier base consolidation. Partnership classification (Section 4.4.2). SCOR collaboration framework (Section 8.4). Product line rationalization.	
PM shortcomings addressed	Efforts to reduce material cost may require subprojects or entirely new projects using the singular project management methodology. Depending on their scope the efforts may be included in the overall supply chain improvement project. Multiple material cost reduction efforts increases the need for singular methodologies that benchmark best practices in the varied technical areas that can come into play in reducing material cost.	
SCM maturity	Stage V of the SCM maturity model for Task 5 requires new behaviors in most companies. However, achieving this level offers the best opportunity for achieving material cost savings in the supply chain.	
Terminology	– ABC inventory classification – Auctions on-line – Certified supplier – Consignment – Integrated supply – Price-taker – Strategic sourcing – Supplier clustering	
Stakeholders	Suppliers representing the highest spend areas are stakeholders. If one's own organization is a key material supplier and a customer has targeted you for cost reduction, your senior management will be fully engaged. This includes top management, finance, sales and marketing, procurement and operations.	

TABLE 15.7

Example Material-Related Symptoms, Root Causes and Indicated Actions

Symptom	Root Cause	Indicated Actions
Material costs are too high	"Over-specification" leading to low supplier yields	Change specification, requalify products. Substitute alternate products. Redesign product. Invest in new processes.
	Volumes are too low	Cancel the product through product line rationalization.
Product too hard to assemble	Too many parts	Combine part functionality reducing the number of parts.
Supplier has proprietary technology	Supplier's technology is designed into product	Find an alternative technology (if possible). Work with supplier on technology advances, share benefits.
Supplier has large aftermarket share	Your company has poor aftermarket supply chain	Create aftermarket supply chain and business arrangement that is attractive to supplier.
Incoming inspection failure rates are high, but supplier quality processes are adequate	Testing process doesn't yield consistent results.	Remove variability in testing procedure. Redesign product features that cause variable test results.

a redesign. If our company is responsible, the ball will be in our court. Not infrequently, a recurring defect will always receive a "use as is" disposition. If this happens, a specification change may be in order.

In some cases, our company's design or preference may impose a poorly performing second tier supplier on our first tier supplier. Making the needed change may require a design change.

15.4.2.3   PM Shortcomings Addressed by Material Cost

This effort doesn't directly fix any of the project management shortcomings described in Chapter 9. Its success, however, does depend on an absence of those shortcomings. Top management support may be needed to enlist suppliers in the effort. If one's company is in a "weak" position, heavily dependent on its partner, top management will certainly want this involvement.

Organization roadblocks are also obstacles to successful implementation. If your organization has a bowtie approach to partnering, not much will get done. Rigidity in its approach to supply chain improvement will also be a roadblock. The variety of solutions available calls for "give and take" with supply chain partners to reach mutually agreeable solutions.

15.4.2.4 SCM Maturity for Material Cost

This process lies in the heart of Stage V for SCM maturity. For companies where noncommodity materials are key for product and financial success, effective execution of activities in this process is vital. A major barrier is the lack of "strategic sourcing" skills in most procurement functions. This obstacle, if it exists, should be addressed to achieve Stage V maturity. Chapter 14 described how to get partners on board. Using Chapter 14 processes, partners must commit to actions likely to involve spending and investments on their part.

15.4.2.5 Terminology for Material Cost

The terms represent some of the efforts used by companies to execute their material cost reduction efforts.

15.4.2.6 Stakeholders for Material Cost

Major suppliers and interfacing organizations are stakeholders. The process design team that identified root causes will likely have to be augmented for this process. Example skill augmentations include product, quality and process design engineers.

5.4.3 OUTPUTS FROM MATERIAL COST (5.4.3)

The principal output of this process is a result, *reduced material costs*. These may not be directly measured in contract prices. For example, the savings may show up in a savings in our own operation. This is because the incoming material has more consistent quality, is easier to assemble, is more available or contains more cost-effective materials or subcomponents.

Accompanying the deliverable may be likely commitments to the supplier for future business or financial support to justify capital investments.

The outputs will be implemented in Phases 3 and 4 of our generic project recommended in Chapter 11.

15.5 DEMAND-DRIVEN SUPPLY CHAIN (5.5)

Implementation of the demand-driven supply chain is the purpose of this process. We cover two of the processes shown in Figure 15.1 in this section. Becoming demand driven requires an assessment of the potential made in root cause analysis (5.3). This assessment can be in two parts: short term and long term. Short-term improvements implement nontechnical changes. Long-term improvements might include new systems for supply chain visibility, supplier network changes and new facilities.

Tables 15.8 and 15.9 summarize the processes for developing the demand-driven supply chain. Table 15.8 is a summary of the overall framework for reaching the demand-driven supply chain. Table 15.9 points to the information systems and other means to create linkages between partners. The two processes should go hand in hand.

TABLE 15.8
Demand-Driven Supply Chain (5.5)

	5.5 Demand-Driven Supply Chain	Executing Process
5.5.1 Inputs	**5.5.2 Process Elements**	**5.5.3 Outputs**
Demand-Driven Potential Assessment (5.3) Process Root Cause Identification (5.3)	**Process definition** Pursue improvements to supply chain operating processes. These will generally support achievement of a supply chain where decisions are based more on actual demand rather than forecasts. The demand-driven supply chain is enabled by changes to the process and information sharing.	*Implemented Supply Chain Operations* *Project Plan Change Requests*
Linkage Requirements (4.1)	**Approaches and techniques** *Decision Support* • Supply chain decision analysis (5.3). Activity-based costing including accounting for inventory and assets. Flexibility framework (Section 3.5.2). *Long to Short Lead Times* • Supply chain network design. Cellular manufacturing. *Flow Model Economics* • Scheduling. Level loading. Setup reduction. Variability reduction. *Replacing Forecasts with Demand* • Postponement. Pull systems like 3C and Kanban. Vendor Managed Inventory (VMI). Demand Flow.[6] Information technology.	
	PM shortcomings addressed Efforts to reduce process cost across several companies may require subprojects or entirely new projects using the singular project management methodology. Depending on their scope the efforts may be included in the overall supply chain improvement project. Multiple process cost reduction efforts increase the need for singular methodologies that benchmark best practices in the varied technical areas that can come into play in reducing process cost.	
	SCM maturity Stage V of the SCM maturity model for Tasks 4 and 5 requires new behaviors in most companies. Despite this obstacle, achieving this level offers the best opportunity for achieving process improvements in the supply chain.	

Terminology

- 3C alternative to MRP
- Demand-Driven supply chain
- Focused factory
- Heijunka
- Kaizen
- Level plant loading
- vMass customization
- Mixed-model production
- Periodic replenishment
- Promotion
- Push system
- Sell-Source-Ship (3S)
- Synchronized supply chain
- Two bin system

- Decomposition (forecasting)
- Disintermediation
- Forecast error
- Independent, dependent demand
- Lean enterprise
- Lot operation cycle time
- Matrix bill of material
- P:D ratio
- Postponement
- Pull system
- Rapid replenishment
- Single Minute Exchange of Dies
- Takt time

- Demand flow®
- Flexibility
- Hedge stock
- Inert stock
- Lean manufacturing
- Lumpy demand
- Min-max
- PDCA
- Product tree
- Push and pull systems
- Replenishment cycle time
- Six sigma
- Third party logistics provider

Stakeholders

Such process improvements should involve upstream and downstream partners in the supply chain. A multicompany process design team should execute the process.

TABLE 15.9
Linkage Definition (4.1)

4.1.1 Inputs	4.1 Linkage Definition	Executing Process
	4.1.2 Process Elements	**4.1.3 Outputs** *Linkage Requirements* *Project Plan Change Requests*
Process definition	Using the process design, define linkages required for the supply chain. Time phase implementation of linkages. Distinguish between short and long-term requirements. Identifying the right linkages is an iterative process done in parallel with designing the demand-driven supply chain.	
Approaches and techniques	Requirements analysis. Process reengineering. Feasibility studies.	
PM shortcomings addressed	Inadequate technical capability and misunderstood technology are directly addressed.	
SCM maturity	Use of the appropriate technology can enable achievement of Stage IV or V for Task 4, Managing information.	

Terminology

- APS (advance planning system)
- Configurator
- Continuous Replenishment Planning (CRP)
- Data warehouse
- Echelon
- Electronic Data Interchange (EDI)
- ATP (available to promise)
- Constant cycle (fixed cycle) reorder model
- CRM (customer relationship management)
- Distribution Requirements Planning (DRP)
- E-commerce
- Event
- BPM (business process management)
- Constant quantity (fixed quantity) reorder model
- CTP (capable to promise)
- Drum-buffer-rope
- ECR
- Forecastable demand

Terminology (Continued)

- Freight forwarder
- Integration
- Key characteristic
- Milk run
- Point of Sale (POS)
- Project manufacturing
- Risk pooling

- Glass pipeline
- Joint replenishment
- Mean absolute deviation
- Partnering
- Point to point integration
- Public warehouse
- SIOP, or S&OP (sales, inventory, operations planning)

- Hosted Software Vendors (HSV)
- Kanban
- Merge-in-transit
- Partnership classification
- Proactive systems
- Pull system
- Supply Chain Event Management (SCEM)
- Web services

- TCP/IP
- XML

- Vendor Managed Inventory

Stakeholders Both line executives, functional managers and technical staff should contribute to the development of linkages. The process design team should oversee linkage design. Technical support staff should assist as needed.

SCOR support SCOR process element best practices and collaboration templates offer suggestions for the use of technology.

15.5.1 INPUTS TO DEMAND-DRIVEN SUPPLY CHAIN (5.5.1)

Inputs include the demand-driven potential described described as poart of Process 5.4. This should set short-term and long-term visions for how demand driven the chain might be. Root cause analysis should indicate how the increased demand-driven level should be achieved. It is likely that several techniques, described in the following section, will be needed to fulfill the vision.

15.5.2 PROCESS ELEMENTS FOR DEMAND-DRIVEN SUPPLY CHAIN (5.5.2)

This process is likely to have the longest duration and require the most resources among all in the supply chain project processes. Process improvement, along with material cost, are the "bottom line" of the overall effort. The process uses inputs from root cause definition and linkage assessment to create the new supply chain design.

15.5.2.1 Process Definition for Demand-Driven Supply Chain

Implementing the short- and long-term visions is essentially a three-step process. The first step seeks to shorten lead times throughout the chain. It relies on outputs from process mapping. The next step uses techniques to implement "flow model economics." This step synchronizes operations along the chain. The vision is to eliminate the bullwhip effect and introduce level production levels. The last step is improving the linkages along the chain so information on end-user demand is transmitted in a timely fashion.

15.5.2.2 Approaches and Techniques for Demand-Driven Supply Chain

Evolution to a demand-driven supply chain follows a process improvement discipline. There are two basic strategies for becoming more demand driven. The first is to shorten the time between the demand signal, usually a purchase, and the point at which a decision to produce is made. The second is to improve communication of demand accurately along the chain, the domain of many software solutions.

The following sections describe the techniques available in each stage of this evolution.

15.5.2.2.1 Decision Support Tools

Multicompany efforts to create a demand-driven supply chain require agreed-to business agreements and process design tools. The decision analysis (Table 15.5) that established the potential to be demand driven is one example. As the project proceeds to implementation, the results of that analysis will be held up for scrutiny and may have to be adjusted. For example, the effort to convert a decision from forecast driven to demand driven might meet obstacles in implementation. We would then have to reevaluate our assessment of demand-driven potential or our approach.

Activity-based costing, described earlier in this chapter, supports business arrangements for risk or reward sharing. The application should capture expenses and capital recovery costs and, if appropriate, work them into prices.

The actions that make a supply chain demand driven also make it flexible. Specifications for the demand-driven supply chain should include the type of flexibility that should be built into operations. Section 3.5.2 described a framework for analyzing the need for flexibility and specifying it in operational terms.

15.5.2.2.2 Long- to Short-Lead-Time Tools

When we mapped our supply chain in process 5.2, we discovered long lead-time processes. Becoming demand-driven requires us to shorten those times as much as possible. Shortening lead time can occur inside the walls of supply chain factories or in the linkages between the factories.

Cellular manufacturing works inside the plant. The approach moves from a functional factory layout, where similar equipment is clustered together, to a layout that puts unlike equipment needed for a product together. This cuts in-plant cycle times because a cell makes the product in one continuous process, while a functional layout requires parts to move from place to place, queuing along the way. Deciding which products have sufficient volume to justify cells can borrow from the SKU ABC Analysis from process mapping.

Supply chain network design might bring suppliers into closer contact with our operation. We also might open distribution facilities or an assembly plant closer to our major customers. At a minimum we would consider overall lead time in decisions about specifying components and determining their source.

15.5.2.2.3 Flow Model Economics

Supply chains suffer from bullwhip effects and work-in-process inventory because they aren't synchronized. Ideally, each partner in the chain will be able to produce at the same rate as end-users consume products. Boeing does this when it sets its production rates for a particular aircraft model at a monthly rate. Everyone in the chain can set its operation to that rate.

Fixed-quantity and fixed-sequence scheduling are tools for improving flow economics. A fixed-sequence, variable-quantity discipline means that replenishment interval is known. An example is the daily trip of the distributor to the retail store. The distributor restocks what has been consumed, a variable quantity on a fixed schedule.

Setup reduction is a common tactic to make smaller batch production on machine tools more economical. A methodical approach minimizes the down time for the equipment reducing the economic batch size. A number of measures are addressed at removing variability from the supply chain. Level loading is one attempt at this. Others seek to improve the reliability of all processes, avoiding the need for contingency inventories in case things do not go well. Another way of removing variability is eliminating suppliers who tend toward unreliability.

15.5.2.2.4 Replacing Forecasts with Demand

Shortening lead times and adopting flow-model economics can be done without large technology investments, as can replacing forecasts with demand. However, this area is likely to be an application where systems play an important role.

For example, short-term measures can utilize postponement. This strategy takes advantage of commonality among end-user products. It does this by postponing a commitment to a final product configuration until the latest time possible. For products where a few components make a variety of products, this can be an effective way to displace forecasts with actual demand in supply chain decision-making. Demand flow is a way to implement this intent by modeling final assembly on a sandwich-stop model in which final products are built to actual order. This is a valuable tool if the products have to be customized for each customer.

Pull systems essentially signal — by some means — upstream operations when consumption occurs downstream. The Kanban is a card that provides this signal. It authorizes the upstream operation to bring another fixed quantity of material. Vendor-managed inventory is like the grocery distributor described above. Replenishment to established levels is left to the vendor, often a distributor of "C" inventory items.

A technique called 3C, meaning *consumption, capacity* and *commonality* is a concept that should find wider application.[5] It is especially appropriate in cases where multiple end products have common components, and forecasting product demand is difficult. From a demand-driven standpoint, it has the virtue of removing forecasts completely from replenishment decisions.

Figure 15.6 illustrates the 3C concept. It depicts a consumption center that uses three components, A, B and C, from three suppliers. The center produces three products that share the three components, reflecting the commonality property. The decision rule sets each component's target inventory at the maximum possible usage rate for the replenishment period. This is determined by physical capacity or peak sales level. For example, for component C, the maximum usage rate is 70. This would occur if only product 2 were sold during the replenishment period, producing a demand for 70. This is certainly conservative since a mix of products will probably be sold in the time period.

This simplified explanation doesn't include other considerations in 3C implementation. However, the straightforward logic can simplify decision-making in many supply chains.

15.5.2.2.5   Information Technology

By placing technology where we have, we might lead the reader to conclude that this book is out of step with most others on the topic of SCM. In those works, technology is front and center. Likewise, Internet-based marketing to those in the supply chain business brings many software pitches. We defend our placement of information technology because technology should support the demand-driven supply chain, not be the main event in its implementation.

Table 15.9 summarizes our coverage of linkages for the demand-driven supply chain. IT application should be coordinated with the steps listed above. For example, it may be tempting to purchase an application that provides supply chain "visibility." However, it may be futile unless the nontechnical solutions described above are not taken first.

15.5.2.3   PM Shortcomings Addressed by Demand-Driven Supply Chain

Like Process 5.4 Material Cost, success in this process demands that the obstacles described in Chapter 9 be absent. This multicompany effort should be run like a

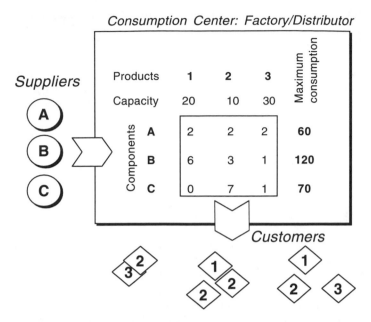

FIGURE 15.6 3C approach to the demand-driven supply chain.

startup enterprise, with flexibility and a willingness to change. The likelihood that technology will be a product of the effort requires an understanding of technology by one's own company and its partners. It also requires the technical competence to implement that technology, not just in one's own company, but also in partner organizations.

15.5.2.4 SCM Maturity for Demand-Driven Supply Chain

Implementing the demand-driven supply chain is indicative of Stage IV and V SCM maturity. Stage IV is primarily cost-reduction focused. Stage V brings additional sophistication, taking into account marketing strategy and utilizing risk–reward sharing among partners.

15.5.2.5 Terminology for Demand-Driven Supply Chain

Terminology focuses on glossary terms related to techniques for implementing the demand-driven supply chain.

15.5.2.6 Stakeholders for Demand-Driven Supply Chain

A process design team, supported by employee front line teams, should complete the process design and test the solutions. All partners in the supply chain whose operations are affected are stakeholders. For longer-term measures like systems and facility changes, providers of outside services will likely support the effort.

15.5.3　OUTPUTS FROM DEMAND-DRIVEN SUPPLY CHAIN (5.5.3)

The principal output is a new process that makes maximum use of actual demand for decisions along the supply chain. Such a supply chain's effectiveness can be evaluated by SCOR metrics, listed in Table 8.2. The supply chain should rank high on both customer-facing and internal-facing measures. Customer-facing metrics include delivery, fill rate, perfect order percentage and lead time. It should also be more flexible and cost effective.

Change requests are another output for the process. These are part of the loop closing needed to update progress on fulfilling the strategy and making needed changes.

ENDNOTES

1. ReVelle, Jack B., Moran, John W. and Cox, Charles A., *The QFD Handbook*. New York: John Wiley & Sons, 1998.
2. This approach was first described in Chapter 12 of the *Handbook of Supply Chain Management*.
3. Ayers, James B. and Malmberg, David R., Supply chain systems: are you ready? *Information Strategy: the Executives Journal*, Fall 2002. pp. 18–27.
4. McAfee, R. Bruce, Glassman, Myron and Honeycutt, Earl D. Jr., The effects of culture and human resource management policies on supply chain management strategy, *Journal of Business Logistics,* Council of Logistics Management, 2002. pp. 1–18.
5. Fernández-Rañada, Miguel, Gurrola-Gal, F. Xavier and López-Tello, Enrique, *3C: A Proven Alternative to MRPII for Optimizing Supply Chain Performance*, Boca Raton: St. Lucie Press, 2000.
6. Demand Flow is the registered trademark of the John Costanza Institute of Technology.

Glossary

3C alternative to MRP A method that uses *capacity, commonality* and *consumption* to control material in the supply chain. The technique decreases the role of forecasts by making inventory decisions based on actual demand and capacity.

5S A foundation for visual controls in a production operation. Characteristic of lean manufacturing. The approach includes the following:

    a. **Sort** (organization): what is needed and not needed

    b. **Stabilize** (orderliness) a place for everything and everything in its place

    c. **Shine** (cleanliness): keeping the workplace clean

    d. **Standardize** (adherence): maintains and monitors the above

    e. **Sustain** (self-discipline): sticking to the rules, scrupulously

    Source: Best Manufacturing Practices Center of Excellence

ABC inventory classification Division of inventory into groups based on decreasing order of annual dollar volume (annual units × projected volume). "A" items are 10–20% of items but 50–70% of dollar volume. "B" items are about 20% of items and 20% of dollar volume. "C" items are 60–70% of items but only 10–30% of value.

The classification points to places where attention can be focused for improvement. The same principle can be applied to suppliers, customers and sales. In classification efforts, one must decide at what level the classification should be completed. This will depend on the product's *configuration.* Adapted from *APICS Dictionary 10th Edition.*

ABCD analysis Technique for analyzing technical and administrative functions. "A" activities add value to the customer and require decision-making discretion. "B" activities require decision-making but don't add value. "C" activities don't require decision-making but do add value. "D" items don't require decision-making and don't add value. The classification is useful for process analysis and deciding how to remove or automate activities.

Action plan A plan that defines a *project* or *projects.* It is part of *programs* or *initiatives.*

Activity (project management context) An element of work performed during a project. It has an expected duration, cost and resource requirement. An activity can be subdivided into tasks. Activity definitions describe what has to be done to produce deliverables. Formerly called a "work item." Adapted from the *PMBOK Guide* — 2000 Edition.

Activity Based Costing, Management (ABC, ABM) A method to plan, measure and control expenses associated with managing and monitoring the supply chain; specific techniques for assigning cost in business processes to activities. ABC is seen to overcome many of the shortcomings of conventional accounting methodologies.

Activity system A term originated by Michael Porter in defining networks of activities that provide a sustainable competitive advantage. These networks can constitute a supply chain. An activity in this context is a feature of the company's strategy that makes it distinctive. Activities, in turn, are supported by supply chain and other company processes.

Agile enterprise Companies that employ rapid customer/supplier partnering to achieve a short product development life cycle. Agility merges competencies in cost, quality, dependability and flexibility. *APICS Dictionary 10th Edition.*

APICS International not-for-profit offering programs and materials for individual and organizational education, standards of excellence and integrated resource management topics. Formerly called American Production and Inventory Control Society. Now The Educational Society for Resource Management.

Application area With respect to project management, an application area is a discipline in which project management theory and practice applies. This book adapts SCM to project management. Other example application areas include construction, defense acquisition and software development.

APS Advanced Planning System. Systems that plan actual logistics and production over short-, immediate- and long-term periods. Can be separate from or built into MRP/ERP systems. The APS can generate different scenarios for decision support. Components include demand planning, production planning, production scheduling, distribution planning and transportation planning. Adapted from *APICS Dictionary 10th Edition.*

As-is The current state, such as how processes in the supply chain process are currently performed.

ASQC The American Society for Quantity Control

Assemble-to-order An environment where products or services are assembled after receipt of an order. This is useful where there are a large number of options consisting of common components. A basket of groceries is an example. Made-to-order computers are another. In a *VAT analysis*, this approach might be tried for "T" type product structures. Adapted from *APICS Dictionary 10th Edition.*

ATP Available to promise. The uncommitted portion of inventory and planned production maintained in the master schedule. Adapted from *APICS Dictionary 10th Edition.*

Auctions on-line On-line negotiations among qualified suppliers. Usually facilitated by software applications.

Balanced Scorecard An approach to measurement that cascades measures from the top down through the organization. The method uses four *perspectives* to achieve balance. These are financial, customer, internal business and innovation and learning.

Bar coding An automatic identification technology that uses parallel dark bars and spaces to represent characters. Bar coding is often an important element in automating the tracking of material in the supply chain.

Batch-and-queue system Refers to a production management system that relies on large batches of material. This leads to long queues while waiting to complete a production step. Such systems are characterized by high work-in-process inventory and low-velocity production.

Benchmarking A search for those best practices that will lead to superior performance. Benchmarking is usually executed with those who perform a targeted activity the best, regardless of the industry they are in. Internal benchmarking makes comparisons within an organization, such as developing best practices from several stores that perform similar functions.

BPM Business Process Management. Broadly, BPM focuses on improving business processes rather than functions or costs. Narrowly, BPMI (Business Process Management Initiative) is a nonprofit group promoting open standards for information technology used in business processes.

BPO Business Process Outsourcing. Contracting out for support services beyond information technology. Examples include human resources, finance and accounting and logistics services.

Branding Vision, position, "space" in the market. Establishing a brand name is a primary way to compete in many industries. SCM can support the strategy for establishing a brand "image."

Breadman A term applied to "automatic" replacement of inventory by third-party logistics providers, normally distributors. The analogy is the bread-man who replenishes stock in the grocery store on a regularly scheduled basis. A related term is "*milk run*." The term can also apply to types of vendor-managed inventory.

Bullwhip effect A term that describes the phenomenon in which small changes in final demand for a product produce wide swings in production upstream in the supply chain.

Business model A model answers question like the following: "Who is the customer?" "What does the customer value?" "How do we make money in this business?" What is the underlying economic logic that explains how we deliver value to customers?" A *strategy* defines how the organization competes. Competing effectively requires being different from your competitors. From Why Business Models Matter, *Harvard Business Review*, May 2002.

Business Process Reengineering (BPR) Taking a holistic customer-focused systems view to changing processes in the organization. BPR encompasses vision for the organization's future, workflow along the supply chain, information technology, organization theory; the Internet, computer-supported collaboration and other approaches.

Capacity strategy A strategic choice for adjusting strategy to business levels. A "leading" strategy adds capacity in anticipation of demand. A "lag" strategy waits until the demand has materialized. A "tracking" strategy means attempts to match capacity and demand. Such a strategy should consider product life cycle position and profitability. Adapted from *APICS Dictionary 10th Edition.*

Cash-to-cash cycle time The time between payments for product components to suppliers to the time customers make payments. This parameter has become an important measure of supply chain performance, reflecting both financial and inventory management process performance. Most have negative measures ranging from 30 to 80 days. Some, notably Dell, have a positive cycle time, meaning it collects payments from customers before it has to pay suppliers.

Category management A structure that focuses on management of products or product families. With respect to SCM, this could also include incoming material, production planning and distribution shifting away from a structure based on commodities or manufacturing plants.

Cause and effect diagram (fishbone diagram) A tool that uses a graphical description of contributing elements to identify root causes of process variation.

Cellular manufacturing A manufacturing process that produces families of parts within a single line or cell of machines with operators who work only within the line or cell. The cellular concept is applicable to administrative and technical process. In this context, it means clustering unlike operations to increase processing *velocity.*

Center of Excellence (COE) A formal or informal committee that focuses on benchmarking and continuous improvement. Has expertise in identifying project management tools. Adapted from *Strategic Planning for Project Management.*

Certified supplier A supplier that has been approved for providing defined components for manufacturing or distribution. Certification levels may have varying conditions related to quality management, such as needs for quality control. Suppliers are often qualified before financial terms are negotiated.

Channel A group of businesses that take ownership title to products or facilitate exchange during the marketing process from the original buyer to the final buyer. Effective SCM requires an understanding of the needs of each customer and segment and the correct channel to reach them.

Channel master The single most powerful company in a supply chain. The channel master dictates terms of trade for the channel. The presence of a master depends on the nature of the industry and competition. Channel mastery is often the goal of SCM programs.

Charter A document that authorizes a project. It enables the project manager to apply resources to project activities. Adapted from *PMBOK Guide — 2000 Edition*

CLM Council of Logistics Management. A worldwide professional organization of logistics personnel. CLM has contributed heavily to the discussion of supply chain issues.

Collaboration Joint planning and execution of supply chain activities. These activities can range from new product development to day-to-day operations. Collaboration includes all aspects of the relationship related to physical movement, information sharing, financial flows and exchange of intellectual property. Collaboration is also defined as internal between people and functions and external between supply chain companies.

Collaborative execution systems Category of application software that enables the effective coordination and flow of information across the entire value chain. Automates tasks required to manage each transaction and providing real-time visibility to information, collaborative execution systems are designed to improve productivity and reliability.

Collaboratory A term coined by participants in the Supply-Chain Council's SCOR Collaboration Technical Committee. It refers to the entity that includes the business, cultural and system environment needed to build and operate a linkage between partners.

Configuration The arrangement of components specified to produce an assembly. — *APICS Dictionary 10th Edition.*

Configuration has a major impact on supply chain design. For example, different configurations affect *postponement* strategies. In application of the *3C* approach, configuration figures in commonality among end items.

Configurator A system used by design-to-order, make-to-order, or assemble-to-order companies. They enable direct customer or sales engineer configuration of the product. Configurators can generate solid models, drawings, costs and bills of material. Adapted from *APICS Dictionary 10th Edition.*

Consignment 1. A shipment by a common carrier. 2. Terms of a contract in which a supplier is not paid until the goods are used or sold. *APICS Dictionary 10th Edition.*

Constant cycle (fixed cycle) reorder model An inventory reorder pattern with fixed time intervals and variable quantities.

Advantages include:
- Establishes a regular rhythm in the supply chain.
- Decreases variability from uncertainty about schedules.
- Can take advantage of set-up economies when set-up times depend on sequence. An example is paint lines where different color sequences require different set-up efforts.

Disadvantages arise when variation in quantities can cause production to run behind. One must also track production through the chain, with a requirement to know usage at various points to signal correct quantity. The approach fits higher-value "A" items.

Constant quantity (fixed quantity) reorder model An inventory reorder pattern with fixed quantity delivered at variable time intervals.

Advantages include:
- Better for close operations with minimal transportation requirements.
- Can take advantage of EOQ economies for operations involving high setup costs.
- Fast, doesn't require counting or tracking of inventory.
- Simplicity. Compatible with visible signaling. Examples are the two-bin system and Kanban approaches.

- Easier to predict time requirements once orders are placed.

The model can cause excess inventory in the system. It is better for low-cost "C" items. Some companies expense items in this category. *Handbook of Supply Chain Management*

Constraint Any element that prevents a system from achieving a higher level of performance. Constraints can be of many kinds, including physical steps in production and the limits on customer desire for the product.

Continuous Replenishment Planning (CRP) The practice of partnering between distribution channel members that changes the traditional replenishment process from traditional purchase orders based on economic order quantities to the replenishment of products based on actual and forecast product demand.

Control points In the theory of constraints, these are strategic locations that are tightly planned and scheduled. Other work centers are not, simplifying scheduling and control. Adapted from *APICS Dictionary 10th Edition.*

Core competence An organization capability that can be applied to a variety of core and end products. The capability is usually technology based, but can also be competence in facets of supply chain management.

Core processes (project management context) Processes with clear dependencies that are likely to be performed in the same order on most projects. These processes may be iterated several times. Examples are *scope planning*, *performance reporting* and *project phase initiation*. Adapted from *PMBOK Guide — 2000 Edition.*

Cost baseline A time-phased estimate of cost. It is used to monitor performance on cost throughout the project. Adapted from *PMBOK Guide — 2000 Edition.*

Cost driver In activity-based costing, volume variable used to calculate the total cost of an activity. The activity cost may be expressed in (cost)/(unit of volume). The unit of volume used is the cost driver.

Cost of quality (COQ) COQ can be viewed as a subset of *activity based costing* and can provide the information necessary to drive service improvements and reduce costs. Components of COQ usually include prevention, detection and correction. Some will divide correction into internal (before the sale) and external (after the sale) components.

C_p, C_{pk} Process capability and the index of capability, respectively. Typically, a process is considered "capable" when capability and/or the capability index are 1.33 or greater.

C_p = (upper — lower specification limit)/6s, where s = standard deviation of process output.

C_{pk} = (mean — nearer specification)/3s

CPFR® Collaborative Planning Forecasting and Replenishment. A set of business processes used for supply chain collaboration. The term is a trademark of the sponsoring organization, the Voluntary Interindustry Commerce Standards (VICS) Association

CPIO Chief Process Improvement Officer. A senior management role to lead the reengineering of processes. Facilitates process improvement across internal and external boundaries. From AMR Research.

Critical path The series of activities that determines the duration of a project. It is the longest path through the project. The Critical Path Method (CPM) is a technique to predict the project's duration by analyzing the path of activities with the least amount of scheduling flexibility. Adapted from the *PMBOK Guide — 2000 Edition.*

Critical to Quality (CTQ) A feature in a product that's important to customers. Such a feature can be translated to processes for delivering the feature. The term is used in connection with Six-Sigma efforts to improve processes.

CRM Customer Relationship Management. "CRM aligns business processes with customer strategies to build customer loyalty and increase profits over time." (From: Rigby, Darrell K., Reichheld, Frederick F. and Schefter, Phil, Avoid the four perils of CRM, *Harvard Business Review*, February 2002, pp. 101–109.)

Computer applications that deal with the "front office" interface between the company and its customers.

CTP Capable to promise. The ability to commit to orders with available capacity and inventory. Adapted from *APICS Dictionary 10th Edition.*

Customer A person or organization that decides to purchase a product or service or receives a product or service if no purchase is involved, such as an internal customer for information. An *end-user* is the person or organization that uses or consumes the product or service. The end-user is not necessarily the customer or buyer.

Customer service ratio In a make-to-stock company, the percentage of items or dollars shipped on schedule. In a make-to-order company, the percentage of items or dollars shipped on time. Synonymous terms include fill rate and customer service level.

Customer-centric organization An organizational structure built around customer segments. Desirable when segments have different requirements, style-driven products with short product lives requiring fast responses and higher margin products. *Handbook of Supply Chain Management.*

Customer-centric supply chain Supply chains or organizations whose construct centers on the requirements of targeted customer segments. Alternatives are functional and product-centric supply chains.

Cycle time CGR views cycle time as a property of processes along the supply chain. The minimum theoretical cycle time for a product's supply chain is the sum of individual process cycle times.

Cycle time reduction is achieved through process reengineering including new technology along the chain. Examples include automated sharing information about final demand, introducing postponement through product design and automation in production processes.

Lead time is a market-oriented property that is driven by competitive forces. A competitor that works to reduce cycle time can end up with the shortest lead time. *Throughput time* is a synonym.

Data warehouse A repository for data organized in a format suitable for *ad hoc* query processing. Data warehouses are built from operational databases used for day-to-day business processes. The operational data is "cleaned" and transformed in such a way that it is amenable to fast retrieval and efficient analysis. A single-purpose data warehouse is sometimes referred to as a "data mart."

Decomposition (forecasting) A method of forecasting where data is divided into trend, seasonal and cyclical components. Another component may be random — where no pattern exists. Forecasts are made using each component. Adapted from *APICS Dictionary 10th Edition.*

Decomposition (WBS, IDEF) Breaking a category down into lower levels for sharper definition of requirements. The term can apply to project scope, activities, tasks and projects. IDEF decomposes functions in a supply chain in a similar way. Adapted from *PMBOK Guide — 2000 Edition.*

Deficiency, discrepancy Failure of a quality system to comply with requirements.

DELIVER processes SCOR processes to provide finished goods and services to customers.

Deliverable Any measurable, tangible, verifiable outcome, result or item produced to complete a project or part of a project. Often refers to a work product delivered to and approved by a sponsor or customer. Adapted from the *PMBOK Guide — 2000 Edition.*

Demand End-user requirements for a product or service. This is what would be consumed if sufficient product were available at prices that yield a profit. End-users aren't necessarily purchasers who pay for a product. A "customer" may buy a product or service on behalf of the end-user.

Demand chain A term sometimes applied to the "outgoing" side of the business. Supply chain, in this context, applies only to the "incoming" side. To the end-user, all activities to produce the product or service are part of the "*supply chain.*"

Demand flow® A technique to speed product final assembly. Demand flow uses the concept of a "pile of parts" that can be assembled in response to actual customer orders. The term is trademarked by the John Costanza Institute of Technology.

Demand-driven supply chain A term developed by CGR that applies to supply chains that use tools that enable decisions to be made on the basis of actual customer demand rather than forecasts. The extent to which a supply chain is "demand driven" is measurable. Most supply chains will require some level of forecasting for advanced planning. However, it is desirable to reduce dependence on these forecasts.

Design team A team, usually of operations managers involved in included supply chain processes, that designs new supply chains. Design teams may be called upon to develop spheres, activity systems, requirements for IT systems and process improvements.

Discounted cash flow A method of financial analysis that recognizes the time value of money as measured by the cost of capital. DCF is used to convert capital costs into "equivalent uniform cash flows." This makes it possible to combine expense and capital items when weighing capital investments.

Disintermediation The elimination of echelons or stages in the supply chain. This can reduce cycle time and operating expense.

Distribution Requirements Planning (DRP) Replenishment procedures at distribution control points. Can use MRP logic or other rules.

Downstream The end of the supply chain nearest to end-users. *Upstream* refers to the beginnings of the supply chain, probably suppliers of components or raw materials.

Driving force A strategic planning concept developed by Michel Robert. The concept holds that there is one and only one driving force around which a company competes. Company management may acknowledge this; however, often it does not.

Drumbeat The pace at which an organization produces product. Used to pace all the operations in a factory or in a supply chain. Similar to *takt time*.

Drum-buffer-rope In the theory of constraints, a generalized process to manage resources to maximize throughput. The "drum" sets the pace of production to match the system's constraint. "Buffers" protect the system from disruption and uncertainty. They are often placed to assure that the constraint always has work. The "rope" communicates between the constraint and the gating operation that controls release of work into the system. The model can be applied at the factory and supply chain levels. Adapted from *APICS Dictionary 10th Edition.*

Early manufacturing and supplier involvement (EMI/ESI) Inclusion of the manufacturing department and suppliers in product design. The result is a more producible and durable design.

Echelon A term that refers to layers of distribution or to stages in the process. Each echelon can include the storage, transportation and handling of the product between the source (presumably a factory) and its point of use. A trend is toward reducing echelons to speed the supply chain and reduce its cost. Also, competitors at any echelon may seek to add services, squeezing out other echelon levels.

E-commerce Electronic commerce has come to mean many different things to many different people. Originally, the term meant selling things online. It has evolved to mean conducting business online, which can include customer service functions, sales, marketing, public relations, advertising and more.

Economic Order Quantity (EOQ) A fixed-order quantity model that determines the amount of an item to be purchased or manufactured at one time. The model minimizes the combined costs of acquiring and carrying inventory. When production rates are closer to consumption rates, as in a synchronized supply chain, the production quantity approaches infinity, or continuous operation.

Economic Value Added (EVA®) The dollar amount of value added by an enterprise over a specified period of time. EVA takes into account the capital employed in the business. EVA is a trademarked term by Stern Stewart. A synonym is *residual income.*

ECR Efficient Consumer Response. Refers to technologies to match supply and demand in the retail sector.

Electronic Data Interchange (EDI) The computer-to-computer transmission of business information between trading partners. The information should be organized in standard file formats or transaction sets following guidelines administered by the Uniform Code Council (UCC). Standards have been developed for all regular business-to-business communication including purchase orders, invoices, shipping notices and funds transfer. By eliminating the clerical, mailing and other costs associated with paper-based information, EDI reduces costs, time delays and errors. Source: ECR Best Practices Report

Enable process A SCOR process that prepares, maintains, or manages information, relationships, or other factors to support planning and execution processes. EP processes enable PLAN processes, ES enable SOURCE processes and so on. EP.1 establishes and manages PLAN rules; ES.1 plans SOURCE rules and so on.

Enable sphere Spheres that involve activities used by product-producing spheres. These are often supporting activities. Customer requirements are set by the needs of the product-producing spheres. Examples can include support systems, organization, logistics services and sourcing.

End-user The person or organization that uses or consumes a product or service. The end-user is at the end of the supply chain. The user is not necessarily the *customer* or buyer of the product or service.

Engineer-to-order Products that need unique engineering design, customization, or new materials. Each order results in a unique bill of material, some unique parts numbers and custom routings. Adapted from *APICS Dictionary 10th Edition.*

Enterprise Resource Planning (ERP) ERP systems are composed of software programs that tie together all of an enterprise's various functions, such as finance, manufacturing, sales, distribution, procurement and human resources. This software also provides for the analysis of the data from these areas to plan production, forecast sales and analyze quality.

Event An occurrence in the supply chain that triggers the need for action. *Supply chain event management* refers to software solutions that monitor operating data to determine whether such an event has occurred.

Execution process A SCOR process that changes the state of material goods. It includes scheduling/sequencing, transforming products through manufacturing processes and moving products.

Executive information system Software providing operating information for direct access by executive users.

Extended product Those features of a product that aren't part of the base, or physical, product. Many supply chain attributes are extended product features like availability of product, method of delivery, customer service, ability to return the product and so forth. Adapted from *Handbook of Supply Chain Management.*

Facilitating processes (project management context) Processes that may or may not be needed, depending on the needs of the project. These are likely to be performed intermittently or as needed. Examples include *staff acquisition, risk response planning, team development* and *solicitation of suppliers.*

Five focusing steps A theory of constraints process to continuously evaluate the production system and market mix to make the most of the system constraints. There are five steps:

1. Identify constraints in the system
2. Decide how to exploit the constraint
3. Subordinate nonconstraints to the constraints
4. Elevate the constraints in the system
5. Return to step 1 if the constraint is broken. Adapted from *APICS Dictionary 10th Edition..*

Flexibility The ability to change or react with little penalty in time, effort, cost, or performance. Categories of flexibility include product mix variation, volume variations, labor flexibility, design-change flexibility and routing flexibility. David Upton, *California Management Review.*

Focused factory A concept originated by Wickham Skinner arguing that factories or parts of factories perform best if they are designed to fulfill customer requirements as efficiently as possible. The focused factory uses manufacturing capability to support strategies for competing.

Forecast error The difference between actual and forecast demand, stated as an absolute value or a percentage. Forecast errors are used to adjust production and inventory plans in supply chains with high dependence on forecasts for decision-making. *APICS Dictionary.*

Forecastable demand Applies to certain patterns of demand that contain enough history to provide a forecast of future demand. The opposite is *"lumpy"* demand, for which forecasting isn't possible.

Freight forwarder This is a manager or handler for the shipment of goods. The responsibilities of a freight forwarder include arranging shipment details and completing documentation. Because of their brokering role, freight forwarders have a good understanding of market trends and insurance and transport alternatives.

Front-line team A group of people working in a process who test new designs and provide recommendations for process design and changes.

Functional organization An organization structure built around functional tasks like marketing, accounting, manufacturing and customer service. Works best where product lines are narrow or mature businesses. Not a good alternative where speed is required or products and customers have diverse requirements. *Handbook of Supply Chain Management.*

Functional product A category of product with lower margins and low uncertainty regarding demand. The supply chains for these products should be designed for the lowest possible cost. (See *innovative product.*)

Fuzzy front end Refers to the beginning of the development cycle, when new product and service concepts are not clear. Many organizations are defining processes and systems to manage the "fuzziness" of the front end of new product development cycle.

Glass pipeline A term describing a supply chain in which the visibility over the status of the product is high. One is able to track physical movement through the pipeline easily.

Greenfield vision An ideal state based on specifications for future operations. The greenfield should ignore constraints inherent in the current situation. It should serve as a "stretch" target for implementing improvements in the supply chain. The use of the greenfield approach is based on the premise that, without ambitious targets, only incremental change will occur.

Hedge stock A form of safety stock implemented for a specific period. Reasons can include interruptions due to strikes, price increases, or a currency reevaluation. Adapted from *APICS Dictionary 10th Edition.*

Heijunka *Heijunka*, or Production Smoothing is a technique used to adapt production to fluctuating customer demand. The Japanese word *heijunka* (pronounced hey June kah), means literally "make flat and level." Customer demand must be met with the customer's preferred delivery times, but customer demand is "bumpy," while factories prefer "level," or stable production. So a manufacturer needs to try to smooth out these bumps in production. The main tool for smoothing is frequent changing of the model mix on a given line. TPS advocates small batches of many models over short periods of time, requiring fast changeovers. Adapted from Frederick Stimson Harriman at FredHarriman.com.

Hosted Software Vendors (HSV) A model of offering software packages over the Internet. The term has supplanted ASP. Applications can be in categories such as accounting and CRM or vertical solutions for specific industries. Adapted from *Infoworld,* January 20, 2003, p. 35.

IDEF Integrated Computer-Aided Manufacturing (ICAM) DEFinition methods are used to perform modeling activities in support of enterprise integration. The original IDEF methods were developed for the purpose of enhancing communication among people who needed to decide how their existing systems were to be integrated. The technique of decomposing a process into activities is useful for supply chain process analysis. The product is a "node tree" of supply chain process functions. IDEF0 modeling is supported by Visio software.

Implosion The process of determining where a component is used. Implosions can be single level, showing only the parents of the next higher level, or multilevel, showing the ultimate top level parents. Adapted from *APICS Dictionary 10th Edition.*

Independent, dependent demand Independent demand is driven by end-user or customer needs. It comes from outside the sphere or enterprise. Dependent demand is derived from independent demand and triggers replenishment within the sphere or enterprise.

Inert stock A term used by CGR to define slow-moving categories of inventory. Components can include defective or obsolete items, "stranded" odd-quantity components with no demand and "*lumpy*" demand items. The inert category can be a large portion of total inventory. Reducing it may require a concerted effort on several fronts.

Initiative A broad program to improve supply chain operations. Initiatives can last several years and evolve with changing requirements. An initiative can have multiple projects. A synonym is *program.*

Innovative product An innovative product has high margins and uncertain demand. The supply chain for such products should be designed for responsiveness to demand, rather than efficiency. (See *functional* product.)

Integrated supply An alliance or long-term commitment between two or more organizations for the purpose of achieving specific business objectives by maximizing the effectiveness of each participant's resources. The relationship is based upon trust, dedication to common goals and an understanding of each other's individual expectations and values.

Integration The extent to which components of the production process are inextricably linked. A software design concept that allows users to move easily between applications.

Inventory turns The number of times each year that the inventory turns over. It can be in units, but is more often in dollars. It is computed by dividing the average inventory level into the annual cost of goods sold.

Issue, Issues List Issues are questions that define the scope of the supply chain strategy. A running list keeps track of these issues and the response implicit in the strategy. Issues are often tracked in categories like Financial, Organization and Measures, Product Development, Processes and so forth.

Joint replenishment Coordination of lot sizing and order release for related items. The purpose is to take advantage of setup, shipping and quantity discounts. It applies to material ordering, group technology production and distribution. The commonality component of the 3C approach is a form of joint replenishment. Adapted from *APICS Dictionary 10th Edition.*

Just in Time (JIT) A philosophy of manufacturing based on planning elimination of all waste and continuous improvement of productivity. It encompasses the successful execution of all manufacturing activities required to produce a final product, from design engineering to delivery and including all stages of conversion from raw material onward. The primary elements of JIT are to have only the required inventory when needed; to improve quality to zero defects; to reduce lead times by reducing setup times, queue lengths and lot sizes; to incrementally revise the operations themselves and to accomplish these things at minimum cost. In the broad sense, it applies to all forms of manufacturing, job shop and process, as well as repetitive. Adapted from *APICS Dictionary 10th Edition.*

Kaizen A Japanese word that means, loosely translated, constant improvement.

Kanban A method of JIT production that uses standard containers or lot sizes with a single card attached to each. It is a pull system in which work centers signal with a card that they wish to withdraw parts from feeding operations or suppliers. The Japanese word *kanban*, loosely translated, means card, billboard or sign. The term is often used synonymously for the specific scheduling system developed and used by the Toyota Corporation in Japan. Adapted from *APICS Dictionary 10th Edition*.

Kano Model The model describes three different types of quality. The first is *basic* quality, items that one assumes is part of a product. The second is *performance* quality. The customer will be able to articulate this type of quality and the quality attributes can be captured by surveys. The third is *excitement* quality, which is unexpected and cannot be articulated by the customer. The supply chain has the potential for assuring all three types of quality. Source: *The QFD Handbook*.

Key characteristic A feature whose variation has the greatest impact on the fit, performance, or service life of the finished product from the perspective of the customer. Key characteristics are a tool to help decide where to focus limited resources. They are used for process improvement purposes. Key characteristics may or may not be "critical characteristics" that affect product safety.

Key process parameter A process input that is controllable and that has a high statistical correlation with the variation in a part key characteristic. Key process parameters are most effectively determined by the use of designed experiments.

Knowledge management Refers to efforts to capture the "knowledge" resident in an organization. Such efforts are often centered on information technology. Some have dismissed knowledge management as a fad, but the concept has value in SCM across multiple enterprises.

Lead time CGR's view is that lead time is associated with a product or service delivered by the supply chain. It is "imposed" on the supply chain by the competitive environment. It is driven by customer expectations, supply chain innovations and competitive pressure. All these factors are in constant motion, moving toward "faster, cheaper, better." Competitors that can't deliver products and services within the established lead time will likely perish. Competitors that have the shortest *cycle time* have an advantage.

Lean enterprise A term coined by James Womack and Daniel Jones to extend the idea of "lean manufacturing" along the supply chain, including production partners. The lean enterprise is operationally synchronized with end-user demand. (Womack and Jones were the originators of the "lean" terminology.) Adapted from *APICS Dictionary 10th Edition*.

Lean manufacturing Production approach based on using multiskilled workers, highly flexible machines and very adaptable organizations and procedures to manufacture an increasing variety of products while continually decreasing costs. "Lean" means more-productive use of labor, material and inventory along the supply chain.

Legacy systems A network or hierarchical database system, usually running on a mainframe. Replacement of legacy systems is often a motivator for installing new supply chain information systems. Implementing supply chain improvements may be limited by the capabilities of legacy systems.

Level (of a product) Components of product structure. Each level is coded with the end item as the 0 level. Level 1 has level 0 components; level 2 has level 1 components and so forth. Also see *Decomposition*. Adapted from *APICS Dictionary 10th Edition*.

Level 1 processes SCOR has five core management processes: PLAN, SOURCE, MAKE, DELIVER and RETURN. There are separate definitions in this table for each. When used in SCOR, these core processes are spelled with capital letters.

Level of Effort (LOE) A support-type activity that is hard to measure. It is usually characterized as a uniform rate of activity. Adapted from the *PMBOK Guide — 2000 Edition*.

Level plant loading Efforts to reduce variability in production at the business unit and supply chain levels. Level plant loading is considered a best practice for achieving effective supply chains. *Drumbeat* and *takt time* are related terms.

Levels (SCOR) SCOR processes decompose to three levels. Level 1 is composed of the five core management processes. Level 2 is the configuration level and depends on supply chain design. Level 2 process examples are a letter and a number, like PP for Plan supply chain and M1 for Make-to-stock. Configuration types include make-to-stock, make-to-order and engineer-to-order. Level 3 activities are process elements supporting level 2. Level 4 processes are company-specific and fall outside SCOR.

Lot operation cycle time Length of time from the start of setup to the end of cleanup for a production lot at a given operation. *APICS Dictionary 10th Edition.*

Lumpy demand An infrequently occurring demand that can't be forecast. The usual result is a need to carry an insurance level of stock. Also called "discontinuous demand."

Maintenance, Repair and Overhaul (MRO) A class of activity occurring after the sale of the product. MRO often demands special supply chain design and can be an important factor in the success of a product that has a long life cycle.

MAKE processes SCOR processes that transform material into finished products.

Make-to-order A production environment where the product is made after receipt of the order. The product is often a combination of standard and custom items. Make-to-order is similar to *assemble-to-order*. Adapted from *APICS Dictionary 10th Edition*.

Make-to-stock An environment where products are finished before receipt of a customer order. The customer orders are filled from stock. Production orders replenish the stock. Adapted from *APICS Dictionary 10th Edition*.

Manufacturing Execution System (MES) A MES is a manufacturing software application, not an "MIS" system. MES focuses on execution and management of production processes. MES provides synchronization of the following as they are used to make the product: labor, machinery and equipment, tooling, other resources, e.g., power, raw material and work in process inventory. MES usually operates in time increments from sub-shift to real-time. MES applications may serve as interfaces between MRP scheduling applications and machine controllers. They also collect quality and production data.

Manufacturing strategy The concept that manufacturing can support other strategies for competing, such as product, marketing and financial strategies. A related term is a "supply chain strategy" where supply chain design contributes to competitiveness.

Mass customization Creation of individual variations of a high-volume product with many options for configuration.

Matrix bill of material (BOM) A method for identifying common components. Components are arranged on one dimension; end products on the other. This is a useful tool for establishing commonality in applying the 3C methodology.

Maturity model A framework for measuring progress toward some goal. The model consists of descriptive "levels" to help users assess their progress toward higher levels of maturity. Harold Kerzner's project management maturity model (PMMM) has five levels: common language, common processes, singular methodology, benchmarking and continuous improvement.

Mean absolute deviation (MAD) The average of absolute values of the deviations between observed and expected values. MAD can be calculated to evaluate forecasting processes as the difference between actual sales and forecasts.

Merge-in-transit A technique for combining order components from various sources while those components are in transit from sources to customers.

Milestone A significant event in the project usually associated with completion of a deliverable. Adapted from the *PMBOK Guide — 2000 Edition*.

Milk run A transportation link in the supply chain characterized by regularly scheduled shipments to one or more points. By combining shipments, more frequent shipments are economically feasible. The milk run lowers the incremental cost of filling an order, enabling continuous flow in the supply chain.

Min-max A type of order point replenishment where the reorder point is the "min" and the "max" sets the order quantity.

Mixed-model production A production scheme where the production line product mix matches what is sold each day.

MRP, MRP II Materials Requirement Planning — a concept developed in the 1970s to make use of the high-speed computers to model the requirements for material for a manufacturing operation. It is viewed as a method for planning all resources of a manufacturing company. It addresses operational planning in units, financial planning in currency and has simulation capability. Output from MRP is integrated with financial reports, purchase commitments, shipping budgets and inventory projections. "Closed loop" MRP implies feedback to keep plans valid with regard to constraints like capacity. Adapted from *APICS Dictionary 10th Edition.*

Network diagram A logical display of project activities. It shows sequence and dependencies among activities. Adapted from *PMBOK Guide — 2000 Edition.*

Operation A step in a process. Can include a changing of physical configuration, a quality control action, temporary or long-term storage, an administrative task or transportation.

Operational excellence (OE) A term used by Michael Porter in discussions of strategy. His contention is that the OE is a necessary but not sufficient condition for sustained competitiveness. It reflects the belief that "you can't save your way to prosperity." Porter advocates the development of activity systems to distinguish the company from its competitors.

Optimization The application of operations research tools to a supply chain function. Examples include distribution planning (warehouse location and transportation planning) and planning or scheduling production. Optimization technology applies in complex supply chains and when the potential for improvement justifies its use.

Order penetration point The point in a product's flow where an item is earmarked for a particular customer. Downstream processes are driven by customer orders; upstream processes are driven by forecasts and plans. However, the plans themselves can reflect actual customer orders in a demand-driven supply chain. Adapted from *APICS Dictionary 10th Edition.*

P:D ratio According to the *APICS Dictionary 10th Edition.* "P" is the manufacturing lead-time. "D" is the customer required delivery time. If the ratio exceeds 1.0, the customer order will be delayed or production will start as a result of a forecast (make-to-stock).

The demand-driven supply chain approach argues that different segments of the supply chain can be driven by either forecasts or actual demand. In general, actual demand is more desirable than forecasts. In this book, we use cycle time to refer to processes for manufacture and distribution and lead-time as a market-driven requirement for delivery.

Partnering A management approach used by two or more organizations, often, but not always, a buyer and a seller, to achieve mutual business objectives by maximizing the effectiveness of each partner's resources. Partnerships can take a number of forms from arm's-length sharing of information to acquisition. Examples include collaboration in design, measures to reduce cost and simplified replenishment procedures.

Partner An entity with which one does business, either upstream or downstream in the supply chain, whose performance is important to your success.

Partnership classification A classification of partnerships has three dimensions: purpose, direction and choice. The purpose defines whether the partnership creates new space. Direction refers to the supply chain. Horizontal means partners are at the same echelon. Vertical is a partnership along the supply chain — probably between customer and supplier. Choice refers to the relative strength of each partner. A "many to one" means your company has many competitors and is seeking a partnership with a dominant partner. *Handbook of Supply Chain Management.*

PDCA Plan-Do-Check-Act. Also called the Shewhart Cycle for implementing process improvement.

Performance-based pricing Basing prices on value to the customer, not necessarily what the product costs. The supply chain can influence value to the customer. Applies specifically to "innovative" products as opposed to "functional" ones, where prices are cost driven in competitive markets.

Periodic replenishment Aggregating requirements to place deliveries of varying quantities at evenly spaced time intervals, rather than variably spaced deliveries of equal quantities. The term *fixed cycle* also refers to this method. The *milk run* is also a tool for implementing this approach. Adapted from *APICS Dictionary 10th Edition.*

Phase A project phase is a collection of logically related project activities, usually culminating in a deliverable. Adapted from the *PMBOK Guide — 2000 Edition.*

PLAN processes SCOR processes that balance supply and demand. PP processes cover long-range planning at the supply chain level. PS, PM, PD and PR cover shorter-term planning for source, make, deliver and return. (these are also referred to as P1, P2, P3 and P4.)

Planning process A SCOR process that aligns expected resources with expected demand.

PMMM Project Management Maturity Model. A five-level model developed by Dr. Harold Kerzner. The levels are common language, common processes, singular methodology, benchmarking and continuous improvement.

Point of Sale (POS) Place where the purchase is made at the checkout stand or scanning terminals in a retail store. The acronym POS frequently is used to describe the sales data generated at the checkout scanners. Source: *ECR Best Practices Report.*
The relief of inventory and computation of sales data at a time and place of sale, generally through the use of bar coding or magnetic media equipment. *APICS Dictionary 10th Edition.*

Point-to-point integration Building a customized computer connection. The software for such integration is usually expensive to build and maintain. When systems change on either side of the connection, expensive changes are needed.

Portfolio, PPM A set of initiatives or projects being pursued to improve supply chains. Portfolio management is deciding the priority of the projects and making resources available for their completion. PPM stands for *Project Portfolio Management.*

Postponement A product or supply chain design strategy that shifts product differentiation closer to the end-user. The approach encompasses identity changes such as assembly or packaging. Adapted from *APICS Dictionary 10th Edition.*

Price-taker A buying organization that typically takes the low price every time. Generally requires a functional supply chain in the face of competitive alternatives. Prices often become the basis for selection in on-line auctions.

Proactive systems An approach to designing information systems to focus on the needs of decision makers. The approach may rely on computer-based tools to disseminate the needed information. Noncomputer-based approaches may also be used.

Process owner The central figure in organizations organized around processes. Owners are charged with end-to-end responsibility and authority for a cross-functional process.

Process type At Level 2, SCOR uses three processes types: planning, execution and enable. Planning processes are preceded by a P, Enable by an E, Execution by S (Source), M (Make) and D (Deliver).

Process, process group (project management context) A series of actions bringing about a result. A process either manages the project itself (a project management process) or creates the output of the project (a product-oriented process). In the former group are Initiating, Planning, Controlling and Closing process groups. Project management processes call for project management knowledge and practice expertise. In the latter are executing processes, which call for application area knowledge and practice expertise. From *The American Heritage Dictionary of the English Language, Third Edition*, Boston: Houghton Mifflin Company, 1992 and the *PMBOK Guide — 2000 Edition.*

Product description In a *project*, the product description documents the characteristics of the physical product, service or result sought in pursuing the project. It is established prior to project initiation and should be embellished as the project progresses. The product description should have sufficient detail to support project planning throughout the project. Adapted from *PMBOK Guide — 2000 Edition.*

Product group, product line, product family A grouping of products or SKUs for planning and forecasting requirements.

Product life cycle A well-known marketing concept that holds that products pass through phases in their market lives. The phases are inception, growth, maturity and decline. The presence of the product life cycle has implications for supply chain design.

Product pipeline, product funnel Visual models of the way new products are developed. The concept implies a repetitive pattern for producing products. SCM should be a part of the product-development process.

Product tree A graphical representation of the product and its SKUs. The tree can also show manufacturing locations and multiple geographic markets for the same or similar SKU.

Product-centric organization An organization structure built around different product lines. Preferred in cases of multiple products with different technologies, homogeneous customer bases, capital intensive and cost-driven businesses. *Handbook of Supply Chain Management.*

Product-centric supply chain Supply chains or organizations whose construct centers on the production of products. Alternatives are functional and customer-centric supply chains.

Product-producing sphere A sphere that produces products for external customers. The other type is an *enable sphere*, which provides a support service. The product-producing sphere is a "business inside the business. It merits its own supply chain design.

Program A group of related projects managed in a coordinated way. A synonym is *initiative*. A program can include project and ongoing operations work. For example, a new-product program includes product design (a temporary project) and ongoing manufacturing and sales (an operation). Adapted from the *PMBOK Guide — 2000 Edition*; *Handbook of Supply Chain Management*.

Progressive elaboration A property of projects that arises from the "temporary" and "unique" nature of projects. At the beginning of a project, the resulting product, service or result is defined broadly. As the project proceeds, the final result is "progressively elaborated." For example, a building project progressively proceeds from concept to design on paper to construction. Adapted from *PMBOK Guide — 2000 Edition*.

Project An organized change effort usually associated with an initiative or program, with a manager, budget, objectives and schedule. A project is temporary and produces a unique product, service or result. Several projects may support an *initiative* or *program*. *Action plans* define the goals for the project. Adapted from *PMBOK Guide — 2000 Edition* and the *Handbook of Supply Chain Management*.

Project life cycle A collection of generally sequential project phases needed for control of the project. Life cycle phases generally include the Initial, Intermediate, and Final phases. Different industries define these differently. For example, the construction industry might call the Initial Phase "Feasibility" and the Final Phase "Turnover and Startup." A software project might start with "Business Requirements" and finish with "Test and Deploy." Adapted from the *PMBOK Guide — 2000 Edition*.

Project manager A person responsible for managing a project. The project management function may rest with an individual for smaller projects and with a larger *project office* for larger ones. The project manager function coordinates the logistics involved in the project, including the activities of steering committees, design teams and employee teams testing new ways of working.

Project manufacturing Manufacturing processes designed for large, often unique, products requiring custom design. These processes require flexible processes and multiple engineering changes. Adapted from *APICS Dictionary 10th Edition*.

Project office A permanent line function for project managers with expertise in project management processes and tools; a repository of lessons learned and a champion for project management methodology. A project office can administer a larger supply chain project. Adapted from *Strategic Planning for Project Management.*

Promotion A term used by CGR to describe *risk pooling* to lower inventories. In promotion, products, product families or SKUs are moved higher in the tree (promoted) to concentrate demand.

Provider Service Models (PSMs) A tool for defining the staffing requirements to meet defined service objectives. Often used in managing the staff required to support operations focused on delivering services.

Public warehouse A warehouse that is rented or leased. Services are provided under contract or on a fee-for-service basis. Adapted from *APICS Dictionary 10th Edition.*

Pull system In production, replenishment only when items are taken for use as a result of a pull signal. For material control, an issue of material is made only in response to a pull signal from a using entity. Similarly, in distribution, a pull signal comes from the downstream warehouses close to the end-user. Adapted from *APICS Dictionary 10th Edition.*

Push and pull systems Production control systems are often described as "push" where decisions are based on forecasts, or "pull" where decisions are based on actual demand. A *demand-driven* supply chain is an example of a pull system. Most organizations try to move from "push" to "pull" decision-making.

Push system In production, replenishment from a schedule driven by forecast requirements. In material control, it is the issue of material based on forecast requirements. In distribution, replenishment is based on forecasts likely to be generated centrally. Adapted from *APICS Dictionary 10th Edition.*

Qualitative risk analysis Use of tools to identify the probability and potential outcomes to identify high-, moderate- and low-risk conditions to set priorities for response planning. Adapted from *PMBOK Guide — 2000 Edition.*

Quality Function Deployment (QFD) A system engineering process, which transforms the desires of the customer/user into the language required, at all project levels, to implement a product. It also provides the glue necessary, at all project levels, to tie it all together and manage it.

Quality standard A set of rules for those seeking to qualify under the standard. Standards are either general or industry-specific. Standards bring consistent practice to large numbers of participants in the supply chain.

Quality threshold The expected features of a product and its supply chain. Any participant must at least operate at the threshold to maintain market share. Those falling below the threshold lose market share and may have to exit the business.

Quantitative risk analysis Measurement of probability distributions and potential results to calculate a distribution of possible outcomes. Adapted from *PMBOK Guide — 2000 Edition*

Quick response program (QRP) A system to speed information flows through the supply chain. The purpose is to respond rapidly to changes in customer demand. Also *rapid replenishment*. Adapted from *APICS Dictionary 10th Edition*.

Radio frequency/automatic data collection Technology frequently deployed in supply chains for rapid processing of operating information.

Rapid replenishment Denotes frequent or fast response to signals for inventory restocking. Rapid replenishment enables demand-driven supply chain approaches.

Reengineering Analysis, redesign and implementation of process changes. Can involve new technology, new methods of performing process steps and organization change to support the process. The idea of reengineering should not be confused with downsizing or staffing cutbacks, although they may occur in conjunction with process change. Also *business process reengineering*.

Replenishment cycle time The total time from the moment a need is identified until the product is available for use. The *APICS Dictionary 10th Edition* uses "lead-time" to define this. Here we refer to cycle time as a physical property and lead-time as a market-determined property or expectation by customers for performance. Adapted from *APICS Dictionary 10th Edition*.

Representative product A typical product flowing through a process used as the basis for process design. The term is applied in developing manufacturing cells. Source: Bourton Group.

Residual income A method of combining the cost of capital assets and working capital with operating expense in calculating supply chain cost. The method converts asset value to equivalent uniform annual cost using discount rates and asset lifetime.

Responsibility assignment matrix (RAM) A matrix that identifies roles in a project for participants by type of responsibility. Appendix B2 is an example.

RETURN processes SCOR processes addressing return and receipt of products for repair, overhaul or refurbishment, or for resale. Includes post-delivery customer support.

Reverse logistics The processing of returned products from end users. This process includes matching returned goods authorizations; sorting salvageable, repairable and nonsalvageable inventories. Reverse logistics may be a neglected function in supply chain design. The flows involved reverse typical flows of physical goods, information and funds in the supply chain.

Risk An uncertain event or condition that could have a positive or negative effect on a project's objectives. Risk identification determines what risks might affect the project; a risk management plan will help manage project risks. Adapted from the *PMBOK Guide — 2000 Edition*.

Risk pooling The process of reducing risk among customers by pooling stock, reducing the total inventory required to provide a customer service level. CGR uses the term *promotion* to describe movement up the *product tree* resulting in pooling of lower levels of inventory. Adapted from *APICS Dictionary 10th Edition*.

Safety factor, safety stock Factor used to calculate the amount of inventory required to provide for uncertainty in forecasts. This is a numerical value based on a service standard, such as 95% certainty that orders will be filled. The factor usually ranges between 1 and 3 and is applied to the mean absolute deviation (MAD) or standard deviation (σ) to compute the safety stock required. The need for safety stock is reduced from *risk pooling*, more frequent replenishment, or taking advantage of commonality among SKU's using the 3C methodology.

Safety stock A quantity of stock planned to be in inventory to protect against demand fluctuations. The level of safety stock is a function of the uncertainty of the demand forecast during the replenishment period and uncertainties in the length of time required for replenishment. High uncertainty (such as for an innovative product) and longer lead times increase the need for safety stock. Also referred to as "buffer stock."

Schedule baseline The approved schedule developed in project planning. It is the standard by which subsequent progress is measured. Throughout the project, the baseline is updated based on actual progress. Adapted from *PMBOK Guide — 2000 Edition.*

SCO Supply chain orientation. A term coined by the University of Tennessee Supply Chain Research Group. It is a management philosophy that recognizes the implications of proactively managing both the upstream and downstream flows of products, services, finances and information.

Scope The sum of the products and services to be provided by a project. *Product scope* includes the features and functions in the products and services produced by the project. *Project scope* is what has to be done in the project to produce those features and functions. Adapted from *PMBOK Guide — 2000 Edition.*

SCOR Supply-Chain Operations Reference-model. An activity model developed by the Supply-Chain Council to standardize descriptions of supply chain processes.

SCPM Supply Chain Event Management. Used to describe software that tracks supply chain operations. Includes Supply Chain Event Management (SCEM) and Supply Chain Performance Management (SCPM). ARC Advisory Group.

Segmentation Breaking the market down into definable subcategories. For instance, Coca-Cola may segment its audience based on frequency (one can per month or five cans per day), location (Bangkok or Bangladesh) and many other criteria. Supply chains should be designed with the differing needs of multiple segments in mind.

Sell-Source-Ship (3S) A supply chain characterization in which the seller doesn't hold inventory. Once an order is placed, the seller channels orders to single or multiple sources. This is the opposite of the Buy-Hold-Sell model in which the seller does hold inventory. Also called "drop ship."

Seven wastes Shigeo Shingo developed these waste categories as part of the Just in Time philosophy: overproduction, waiting, transportation, stocks, motion, defects and processing.

Single Minute Exchange of Dies (SMED) A theory and the techniques for performing setup operations in fewer than 10 minutes, the number of minutes expressed in a single digit. The SMED philosophy is important in moving from "batch-" to "flow-oriented" supply chains.

SIOP, or S and OP Sales, (inventory) and operations planning. Processes for matching supply and demand. Usually an intermediate planning horizon. Also refers to a category of software to perform these tasks. Often these consist of several modules.

Six Sigma Sigma is a letter in the Greek alphabet. The term "sigma" is used to designate the distribution or spread about the mean (average) of any process or procedure. For a business or manufacturing process, the sigma value is a metric that indicates how well that process is performing. The higher the sigma value, the better. Sigma measures the capability of the process to perform defect-free work. A defect is anything that results in customer dissatisfaction. The sigma scale of measure is perfectly correlated to such characteristics as defects-per-unit, parts-per million defective and the probability of a failure/error. A Six-Sigma capability means no more than 3.4 parts per million defects. Recently, Six Sigma programs have become more general in their approach, reflecting overall efforts to make improvement as well as error-free production.

SKU (Stockkeeping unit) An inventory item whose status is maintained in an inventory tracking system. In the distribution system, different SKUs may represent the same item at different locations. Pronounced "skew." Adapted from *APICS Dictionary 10th Edition.*

SOURCE processes SCOR processes related to incoming material and services.

Specification A description of performance required from the supply chain for a process based on an evaluation of the as-is. The specification states only what is required, not how that goal will be reached.

Sphere A description of entities derived by dividing complex supply chain operations for the purposes of improvement. A sphere consists of market–product–operations combinations, or "businesses within the business." There are two types of sphere: *product-producing* and *enable.* The former has external customers. The latter provides support to multiple product-producing spheres and has internal customers. A related, but not synonymous, term from the Supply-Chain Council is "threads." *Handbook of Supply Chain Management.*

Sponsor An executive champion for a supply chain improvement effort. The level of the individual will depend on the level of the project — functional (department level), business unit level or supply chain level.

Stage 3 supply chain organization Stage 3 refers to the multicompany organization needed to implement supply chain level changes. A common goal, multicompany staffing, a third party "honest broker," creative win-win contracting and a senior management steering committee mark stage 3.

Stage gate approach to product development Formal processes used for the development of new products and services in companies of all sizes. It includes: (1) clearly defined stages in which specific tasks are undertaken,

(2) the development of compelling, comprehensive business cases, rigorous and demanding, (3) go/no go decision points at the end of each stage using clearly defined measurable criteria and (4) the objective review of actual vs. planned performance for every new product after its introduction to the marketplace. Adapted from *Winning at New Products* by Robert G. Cooper.

Statement of Work (SOW) A narrative description of products or services to be supplied, often part of contract terms. Adapted from the *PMBOK Guide — 2000 Edition.*

Statistical Process Control (SPC) A set of techniques and tools that help characterize patterns of variation. By understanding these patterns, a business can determine sources of variation and minimize them, resulting in a more consistent product or service. Many customers are demanding consistency as a measure of high quality. The proper use of SPC provides a powerful way to assure that the customer gets the desired consistency time after time.

Steering committee An executive-level group responsible for SCM projects. The steering committee makes decisions and sets policies. Membership depends on the levels represented: Level 1 is functional, or departmental; Level 2 is the business unit level; Level 3 is the multicompany or supply chain level. The steering committee is responsible for project results. It will also make important organization-related decisions. A project may have two steering committees. The first is inside the company that initiates the project. Later, a multicompany steering committee may oversee intercompany relationships, including processes and terms of agreements.

Strategic sourcing The use of the overall acquisition function as a tool for strategic improvement rather than one focused on transactions only. Involves both cost reduction from better purchasing and effective partnerships across the supply chain.

Strategy The ways in which the company will be different from competitors. *Strategy* is different from a *business model*, which defines the customers, their needs and the underlying economic logic for the organization. From Why Business Models Matter, *Harvard Business Review*, May 2002.

Subproject A smaller portion of a larger project. A subproject is likely to be managed just like a standalone project. Adapted from the *PMBOK Guide — 2000 Edition.*

Supplier clustering Deliberate sole sourcing of remote suppliers within a small geographic area to gain economies in shipping. Adapted from *APICS Dictionary 10th Edition.*

Supply chain Life cycle processes composing physical, information, financial and knowledge flows whose purpose is to satisfy end-user requirements with products and services from multiple, linked suppliers. *Handbook of Supply Chain Management.*

The global network used to deliver products and services from raw materials to end customers through an engineered flow of information, physical distribution and cash. *APICS Dictionary 10th Edition.*

Supply chain design According to the *APICS Dictionary 10th Edition*, facets of design include selection of partners, location and capacity of warehouse and production facilities, the products, the modes of transportation and supporting information systems.

Supply Chain Event Management (SCEM) Software feature that monitors supply chain transaction data for predefined "exceptions" or events that require intervention. An example could be a late order. In such a case, the SCEM software would alert designated parties to inform them and suggest interventions.

Supply Chain Management (SCM) Design, maintenance and operation of supply chain processes for satisfaction of end-user needs. *Handbook of Supply Chain Management.*

The design, planning, execution, control and monitoring of supply chain activities with the objective of creating net value, building a competitive infrastructure, leveraging worldwide logistics, synchronizing supply with demand and measuring performance globally. *APICS Dictionary 10th Edition.*

Supply chain strategy The idea that supply chain design should support overall strategies for competing.

Supply-Chain Council (SCC) A trade association of companies interested in SCM. The Council was incorporated in June 1997 as a not-for-profit trade association. It offers members an opportunity to improve the effectiveness of supply-chain relationships from the customer's customer to the supplier's supplier.

Synchronized supply chain A general vision of having all links in the supply chain producing at the same rate as customer demand. Obstacles include coordination, batch-size limitations in production and inability to share information. However, synchronization is a useful goal, as it is likely to provide high levels of customer service at lower cost than unsynchronized supply chains. The term is somewhat synonymous with a *lean supply chain.*

Takt time The interval that sets the pace of production to match the rate of customer demand. It is the "heartbeat" of the lean production system. The term is derived from the German expression for a metronome beat. Adapted from *APICS Dictionary 10th Edition.*

Target costing A strategic profit planning and cost management system that incorporates a strict focus on customer wants, needs and values and translates them into delivered products and services. A variation is using cost as a design criterion in product development.

Task The lowest level of effort on a project. Not included in a work breakdown structure, but could be part of the decomposition of work by individuals responsible for the work. Adapted from the *PMBOK Guide — 2000 Edition.*

TCP/IP Transmission control protocol/Internet protocol. The communications protocol used by the Internet.

Template An activity list containing skills, resources, deliverables, dependencies and risks that is appropriate for reuse from one project to another. Adapted from *PMBOK Guide — 2000 Edition.*

Theory of Constraints (TOC) A portfolio of management philosophies, management disciplines and industry-specific "best practices" developed over the past 20 years by physicist Dr. Eliyahu M. Goldratt and his associates.

Third party logistics provider A company specializing in performing logistics-related services for its customers. Examples include warehouse, transportation and product assembly. Also called "3PL."

Thread A multientity supply chain that uses different Level 2 SCOR execution processes. For example, a make-to-stock company supplies a make-to-order company. *Sphere* is a related work with a broader meaning.

Throughput In the theory of constraints, the rate at which the system generates money through sales. This does not necessarily mean output in terms of physical production so excludes inventory building. Adapted from *APICS Dictionary 10th Edition.*

To-be The future state, or how a supply chain process will be performed in the future. Determined after examining trade-offs between an ideal goal (*greenfield*) and constraints standing in the way of implementing that ideal.

Total Cost of Ownership (TCO) All the costs associated with buying, supporting and operating a product or a component.

Total Productive Maintenance (TPM) A systematic approach for minimizing machine "downtime" resulting from unexpected breakdowns. TPM emphasizes the role of the machine operator who becomes more involved with routine checks and fine-tuning. TPM enables machinery to operate more efficiently and reliably, decreasing the risk of a "broken link" in the supply chain.

Total Quality Management (TQM) An approach that involves all employees in continually improving products and work processes to achieve customer satisfaction and world-class performance. TQM is generally associated with "bottom-up" incremental improvement.

Toyota Production System A manufacturing process model developed by Toyota that contributed to its reputation for quality in the auto industry. The Toyota production system was built on three key factors that differentiated it from practices being employed by their competitors in the auto industry: (1) reduced lot sizes, leading to production flexibility; (2) controlling parts required in production to enable them to be provided when and where they are needed for specific tasks; (3) arranging production equipment in the order that people work so that value is added instead of grouping by equipment function. All these elements involved suppliers and customers to some extent.

Traceability An attribute that allows for ongoing location of items in the supply chain.

Tracking signal A signal that forecasting techniques should be reevaluated. *Handbook of MRP II and JIT.*

Transfer pricing The pricing of goods and services between entities in the supply chain. These entities can be internal or with outside organizations. Supply chain partnerships require agreements on pricing.

Trigger, trigger events An indication a risk has occurred or is about to occur. A trigger may activate a risk response or a replanning of supply chain operations.

TRIZ Russian acronym for Theory of Incentive Problem Solving. TRIZ is a methodology for eliminating conflicts that arise in product design. *QFD Handbook* by Revelle, Moran and Cox.

Truckload/less than truckload carriers (LTL) Carriers that cater to the needs of different classes of shippers. Truckload-only carriers generally serve larger shippers. LTL carriers generally serve smaller shippers.

Two bin system An inventory rule that calls for a new order when one bin (either real or conceptual) runs out. The second bin then becomes the source of new requirements. The reorder quantity is equal to the bin size and depends on lead times and usage quantities. The method is one of the simplest to implement and lends itself to visual approaches.

Upstream A reference to the "front end" component and raw material suppliers in the supply chain. *Downstream* is the end of the supply chain nearest to end-users.

Value chain The source of strategic advantage within the firm. It stems from the many discrete activities a firm performs including those associated with the supply chain. Value is created through cost efficiencies or differentiation from competitors. Adapted from *Competitive Advantage: Creating and Sustaining Superior Performance* by Michael Porter.

Variable costing An accounting approach to support management decision-making. Variable costs normally consist of direct labor and material plus variable overhead. Fixed overhead, which is allocated, is not included, although it is included in the cost of goods sold, the basis for inventory costing.

Variable costing is more valid in making decisions related to make or buy, economic order quantities and other decisions. Supply chain design may transform variable into fixed costs. For example, a *milk run* will be made regardless of a decision to replenish for any single SKU. Therefore, the reorder cost (including transportation) assumption related to the decision should be reduced accordingly.

The approach is consistent with the theory of constraints, which maintains that operating expense is relatively fixed over a range of production.

VAT analysis Analysis of product structure from the *theory of constraints.* A "V" structure has few raw materials and many products. An "A" structure has many raw materials and few end products. A "T" structure has numerous similar finished products assembled from common components. An understanding of the product structure is a foundation for supply chain design. Adapted from *APICS Dictionary 10th Edition.*

Velocity A term that describes how much time a unit of production spends in actual process steps as a percent of total time in the process. Low velocities mean much of the time required for processing is spent in waiting on value-adding steps in the process. A goal of supply chain design is often to increase velocity. The term is increasingly applied to administrative as well as physical processing.

Vendor Managed Inventory (VMI); Vendor Managed Replenishment (VMR) The practice of partnering between distribution channel members that changes the traditional replenishment process from distributor-generated purchase orders, based on economic order quantities, to the replenishment of products based on actual and forecast product demand. Source: CRP Best.

A process by which a supplier automatically replenishes customer stock based on actual sales or shipments. Also called continuous replenishment. *APICS Dictionary 10th Edition.*

Some practitioners view VMR as an enhancement of VMI, requiring more collaboration.

Virtual enterprise A team of individual companies organized to meet a market opportunity as if they were all part of the same company with a common goal.

Virtual private network (VPN) A private network that uses Internet technology. It is accessible only by authorized users. It is seen as a cost-effective alternative to dedicated lines.

Virtual value chain The virtual information-based equivalent of the value chain model where value is created by gathering, selecting, synthesizing and distributing information. Rayport, J.F. and Sviokla, J.J. Exploiting the virtual value chain, *Harvard Business Review*, November–December, 1995.

Voice of the customer A component of Quality Function Deployment (QFD) that uses customers' requirements as the basis for design of a product or process.

Wall-to-wall inventory A technique in which material enters a plant and is processed into finished goods without entering a formal stock area. Also four-wall inventory. *APICS Dictionary 10th Edition.*

Warehouse Management System (WMS) A system that tracks and controls the movement of inventory through the warehouse, from receiving to shipping. Many WMS systems also plan transportation requirements into and out of the warehouse. The WMS allows visibility to the quantity and location of inventory, as well as the age of the inventory, to give a current and accurate picture of the Available to Promise (ATP) stock.

Web services Supply chain applications delivered over the Internet. These reduce the cost and complexity of forming links between supply chain partners and customers for products in the chain. They use shared standards to speed the job of developing links. Adapted from "The Strategic Value of Web Services" from the *McKinsey Quarterly* and Business Processes and Web Services by Alan Kotok at http://www.webservices.org.

WERC The Warehousing Educational and Research Council. An international professional association dedicated to the advancement and education of people involved in the management of warehouses and distribution facilities.

Work Breakdown Structure (WBS) A deliverable-oriented grouping of project elements that organizes and defines the total work scope of the project. Descending levels add detailed definition to the project work. Adapted from the *PMBOK Guide — 2000 Edition.*

Work flow A class of software applications that includes automation of the flow of information according to process rules. Similar to, but not as encompassing as, a proactive systems approach in which the requirements of decision makers are part of the redesign of the supply chain.

Work in progress (WIP) Units of production that have started — but not finished — the production process. Material entering the factory usually starts as raw material, then becomes WIP and then proceeds to finished goods. High WIP levels are characteristic of long *cycle times* or low *velocity* in production.

Work package A deliverable at the lowest level of the Work Breakdown Structure, when that deliverable may be assigned to another project manager. A work package can be divided into activities. Adapted from the *PMBOK Guide — 2000 Edition.*

World class Being best in your industry on enough competitive factors to achieve profit goals and be considered one of the best in satisfying customers.

XML Extensible markup language. This is a flexible cousin of HTML, the format for web pages. HTML just describes how the document will look. XML describes what's in the document and is not concerned about the display but the organization of the information. XML enables transfer of data among databases and websites without losing descriptive information. It also speeds searches because the search engines can look at tags rather than lengthy text. A standard syntax is required to allow companies to share information. Explaining XML, *Harvard Business Review*, July–August 2000.

Yield management Using price and other promotions to maximize return on investment. Usually implies a fixed capacity, such as airline seats, to be filled with customers from segments paying different prices.

Bibliography

A Guide to the Project Management Body of Knowledge (PMBOK Guide®), Newtown Square: Project Management Institute, 2000.

Ayers, James B., Gustin, Craig and Stephens, Scott, Reengineering the supply chain, *Information Strategy: the Executive's Journal,* Fall 1997 (14/1), pp. 13–18.

Ayers, James B. and Malmberg, David R., Supply chain systems: Are you ready? *Information Strategy: the Executive's Journal,* Fall 2002, pp. 18–27.

Ayers, James B., *Handbook of Supply Chain Management,* Boca Raton: St. Lucie Press/APICS, 2001.

Ayers, James B., *Improving Your Competitive Position: a Project Management Approach,* Detroit: Society of Manufacturing Engineers, 1990.

Ayers, James B., *Making Supply Chain Management Work: Design, Implementation, Partnerships, Technology, and Profits,* Boca Raton: Auerbach Publications, 2002.

Ayers, James B., Supply chain strategies. *Information Strategy: The Executive's Journal,* (15/2) Winter 1999, pp. 2–10.

Ayers, James B., What smokestack industries can tell us about reengineering, *Information Strategy: The Executive's Journal,* (11/2) Winter 1995, pp. 20–26.

Ayers, Jim and Bonhag, Robert, Work performance follows human enhancement, *Administrative Radiology Journal,* November, 1998 (17/11), pp. 27–32.

Beavers, Alex N., *Roadmap to the e–Factory,* Boca Raton: Auerbach Publications, 2000.

Bensaou, M. and Earl, Michael, The right mindset for managing information technology, *The Harvard Business Review,* September–October, 1998, pp. 119–128.

Bermudez, John, Supply chain management: More than just technology, *Supply Chain Management Review,* March–April 2002, pp. 15–16.

Bhote, Keki R., *Strategic Supply Management: A Blueprint for Revitalizing the Manufacturer–Supplier Partnership,* New York, AMACOM, 1989.

Bovel, David and Sheffi, Yossi, The brave new world of supply chain management, *Supply Chain Management Review,* Spring, 1998, pp.14–22.

Bower, Charles C. and Reiter, Stephen E., *Supply Chain Optimization: Building the Strategic Total Business Network,* Barrett-Kohler, 1996.

Bowersox, D.J. and Closs, David J., *Logistical Management: The Integrated Supply Chain Process,* McGraw-Hill, 1996.

Burt, David N., Managing suppliers up to speed, *Harvard Business Review,* July–August, 1989.

Cahill, Joseph B., Whirlpool experiences shipping delays over computer glitches in SAP software, *The Wall Street Journal,* November 3, 1999, p. A3.

Camp, Robert C. *Benchmarking,* Milwaukee: ASQC Quality Press, 1989.

Cavinato, Joseph L., What's your supply chain type? *Supply Chain Management Review,* pp. 60–66, May/June 2002.

Cliffe, Sarah, ERP implementation; How to avoid $100 million write-offs, *Harvard Business Review,* January–February 1999, pp. 16–17.

Cooper, Robert G., *Winning at New Products,* 2nd ed., Addison–Wesley Publishing Company, Reading, Massachusetts, 1993.

Cooper, Robin and Chew, W. Bruce, Control tomorrow's costs through today's designs, *Harvard Business Review*, January–February, 1996.

Copacino, William C., *Supply Chain Management: The Basics and Beyond*, Boca Raton: St. Lucie Press, 1997.

Costanza, John R., *The Quantum Leap in Speed to Market*, 3rd ed. Englewood, Colorado, John Costanza Institute of Technology, 1996.

Cox III, James F. and Blackstone, Jr., John H., *APICS Dictionary*, 10th ed., Alexandria: APICS – The Educational Society for Resource Management, 2002.

Doherty, Katherine, How far to supply chain paradise?" *Food Logistics*, September, 1998, No. 14, 23–32.

Dyer, Jeffrey H., How Chrysler created an American keiretsu, *Harvard Business Review*, July–August, 1996.

Eisenhardt, Kathleen M. and Brown, Shona L., Patching: Restitching business portfolios in dynamic markets, *Harvard Business Review*, May–June, 1999, pp. 72–82.

Feitzinger, Edward and Lee, Hau, Mass customization at Hewlett–Packard: The power of postponement, *Harvard Business Review*, January–February, 1997, 116–121.

Fernández-Rañada, Miguel, Gurrola-Gal, F. Xavier, and López-Tello, Enrique, *3C: A Proven Alternative to MRPII for Optimizing Supply Chain Performance*, Boca Raton: St. Lucie Press, 2000.

Fisher, Marshall L., Hammond, Janice H., Obermeyer, Walter R. and Raman, Ananth, Making supply meet demand in an uncertain world, *Harvard Business Review*, May–June, 1994.

Fisher, Marshall L., What is the right supply chain for your product? *Harvard Business Review*, (75/2), March–April, 1997, pp.105–116.

Fites, Donald V., Make your dealers your partners, *Harvard Business Review*, March–April, 1996.

Geary, Steve, Childerhouse, Paul and Towill, Denis, Uncertainty and the seamless supply chain, *Supply Chain Management Review*. July–August 2002, pp. 52–61.

Gilliland, Michael, Is forecasting a waste of time? *Supply Chain Management Review*. July–August 2002, pp. 16–23.

Goldratt, Eliyahu M. and Cox, Jeff, *The Goal*, Croton–on–Hudson: North River Press, 1984.

Goldratt, Eliyahu M. and Fox, Robert E., *The Race*, Croton–on–Hudson: North River Press, 1986.

Gouillart, Francis J. and Sturdivant, Frederick D., Spend a day in the life of your customers, *Harvard Business Review*, January–February, 1994.

Hagel III, John and Brown, John Seely, Your next IT strategy, *Harvard Business Review* *(79/9)*, October, 2001, pp. 105–113.

Hamel, Gary and Prahalad, C.K., Strategic intent, *Harvard Business Review*, (67/3) May–June, 1989, pp. 63–76.

Hamel, Gary and Prahalad, C.K., The core competency of the corporation, *Harvard Business Review*, (68/3) May–June, 1990, pp. 79–90.

Harbison, John R. and Pekar, Peter, *Smart Alliances: A Practical Guide to Repeatable Success*, San Francisco: Jossey–Bass, 1998.

Hauser, John R. and Clausing, Don, The house of quality, *Harvard Business Review*, (66/3), May–June 1988, pp.63–73.

Haverly, Richard C. and Whelan, James F., *Logistics Software: 1998 Edition, Volume 1*, Council of Logistics Management. (Compact Disc).

Hayes, Robert H. and Pisano, Gary P., Beyond world-class: The new manufacturing strategy, *Harvard Business Review*, January–February, 1994.

Hayes, Robert H. and Wheelwright, Steven C. *Restoring Our Competitive Edge: Competing Through Manufacturing*, New York, John Wiley & Sons, 1984.

Hayes, Robert H., Wheelwright Steven C. and Clark, Kim B. *Dynamic Manufacturing: Creating the Learning Organization,* New York: Free Press, 1988.

Hicks, Douglas T., *Activity–Based Costing: Making it Work for Small and Mid–Sized Companies*, 2nd ed., New York: John Wiley & Sons, Inc., 1999.

House, Charles H. and Price, Raymond L., The return map: tracking product teams, *Harvard Business Review*, January–February, 1991, pp. 92–100.

Iansiti, Marco and West, Jonathan, Technology integration: Turning great research into great products, *Harvard Business Review*, (75/3), May–June, 1997, pp. 69–79.

Imai, Masaaki, *Kaizen,* New York: Random House, 1986.

Jennings, Dana and Kling, Greg, Integration of disparate enterprise IT systems, presented to Supply–Chain World Conference sponsored by the Supply–Chain Council, April, 1999.

Juran, J.M., *Juran on Quality by Design*, New York: The Free Press, 1992.

Kaplan, Robert S. and Norton, David P., The balanced scorecard — measures that drive performance, *Harvard Business Review*, January–February 1992, pp. 71–79.

Kerzner, Harold, *Project Management: A Systems Approach to Planning, Scheduling, and Controlling, Seventh Edition*, New York: John Wiley & Sons, Inc., 2001.

Kerzner, Harold, *Strategic Planning for Project Management: Using a Project Management Maturity Model*, New York: John Wiley & Sons, Inc., 2001.

Kim, W. Chan and Mauborgne, Renee, Creating new market space, *Harvard Business Review*, (77/1), January–February, 1999, pp. 83–93.

Kumar, Nirmalya, The power of trust in manufacturer–retailer relationships, *Harvard Business Review*, November–December, 1996.

Lee, Hau L. What constitutes supply chain integration? *IEEM Network News*, Stanford University School of Engineering, Summer, 1998.

Lewin, Marsha, Kennedy, Keith, and Ayers, Jim; Transformation through proactive systems: a case study, *Information Strategy: The Executive's Journal*, (12/3), Spring 1996, pp. 29–35.

Lutz, Robert A., *Guts*, New York: John Wiley & Sons, Inc., 1998.

Magretta, Joan, Why business models matter, *Harvard Business Review,* pp. 87–92, May 2002.

McGrath, Rita Gunther and MacMillan, Ian C., Discovery-driven planning, *Harvard Business Review*, July–August, 1995, pp. 44–54.

Monden, Yasuhiro, *Toyota Production System*, Norcross, Georgia: Institute of Industrial Engineers, 1983.

Montcrief, Bob and Stonich, Mark, Supply-chain practice maturity model and performance assessment, a presentation by the Performance Management Group (PMG) and Pittiglio Rabin Todd and McGrath (PRTM), November 6, 2001.

Morris, Steven A. and McManus, Denise Johnson, Information infrastructure centrality in the agile organization, *Information Systems Management*, Fall 2002, pp. 8–12.

Nagel, Roger and Dove, Rick, *21st Century Manufacturing Enterprise Strategy*, Iacocca Institute, Lehigh University, November 1991.

Narus, James. A. and Anderson, James C., Rethinking distribution: adaptive channels, *Harvard Business Review*, July–August, 1996.

Nelson, Emily and Ramstad, Evan, Hershey's biggest dud has turned out to be its new technology, *The Wall Street Journal*, October 28, 1999, p. A1.

Nyman, Lee R., *Making Manufacturing Cells Work*, Detroit: Society of Manufacturing Engineers, 1992.

Petroff, John N., *Handbook of MRPII and JIT: Strategies for Total Manufacturing Control,* Englewood Cliffs: Prentice-Hall, 1993.

Poirier, Charles C., The path to supply chain leadership, *Supply Chain Management Review,* (2/3), Fall, 1998, pp. 16–26.

Poirier, Charles, Achieving supply chain connectivity, *Supply Chain Management Review, November/December 2002,* pp. 16–22.

Porter, Michael E., *Competitive Advantage: Creating and Sustaining Superior Performance,* New York: The Free Press, 1985.

Porter, Michael E., *Competitive Strategy: Techniques for Analyzing Industries and Competitors,* New York: The Free Press, 1980.

Porter, Michael E., Strategy and the Internet, *Harvard Business Review,* (79/3) March 2001. pp. 62–78.

Porter, Michael E., Strategy and the Internet, *Harvard Business Review,* pp. 62–78, March 2001.

Porter, Michael E., What is strategy? *Harvard Business Review,* (74/6) November–December, 1996, pp. 61–78.

Project Management Institute, *A Guide to the Project Management Body of Knowledge (PMBOK Guide — 2000 Edition),* Newtown Square, Pennsylvania: Project Management Institute, 2000.

Ptak, Carol A. and Schragenheim, Eli, *ERP: Tools, Techniques, and Applications for Integrating the Supply Chain,* Boca Raton: St. Lucie Press, 2000.

Rayport, Jeffrey F. and Sviokla, John J., Exploiting the virtual value chain, *Harvard Business Review,* November–December, 1995.

ReVelle, Jack B., Moran, John W., and Cox, Charles A., *The QFD Handbook.* New York: John Wiley & Sons, 1998.

Rigby, Darrell K., Reichheld, Frederick F. and Schefter, Phil, Avoid the four perils of CRM, *Harvard Business Review,* February 2002, pp. 101–109.

Riggs, David A. and Robbins, Sharon L., *The Executive's Guide to Supply Chain Management: Building Supply Chain Thinking into All Business Processes,* New York, AMACOM, 1998.

Robert, Michel, *Strategy Pure and Simple II,* New York, McGraw-Hill, 1998.

Roche, Eileen, Explaining XML, *Harvard Business Review,* (78/4), July–August 2000, p. 18.

Ross, David F., *Competing Through Supply Chain Management: Creating Market-Winning Strategies Through Supply Chain Partnerships,* Chapman and Hall Material Management Series, 1997.

Ross, Jeanne W. and Weill, Peter, Six IT decisions your IT people shouldn't make, *Harvard Business Review,* November 2002, pp. 85–91.

Roztocki, N. and Needy, K.L., An integrated activity-based costing and economic value added system as an engineering management tool for manufacturers, 1998 ASEM National Conference Proceedings, Virginia Beach, October 1–3, 1998, pp. 77–84.

Skinner, Wickham. The focused factory, *Harvard Business Review,* May–June, 1974.

Slater, Derek, The ties that bolt, *CIO Magazine,* April 15, 1999.

Tinnirello, Paul C., *Project Management,* Boca Raton: Auerbach Publications, 2000.

Turbide, Dave, What is APS? *Midrange ERP,* January/February, 1998.

Upton, David M. and McAfee, Andrew, The real virtual factory, *Harvard Business Review,* July–August, 1996.

Upton, David M., The management of flexibility, *California Management Review,* (36/2), Winter 1994, pp. 72–89.

Upton, David M., What really makes factories flexible, *Harvard Business Review,* July–August, 1995.

Walton, Mary, *The Deming Management Method*, The Putnam Publishing Group: New York, 1986.

Wheelwright, Steven C. and Clark, Kim B., *Revolutionizing Product Development*, New York: Free Press, 1992.

Womack, James P. and Jones, Daniel T., Beyond Toyota: How to root out waste and pursue perfection, *Harvard Business Review*, September–October, 1996, pp. 140–158.

Womack, James P. and Jones, Daniel T., From lean production to the lean enterprise, *Harvard Business Review*, March–April, 1994, pp. 93–103.

Woods, John A. and Marien, Edward J., *The Supply Chain Yearbook, 2001 Edition*, New York: McGraw-Hill, 2001.

Appendix A1:
Change Management in a Complex Supply Chain Configuration Project

Ted Pollock

This project illustrates the problems of gaining internal cooperation in a large company. The North American operations of a $2 billion consumer packaged-goods company reached that level of revenue through several recent and substantial acquisitions. Combined with two base businesses, the acquisitions grew the supply chain network to almost 100 plants, co-packers and warehouse sites ... some in the same metropolitan areas.

The acquired companies were all quickly absorbed into three business units. While all three produce beverages in bottles and cans, the supply chain strategies of each differed in one form or another. An example was related to decisions about outsourced vs. company-owned production. Another entailed the path to market, whether through sales to bottlers or through distributors or direct to retail chains.

The parent company recognized that the network was growing with no strategic plan in place. It was assumed that significant cost savings opportunities were embedded in the network configuration, with the major portion being in manufacturing realignments.

A1.1 THE CHALLENGES

Two principal challenges stood in the way of achieving the expected benefits. First, it was clear that a network modeling approach using network modeling software was necessary. The model to be developed would be one of the most ambitious ones from the perspective of the author and also the software firm who developed the model. It would include all existing plants, co-packers and warehouses, plus candidate sites for mixed business unit production in several strategic locations throughout the country.

For new plant sites, the model design also included a fixed cost for production lines and the plant in general such that the model could choose to open any number of lines in a plant, if it found the tradeoff of new fixed costs vs. lower variable costs to be acceptable.

A second challenge was that the three independent business units would need to consider a new strategic direction, namely participation in shared facilities. As is the case in any multibusiness unit study of this nature, the potential exists for one business unit, in one site, to be the point of meaningful cost-savings leverage while another business unit does not expect to reap significant rewards.

For example, it may be that a new plant is not feasible without two or more production lines absorbing the overhead. Business unit "1" might reap tremendous rewards based on variable cost (production and freight) improvements. Business unit "2" might not. However, both operating together yield a feasible solution. So benefits had to be evaluated based on the total business, not just individual profit centers.

A1.2 EARLY INTRODUCTION OF CHANGE MANAGEMENT

These challenges might seem to "simply" suggest the need for a rigorous analytical methodology. However, what was perhaps as important was the need to start the change management process during the project rather than what is more typical — as an implementation afterthought.

The change management process essentially embodied consensus development that included the following elements:

- Starting at the proposal presentation where all business units were present and had equal "voting" privileges regarding the project's scope, technical approach and selection of the consultant.
- "Playback packs" — reports summarizing data analysis that each business unit provided — sent to each business unit. This enabled them to perform sanity checks, make changes and, in general, be confident that the model was using data that properly reflected their operations.
- Weekly telephone conference calls regarding status against plan and, more importantly, issues surrounding data collection or interpretation.
- Formal milestone presentations conducted ensuring each of the business unit executives an opportunity to question, challenge and suggest.
- Participation in the modeling effort of the logistics executive of the business unit with the most to gain. This provided the opportunity to review model runs and suggest changes "on the fly."

All too frequently, the words "involvement in the project" are hollow. It is clear that while this factor may not ensure a successful study result, the absence of this early component of change management almost invariably leads to surprises and disappointment. Build the change management process into the project plan. Start the change management process on day one.

Appendix A2:
Supply Chain Facility Network Design

Peter A. Crosby

A2.1 THE COMPANY AND ITS SCM PROJECT

The company is an international manufacturer and distributor of frozen consumer products through retail outlets it owns and franchises. The company is organized in the form of a typical process manufacturer from the production side with plants providing the products they make best. The organization also includes a division that franchises retail outlets and manages company-owned and -operated retail outlets.

Raw materials and ingredients are purchased from independent suppliers. The primary raw material is sourced close to the plants. Some ingredients are stored and consolidated in central third-party logistics company locations with stock moved to the plants when needed.

The importance of manufacturing comes from the increased control the company has on its upstream cost of manufactured goods. Production control is important to maintain consistently high quality standards to "delight" consumers.

The supply chain is complex. Challenges to a project to change the supply chain arise from several causes, including the following:

- There are 10 domestic outsourced co-packers as well as company-owned and -operated plants. Coordination and planning for a "mixed" system at many locations requires a significant central planning and scheduling staff at the corporate headquarters.
- The company has a foreign parent that manages other product lines and companies. Organizationally, one "family" of product line managers who specialize in dry, ambient product has attempted to dominate and control a dominant frozen-product "culture." This provides challenges in training and communication between the parent and managers.
- The supply chain used third-party logistics operations as well as company-owned and -operated warehouses and truck fleets. As in a mixed plant configuration, a partially outsourced distribution system requires more effort than a single type of logistics organization.

- The company has both franchised and company-owned stores. Company outlets are easier to manage and control than franchisees.
- Sources of supply were unstable and government regulated. Switching suppliers presented challenges in procurement-sourcing consistency and incoming quality control.

The company's industry environment is characterized by intense competition and continual change. Companies in the industry exchange ownership frequently. There are also consolidations and new entrants in the marketplace. Alternative distribution channels, such as the mass merchandiser channels, vs. the restaurant channels, are evolving. Also, competitors are developing improved quality products commanding higher prices sold through retail chains.

The company's supply chain objectives are to take as much cost from the chain as possible to maintain margins and to remain competitive in retail pricing. The supply chain project undertaken by the company conducted a diagnostic study to identify areas for cost reduction and operational improvement. The diagnostic study included:

1. Developing an "as-is" profile of the supply chain, including mapping current processes, volume flows and costs
2. Evaluating the "as-is" supply chain. Setting specification for a new supply chain
3. Identifying alternative supply chain scenarios using the specifications
4. Designing the "ideal" supply chain for the company
5. Determining the cost and resource trade-offs to come up with the "to-be" supply chain
6. Developing an implementation action plan for the "to-be"

The president assembled a team of executives that included the following roles:

- **Project Steering Committee**, consisting of a project executive sponsor, the president and CEO, a day-to-day project liaison, the CFO and a consultant manager
- **Project Liaison:** Director of Operations
- **Contact personnel:** From the production, distribution, finance, MIS and marketing departments

A2.1.1 SUCCESSES

This case illustrates both success and lack thereof in implementing supply chain change. Successes were achieved in the following areas:

- Improving the process flow of products throughout the supply chain, thereby reducing cost by approximately 5% and increasing product quality by having fresher product in the outlets

- Reallocating product production from one plant to the other (a plant that represented about 25% of the total company plant capacity was proposed to be closed and its production shifted to underutilized plants)
- Realigning territories served by facilities
- Establishing new warehouse locations closer to clusters of cuxtomer-outlets
- Lowering product delivery costs by 10% by using fuller trailers
- Identifying opportunities for outsourcing both production and distribution (lowering production costs by up to 5%)
- Identifying opportunities for leveraging underutilized assets by collaborating with other frozen-product companies

A2.1.2 Shortfalls

Lack of success was evident in the work because:

- Plant closures that would generate major operating expense savings were not implemented on a timely basis due to resistance to change in personnel status, accounting write-offs, severance cost avoidance and the low value of plant equipment.
- The desire to maintain the "status quo" with entrenched, long-term employees was stronger than the logic with savings and ROI projections. A more persuasive argument should have been made from a marketplace-competition standpoint.
- Outsourced opportunities were also very slow to be implemented, due to resistance to organizational change and the required personnel status changes. Eventually, after a few years, production and distribution were all outsourced, so the company could focus on its core competencies of franchising, outlet growth, product development, marketing and promotion of the brand. Again, a more aggressive case for the benefits of outsourcing should have been made.

A2.1.3 Root Causes

Management faced a series of challenges. For example, outsourcing production and distribution was counter to the current company culture of "do it ourselves." The culture was strongly against personnel termination or relocation and facility closure or relocation. Management was highly resistant to change. These feelings involved overcoming psychological barriers and avoiding a resulting feeling of losing control of the business.

Companies are always suspicious of accepting advice from advisory services. They believe they know the business best and an outsider can't possibly understand their company. Dealing with difficult personalities within the entrenched management ranks is also a challenge. Arranging strategic alliances with other companies in similar businesses requires new levels of collaboration not familiar to employees who are experienced working only within their own internal company structure.

The options open to management to address these challenges were many. The status quo could be maintained, or a partial or complete outsourcing of production and distribution facilities could be arranged. Fleet rolling stock and drivers could also be outsourced. Transportation resources could also be shared with another frozen-products company. The fleet backhaul program could be expanded to offer for-hire transportation.

Also, changes in physical product flows between facilities could be made to improve product quality, reduce cost and reduce inventory. Company facilities could be reconfigured, or new facilities could be opened. Outlet service territories from existing facilities could be recast and reallocated. Forecasting, production scheduling and inventory management processes, rules and methods could also be altered.

Changes made to the project approach in response to the situation included working more closely with the president and CEO in order to use the leverage of the top executive to facilitate change. Less reliance was made in leaving implementation to middle management executives, the project liaison and design team members, who didn't have the organizational clout to facilitate change on a timely basis.

A2.2 OUTCOME AND LESSONS LEARNED

A major benefit of the effort was improvement in competitive position. Product unit prices in the market were held constant for a longer period of time. Price increases were avoided for as long as possible. This helped to maintain market share and outlet sales, in the face of competition from alternative channels of distribution and from products with similar characteristics but varying levels of product quality.

Overall, the project was a success. Over a 10-year period, all recommendations were implemented, but were a result of an ownership and management change that took place after the formal implementation phase of work was completed. The biggest lesson learned is that change does not happen overnight.

Appendix A3:
Lessons from a Failed Supply Chain Initiative

Louis J. De Rose

A3.1 THE COMPANY

Xerxes, a real company but a fictitious name, is a midsize producer of semiconductors for the networking and telecommunications industries. The company is a subsidiary of a larger parent that is headquartered in another state, but which does business worldwide through multiple divisions and affliates.

Xerxes is a "fabless" semiconductor manufacturer. This means it designs the devices. It then contracts out capital-intensive wafer production and testing, as well as assembly and packaging, usually to companies in Asia and Latin America. Due to fast growth in developing markets, the company's product mix is extensive and steadily expanding. Given the prospects for continuing growth and the complex structure of its supply base, Xerxes decided to initiate an SCM project.

An SCM task force comprising representatives from the Engineering, Marketing, Operations, Procurement-Logistics and Finance departments was assembled and met on a weekly basis. Its mission was to study the supply chain situation and come up with an action plan in 3 months' time. An outside consulting firm assisted the task force and guided it through the study phase to the point of implementation. The 3 months stretched out to 5 months and "supply chain management" remained more a theoretical concept and less an "implementable" initiative.

As a consultant retained to assess the company's procurement and logistics operations, I saw first-hand the reasons for that initiative to fail. Here are a few of those reasons:

- There was little real commitment from senior management to make the project succeed. Lip service was paid to the SCM concept, but management's prime concerns were increasing market share, speeding up new-product introduction and meeting the profit projections made to the parent company for the next few fiscal quarters.
- At the task force level, there was continuing debate as to the scope and extent of the supply chain model and structure. Operations insisted it

began when wafers were tested and received from foundries. Procurement-Logistics argued that it must begin at the product design stage. Clearly, it contended, once Engineering qualifies wafer, test and assembly sources, they are locked into the company's supply chain, for better or for worse. Hence, to ignore Product Design as an integral factor in the supply chain paradigm would be to invite failure.

In Xerxes' period of fast growth and high-capacity utilization, management's priority was to build to total demand, regardless of distinctions in product mix, market segments, or specific customer demand patterns. Considerations of revenue contribution, high- vs. low-volume demand, standard or unique application, susceptibility to engineering change, or early obsolescence were ignored in the planning and scheduling process. The consequence was that, when business fell off, revenue and inventories were badly misaligned. This led to write-downs on excess inventory, price-cutting and reduced margins on saleable product and serious budgetary and cash flow problems.

Xerxes' information systems included software from multiple vendors, each addressing one or another element of the supply chain process. Further, with no common platform to integrate them, there were serious disconnects between one element and another. For example, one system generated forecast information, inventory levels, projected demand by product and customer, all in quantitative terms. Another system reported inventory in terms of dollars, enabling management to monitor bookings, billings and inventory levels from a macro-financial level. This disconnect made for problems at the operational level in prioritizing resources and capacity, as well as scheduling day-to-day production. Do we build what the forecast and experience tell us to build, or do we react to Marketing's or Finance's sense of priority?

Much of the planning and scheduling at Xerxes was manual. Although there was computer-generated information on billings, forecast demand, finished and in-process inventory, planners still used spreadsheets and personal judgment to fill the gaps.

For example, by analyzing the forecast, planners might determine a requirement for a specific die type (a die is separated out of the wafer and becomes the base for assembly and final product). Accordingly, an appropriate number of wafers would be ordered from the foundry. Devices A, B, or C can be built from the same die and the forecast may show requirements of 1,000 for each device, or 3,000 in total. However, bookings may come in differently. Actual demand for device A may be 2,000 and for devices B and C, it may be 500 each. The result is that customers for device A would be shorted, while quantities for device B and C would be greater than needed.

The parent company introduced a customer relations management (CRM) system to integrate inventory information from all divisions and subsidiaries. The system was designed to enable the parent to provide real-time information on availability to customers and prospective customers worldwide and across its total product mix. By doing so, it was believed that field sales staffs could be reduced, while demand could be more effectively determined through a centralized corporate marketing activity. It was also believed that, by centralizing demand information, planning operations at Xerxes could also be reduced. Whereas before, field sales could assess from personal contact the reality of customer demand projections and where planners could manually allow for unforeseen demand fluctuations, the only information now provided to Planning was CRM extrapolations of past demand. All too often, these proved to be unrealistically high or low.

A3.2 LESSONS LEARNED

From just these few examples, there are clear and powerful lessons to be learned about contemplating and initiating an SCM improvement project:

1. Make absolutely certain there is strong and continuing support for the SCM initiative from senior management before initiating a project. Without that support, the project will degenerate into a theoretical exercise, or worse, be seen simply as just another "management fad."
2. Create a cross-functional team or task force with strong, clearly identified leadership to guide and direct the conceptual and implementation phases of the project. Without that leadership, the project will flounder, go off course or merely cease to function.
3. Establish clearly spelled-out goals as to what the SCM project will accomplish, with specific metrics for results and clear time frames to ascertain results.
4. Make certain that the SCM initiative is aligned with the company's business objectives and current information technology (IT). Although SCM demands use of IT, its aim is not to advance technology. The aim is to achieve business and operational goals. Further, the technology employed must be compatible with systems and programs across the entire business spectrum.
5. Finally, for so complex a process as SCM to succeed, human oversight and intervention are essential. Software systems and codes are no substitute for knowledgeable judgment and functional experience.

CRM systems cannot supplant the information and insights on true customer demand that continuing face-to-face contact with customers can provide. MRP systems cannot always address beforehand the consequences of "what if" scenarios concerning supplier quality or delivery problems, engineering changes, market volatility or sudden changes in customer buying pattern. And, unless an Enterprise Resource Planning System is state of the art and employed much beyond today's current capabilities, there will be serious disconnects between engineering, financial, production and procurement-logistics information bases and information needs.

It is a prime task of SCM project leadership to identify areas of IT weakness and to compensate for that weakness through timely human and functional input.

Appendix A4:
Adapting to a New Supply Chain Role

Don Derewecki and Emile Lemay

A4.1 THE COMPANY

Lantis Eyewear Corporation is a leading designer, marketer and distributor of quality eyewear products, primarily sunglasses and optical frames. Its licensed and proprietary brand name products are known throughout the United States and internationally. Lantis distributes through mass merchants, department stores, drug stores and eyewear specialty stores. The firm ships about 30 million units each year.

Most of Lantis' products are imported from the Far East, with some specialty products manufactured domestically. Scheduling product to meet demand seasonality without overwhelming the distribution center is a supply chain management requisite.

Executing an expanded volume of multistep value-added services demanded by customers is also a critical supply chain requirement. This includes tagging, labeling, security device application, repacking and display assembly. The flexibility to deliver large and small custom orders on short notice — often the same day — is necessary to meet customer expectations.

Lantis' legacy operation was spread over four facilities with separate functions totaling 168,000 square feet. The facilities included the following:

- 86,000-square-foot primary operations facility including receiving, storage and shipping, prep area, picking and optical area.
- 60,000-square-foot second facility with preticketed merchandise for Wal-Mart, collateral products, displays, samples, returns and reclamation
- 12,000-square-foot third facility for premium brands
- 10,000 square feet of public warehouse space

Having operations spread among four facilities resulted in a hard-to-control network with limited opportunities for labor flexibility. The combined hourly staff labor totaled 250 during nonpeak times and 500 during peak times, with half of these working on customization of customer products.

Lantis management wanted to retain its labor force, so relocating to another region was not considered. Additionally, Lantis wanted to stay close to the home office in Manhattan and build 50,000 square feet of office space to relocate some of the home office staff to less expensive space.

A4.1.1 THE FACILITY CONCEPT

Given the shortage in northern New Jersey of undeveloped property of the size required, the company's options for potential sites were limited. Although a suitable site was located, the challenge of designing an efficient operation in a long, narrow building planned to fit the site had to be addressed.

The various functional operations within the distribution center were designed with the objective of maximizing productivity, throughput and flexibility within the fixed envelope of space. A detailed conceptual design was developed that met design-year requirements for throughput, deferred customization, inventory and SKU facings (location of items in the facility). These optimized the building configuration without requiring compromises to operations.

The design also incorporated requirements for future flexibility to expand various functions without disrupting operations. All of the physical systems were selected to take full advantage of the robust functionality of a warehouse management system (WMS) upgrade to be implemented after the building was completed.

A4.1.2 SPECIFICATIONS FOR THE FACILITY

The requirement for the new facility was determined to be 300,000 square feet of 36-foot clear height space. This space could accommodate growth and surges in inventory to satisfy seasonal demand.

Functional requirements for the new facility included:

- Receiving and quality control inspection
- Storage capability:
  1. Individual cartons of unprocessed products
  2. Individual cartons of processed products (Lantis arranges with contract manufacturers to configure product to specifications for much of Wal-Mart's product)
  3. Standard pallet loads with product only
  4. Large pallet loads with bulky display materials
- Value-added services capability:
  1. Tagging
  2. Labeling
  3. Security device application
  4. Repacking (changing case pack and inner pack configurations to meet customer requirements)
  5. Display assembly (customized displays, both retailer- and Lantis-designed)

- Order assembly
  1. Batched piece order picking (picking preprocessed SKUs from a fixed location into a group of store cartons)
  2. Batched piece order "putting" (reverse picking — taking customized units of a single SKU and placing them in store cartons)
  3. Picking full cartons of preprocessed merchandise
- Checking and manifesting
  1. Scan verification of SKUs and piece counts
  2. Validation of customers' value-added processing requirements
  3. Generation and application of labels in compliance with customer specifications
- Dunnage fill and carton sealing
  1. Proper product protection
  2. Carton sealing for a wide variety of sizes
- Automated scanning, check weighing and sortation
- Palletizing, staging and loading

A4.2 SPECIFIC SCM SOLUTIONS

Flexibility, which had to consider the need to handle seasonal peak levels of flow, was important in the facility design. It also had to handle expected changes in the mix of product that would occur over time. Flexibility was also required in terms of staff utilization. Quick turnaround and labor efficiency were more important than utilizing space.

To address the peak inbound flow and inventory build-up, which occurs about a month prior to peak shipping activity, sufficient dock doors and dock operations area were provided. Secured trailer and ocean-container parking spots were designed into the site plan to add flexibility to inbound operations.

Storage modules were planned to accommodate the present inventory mix. That mix ranges from small lots of cartons to multiple pallet quantities of tall pallets. A combination of decked shelf-rack modules and two opening sizes in pallet racks were designed. The startup design allowed for open space between the two sets of modules for future rack expansion that would accommodate changes in the inventory mix.

The tailored value-added processing requirements of the various customers were considered in the material flow and workstation designs for the processing stations. The flexible use of workstations was a primary consideration. The philosophy of the process design was to have more workstations than staff to allow dedicated workstations to be set up in advance with all the materials needed for a particular order. When a processing crew finishes one job, they leave the finished work for a material-handling crew to remove and they move to another set of workstations that has been set up for the next production order.

Light directed picking at three rack levels and "putting" zones with conveyor takeaways from incoming docks were designed for maximum productivity and throughput capacity. The process designs for the modules are intended to economically absorb the huge surges in demand and seasonal requirements maintaining very strict order accuracy and control standards.

The supply chain compliance requirements include 100% order accuracy, shipping-carton contents manifesting and customer-specific shipping labeling. Ergonomic workstation designs for checking and manifesting included the following components: conveyor input to and takeaway from the stations to eliminate any lifting, scanning capabilities, screen displays to validate the processing requirements specified by the customers and shipping-label printers.

The mechanized workstations for the dunnage fill and carton sealing workstations were designed around the supply chain requirements for surge and seasonal volumes, protective packaging of fragile products and variable shipping carton dimensions.

The automated conveyor sortation and shipping system design were based on supply chain requirements for surge and seasonal volumes for both package carrier and LTL shipments, validation of complete shipments (scan verification of each carton and validation of check weights), confirmation of pallet contents for multiple pallet orders and sufficient throughput capacity.

A4.3 LESSONS LEARNED AND OUTCOME

Among the lessons learned during the project, the ones that stand out are the following:

- The importance of having the right Lantis staff, the realtor, the consultant, the developer and the system integrator for the WMS and equipment on the project team
- The savings that can be achieved by value-engineering the material-handling system to fit operations requirements and capital budget constraints
- The level of control that can be maintained by phasing-in changes
  a. The operation in the new building was started with the legacy paper-based system — the light-directed system was activated about 3 months after the initial startup.
  b. To simplify the implementation, the decision was made to activate the WMS about 8 months after the startup.
- The benefits of having a custom building that satisfies the specific business requirements
- The importance of reviewing plans with insurance and other "compliance" entities early in the process

The facility is fully operational and is exceeding expectations for customer service, productivity, control and throughput capacity. Distribution center managers feel that the hourly staff is motivated to do better work because they have the right tools. Target goals for productivity, accuracy and throughput are already being surpassed. Senior managers are now confident they can consistently meet or exceed their customers' supply chain performance criteria.

Appendix A5: Chasing Low Labor Production — Words of Warning

Fred Neu

A5.1 THE COMPANY

A company located in Southern California manufactured and distributed medical equipment products throughout the United States. Its products include wheelchairs, oxygen concentrators, hospital beds, homecare beds and walkers. The company was nonunion and had a very senior and experienced workforce, with many employees having been with the company 20 years or more.

All its products were manufactured at its Southern California headquarters location, from which it shipped finished goods to customers in the western United States and service parts to the entire United States. It also shipped finished goods to distribution centers located in Illinois, Georgia and New Jersey, which then distributed products to customers in their geographic areas.

A5.1.1 SUPPLY CHAIN PROJECT OBJECTIVES

Due to cost and environmental issues, the company decided to source chrome-plated component parts and certain complete finished goods products from Asia. Approximately 72% of the company's business was wheelchairs, and chrome-plated parts made up approximately 87% of the value of each wheelchair. The other component parts included vinyl-padded armrests and legrests, vinyl upholstery, rubber tires and miscellaneous fasteners such as nuts, bolts and screws.

Due to the high percentage of customers being in the eastern United States, the company decided to relocate to a state on the Mississippi River, where it was determined that labor rates were cheaper, shipping costs to most customers would be less and delivery times to most customers would be decreased.

The planned duration of the move was 7 months, which included preparing the new facilities and relocating all departments. Expected benefits were to reduce labor costs by 34%, facility costs by 60% and distribution costs by 27%. The expected cost savings from these efficiencies were $2.6 million per year, plus a one-time windfall incentive of $500K from the state government to which the company relocated.

A5.2 LESSONS LEARNED

Quality was initially not adequately controlled at the manufacturing locations. The manufactured component parts from Asia were poorly loaded into the ocean containers and not properly identified. This resulted in scratching of the chrome-plated surface of many parts that had to be scrapped, plus excessive labor was required to sort and identify the various parts.

Approximately 22% of all chrome-plated parts received in the first five 40-foot ocean containers were scrapped. An agreement was negotiated with the Asian suppliers to replace those parts. The quality of the chrome plating was excellent; however, many of the component parts were out of tolerance, therefore they were difficult or impossible to assemble.

The company also underestimated the ramp-up time it would take to get a new workforce trained where it relocated. It was also not prepared to adequately prevent a successful union campaign within the first 2 years after the relocation. This resulted in higher labor costs and lower employee flexibility and utilization than had been anticipated. Rather than a 37% labor cost reduction, the company realized only a 28% reduction due to the labor agreement and the cost for relocating more employees than had been originally planned.

A5.3 PROJECT OBSTACLES

The company wanted to coordinate an efficient phase-out of manufacturing chrome-plated parts and the phase-in of having those parts manufactured and shipped from Asia. It wanted to relocate without sacrifice to customer service. It especially didn't want interruption in the timely delivery of products to customers.

A challenge related to the relocation was that the buyer of the vacated facility in Southern California demanded occupancy sooner than the company wanted to leave, having hoped to have sufficient time to properly arrange for an orderly move. The relocation was completed in time to meet the requirements of the buyer, but certain departments were slow to get fully operational at the new facility due to rushing without thorough planning. Fortunately, there was very little disruption in orders and it was possible to fill orders for custom-made products.

There were significant morale issues with employees who were not given an option to relocate, or were fearful of possibly losing their jobs due to sourcing offshore in Asia. Approximately 17% of the workforce relocated, including management personnel. Approximately 255 were offered relocation packages. An additional 12% of the factory workers relocated for an 8-week training and transition period. Options considered for the move were to either have a total shutdown of the business for 2 to 3 weeks to make the move, or phase the move of departments over a 4- to 6-week period.

To address quality issues, the company considered relocating certain employees to live near the main Asia manufacturing facility, either on a temporary basis or permanently.

A5.4 PROJECT MANAGEMENT SOLUTIONS

The company relocated two key company employees to temporarily live near the main manufacturing location in Asia until all the issues were resolved, which took almost a year. One employee developed quality control procedures, provided education and training of employees and monitored implementation of the procedures to ensure they were followed and would continue to be followed after his departure.

The other employee developed procedures for properly packing ocean containers. The purpose was to ensure that products were not damaged in transit and that they were identified to facilitate unloading and moving the parts to the proper location when they arrived at the U.S. assembly plant.

The company relocated all the support functions, one or two departments at a time, over a 5-week period. It arranged for temporary relocation of key individuals in each department for training and performing day-to-day functions until the new staffs were hired, trained and performing adequately.

The option chosen was to phase the move of departments. Of course, certain departments were easier to move, including most of the support areas, for example, all the accounting departments. In many cases, employees were working at both the old and new facilities until it was determined that the employees at the old facility were no longer needed.

The company moved approximately half of every service part from the picking location flow racks and placed them on the floor, where the picking locations were identified with marking pens so orders could be processed. Once the picking-location flow racks were set up at the new facility, the balance of the service parts was moved there.

A5.5 RESULTS

Although it took 3 months longer than expected to complete the move, the overall supply chain changes were beneficial. Once the planning, quality and flow of component parts and products from Asia were properly controlled, certain products could be sold at lower costs than previously, while maintaining the same profit margin. This resulted in gaining additional market share with those products, and the company still realized a 7% overall profit increase.

Once the relocation was complete and the new workforce was trained and productive, the company eliminated the distribution centers in Georgia, Illinois and New Jersey, which saved millions of dollars per year. Although top management expected this to happen, the planned elimination of the distribution centers was kept a closely guarded secret until time came for their elimination. East Coast customers were happier because shipping costs were less and delivery lead times were reduced.

Appendix A6:
Acoustic Systems, Inc.

Douglas Hicks

A6.1 THE COMPANY

Acoustic Systems, Inc. (ASI) is a Tier 1 supplier to the U.S. auto industry. (ASI is a real company whose name has been changed.) The company manufactures automotive interior trim and acoustic components in several facilities located in the United States.

In recent years, its high-level managers have consistently impressed upon the customers that they are an important part of "the team" — a long chain of supply to the ultimate vehicle customer. In real life, however, ASI's day-to-day contact with its customers is through buyers whose emphasis is seldom a reduction in the overall cost of an end product, but on a reduction in the cost of the component part they are buying.

One buyer was particularly persistent in his efforts to reduce part cost. This nonengineer made frequent technical suggestions for reducing cost that ASI's engineers were obliged to investigate. These follow-up investigations were costly and time consuming and took time away from the company's efforts to uncover cost-reduction opportunities.

Despite that, one of the buyer's suggestions had promise — at least for ASI. The buyer suggested that an "under-dash panel," a sound-suppressing barrier between the engine compartment and the dash, be made from polyethylene instead of its current primary material. From ASI's standpoint, this change would be great. It would free up one of the company's "bottleneck" processes, use a process that was being underutilized, and, although the total price of the part would be reduced, the company's profit would be the same. The same profits on lower sales — freeing up bottleneck operations — not a bad deal.

Unfortunately, ASI's engineers also anticipated a problem on the customer's end. The material change would result in a less rigid part. Instead of producing a precisely molded, rigid, fibrous product, it would be providing the customer with a precisely molded — but flimsy — "foam in a plastic bag" product.

The rigidity of the current under-dash panel makes it possible for a single worker to install it on the customer's assembly line. One worker positioned on either side of the vehicle can easily line up the panel's eyelets with the appropriate posts for fastening. The polyethylene part, however, would require at least two workers —

one on each side of the vehicle to hold it in position as they coordinate their efforts to align the panel's eyelets with the posts.

In addition to the manufacturing problems, the "foam in a plastic bag" approach would result in a component with a lower sound-suppression capability — the vehicle's operator and passengers would be subjected to more engine noise.

ASI's engineers pointed out the manufacturing and performance problems to the buyer. They estimated the impact on the customer's total cost using known production statistics and the wage and fringe rates existing at the customer's assembly facility. The resulting overall cost would be higher with the lower-cost component than with the current higher-cost one.

The buyer didn't care about the potential manufacturing or performance problems. His performance was measured by how he reduced the cost of the products he buys — manufacturing and performance were someone else's problems.

ASI's sales, engineering and quality personnel invested the resources to put together the package to submit the proposed change to the auto manufacturer. After investing time and effort in evaluating the proposed change, the auto manufacturer rejected the idea because it would increase assembly cost by more than the material cost reduction. The net result was "a lot of wasted effort to make the buyer look good!"

Appendix B1: Summary of Inputs and Outputs for a Supply Chain Project

The following table summarizes inputs and outputs for the supply chain project. Most entries in the "Inputs/Outputs" column are outputs of the processes where they are listed. Inputs, which are in italics, are identified along with their source.

Section	Process #	Process Name	Inputs/Outputs	Where Used
12.1	1.1	Chartering the supply chain effort	*Customer and Product Briefing (external input)*	1.1, 1.3
			Strategy (external input)	1.1, 1.3,
			Environmental Briefing (external input)	1.1, 1.3, 1.4
			Issues (external input)	1.1, 1.3, 1.4
			SCM Charter Elements	1.2
			Project Management Charter Elements	1.2
12.2	1.2	Project plan development	SCM Plan	1.3
			Project Management Plan	1.3
12.3	1.3	Sphere definition	Enabling Process Definition	1.4
			Supply Chain Sphere Definition	1.4
12.4	1.4	Activity system design	Activity System Designs	1.5, 1.6, 1.7, 2.4, 3.2, 3.3, 3.4, 5.1
12.5	1.5	Organization alignment	Organization Design	2.1, 2.3, 2.4, 3.1, 3.4
12.6	1.6	Collaboration strategy	Collaboration Strategy	2.3, 2.4, 3.1, 3.2, 3.3
12.7	1.7	Integrated change control	Implementation Progress	
			Various inputs from 1.4, 2.5 3.5, 3.7, 5.1	
			Environmental Updates (external input)	
			Review Meetings (external input)	
			Partner Inputs (external input)	
			Changes	1.2, 4.1, 5.4, 5.5
12.8	1.8	Phase closure	Deliverables	

Section	Process #	Process Name	Inputs/Outputs	Where Used
13.1	2.1	Organization planning	Organization Implementation Plan	2.2
13.2	2.2	Staff acquisition	*Staff Acquisition (external input)*	2.2
			Staff Resources	2.3, 5.1
13.3	2.3	Organizing for activity system implementation	Implemented Organization Plan	2.4
			Organization Plan Implementation Progress Reports	2.5
13.4	2.4	Supply chain metrics	Project Control Metrics	2.5
			Supply Chain Metrics	5.1
13.5	2.5	Schedule control	Organization Changes	2.1
			SCM Change Requests	1.7
			Project Management Change Requests	1.7
14.1	3.1	Communications planning	External Communications Plan	3.2, 3.3
14.2	3.2	Supplier base	Level 3 (Multicompany) Organization Design — Supplier Base Implementation	3.4
			Collaboration Plan Change Suggestions (suppliers)	3.1
14.3	3.3	Customer base	Level 3 (Multicompany) Organization Design — Customer Base Implementation	3.4
			Collaboration Plan Change Suggestions (customers)	3.1
14.4	3.4	Stage 3 (multicompany) organization	SCM Subprojects	3.5, 3.6, 3.7, 5.1
			Multicompany Project Staffing Requirements	3.5, 5.1
			Multicompany Risk Sharing Plan	3.5, 3.6, 5.1
14.5	3.5	Risk sharing	Partner Business Arrangements	3.7, 5.1
14.6	3.6	Project staffing	Staffed SCM Projects, Subprojects, or Project Extensions	1.7, 5.1
			Staff Plan Exceptions	1.7
14.7	3.7	Partner scope verification	SCM and Project Management Change Requests	1.7
15.1	5.1	Process improvement initiation	Process Improvement Initiation	5.2
			SCM Change Requests	1.7
15.2	5.2	Supply chain mapping	Process Analysis	5.3
15.3	5.3	Identifying root causes	Process Root Cause Identification and To-Be Process Design	5.4, 5.5
			Action Plans	
15.4	5.4	Reducing material cost	Reduced Material Costs	
15.5	5.5	Demand-driven supply chain	Implemented Supply Chain Operations	4.1
	4.1	Defining linkages	Linkage Requirements	5.5

Appendix B2: SCM Project Responsibilities

The Responsibility Assignment Matrix lists the SCM processes and suggested assignments. Its purpose is to clarify "who does what" in the project.

Section	Process #	Process Name	Project Manager/ Project Office	Company Steering Committee	Multicompany Steering Committee	Supply Chain Design Team	Sphere Design Team	Process Design Team	Company Internal Departments	Partner Internal Departments
12.1	1.1	Chartering the supply chain effort	R	A					C	
12.2	1.2	Supply chain scope planning	R	A		C			C	
12.3	1.3	Sphere definition	I	A		R			I	
12.4	1.4	Activity system design	I	C		A	R		C	C
12.5	1.5	Organization alignment	I	A		R	C		I	
12.6	1.6	Collaboration strategy	I	A		R	C		I	C
12.7	1.7	Integrated change control	R	A	I	I				
12.8	1.8	Phase closure	R	A		I				
13.1	2.1	Organization planning	A	I		R			C	
13.2	2.2	Staff acquisition	A	I		I				
13.3	2.3	Organizing for activity system implementation	R	A					C	
13.4	2.4	Supply chain metrics	A	I		R	C		A	C
13.5	2.5	Schedule control	R	A						
14.1	3.1	Communications planning	I	A	C	R			C	C
14.2	3.2	Supplier base	I	A		R	C		C	C
14.3	3.3	Customer base	I	A		R	C		C	C
14.4	3.4	Stage 3 (multicompany) organization	I		A	R			C	C
14.5	3.5	Risk sharing	I	I	A		R			C
14.6	3.6	Project staffing	R	I	A				C	C
14.7	3.7	Partner scope verification	R	I	A					
15.1	5.1	Process improvement initiation	R	A	C			C	C	I

Section	Process #	Process Name	Project Manager/ Project Office	Company Steering Committee	Multicompany Steering Committee	Supply Chain Design Team	Sphere Design Team	Process Design Team	Company Internal Departments	Partner Internal Departments
15.2	5.2	Supply chain mapping	I	I	A	C		R	C	C
15.3	5.3	Identifying root causes	I	I	A	C		R	C	C
15.4	5.4	Reducing material cost	I	A	C	C		R	C	C
15.5	5.5	Demand-driven supply chain	I	A	C	C		R	C	C
15.6	4.1	Defining linkages	I	A	C	C		R	C	C

Legend: **A** = Accountable — Has decision-making authority. Assigns responsibilities. Is accountable for project results; **R** = Responsible — Assigned to complete certain project processes; **C** = Consulted — Provides input to those responsible or accountable. Tests solutions to confirm feasibility; **I** = Informed — Provided with progress reports or information on the products of the project.

INDEX